Second Edition

Technology Strategies for the Hospitality Industry

Peter D. Nyheim
The Pennsylvania State University

Daniel J. Connolly
University of Denver

with

Lesley Holmer

Steven Durham

Prentice Hall

Boston   Columbus   Indianapolis   New York   San Francisco   Upper Saddle River
Amsterdam   Cape Town   Dubai   London   Madrid   Milan   Munich   Paris   Montreal   Toronto
Delhi   Mexico City   Sao Paulo   Sydney   Hong Kong   Seoul   Singapore   Taipei   Tokyo

Editorial Director: Vernon R. Anthony
Senior Acquisitions Editor: William Lawrensen
Editorial Assistant: Lara Dimmick
Director of Marketing: David Gesell
Marketing Manager: Thomas Hayward
Marketing Assistant: Les Roberts
Senior Managing Editor: Central Publishing
Production Project Manager: Clara Bartunek
Creative Art Director: Jayne Conte
Cover Designer: Suzanne Duda
Cover Art: Fotolia
Full-Service Project Management: Jerusha Govindakrishnan
Composition: PreMediaGlobal
Printer/Binder: STP/RRD/Harrisonburg
Cover Printer: STP/RRD/Harrisonburg
Text Font: 10/12, Minion Regular

Library of Congress Cataloging-in-Publication Data

Nyheim, Peter D.
Technology strategies for the hospitality industry / Peter D. Nyheim, Daniel J. Connolly; with Lesley Holmer, Steven Durham.—2nd ed.
    p. cm.
  Includes index.
  ISBN-13: 978-0-13-503802-4
  ISBN-10: 0-13-503802-2
  1. Hospitality industry—Data processing.   2. Information technology.   I. Connolly, Daniel J.   II. Title.
TX911.3.E4N95 2011
338.4'7910285—dc22

                                                                                                    2010050341

10 9 8 7 6 5 4 3 2

Prentice Hall
is an imprint of

www.pearsonhighered.com

ISBN 10:   0-13-503802-2
ISBN 13: 978-0-13-503802-4

CONTENTS

PREFACE

Hospitality organizations, like all others, have gone digital. Whether it is with a customer, supplier, or coworker, our industry is expected to operate to a large degree digitally. Remember those words from the first edition? They ring even truer today! **We are happy to be back with an even more powerful second edition!** In an industry where presentation is everything, this must be accomplished seamlessly, even though numerous boundaries and multiple parties are involved. Take heed that if along the way it breaks down, it is the property where the customer is located that suffers. If it works properly, well that was expected in the first place. The second edition of *Technology Strategies for the Hospitality Industry* not only takes away the confusion surrounding technology in our industry, but it also gives you the tools to succeed.

Obviously, the role of information technology (IT) or information systems (IS) is important and challenging for managers today. From daily operations to future planning, it is hard to find a process where some form of technology is not involved. Do you wish to understand it?

Ours is a fast-moving industry, where serving the customer right away often takes precedence over all other considerations. For this and other reasons, oftentimes the uses and advantages of technology are not employed to their fullest potential. With the entrance of smartphones, today's customers are even more empowered and demanding. Given the competitive nature of our industry and the fact that technology will not go away, today's manager has no choice but to understand it. Simply put, technology is part of doing business in the new millennium.

Information technology (IT), information systems (IS), management information systems (MIS) . . . just what is the difference? The first two are often used interchangeably in this book and elsewhere; however, MIS is very different. The *M* in MIS stands for *management*. Managers are concerned with getting things done through other people. Managers are also evaluated on revenue and expenses. Although IS and IT are used, their purpose is to lead the reader in understanding technology within a management context, or MIS.

From a human resources perspective, those managers with this IT understanding find themselves with a leg up on their competition and often a brighter career path. Whether your role or career aspirations focus on food and beverage (F&B) management, asset and space management, marketing and sales, consulting, or perhaps even MIS, your specialty will only be enhanced with the right MIS knowledgebase resulting in your becoming a coveted "knowledge worker."

CHANGING ROLES IN HOSPITALITY MANAGEMENT

In the past day-to-day operations in our industry involved pens, paper, and files. Although they are obviously still used, the focus has shifted towards technology. Managers find themselves using technology daily. Almost all departments have department-specific software and systems through which an organization is managed. Take, for example, the purchasing environment. Today, e-commerce has enabled hospitality organizations to purchase needed items from a vendor or supplier over the Internet. iPad anyone? Other examples include the systems and applications used in a restaurant or catering environment. No longer is a stand-alone cash register or paper seating chart enough. Now, enterprise, meaning companywide, systems have been put in place to take advantage of data collection and collaboration across different locations. On the lodging side, properties are now managed by entire systems that track the status and charges of specific spaces and allocate costs and supplies accordingly, all the while interfacing with the outside world. The use of the emerging technologies plays a large role in this edition of *Technology Strategies for the Hospitality Industry*.

AUDIENCE

If you are a current hospitality management student or a hospitality professional wishing to better your MIS knowledge, you can use this textbook. With an expanded thirteen-chapter layout and specific emphasis on aligning technology to business strategy, this text presents both specific and conceptual themes.

NEW LAYOUT/UNIQUE FEATURES

This text is a collaboration among authors who have been there. Further, the living world of hospitality technology is incorporated via interviews at the beginning of each chapter with leaders in our industry. Take a look at the begining of each chapter to see if you recognize anyone. Through these interviews, we take a look at hospitality technology from two main vantage points. From Par to Micros, we first seek to understand *Technology Strategies for the Hospitality Industry* from a vendor's perspective. Second, we look at these systems and applications from the view of those who purchase and use it every day in hospitality, be they a general manager or a director of technology for a specific property. Through these two views, the reader is able to fully capture the function and use of technology in the hospitality industry.

ENTREPRENEURIAL

Regardless of the economy, the drive and execution of innovative ideas play a vital part in our industry and are presented throughout the book. From the ability to make a restaurant reservation over the Internet from companies such as Open Table, Inc. to new smart phone applications, new technologies are giving more capability to both managers and customers.

Layout

After the opening interview, the subject matter is detailed in the chapter itself, with a case study and learning activity at the end. After reading the chapter, we recommend that you reread the interview with your newly gained knowledge.

The text opens with a foreword written by Richard G. Moore, Professor Emeritus at Cornell University. The thirteen-chapter updated text is divided into two parts. Chapters 1 through 4 form Part I and constitute *fundamentals* of knowledge and usage. Chapters 5 through 13 make up Part II and look at specific software and systems in hospitality.

As in the first edition, Chapter 1 welcomes you to the world of hospitality information technology, and Chapter 2 shows how we can use it for competitive advantage. These two chapters set the tone for the rest of the book, while presenting to the reader what career and business opportunities are available through technology understanding and usage. These points are reinforced throughout the book and serve as its major themes. Rounding out the fundamentals section are Chapters 3 and 4 with a description of computing essentials and networks, requisite knowledge for the next section.

Chapter 5 begins Part II with a detailed discussion of e-commerce and the way in which the Internet and smart phones have changed the way we do business. Chapters 6 and 7 again detail operational-specific applications for both the F&B and lodging sides. Chapter 8 is our most detailed chapter and is a thorough analysis of the global distribution system (GDS), where and through which much of our customer data originates and travels. Chapters 9 and 10 round out the text with a discussion of databases and customer relationship management (CRM) (Chapter 9) and the efficient usage of information through such systems as executive information systems (Chapter 10). New chapters on casino technology (Chapter 11) and meeting and events technology (Chapter 12) have also been added. We close our text with a chapter on technology investment (Chapter 13) and an appendix with a sample request for proposal (RFP) which may also be used in the investment discussion.

CAREER

The authors encourage those who are seriously considering hospitality technology as a career to pursue the industry's certification, Certified Hospitality Technology Professional (CHTP). This certification is offered from the Hospitality Financial and Technology Professionals (HFTP). More information can be found at *www.hftp.org*.

FOREWORD

A chief information officer (CIO) of one of the major hotel chains once told me that IT has two functions. The first is to drive revenues, and the second is to contain or reduce costs. However, the use of IT in the hospitality industry has dramatically changed over the past several decades, shifting from a back-of-the-house support role to one of strategic significance. It has also become a key means by which we interact with our guests. IT is now requisite in all aspects of any hospitality business. It is an important consideration in most business decisions and a key element in delivering exceptional guest service. IT has evolved from a focus on performing manual processes more cost-effectively to an emphasis on knowledge-based systems that can help drive revenues, make better business decisions, and create competitive advantage.

To help put things in context and understand the present state of the industry with regard to IT, it is important to take a historical perspective. Within the hotel industry, hospitality IT usage has followed two major paths: (1) the use of technology to distribute hotel products or rooms through as many channels as possible and (2) the use of technology to automate specific processes and tasks. Because of the relative high cost of early technology, initial applications focused on business opportunities where the costs of IT could be spread over many hotels or many hotel rooms to create economies of scale. The HOLIDEX reservation system developed by Holiday Inns in the mid-1960s was a prime example. This landmark reservation system was developed before the free 800 number system proved that existing IT could be used to process reservations in a cost-effective manner. One could also argue that HOLIDEX was not only a reservation system but also a marketing system to sell Holiday Inn franchises. Every major chain soon realized that a central reservation system (CRS) was critical to their survival and success. Today, a hotel chain's CRS is the major component in a highly complex distribution system that encompasses the GDSs developed by the airlines and the World Wide Web (WWW).

Initial in-house hotel automation projects focused on large hotels—those with one thousand rooms or more. In the mid-1970s, the number of hotels that had a property management system (PMS), the heart of most hotel property technology, could be counted on both hands. These systems were justified mainly because of personnel reductions and better accountability for reservations and room inventory. A smart phone or tablet today has many times the processing capability of these early million-dollar systems—and at a mere fraction of the cost, which goes to show how much technology has progressed. As technology became more affordable, companies developed systems that focused on automating the many manual, repetitive tasks found in hotel operations to create efficiencies and reduce overhead costs. Examples ranged from in-room mini-bar management and labor scheduling to managing the food and beverage inventory and determining pricing strategies. As systems were developed for narrow and specific tasks, the need to pass on information to other systems or get information from other systems was discovered. This introduced another complexity in managing IT in a hospitality organization. The guest who viewed a pay-per-view movie needed to have the charge posted to his or her folio. Interfaces were built to connect systems. These early interfaces were custom designed and required constant tweaking. They were expensive to buy and maintain, something which is still true today. A diagram of the many systems in a typical hotel today looks like a large bowl of spaghetti and meatballs, with the meatballs representing systems and the strands of spaghetti between the meatballs representing interfaces. There have been successful initiatives to develop interface standards, but more progress is needed to achieve true systems integration. Standards help to lower the costs of technology and reduce the barriers to upgrading or replacing technology.

Hotel and restaurant operations can be highly complex, involving far-reaching and multi-faceted decisions. IT has evolved to where we can make better business decisions; for example, a centralized revenue management system (RMS) helps us answer the question "what rate should we set for our hotels in a city for a specific market segment on a particular date?" IT has also developed so that we can process more complex tasks. For example, a customer planning a last-minute sales meeting might ask, "I need a meeting room for thirty people and twenty-five sleeping rooms for the night before at a major airport hotel two days from now. What do you have available?" IT has also evolved to help us know our customers better. Each customer has a different lifetime value to us. Our CRM systems allow us to tailor a unique experience for each customer or guest to maximize that value. IT is the enabler that allows us to recognize a customer from one property in the chain to another and provide amenities and service that make his or her stay unique. As progress continues, IT is increasingly becoming integral to the guest experience in every facet of the guest life cycle. Just consider the opportunities and impacts associated with mobile technologies, the Internet, self-service technologies, and consumer electronics and how they are transforming the ways in which guests shop for and interact with hospitality suppliers and what they expect during their stays.

IT issues facing managers continue to expand and now largely involve embracing the Internet and mobile technologies, creating the enabling infrastructure which powers the technology, addressing security, integrating systems, taking on large-scale projects like CRM and Web 2.0 interaction, and more. The list of issues and the many considerations one must take into account are growing, requiring every manager to have a keen sense of what IT can and cannot do and when it should be used and when it shouldn't.

One could argue that IT has contributed to a change in the structure of the hospitality industry. IT has been an enabler of the consolidation of the industry into a few mega brands. If we use a store analogy, we can say that the mega brands present different storefronts to each market segment based on the price and service preferences of the customers. However, when one looks at the back-of-the-house infrastructure, one can see the same reservation system, the same purchasing system, the same accounting system, the same CRM system, and so on driving all the brands. Revenue (yield) management on a regional basis across brands is possible because of common reservation and RMSs capable of aggregating and processing large volumes of data very quickly. The ability to cross-sell and up-sell from one brand to the next is IT based, "I'm sorry rooms aren't available at the property you requested, but our sister property across the street has rooms available."

Why is this book needed? We have reached a point in time where IT as a discipline is growing up. Competition in the industry is increasingly driven by IT. With most hospitality companies dependent on IT, it is incumbent upon all managers and managers in training to understand IT, how it ties to the business, and its ramifications on various business decisions. It is also capital intensive. Thus, managers must know how to wisely pick and choose the appropriate solutions given the needs of their businesses, how to estimate the cash flows, and how to assess the associated risk.

Non-IT in hotels is stable and well understood. Elevators, HVAC (heating, ventilation, and air-conditioning) systems, plumbing and electrical systems, while also very capital intensive, need little more than routine maintenance, and if well cared for, can last for decades. IT, conversely, evolves in a much more rapid fashion, and the decisions facing today's manager are more complex and far-reaching. The wiring network selected two years ago is technologically obsolete today and unable to handle guests' incessant needs for more and faster bandwidth to handle their applications and entertainment. What is the impact on guest service, the overall guest experience, and in-house system performance? Should you select a new PMS, and if so, should you consider an above-property option based upon a cloud computing model? How do you prevent a hacker getting into your systems and stealing all of your guests' credit card numbers? These are some of the many concerns facing industry leaders now and in the forseeable future.

IT is an investment, and like any other asset, it requires continual upkeep and ongoing expenditures to sustain its useful life. Today's manager needs to have fundamental knowledge about hardware, software, databases, networks, and security. He or she does not necessarily need to be a technical expert but does need to be IT literate to understand how systems work and their implications on the business. Today's manager needs to be able to understand the technical person, but more importantly, he or she needs to understand the business and customer impact of technology decisions.

This book gives the reader the knowledge and perspectives necessary to thrive in a competitive and ever-changing environment, one in which IT will greatly determine or contribute to an organization's and an individual's success. This book covers the key topics that should be foremost on any manager's mind and does so in a way that is easy to understand and relevant to industry practice. It blends theory and strategy with application and how-to. It raises awareness for important investment considerations that must be asked by chief financial officers, asset managers, and property owners to ensure their organizations are deriving the maximum value from IT. It helps to raise important questions all hospitality managers should ask when facing important business and technology decisions. It also opens the doors to many career opportunities within the industry involving IT.

In short, this book is a must-read for all hospitality professionals and students of the industry, even if IT is not one's primary career focus. One can no longer afford to ignore the impacts of IT or delegate responsibility for this important function to others. IT must be part of anyone's core competencies who wishes to be an industry leader.

Professor Richard G. Moore
Emeritus
Cornell University's School of Hotel Administration

BIOGRAPHIES AND ACKNOWLEDGMENTS

Peter D. Nyheim is a Senior Instructor of Technology in The School of Hospitality Management at the Pennsylvania State University.

Leading this charge a second time has been quite an endeavor and aside from my coauthors, publisher, and interviewees, many deserve praise. I would like to thank all the many companies, colleagues, and individuals who helped with this project. Take a look inside the book to see them all!

Dr. Daniel J. Connolly is the Associate Dean for Undergraduate Programs at the University of Denver's Daniels College of Business. He also serves as an Associate Professor of Information Technology with a dual appointment in the Fritz Knoebel School of Hospitality Management and in the Department of Information Technology and Electronic Commerce. In August 2008, he was named by *Lodging* magazine as a hospitality technology leader and visionary. His work is widely published in academic and industry journals and presented at conferences around the world. Dr. Connolly, a former information technology professional with Marriott International, earned his Ph.D. from Virginia Tech, his M.B.A. from American University, and his B.S. from Cornell University.

A book is a large undertaking that requires the help and support of so many people. I wish to thank my colleague and coauthor Peter Nyheim, all those who provided content for this book as contributing authors and interview participants, and the Prentice Hall team for its great work from start to finish. Additionally, I'd like to thank my industry and academic colleagues, my coworkers, and my students for challenging me, teaching me, and inspiring me. Finally, I'd like to thank Professors Michael Olsen and Richard Moore for serving as my mentors, and my family for all of its love, support, and many sacrifices during the writing of this second edition.

CHAPTER 1

If You Think You Don't Need to Know About IT, Think Again!

INTERVIEW

Jason Rotter is an account manager with the Denver-based Four Winds Interactive, a company specializing in digital signage for the hospitality industry. Jason is a 2008 graduate of the University of Denver's Fritz Knoebel School of Hospitality Management.

Q: Please provide a brief background and introduction to yourself and share what inspired you to pursue a career involving hospitality information technology (IT) rather than pursuing some other aspect of the hospitality industry.

A: I knew early on that I was interested in the hospitality industry. My dream as a teenager was to own and operate my own restaurant. About that same time, I got my first computer and became fascinated with technology and all that it could do. It wasn't until I was in college that I discovered it was possible to combine my interests in hospitality with my love for using computers—and not have to be a programmer or on the technical side of computing like what a computer science major would be. Through my coursework, internships, and professors, I began learning the importance of technology in the hospitality industry and various career opportunities that would allow me to fuse my passions so that I wouldn't have to make choices between them. This unique combination of interests set me apart from my University of Denver graduating class. Most of my peers pursued management training programs with chain operators in hotel or restaurant operations. I took a different route, accepting a position with a digital signage company. Since many of its clients are in the hospitality industry, I am still connected while gaining exposure to new technologies and how they can be used within the business to improve the quality of hospitality and service. I still want to own my own restaurant someday, but for now, that dream will have to wait.

Q: What is Four Winds Interactive, and what do you do in your role within the company? What do you find most rewarding about your job and the digital signage industry?

A: Four Winds Interactive (FWi) is a leading provider of interactive kiosks and digital signage solutions. Digital signage is the industry term for using digital display technology such as LCD, plasma, and LED displays to communicate with a target audience. Digital signage can be noninteractive or interactive through the use of touch screen, barcode scanner, card swipe, RFID, and other input devices. Digital signs provide visual appeal that can help break through clutter to engage audiences. They provide our clients with a unique, fun, and informative means to communicate their brands to their guests.

As a dedicated account manager, my main role is to ensure that our clients are happy with their FWi experience and our products. I am also responsible for making sure they are knowledgeable about how to use our software to its fullest to maximize the benefits our products have to offer. I am trained in all aspects of our software, which enables me to provide product support and training to our clients, either remotely or on site.

In addition to working with technology, an exciting part of my job is that I get to travel extensively to meet and support our clients. I consider myself fortunate to have found this great opportunity through my college mentor and that I am able to work with cutting-edge technologies in a growing industry with an innovative employer.

Q: Where do you see your future career path heading?

A: One important thing that I learned in college is to keep an open mind; that is to look for opportunities that you never knew existed. It was not until 2007, when I learned about digital signage and the way it is revolutionizing hospitality. It is providing new career opportunities for business-minded professionals who are interested in the application of technology versus the technical programming of technology. I enjoy having found a career that is cutting-edge, creative, and people oriented. Digital signage provides me with the unique opportunity to engage with technology and people at the same time.

Q: Information technology is constantly changing. How do you keep up with the latest trends and avoid obsolescence? Where do you suggest looking to monitor hospitality industry trends and technology developments?

A: I find that the best way to stay abreast on current trends is by speaking with and listening to FWi clients. Listening to them provides me with unique insight into their business needs and objectives. In addition, I utilize the latest RSS technology and iPhone applications to seek out information and read industry trade publications.

Q: What do you consider to be the most important skills and knowledge for someone to possess who is interested in pursuing a career in hospitality IT and why? How will these skills likely be used in one's career?

A: Passion and curiosity are absolutely critical. Technology changes are pushing the hospitality industry in new and exciting directions. In order to keep up with all of these exciting changes, one must love hospitality and IT and constantly seek ways to learn about technology, business, and consumer trends. My passion for both hospitality and information technology prompts me to ask *how* and *why* questions that enhance my own understanding and enable me to be successful.

Q: Where do you see the future opportunities in hospitality IT to be? What will be the hot technologies, skills, and industry sectors on which one should focus?

A: Hospitality venues are jumping on the digital signage bandwagon. It is revolutionizing the way the hospitality industry relates with its clientele. For example, a hotel guest can digitally view a meeting schedule, receive directions on how to get to the meeting place, and even print out driving directions to a restaurant for drinks with coworkers. In essence, digital signage personalizes a guest's experience while acting as a convenient, virtual concierge. Digital signage is a great industry with products that have created jobs that did not exist a decade ago.

Q: What advice or parting thoughts can you share with aspiring hospitality business professionals?

A: The following are tips I have learned over the years that have served me well to this point:

- Keep an open mind.
- Learn from your peers.
- Accept feedback willingly.
- Never stop asking questions. They help us learn.
- Find a mentor.
- Experience the field firsthand. Get as many different internships as possible.
- Seek roles outside traditional hospitality positions.
- Always remember that you are catering to a people-business. It's all about relationships and service.

1. INTRODUCTION

At the start of each new academic term, the number of students enrolled in our classes seeking careers in hospitality information technology (IT) is generally small. Yet, after comparing IT salaries to those for traditional positions in hospitality operations (e.g., management positions, sales, and human resources), one may want to rethink his/her career path. Money aside, the reality is that for most careers, IT is an important, integral, and necessary component. Thanks to the convergence of various forms of technology (e.g., computers, software, and telecommunications), the rise in electronic business (e-business), and a growing number of enterprise-wide technology initiatives, technology is a critical aspect of almost any job (see Table 1-1). It has become an essential element in almost every business process, disrupting functional silos and creating the need for boundary spanners. Simply put, IT is changing everything—from guest expectations and needs to industry structure to how we perform our jobs and what skills we will need to be successful. In fact, it is changing the very nature of how services are delivered. Consequently, IT is inescapable and must be a core skill for any aspiring hospitality manager or executive. Management guru Peter Drucker often stated that everyone in the firm is responsible for marketing the firm and ensuring customer satisfaction. In a similar vein, because of the confluence of business process, competitiveness, and technology, everyone in today's organization, by default, must be responsible for IT and think and act like a chief information officer (CIO). Congratulations, you have just joined the IT team—whether you like it or not!

It's true. Take marketing, for example. It is tough to be a great marketer without IT. In today's high-tech era, IT is a prerequisite to marketing and must go hand in hand. One cannot make marketing decisions in a vacuum without in-depth knowledge about the capabilities and limitations of IT. Global distribution, supply chain management, customer relationship management (CRM), electronic commerce (e-commerce), customer segmentation, revenue management, and so on are all underpinned by IT applications. Thus, a good marketer, by default, must be well versed in IT.

The same could be said for every other discipline, including human resources, finance and accounting, management, and operations. You can't make decisions about the business without using IT (or information generated from IT systems) and without factoring in IT considerations. Front desk managers must be intimately familiar with property management system (PMS), revenue (yield) management, central reservations system (CRS), call accounting and the private branch exchange (PBX), voice messaging, guest locking systems, concierge systems, energy management systems, and more. Similarly, restaurant managers must be proficient in point-of-sale (POS) technology, inventory management systems, menu engineering, and the like, and all managers must be intimately familiar with the risks of using technology in business and appropriate ways (including policies, procedures, and training) to safeguard against these risks.

Table 1-1   IT Is Important to Every Hospitality Position

Position	Brief Description of Duties	IT Knowledge Requirements
General Manager (GM)	Responsible for overseeing the entire operation.	• Operational systems, business intelligence, and reports to manage, control, and direct the business • Technology to track and communicate with customers, suppliers, employees, regional and corporate management, and owners • Balanced scorecard • Big picture knowledge related to all aspects of the business and systems used throughout the business in order to make decisions and determine how best to allocate resources • Microsoft Office
Controller	Responsible for the accounting and financial aspects of the operation. Establishes and manages budgets, maintains the books, prepares financial reports, acquires funding for capital projects, and controls against theft and waste.	• Spreadsheets • Data analytics • Business intelligence tools • Balanced scorecard • Project management software • Back-office accounting system • Security surveillance and audit trails • Time and attendance • Payroll • Intranet • Microsoft Office

Position	Brief Description of Duties	IT Knowledge Requirements
Director of Rooms Operations	Responsible for all guest service functions in a hotel; including front desk, reservations, bell staff, housekeeping, concierge, and telephone operators.	• Property management system • Reservation system • Revenue management system • Distribution and channel management • Customer relationship management and loyalty program • Telephone and call accounting systems • Guest lock system • Guest response system • Concierge system • In-room guest amenities (e.g., movies, high-speed Internet access, mini bars, guest safes) • Microsoft Office
Revenue Manager	Responsible for setting rates, restrictions, and selling strategies for hotel rooms and managing room inventory allocated to the various distribution channels used by the hotel.	• Revenue management system • Reservation system • Distribution and channel management • Property management system • Sales and catering system • Business intelligence • Microsoft Office
Director of Sales and Marketing	Oversees the sales and marketing activities of the operation and its advertising and promotion materials; typically responsible for group business (i.e., corporate accounts, reservations involving 10 or more guestrooms, meetings, and conventions).	• Sales and catering system • Lead generation and tracking databases • Sales force automation • Customer relationship management and loyalty program • Web site and e-commerce • Reservation system • Content management system • Social media • Distribution and channel management • Revenue management system • Meeting room layout and design software • Microsoft Office
Food and Beverage Director	Oversees all food and beverage operations. Manages day-to-day operations, purchasing, and inventory management.	• Point-of-sale technology • Inventory management • Recipe management • Purchasing and receiving system • Table management • Restaurant reservations • Labor forecasting and scheduling • Menu engineering • Microsoft Office

(continued)

Table 1-1   IT Is Important to Every Hospitality Position (*Continued*)

Position	Brief Description of Duties	IT Knowledge Requirements
Director of Human Resources	Responsible for all aspects of staffing and team building. Duties include hiring and termination decisions, benefits administration, payroll, policy compliance, training, promotions, special programs, and succession planning.	• Human resources information system • Labor forecasting and scheduling • Time and attendance • Payroll • Benefits • Online training • Intranet • Microsoft Office
Director of Security	Oversees the security operations for the organization to ensure the safety of guests and workers alike.	• Access control systems and guest locking system • Surveillance systems • Fire alarm system • Biometrics • Microsoft Office
Director of Engineering	Oversees the facility, maintenance, and equipment	• Heating, ventilation, and air conditioning (HVAC) system • Energy management system • Preventative maintenance system • Work order management system • Microsoft Office
Director of Housekeeping	Oversees the cleanliness of the facility, including all public space, administrative offices, and guestrooms.	• Property management system • Labor forecasting and scheduling • Microsoft Office
IT Manager	Oversees, maintains, and secures the various computer systems used throughout the organization; provides support to end-users; and assists with the selection, procurement, and implementation of computer applications and hardware.	• Operating systems • Hardware platforms • Programming languages • Network and communications architecture (both wired and wireless) • Project management software • Electronic mail (e-mail) server • Systems security • Antivirus and malware detection tools • Backup and recovery • Database administration • Report writer tools • Technology trends • All systems used throughout the business • Microsoft Office

How can a hospitality executive determine how to maximize value for the firm if he or she is faced with resource constraints and must decide between, say, a new sales and catering system and the renovation and re-theming of a restaurant outlet? How can one possibly estimate cash flows, assess risks, assign risk premiums, and calculate returns on investment (ROI) without fully comprehending IT? It would be rather difficult to evaluate the pros and cons, quantify the benefits, and understand the strategic opportunities associated with each option to make a well-informed business decision without having a solid grasp of IT. From your perspective as an aspiring manager or executive, how can you lead others, make hiring decisions, and mentor and develop people without understanding the technological future of the industry?

Just think about this question for a moment. Many are quick to say that they don't need to become proficient in a particular area because they can hire someone else to handle those responsibilities or because they can outsource those functions. Generally speaking, this type of thinking is shortsighted, and when it comes to IT, it can be outright dangerous—especially considering the stakes involved. IT tends to rank among the top expense categories of most firms. It also tends to be one of the most pervasive and enabling—or confining—resources in the firm. Therefore, every manager or executive must strive to understand how to use IT, see its strategic potential, and recognize its limitations so as not to be bamboozled by it, led astray, or be constrained by the limitations of the firm's IT infrastructure. While hiring experts or outsourcing may be a viable approach and help to reduce the amount of expertise you must have in this area, it does not completely absolve you from having proficiency and a solid understanding of what technology can and cannot do and what questions to ask. Like anything, understanding and using IT require investment (of both time and money), commitment, and diligence. Your knowledge in this area will reduce your dependence on others and improve your ability to ask the *right* questions so you can properly lead your firm.

2. WELCOME TO THE WORLD OF IT!

The discussion in the previous section suggests a very clear message. IT is one of the greatest forces driving change in almost any industry, especially the hospitality industry—so get used to IT! Unfortunately, human bandwidth, that is people's ability to grasp IT and understand how to effectively use it and apply it in business, is one of the greatest barriers to a firm's ability to successfully adopt IT and realize its many benefits. The IT wave will likely continue for the foreseeable future for several reasons. First, the pace of change and the expected number of technological advances continue to grow at alarming rates. Second, the technological demands of guests continue to rise. This is especially true of the Millennial Generation (Gen Y), which has practically been reared on technology. Third, the competitive environment is growing in intensity with increased investment in and emphasis on IT. Fourth, labor issues continue to plague the industry. Both the cost of labor and the scarcity of people willing and able to fill industry positions require greater focus on technology as a viable alternative to run the business and service guests. For these reasons, IT is quickly becoming one of the most important skills industry managers and leaders need to possess and one of the most important competitive methods a hospitality firm can exploit to gain advantage in an increasingly competitive business. These advantages come in many forms including, but not limited to, differentiation, efficiency (economies of scale), resource capabilities, cost reduction, and information asymmetry. Despite their diversity, these advantages all have one thing in common; they are all enabled by IT. Thus, whether you are interested in pursuing a career in IT or not makes little difference. The underlying premise is the same;

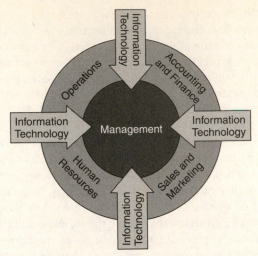

FIGURE 1-1   IT Pervasiveness Creates the Need for Boundary Spanners and IT-Savvy Individuals

no matter what you choose to do as a profession, you need to become proficient in IT at the personal, intraorganizational, and interorganizational levels.

By default, your career will involve IT. IT transcends today's organizations by crossing and blurring all traditional departmental, organizational, and geographic boundaries. This is especially true with large-scale initiatives such as e-business, enterprise resource planning (ERP), and CRM. The illustration in Figure 1-1 helps bring this reality to life. IT-related decisions require input from multiple perspectives within the organization since IT is pervasive throughout the firm's **value chain**, all of the primary and support activities of the firm required to produce products and services that generate revenues and drive profits. Consequently, if the organization is to exploit IT for competitive advantage, business leaders, regardless of the discipline (e.g., management, marketing, finance, accounting) they represent, must (1) focus on enterprise-wide solutions, (2) be able to serve as **boundary spanners** (people who can cross multiple disciplines or areas of knowledge), and (3) become technologically savvy. Decisions involving IT cannot be made in a vacuum, and because of their reach, cost, and strategic implications, they should *not* be delegated to others. They require commitment from the top, insight from all aspects of the business, and the involvement of those possessing specific expertise in IT.

3. MANAGING YOUR CAREER

Unquestionably, this is an exciting time to pursue an IT career within the context of the hospitality industry. Hospitality and tourism are among the largest and fastest growing employers worldwide and they offer a rich, yet diverse, set of possibilities. IT, despite the temporary slowdown in the economy (especially in the technology sector) and the number of dot.com crashes, is also among the fastest growing areas of employment and one of the economy's great contributors, a trend expected to continue well into the future. The intersection of these great industries offers much excitement, opportunity, and new careers for those who seek and would like to take advantage of them. Are you interested?

Moving forward, IT will continue to be one of the greatest forces driving transformation in almost any industry, including hospitality. Consequently, everything will continue to change—from how we work and learn to how we transact business with our guests and employees to the technological amenities and infrastructure found in our establishments. Moreover, technology will redefine the very nature of what constitutes good service and how services are delivered. With the rise in e-business, self-service, and mobile technologies, these changes have only become more pronounced and more commonplace—moving the industry to new heights technologically while expanding the globalization of the hospitality industry. Certainly for those seeking careers in this industry, exciting opportunities abound, and because of IT, many new career possibilities have surfaced, just as Jason Rotter discovered when embarking on his career (as discussed in the chapter's opening interview). You are encouraged to explore IT-based careers for many reasons—not just for the salaries but also for the diversity of career options, the challenges and intellectual stimulation, and the overall quality of work life (i.e., better and more predictable hours than careers in hospitality operations).

To excel at your career, you need to have passion and enjoy what you do. You also need to continue to develop yourself and your skills. Learning should be a lifelong journey and a regular part of your job. The hospitality industry has become so complex and continues to change at a rapid pace. Thus, you, too, need to change, adapt, and stay current with all aspects of the business—and especially with IT. One of the nice things about IT is that there is a built-in mechanism or incentive that forces you to stay current if you want to stay employed—the very desire to stay marketable and relevant.

Remember that career paths for most people seldom resemble straight lines. They often take many twists and turns, but these twists and turns are largely up to you and often offer many wonderful developmental opportunities that can lead to new, exciting, and very different career opportunities than what you may have initially thought possible. It is your responsibility and obligation to yourself to manage your own career. While others can help you with this important task, no one can do this for you as well as you can do it for yourself. After all, you know yourself best, particularly your interests, your goals, and what motivates you and gives you personal satisfaction.

At this point in your career, one of the best things you can do is to conduct a self-assessment or **SWOT (strengths, weaknesses, opportunities, and threats) analysis**. Determine what you like and what you don't and inventory your skills and core competencies. Be sure to think about what you would like to do long-term and what skills will be required to achieve your goals. Where are you strong, and where is there room for improvement? What skills are you lacking, or which ones need further development? How prepared are you for the digital economy? What are the job opportunities like presently, and where will they be in the next five, ten, or fifteen years? In essence, you want to create your own personal balance sheet that identifies your assets (strengths) and liabilities (weaknesses) relative to the marketplace you will enter. Then, just as you would do if you were managing a firm's balance sheet, figure out how to improve your assets through value creation (adding something for which people are willing to pay that wasn't there before and will provide a noticeable advantage) while reducing, and hopefully eliminating, your liabilities. Look for jobs that will serve as springboards to new opportunities and help you progress and achieve your ultimate career dreams. Each position you take should help you acquire new skills and serve as a stepping-stone or springboard to the position you ultimately desire. When it comes time to interviewing for a job, be prepared to address with conviction the question, "What value do you bring to the table?"

4. DECISIONS, DECISIONS, DECISIONS

One of the hard parts about planning a career is knowing what options exist. Awareness of these options allows you to prepare better and take the necessary steps to gain the skills and knowledge required for a desired career path. The beauty of IT is that it is broad and far-reaching. While attractive, these attributes often create discomfort among students. Because of the number of choices, the decision-making process can become overly complex and downright confusing at times. There are so many options and possibilities. Having to make such an important decision that can alter the course of a life seems daunting. While true, the good news is that you do have options. These are the kinds of decisions you like to have. This type of flexibility and diversity, which many people find attractive when developing their career paths, helps to keep you marketable in a volatile and ever-changing economy.

There are many types of IT-related careers from which to choose. You may be interested in operations, consulting, Web design, e-commerce or e-business, distribution, search engine optimization, project management, system development, database management, computer programming, electronic marketing, distribution, CRM, training, system management, digital signage, and so on or perhaps something more entrepreneurial. These are just some examples, but in reality, the possibilities are almost endless. For manageability, let's consider three basic career path options, as depicted in Figure 1-2. Within the hospitality industry, there are numerous avenues for exploring a career involving IT. However, at the macro level, careers can be defined as those involving (1) the managerial aspects of IT, (2) the technical aspects of IT, or (3) a non-IT managerial position that relies extensively on IT.

IT Managerial

For those seeking an IT managerial position, it is important to understand both the hospitality business and IT. Although there is no definitive mix, many would agree that business knowledge is just as important as the knowledge of technology or the technical skills. The appropriate mix will likely vary with each position and set of responsibilities. Since we are talking about business here, you must possess the ability to develop sound strategies, make rational and informed decisions, and allocate and manage resources appropriately to generate business value (i.e., profits and competitive advantage) and shareholder returns. You must be a skillful and persuasive communicator and an agent of change. IT is a resource or tool that should be applied as a competitive method and aligned with the firm's strategy. Those who are able to utilize IT and its by-product information to solve business problems and create new business opportunities will

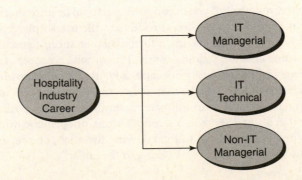

FIGURE 1-2 Career Path Options

be in a position to drive strategy and generate strong business value. Clearly, managers of today and tomorrow must be exceptional in all facets of the business, analytical in nature, and great users of information.

As technology becomes more pervasive and influential, it will become an underlying part of nearly every business decision, business process, and the entire value chain. Therefore, thinking is shifting away from pure technology projects in favor of business projects that involve IT. In effect, people who assume these roles need to be great managers and leaders, but they must also be able to serve as liaisons between the various aspects of the business and the functional disciplines (e.g., sales and marketing, finance and accounting, human resources, operations) and the IT staff (i.e., the programmers and software engineers or architects who design and develop the applications). To do this, it is important to be able to speak the languages of both business and technology (yes, all those acronyms) and to do so decisively and convincingly. Being able to recognize needs, find solutions, and then develop, pitch, and defend persuasive business cases are requisite skills. Often, one must translate business requirements into technical solutions as well as have the ability to find new business opportunities using technology to drive revenues, gain market share, or reduce overhead costs. Needs analysis, business case development, and risk assessment are important and frequent aspects of the job. It is also important to understand, recognize, and balance the needs of competing stakeholders that include customers, employees, owners and investors, franchisees, suppliers, and the community. If projects are not managed well, they can quickly become derailed—over budget, late, or short on functionality. Therefore, the ability to manage projects (including resources, budgets, and functional scope) is essential. Projects involving IT can quickly become political due to the many variables, stakeholder groups, resource requirements, and the stakes (i.e., costs, risks, organizational impact, and complexity).

The position of **chief information officer (CIO)** represents the ultimate business–IT liaison and should report to the organization's chief executive officer (CEO), although this reporting relationship may vary from company to company. This individual must understand the ins and outs of the business completely and know when (and when not) to apply technology to achieve business results (e.g., higher customer retention, more market share, increased profits, decreased costs, greater employee productivity, stronger shareholder value). This person must also possess a global perspective and have a significant amount of large-scale, multinational project experience, including justification, systems design and development, rollout, implementation, and benefits tracking. Other positions, to name a few, include IT directors, managers, consultants, and business analysts.

To prepare for an IT managerial career, you must understand all of the relevant business aspects of the hospitality sector you plan to enter. Strong operational experience with cross-functional exposure is an absolute must. In this industry people work their way up to the top. Start early to begin paying your dues and learn the nuts and bolts of the industry, both the craft or service aspects of hospitality and the business acumen and technical know-how required. Then, continue to seek more exposure and positions of greater responsibility that will allow you to strengthen and develop your management skills. While in school, enroll in classes that will allow you to develop your analytical and critical reasoning, communications, leadership, financial management, and strategic thinking skills. In addition, take classes and look for experiences that will help you master technology as a user and a person seeking ways to apply it. These include courses in programming, office applications (especially spreadsheets), database management, project management, web design, networking, security, e-commerce, collaboration software (groupware), and IT strategy. Generally, it is a good idea to accept one or more jobs that will immerse you in the technical side in order to establish yourself and build your technical credibility. As with anything, it is easier to manage something if you are completely knowledgeable about that which you are managing, and having served in the trenches can give you a great credibility boost with people on your team.

It is important to be comfortable with technology and capable and willing to explore its outer bounds while understanding and managing costs and risks. As you understand both the business and the technology, your value-add and competitive differentiator will be your ability to marry the two to come up with creative and effective combinations that will give your firm competitive advantage. Perhaps your biggest and most overwhelming challenges will be to stay current and abreast of extremely dynamic environments, to see opportunities for marrying technology solutions to business problems before others, and to convince others that your ideas have merit. In an IT managerial capacity, you must continuously monitor and follow key trends for all aspects of your business (i.e., sales and marketing, operations, human resources, finance and accounting, and management) as well as the technology trends. You will need to know how to evaluate emerging trends and technologies, assess their impacts, and know when to embrace them and when not to. Although these tasks can be overwhelming and a lot of work, they are essential to survivability; failure to do so will render you ineffective in your job and ultimately obsolete. So, if you don't want your career to end prematurely, you must make continuous learning and trend-tracking key parts of your job responsibilities and regular routine.

As you progress on your IT managerial career track, you will likely find it worthwhile to pursue a graduate degree, most notably a Master of Business Administration (MBA) with a concentration or specialization in IT and e-business.

IT Technical

For those of you who are attracted to the computer science or software engineering aspects of IT, you may wish to pursue a technical career track. In our careers, we have come across a number of individuals who love to write software applications, design databases, and deal with technology infrastructure, network topology, and data networking and security issues. Many of these people have no real interest in managing people per se. Instead, they prefer to deal with, develop, and manage technology. These are important people to have on staff because without them, we, as an industry, would not have the technology applications and solutions that we use today. For people serving in these roles, it is important to understand the particulars of the hospitality business with a keen sense of the guest and guest service. Unfortunately, being a great programmer is not sufficient due to the many complexities and nuances of our business. What many don't realize is that some of the hospitality industry's systems are among the most complex in the world, given the number of transactions they must process, the diversity of guests and properties they must serve, the volume of data that must be tracked, the number of disparate systems that must be integrated, and the sub second response times required. To gain the necessary skills and competencies, one should seek training, coursework, and jobs involving computer programming, data networking, telecommunications, wireless communications, Web design and development, database design and management, systems analysis and design, IT security, and enterprise architecture planning coupled with industry exposure through coursework and practical (i.e., hands-on) work experience.

The ultimate technical position is that of **chief technology officer (CTO)**. This individual typically reports to the CIO and is responsible for the firm's technology infrastructure, network typology, standards, architectural decisions, computer security, computer usage policies, and computer operations. Having the *right* (i.e., fast, capable, responsive, integrated, stable, reliable, and secure) technology in place is the foremost responsibility of this individual. This person typically manages the technical staff of application developers (programmers), database administrators, network administrators, computer operators, etc. As such, someone in this role must possess a strong set of technical skills and in-depth knowledge of the business. However, the order of priority is reversed from that of the CIO. The technical skills take on greater priority followed closely by knowledge of the business. This person must also possess a significant amount of system development and rollout experience for large-scale, multinational projects. A graduate degree is strongly recommended. Examples of other technical positions include database manager or administrator, Web developer, network operations manager, data center manager, system manager, technology director, senior programmer, technology/application specialist, systems analyst, technology architect, technical writer, quality assurance specialist, and help desk/support analyst.

Non-IT Managerial

IT, by its very nature, is multidisciplinary, especially since IT is becoming such a major component of every discipline and every business process. As stated earlier, it is difficult to carry out a particular job function without understanding the opportunities of IT and recognizing its limits. Also, it is important to understand IT in order to spend wisely and not needlessly on IT. Thanks to many recent technological developments like CRM, ERP, mobile applications, and e-business, most hospitality jobs are being affected by IT, and the people fulfilling these jobs are increasingly being required to play more active roles in technology decision making, direction setting, project development, and implementation. Moreover, employee compensation is often tied to the outcomes of IT-enabled initiatives.

Currently, in many companies, most of the major requests for technology funding are made and decided by the business executives who are considered to be a project's client base or primary users or beneficiaries of the system. Business executives are responsible for the company's financial assets, marketing initiatives, and operations. Although the CIO, the CTO, and other IT staff provide support and guidance, make recommendations, and work closely with these individuals, it is up to these executives to develop, defend, and *own* the business cases. They must then execute the project upon successful approval and funding. They are required to take an active managerial role rather than simply providing moral support and hiding behind the IT staff who, in the past, often became the scapegoat whenever a project got derailed. In fact, their compensation (i.e., bonuses and merit increases) is often based on the successful outcome of IT projects. With that kind of vested interest (or "skin in the game"), it is incumbent upon business executives to learn about and understand IT and how it can be used, when to use it, when not to use it, and then, to subsequently promote its use and adoption throughout the organization. Thus, we see more of a partnership rather than an adversarial role developing between the business units and IT, which results in a higher success rate and greater realized benefits for all IT-related initiatives.

Because of their rank and positioning in the organization, the business executives are influential in determining the organization's culture and attitudes towards IT. They play an important role in affecting the success of initiatives involving IT. They also serve as important role models and mentors for others in the organization—by seeking ways to grow and prepare for future trends, trying to grapple with change and understand IT, and looking to be more open-minded or think "out of the box" to develop innovative and creative solutions that will lead to competitive advantage (and personal promotion). In short, they should be technology advocates and consider IT as an important aspect of their job responsibilities. They should also be early adopters of new technology and demonstrate by example how technology can enable individuals and the business to make great things happen.

To climb the rungs of the corporate ladder at a faster rate, you are advised to attain a graduate degree such as an MBA. To be successful in a business executive position, you must demonstrate a proven track record (i.e., string of successes) and have a strong sense of the business, a global perspective, and a good working knowledge of IT, at least from a macro level. It is not necessary to know specifically which buttons to push on the computer to make something happen. Instead, it is important to be able to define and articulate needs, specify functional requirements, recognize opportunities for applying IT to achieve business success, and prepare compelling business cases to secure funding and resources to make IT happen. You must also be willing to assume risk, experiment, and think strategically and creatively. People serving in these capacities must, like their IT managerial counterparts, serve as liaisons, strategic thinkers, agents of change, and boundary spanners. They must seek to understand foreign ground—the world of IT—and then apply it in a given context to their specific area or areas of the business. These individuals must be strong managers who are able to toe the line, ask good questions, hold others accountable for deadlines and deliverables, and be held accountable and able to deliver projects themselves—on time and on budget according to the agreed-upon specifications.

A while back, IBM ran a series of great commercials that helped to put all of this into perspective. In one commercial, the setting is the conference room of a major, multinational corporation. Sitting around the table are a number of executives who are trying to troubleshoot, address the aftermath of a major system outage, and prevent such a catastrophe from reoccurring. The executive in charge is polling her direct reports as to the problems, trying to determine what led up to the calamity, and to establish accountability so that appropriate disciplinary action can be taken. As she fires through her litany of questions, the shift of blame moves around the room. The answer to each question puts her closer and closer to the source. Ultimately, she hones in on the source of the problem and asks who was responsible. After a deafening moment of silence, one timid member of her staff sitting beside her politely whispers to her that the direct responsibility for the problem rested with her. What a moment of truth and an embarrassing realization that was for that manager—although humorous for the audience—to find out that she was responsible for something about which she had no idea, not even a clue!

In another commercial, the media and members of Wall Street are grilling a CEO of a Fortune 500 firm regarding his company's future plans and strategy. The executive responds to inquiries about his company's technology infrastructure, a topic which, judging by his nervousness, he is clearly ill-prepared to address. Nevertheless, he makes several lofty and senseless promises that his staff, who are watching the televised interview in a nearby conference room, doubt can ever be realized. The interrogators take note of the promises made and indicate that they will hold the CEO accountable. When the interview is over, the CEO joins his staff in the conference room and asks one simple question: "What is infrastructure?" In that very moment, he confirmed his very ignorance, something his staff feared and knew all along. Ignorance can get businesses into trouble by misusing company resources and overspending. It can also, lead to constrained growth at some point in the future and limit-overall competitiveness in the marketplace.

While many may find these commercials amusing, they can also see their instructive value because they represent some very serious issues and considerations that are relevant business and career issues. What can you do to save yourself from similar humiliations and from becoming a discredited leader or manager? Assume that there are no second chances; you have only one chance to get it right. Every job involves IT, so take action now to understand IT, how it affects your job, and what control and responsibilities you have with respect to IT so that you are not caught off guard or making uninformed decisions like the characters depicted in these IBM commercials.

Unfortunately, according to statistics commonly cited in the trade literature, the majority (about two-thirds) of all IT-related projects result in failure. They are either late, over budget, or fail to deliver the functionality that was originally specified. This does not have to be the case and would not be the case if more people took the time to learn about and understand IT. Be sure to do your part to develop your IT skills and knowledge and contribute to your organization's IT success. Remember, your success depends on IT!

5. Summary

As professors, we are often asked what skills are required to succeed in the hospitality industry. There are five principal areas we always advise our students to consider, regardless of specific career focus. These include (1) developing business acumen and leadership skills, (2) establishing a strong-technical skills foundation (i.e., financial and statistics, communications, interpersonal), (3) becoming technologically savvy, (4) understanding the art of service management (the craft elements of the business), and (5) being socially and ethically responsible. The industry is highly complex and extremely competitive. Customers and investors are becoming increasingly more demanding. Keeping pace with the demands and making sound business decisions to respond accordingly require strategic thinking, strong analytical and financial skills, and a keen sense as to where the business is heading. Leadership, interpersonal, and communication skills are also essential since we are in a people business. Remember, human resources are our most important strategic assets. We need good, capable, and caring people to accomplish what we do. The thesis of this chapter focused on the technology aspects and why you must master these to be a successful business professional and industry leader. Because the hospitality business is service oriented, the customer or guest must take center stage in all that we do and plan. In order to create unique, memorable experiences, we must also understand the dynamics of service management and how to blend high tech with high touch to provide the right information at the right time to the right people to create the right experience or service as required by the guest at any given circumstance. We are solution providers. As such, it is up to us to make what is seemingly impossible possible—and with ease. In the end, we, as leaders and business professionals,

need to know how to use the many business tools (technology or otherwise) available to us to flawlessly execute our service mission in an ethical and socially responsible manner and with an eye towards profits and shareholder value—every time and with every guest. To do this, we need to be well-rounded and understand as many aspects of the business we can to know how to lead and direct. Your skills assessment and career planning are vital to your future and making sure you are well prepared, so get started on these immediately.

We should take to heart the words of two of history's greatest people: Thomas Edison and Franklin Delano Roosevelt (FDR). In the words of Thomas Edison, "If we all did the things we are capable of doing, we would literally astound ourselves." Engraved on one of the walls of FDR's memorial in Washington, D.C., is the following quote from an undelivered Jefferson Day speech which he was to give within days of his death: "The only limit to our realization of tomorrow will be our doubts of today. Let us move forward with strong and active faith." These quotes are appropriate and offer many insights when thinking about and launching a career. Anything is possible if we set our minds to it. More often than not, we are our own worst enemies and the greatest barriers to realizing what is possible. As you go forward in your studies and your career, just think of what is possible and what we are capable of doing. Channel your energies and creativity to make great things happen. IT's up to you!

Miniaturization, portability, and the convergence of powerful computers, intelligent software, and high-speed, global telecommunications networks and wireless communications are creating a new climate for conducting business throughout the world. IT is transforming virtually every aspect of the industry, from business models and value chains to customer service. Clearly, IT is not a panacea or the Holy Grail, but it is here to stay and will play an important role in both your professional career and personal life. You need to know what it can do for you and your company, recognize opportunities to apply it to gain advantages, understand how it is reshaping business processes, and know when there might be other non-IT alternatives that should be exercised instead. The new source of competitive advantage will be based on intellect rather than on just assets and capital. While the latter two resources are necessary, they are no longer sufficient in a dynamic, high-tech world where the customer is king (i.e., more demanding, more informed, and value conscious). To survive and thrive in the long run, the hospitality organization of the future will need to be a learning organization, one that must always reinvent itself to create value and provide the ultimate in individualized, personalized service. Knowledge will be the basis of competition in the future. The dichotomy between the "haves" and the "have nots" will be exacerbated by the bipolarization between those who know and those who know not (especially when it comes to IT), in what could be categorized as the great digital divide. In other words, it is not sufficient to have the latest in tools and technology. In order to prosper, one must know how to effectively use and deploy these tools and technologies and exploit their capabilities in such a way that competitors cannot easily duplicate.

Ultimately, the challenge will be to creatively implement new technologies to effectively and efficiently treat each consumer as an individual segment (i.e., providing a highly customized, unique experience) while simultaneously creating shareholder value. Information and communications technologies will drive these opportunities—but only if the *right* infrastructure is first established. What is right, of course, will be organization-dependent, but it is clear that the technology architecture in any organization must be flexible and capable of being upgraded to meet changing business needs and take advantage of newer technology innovations. To reach this state, a well-thought strategy must be developed; this can only be done if the events shaping the future are identified and understood. Hence, the need to focus on IT and the resulting convergence is not only timely but also essential to the industry's future. The timing is now to begin this planning effort if the industry is to proactively manage the changes that will inevitably occur and if you are to prosper in your career.

Without question as you will learn from reading this book, the IT requirements of today's marketplace are raising the level of investment and level of knowledge required to compete successfully. In an information economy, everyone in the organization must think and act like a CIO—otherwise, no one is doing his or her job! As previously indicated, IT ofen ranks among the top capital expenditures of a hospitality firm, is quickly becoming pervasive with its impacts spanning all aspects and levels of the firm, and is clearly becoming inescapable as it touches upon all aspects of our lives, both personally and professionally. Its role has shifted from that of support or utility to that of strategic enablement. It is no longer a cost to be contained but rather, a competitive lever to create strategic value. It is an investment in a firm's long-term prosperity and viability. Because of the scope, cost, reach, and strategic implications of most IT projects, it is unacceptable and inexcusable for any hospitality manager not to be involved and adequately prepared to handle such decisions. As you are entrusted with managing the firm's assets with the goal of maximizing shareholder value, it is your fiduciary (i.e., legal) responsibility to carry out your duties to the best of your abilities. You can only fulfill your obligations if you have prepared yourself properly, are well versed in what you manage, and continue to keep yourself current. In an Information Age, this requires knowledge of and competence in IT and continuous learning regardless of the type of career you seek. Are you ready? Go for IT—and remember, it is up to you to make IT happen! Good luck to you as you explore the wonderful world of hospitality and embark on your career!

6. Case Study and Learning Activity

Case Study

Career paths vary widely and often are discovered. Here is how Dr. Daniel Connolly, associate professor of information technology and electronic commerce at the University of Denver's Daniels College of Business, discovered his career calling. While his career choices and interests may differ from yours, there are many relevant lessons which should benefit you in your journey. What follows is Professor Connolly reflecting on portions of his career—the decisions he made and how he came to pursue a career in hospitality IT.

Let me take a step back and share with you how and why I came to pursue a career in hospitality IT—not because I am the exemplar—but because I took a sort of serendipitous route and because many of the decisions I had to make along the way might be similar to those you presently or will soon face. Ironically, when I entered college, I wanted nothing to do with IT. My real goal when I set off for college was to own and operate my own family-style restaurant, much like the one I had worked in as a kid. It was this goal that led my college selection and major. I took—or should I say struggled through—my first computer course in high school. It was a course in computer programming. Although the course was interesting and challenging, I found it to be extremely frustrating. For some reason, my programs never seemed to work properly after the first, second, or even third attempt. In most cases, I found it easier and faster to do the work myself rather than to program the computer to do the tasks for me. At the time, I could neither understand nor appreciate the power and potential of computers, but, as a result of the experience, I did develop some great analytical skills.

Upon entering Cornell University's School of Hotel Administration as a freshman, I once again found myself faced with having to take another computer course. Needless to say, my anxiety level was at an all-time high. However, this course became a defining moment for me,

thanks in part to an instructor who inspired and challenged me to expand my thinking and comfort zone. It was during this course that I began to understand the benefits and potential time-saving applications of computers. I began to see the computer as a tool. As many of my classmates were struggling through their first computer programming experiences, I was building on what I had already learned. In fact, I was beginning to actually understand and appreciate what I had learned in high school in my previous computer course. I was so intrigued that I was constantly looking for new ways to apply the computer in my everyday life. I would write short programs to help me carry out basic tasks more efficiently. What had previously seemed like tedious tasks became fun because I was experimenting and learning while doing my work. At the end of the term, I was convinced that computers would be an important part of the hospitality industry, and that for an aspiring manager, I would need to understand this phenomenon in order to become the industry great I had hoped to be. I then began to seek out additional courses to build my skills so that I would be well positioned for what has become known as the Information Age or Information Economy.

What really turned me on to computers and ultimately a career in hospitality IT is the pervasive nature of IT. During my years at Cornell, I was studying many subjects and developing proficiencies in key areas like accounting, finance, and operations to become a successful businessman. My problem at the time was deliberating over a question that everyone faces: "What career should I ultimately pursue?" At first, as I noted earlier, my interest was in the restaurant industry. Over time, I had developed interests in hotels, sales and marketing, and accounting. Clearly, I could not do everything and would have to make some difficult choices.

As graduation neared, I was debating between careers in lodging, food and beverage, and accounting. With the help of a good faculty mentor and countless hours of advice from friends and family, the light started to become clearer. I realized that I did not necessarily have to give up any of my many interests. If I pursued a career in hospitality IT, I could simultaneously pursue, albeit in a different way, my interests in lodging, restaurants, accounting, and sales because IT was quickly becoming an important ingredient in each of these areas. Thus, what appeared to be a difficult choice became rather obvious.

Upon graduation, I joined the Marriott Corporation (now Marriott International) as a programmer/analyst at its corporate offices in Bethesda, Maryland—and I never looked back. Ever since then, I have found myself exposed to many different facets of the industry and always faced with a new set of interesting challenges to keep me learning and growing. My knowledge of and experience in IT have given me access to many aspects of the hospitality industry, including hotels, restaurants, institutional foodservice, healthcare, retirement communities, and, now, education—and my travels have taken me around the world exposing me to numerous cultures, technologies, and innovative applications of technology. I relish in the challenges of understanding the business—identifying problems and opportunities, and then finding technology solutions.

Clearly, there are great opportunities to be had for anyone interested in and willing to develop the skills and knowledge required to pursue a career in hospitality IT, but it is important to remember that IT is only a tool—an enabler—to make many things possible. To be successful, you must possess skills in three areas: business acumen, technology, and service (the craft elements of the business). A solid grasp of these three areas is requisite to becoming a strong leader and decision maker. IT is important, but by itself, it is of little value if it cannot be applied effectively in the appropriate industry contexts. To effectively apply IT, you must understand how to respond to changing business conditions, think in both strategic and financial terms, and focus on customer service and value creation.

I offer this story to help you appreciate some of the many doors IT can open for you, to get you to think about your own interests and the possibilities IT may play for you, and to focus your attention on important decisions with which you will be faced so that when the time comes, you can make informed choices that take into account your best and long-term interests. There are a few themes you should take away from this account regardless of the type of career you may be considering or the industry in which you seek to work. First, interests change with time, exposure to new subjects, and work experiences. Therefore, keep your mind open and be receptive to new possibilities, even if you do not readily see the fit and even if you think—or are certain like I was—that you already know what you want. Also, pursue multiple career tracks and opportunities simultaneously. That way, if market conditions change or if one possibility dries up, you will have other alternatives to pursue. Second, look for opportunities that will allow you to combine multiple interests and that will offer great flexibility long-term for you and your career. Third, just because you struggle with a subject does not mean you should give up and write it off. Be willing to give it another try and push yourself to achieve new levels. Finally, make career decisions with an eye towards the future. Look for opportunities that will offer growth and open new doors down the line. When I was in college looking to the future, I saw great potential for people well versed in IT. I also saw that it could open many doors and offer many opportunities to branch into new areas that I had not previously considered. I am so fortunate to those that have helped me along the way to recognize and begin pursuing my passion and now my vocation. As poet Robert Frost once wrote, combine your avocation and your vocation. If you do so, you will thrive and love every minute of your work.

Learning Activity

1. What are the key learnings you take away from Professor Connolly's story? How can you apply them to your own career planning?

2. Scan industry job postings from a variety of online and offline sources in search for hospitality managerial positions, IT and non-IT alike. What positions are available? For each position, list and discuss the stated qualifications, skills, job duties, and IT expertise required to perform the job. Which positions are most appealing to you and why?

3. Interview a hospitality business professional in the area of the industry that interests you most and find out in what ways IT affects his or her job and abilities to effectively manage and compete in today's complex and challenging world. What advice can this person offer you in terms of developing your skills and preparing yourself for a future industry career?

4. Define and develop what you would consider to be the ideal career path for you. What steps will you need to take to achieve your goals?

5. Debate with a group of friends or classmates the chapter's thesis that IT is an essential part of every hospitality business professional's career. Do you agree with the chapter's premise? Why or why not? What evidence can you provide to support your position? How would you counter the opposing view?

7. Key Terms

Boundary Spanners

Chief Information Officer (CIO)

Chief Technology Officer (CTO)

SWOT Analysis

Value Chain

8. Chapter Questions

1. Identify at least three examples of hospitality businesses that rely heavily upon technology. For each example, discuss how technology is used, why it is used, and the benefits it affords each organization.

2. What does it mean to be a boundary spanner?

3. What are the different career options available within the hospitality industry for those wishing to explore a career involving IT? How do these options and the skills required vary across industry segments?

4. How would you advise someone interested in pursuing a career in (a) hospitality IT and (b) hospitality management? For each, what steps should he or she take to prepare? What schooling and coursework would you recommend? What types of work experience or jobs would you advise? What skills should be developed and why?

5. Define what the hospitality industry might be like in twenty years. How will business be conducted? What roles will technology play? What will be the hot issues keeping managers awake at night? How will you prepare for these?

CHAPTER 2

Using Information Technology to Drive Competitive Advantage

Chapter Contents

INTERVIEW

Abigail Lorden is editor-in-chief for *Hospitality Technology* magazine which reports on the latest trends and headlines related to technology issues and applications in the hospitality industry.

Q: Please share a brief overview of your background in terms of your education, work experience, and current role and responsibilities in working with hospitality information technology.

A: As editor in chief of *Hospitality Technology,* I regularly monitor and report on industry news and trends that are relevant to hotel and restaurant technology professionals. I call upon industry executives to share their insights, and I analyze the overall travel and consumer landscape for information that is relevant to my audience. In my role,

I provide strategic direction for all of the publication's content, the Web site, and several industry educational events. I have been with the publication for more than five years, and before that, I covered travel industry trends for AAA (American Automobile Association). I hold a BA in Communication from Rutgers University.

Q: Given the state of the economy, it is no longer business as usual. How is information technology reshaping the hospitality business landscape and the service delivery process?

A: Economic conditions have forced many hospitality companies to cut budgets, reduce staff, overhaul their menus, and even close locations. When used in the right ways, information technology has the potential to help organizations use their resources for the greatest operational efficiency, which can offset the potential negative impact of a reduction in internal resources. In addition, IT can help hospitality companies better respond to guests' needs. This is really critical today since consumers are so price and value conscious and willing to shop around to find deals.

Q: What roles should information technology play in the hospitality industry? What are the critical success factors, and how can the value derived from information technology be effectively measured?

A: In short, information technology should be used to create better guest experiences, in ways that are economically sound for the hospitality operator. For example, IT should be used to add efficiency, accuracy, and personalization to the guest experience; it should also be used to create meaningful, lasting experiences for guests, allowing them to take as much control over their interactions as they desire, without detracting from the level of personal touch that they seek.

    Critical to success are guests' ability to use any guest-facing technologies with relative ease and minimal instruction. In addition, the technology must provide a return on investment (ROI) to the hospitality operator. This return can be "hard" (measured in dollars and cents) or "soft" (measured through improvements in the guest experience, customer feedback, customer loyalty, employee retention, etc.).

Q: How can hospitality organizations use information technology to create *sustainable* competitive advantage and drive business value?

A: Specific tools such as business intelligence (BI) and inventory management are great examples of areas in which information technology can provide competitive advantage. For example, if a restaurant operator can predict the number of employees it will need for a particular dinner shift and accurately monitor its product inventory to ensure it will have enough fresh salmon on hand for that shift, that restaurant will be able to better serve its guests without overspending on labor or having to inform customers that the restaurant has run out of salmon. This kind of information comes from having fully integrated systems that monitor sales, on-hand inventory, delivery lag times for food inventory, and much more. Integrated business intelligence across all areas of the operation has tremendous value for the restaurant.

Q: Where should hospitality business leaders look for new ideas and innovations?

A: New ideas are born every day—in board rooms, in test labs, in hotel guest rooms, in a technology manufacturer's research facility, or scribbled on the back of a napkin during a business lunch. (I've seen that one firsthand!) To learn about these innovations, business leaders should attend industry educational and networking events, stay active in industry associations, subscribe to industry trade magazines, network with their peers online via social media channels, and communicate with their technology partners.

Q: In looking over the next three to five years, what do you see as the top industry trends and strategic priorities for hospitality companies?

A: I predict there will be greater integration of guests' personal mobile telephones into their dining and lodging experiences—in fact, so much so that these devices will become an integral part of hotel and restaurant operations. Some examples of applications include room check-in devices, shopping and reservations/purchasing tools, location-based services, marketing platforms, and much more.

I also see that guests will continue to want control over how they do business with hotels and restaurants; that is, when, where, and how they interact with hospitality providers—all on their own terms and increasingly through their smart phones. This will lead to ongoing involvement in social networking channels on a highly localized level and to even yet unexplored ways of inputting preferences and making purchases. For example, with location-based services enabled on a guest's smart phone and opt-in preferences set with frequently used hospitality providers, a guest can automatically receive relevant information and offers after arriving in a certain city, say a text message from a favorite restaurant company with directions to its nearest location plus special offers or discount coupons.

A third, yet continuous trend is that guests will be more inclined to patronize hotels and restaurants that can provide personalized services and experiences based upon their preferences and past purchase history. Hospitality is all about the experience; it is not simply a transaction.

Q: Whom do you consider to be on the forefront of these trends (i.e., the players to watch) and why?

A: In general, the lodging industry has been able to build more lasting and personalized relationships with guests than the foodservice industry due to the longer periods of time that guests stay at a hotel versus at a restaurant; however, both have much room for improvement and growth. On the lodging side, several hotel brands tend to be on the cutting edge of guest-facing technology. Mandarin Oriental Hotel Group, Fairmont Hotels and Resorts, and MGM Resorts International (formerly MGM MIRAGE) represent a few innovators. On the foodservice side, companies such as Pizza Hut and Chipotle have done very well in designing useful and dynamic applications for guests' iPhones and iTouch devices.

Q: What do you consider to be the greatest challenges or barriers to information technology adoption in the hospitality industry?

A: In the current climate and for the next twelve to eighteen months, budget constraints will continue to pose a challenge to technology adoption in the hospitality industry. Looking longer term, limitations with the technology itself and integration between systems will be major challenges. Hospitality operators run vast numbers of systems (e.g., POS, CRM, inventory, payment processing, back office, labor.) from disparate vendors within their operations. These different systems don't currently integrate at the level necessary for hospitality operators to have one guest record containing all information of the relevant guest information. In addition, on the lodging side, consumers are installing high-tech multimedia systems in their homes with access to things like high-definition content, digital records, streaming content from the Internet, and vast audio libraries. It is proving challenging for hotel operators to keep up with the pace of technology adoption in their guest rooms that consumers have in their homes.

Q: What parting words of advice can you share with current and aspiring hospitality business professionals?

A: Remember to stay focused on the most important element of the hospitality industry: the guest experience.

1. INTRODUCTION

Information technology (IT) is an important resource for any firm. In today's era, it is hard to imagine how any business, especially a hospitality business, could operate without the assistance of IT. IT applications are seen throughout an entire firm—integrated with almost every business discipline and process, a useful resource for decision making, and increasingly a key ingredient in driving business value. As such, IT must be viewed holistically with the business in mind and be a topic of discussion in nearly every business decision, particularly those involving business strategy, marketing and distribution, operations, and future growth planning. Also, all business leaders should have some proficiency working with IT and an understanding of how to use it effectively to solve business problems, serve business needs, and create new opportunities. As such, the IT function should be represented at the executive-suite level with the chief information officer (CIO) occupying a seat at the decision-making table with visible support and participation from all top-level executives. These factors will ensure that IT is factored into decisions early on and for the right reasons—to create business value and advantages.

Within the hospitality industry, IT represents one of the largest areas of capital expenditure. To some, IT might be viewed as a rather large expense, but it should be viewed as a strategic opportunity. In reality, IT is both a support tool and a strategic enabler. IT should never be used for the sake of IT itself or just because it is the latest and greatest. Instead, IT should be used purposefully with the end business goals in mind. It should be used to solve business problems. If not used correctly, IT can become nothing more than an unwanted expense, a source of frustration, or an inhibitor to change, but when used correctly, many exciting possibilities can result—from service enhancements and product differentiation to new revenue streams. Moving forward, hospitality executives must continually look towards the strategic opportunities technology offers and use technology as a **competitive method**—or as a tool—to differentiate and create **competitive advantage**. Thriving in today's competitive world is all about doing things better, faster, cheaper, and differently than anyone else.

The creation of competitive advantage must involve multiple aspects of the firm coming together. In this chapter, we want to explore the use of IT for creating—or at least contributing to—competitive advantage in a hospitality firm. If you look at history across the general business landscape, you can find many great companies that have creatively and strategically deployed IT to create competitive advantage. Some of the many examples include American Airlines and its reservation system, SABRE; FedEx and its shipping and package tracking software, PowerShip; Wal-Mart and its supply chain management technology; Hertz and its system for driving directions and use of mobile technology to support quick car returns; and Dell Computer's self-ordering system for customized personal computers. More recent technology innovations include McDonald's kitchen production and management system to support efficient and low-cost operations, Marriott's reservations and revenue management systems to achieve rate premiums and higher occupancy rates than industry averages, Mandarin Oriental's in-room guest technology to create memorable guest experiences, Southwest Airline's Ding! application to push special promotions to customers and sell distressed (i.e., last-minute) inventory, Harrah's customer relationship management (CRM) to personalize services and promotions, and InterContinental Hotel Groups' use of mobile technologies to enable and support guest services for people on the move. These are just a sampling of some of the many creative and successful applications showing how technology can drive competitive advantage and differentiation. They illustrate how crucial technology has become in driving the competitive and very dynamic landscape. The magnitude of these initiatives also suggests the need for a great deal of vision, competencies, and capital resources to make things happen through IT.

Our challenge as hospitality managers is to find new opportunities—just as these exemplar companies did—in which IT can be used to solve business problems, create better service experiences, provide cost and/or informational advantages, and create distinction in the market place. Ultimately, technology should be used to lower cost structure, increase revenues and market share, create unique value propositions for guests, and generate unprecedented returns for investors or shareholders. Certainly, these sound daunting—and they are! Creating competitive advantage requires creative, out-of-the-box thinking. Like Apple's CEO Steve Jobs, one must think differently. This requires seeing the future first, taking some calculated risks, and doing things that no one else has attempted. To do so requires dedication, determination, focus, and consistent allocation of resources. Sometimes, one can stumble from time to time, but if one learns from his or her mistakes, progress can be made. If creating competitive advantage were so easy, then every manager would have already thought of all the great ideas possible, and every company would have implemented them by now. Creating competitive advantage requires you to see things that others cannot or do not see and then act on these opportunities to make them happen, but it does not stop there. Once the competitive advantage has been created, the challenge shifts to sustaining that competitive advantage or destroying it and either reinventing it or replacing it with something else before anyone else has time to copy it and catch up to your lead. There is no resting on your laurels. This is a complex and never-ending game. Therefore, you, as a manager, must be prepared to play aggressively, think quickly and creatively, and be in the race for the long haul. Are you ready? Will you think differently, and act quickly?

2. TECHNOLOGY TAKES CENTER STAGE

One of the most significant developments related to technology over the past few decades (and for the foreseeable future) is the concept of **digital convergence** (Tapscott, 1996; Negroponte, 1995)—the coming together of numerous technologies to make great things happen. At the core of this convergence, as shown in Figure 2-1, are IT (i.e., computer hardware, software, databases, mobile devices, etc.), telecommunications and telephony (i.e., voice, data, cable, and wireless networks; telephones, facsimile, and telephone answering devices), interactive, multimedia content (i.e., text, voice, graphics, digital photos, sound, and video), and broadcast media (i.e., radio and television).

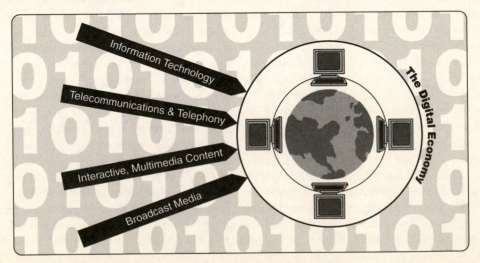

FIGURE 2-1   The Great Convergence Gives Rise to the Digital Economy

This digital convergence, supported by miniaturization, mobility, declining costs, push technology, constant connectivity to the Internet, and more powerful applications, is part of a trend driving computers to ubiquity in everyday life—so much so that computers are deemed essential or required for survival in today's world. As such, technology is reshaping everything we do—from how we work, play, and learn to how we communicate with others. IT is redefining communications among our employees, guests, and suppliers; changing the nature of business transactions; and increasing the technology needs and amenity expectations of our guests. We must, therefore, learn to embrace technology and use it creatively to win over customers and provide our employees with the appropriate tools to perform their job responsibilities. We must constantly stay abreast of the developments taking place in and outside of our market space and remain alert to signals of change and opportunity. Lack of vigilance, however brief, could allow a competitor or outsider to move in, capitalize on new opportunities, and leave us in a trail of dust.

As a result of digital convergence, the competitive landscape is drastically and constantly in a state of flux. Speed, agility, connectivity, and the ability to amass and subsequently employ knowledge are key competitive ingredients to long-term survivability, but we must not seek merely to survive but to thrive under these conditions. This calls into question the competitive nature of business, the skills required to succeed, and what this will mean to managers serving as stewards of their companies and working to guide their companies to prosperity and vitality. Needless to say, the effects of digital convergence are both impressive and exciting—offering new opportunities and capabilities limited only by our imaginations. How we tap into this digital convergence will set us apart from others and allow us to create competitive advantage.

As Porter (1985), Quinn (1988), Burrus (1993), D'Aveni (1994), and others have astutely observed long ago, IT undermines traditional forms of competition, strategic management, organizational structure, governance, and economic policy making. The resulting environment is one of hypercompetition, where shorter transaction times, nontraditional competitors, volatility, surprise, and new alliances are the norm. For the hospitality industry, the implications are also profound: higher capital costs, more sophisticated and discriminating customers, knowledge gaps, more complex business operations, more demanding investors, new competitors, and new operating paradigms. Therefore, in the new business climate, continuous change, lifelong learning, and innovation will become standard components of everyone's job responsibilities.

Bounded by Tradition

Conventional thinking suggested that services were less technologically advanced than their manufacturing counterparts (Quinn, 1988). Under this traditional paradigm, IT was viewed as a support tool. Over the years, this thinking influenced IT spending, investment, and usage throughout the industry, placing the primary emphasis on tactical systems with calculable ROIs. Until recently, seldom did strategic vision or a **preemptive** (i.e., proactive) strategy drive investment decisions in IT. In a study of three prominent, multinational hospitality companies, Cho (1996) found that cost-benefit criteria consistently outweighed strategic preemptiveness when considering IT investment decisions. In essence, IT expenditures were typically viewed as discretionary spending and, therefore, subjected to intense scrutiny (Antonucci and Tucker, 1998). Moreover, pressures from Wall Street and the investment community to focus on earnings resulted in a short-term orientation at the expense of long-term benefits and positioning. Further hindering the implementation of IT were management's lack of understanding of technology (i.e., applications and capabilities of IT) and the uncertainty surrounding the effectiveness of an organization's investment in IT (Andersen Consulting and American Hotel & Motel Association, 1989).

These factors led to six prevailing philosophies regarding IT investment within the hospitality industry. IT projects typically fell in one of the following six categories: (1) projects that were essential to survival; (2) projects requiring an act of faith (or gut feeling) that an investment will prove beneficial to the firm over the long term; (3) projects with an intuitive appeal and seemingly obvious outcomes; (4) projects that were required or mandated (either by law, by regulation, or by top management); (5) projects in response to moves by competitors to achieve parity or protect market share; and (6) projects that had to undergo intense scrutiny and analysis due to the high degrees of risk and uncertainty—either perceived or actual. Notice that none of these categories addressed innovation or the strategic capabilities of technology. These categories were testament of the reactionary tendencies that used to characterize and plague the hospitality industry.

This thinking often slowed the deployment of IT within the hospitality industry, especially with respect to the use of IT for competitive advantage. Shying away from preemptive strategies was further reinforced by the continuing trend towards decreasing costs for IT equipment, which encouraged managers to wait or defer technology-related decisions until the technology became more affordable (Post, Kagan, and Lau, 1995). Finally, IT capabilities were hampered by the lack of industry-specific applications and proven solutions. Since many applications were adapted from other industries (e.g., airlines), they were considered inadequate or clumsy because of their poor fit and their inability to address hotel-specific needs (Hensdill, 1998).

Enlightenment

Fortunately, the sentiment towards the application of IT is changing and the technology is greatly improving, although these have been a long time in coming. The foremost forces driving technology applications in the hospitality industry are the quality of the guest experience, the advances in consumer technology, and competitive pressure. In 1985, Porter recognized the potential and value of IT for driving competitive positioning. Porter wrote that technological change was among the most prominent forces driving competition (Porter, 1985). It took more than a decade for this same realization to become apparent in the hospitality industry (Olsen, 1996; Cline and Blatt, 1998; Hensdill, 1998). As Palmer (1988, p. 26) commented:

> Pricing strategies will always be a major determining factor, but below the surface the battles in the travel business are being fought with a more subtle weapon, information technology.

Hensdill (1998) wrote that investing in technology simply to manage a hotel was no longer sufficient. This is especially true today. We are now at a point where information becomes the catalyst for competitive advantage. While location and physical assets are important to competitiveness, they are not enough. Companies must look to deploy technology that will help their employees learn faster and know more than anyone else about their businesses, customers, and competition, and then use this information to compete more effectively and more aggressively than their competitors—and in ways that create customized and personalized services and experiences that can't be duplicated easily.

In an information economy, knowledge about and access to customers are critical success factors (Cline and Blatt, 1998). However, these critical success factors can only be realized through IT and competent, knowledgeable workers. IT can assist with data collection, storage, and analysis, but it is up to employees to interpret the data, convert it to usable information, and then put it to work in unique ways. An important industry trend is to proactively apply IT in the area of guest services, a necessity that has resulted from increased competition, consumer demands, and shareholders' focus on **asset optimization** (i.e., getting the most value from firm resources or assets as measured by return on assets). The historical debate between high tech and high touch is dead. Service quality is perceptual and differs greatly from consumer to consumer based upon a variety of factors including generational upbringing, comfort levels, knowledge, and access to technology. Technology is a service enabler. In today's sophisticated market place, it is nearly impossible to achieve high touch without high tech. That said, IT is an important resource vital to a firm's success. No longer can it be viewed simply for its support and utility roles characteristic of tactical applications that focus on the use of IT to gain efficiencies, reduce costs, decrease labor, and improve productivity. Instead, IT must play more strategic roles in organizations that involve creating competitive advantage, differentiating products and services, building and sustaining core competencies, and enabling new business opportunities.

The focus is on value creation, not just cost containment. This transformation in management's thinking is summarized in Figure 2-2. Please note, however, that this shift in thinking does not diminish the importance of reducing or containing costs. This is important, but costs can only be cut so far. Thus, to grow the business, one must look externally and strategically to create new opportunities. This mindset shift represents a transition from investing in technology as a means of surviving or maintaining competitive parity to one of conquering new ground and to creating competitive advantage. The focus must be proactive rather than reactive, strategic versus support-oriented. Consequently, the basis of competition is not just about assets and resources. It's also about agility and intellectual prowess to outfox the competition.

Hospitality executives must view IT in a positive light to truly harness its power and capabilities. Instead of waiting for other companies to pave the way, hospitality professionals must look for creative ways to marry technology, people, and opportunity to creatively solve business problems. This is necessary to both survival and competitiveness. To be in a position to prosper from technology requires significant investment of both time and money in IT and a consistent allocation of resources to create a capable and secure IT infrastructure and to master the steep learning curve typically associated with IT. The IT function must also be well aligned with the firm's overall strategic initiatives and those of each of the core disciplines, namely sales and marketing, accounting and finance, human resources, management, and operations. IT and strategy of the firm must be intertwined and evolve in definition together, not separately to generate value and so that the benefits of technology can truly be realized. The best results from IT are usually derived when IT is viewed as an integral part of the business and the projects in

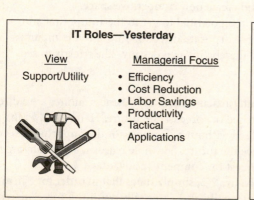

FIGURE 2-2   Shifting IT Roles in Organizations

which it is involved. In these cases, the focus is on the business outcomes (usually something related to the guest experience), generally not the technology itself (unless, of course, the project is infrastructure related). Technology is not the end game, but rather, a tool or enabler to help arrive at the end goal or goals. It is one important piece among a number of pieces to play the competitive game. The fundamental question to be asked is "How can IT help?" Because there is a significant lead time associated with IT development and implementation, a firm must continuously focus on IT (specifically its capabilities and limitations) at the very inception of any business opportunity or problem assessment if IT is to contribute positively to the value of the firm and result in the desired benefits. The earlier IT can be brought in on a project, the greater the likelihood the organization will achieve success from IT; the better the fit will be, and the more people will embrace the solution. One must also remember that it is not the technology itself that provides the competitive advantage in a firm, but rather, how that technology is used, what it enables the firm and its employees to do, and what that technology can deliver in the future that makes a competitive difference. It's all about people, business processes, information, and technology coming together in a unified way to make great things happen in a timely manner.

3. THE CONCEPT OF CO-ALIGNMENT

To understand the essence of strategy and the concept of competitive advantage, it is important to study the **co-alignment principle**, which is the theoretical underpinning of these subjects. Firms are often viewed as living organisms that must adapt to their environments to survive and thrive. This concept builds on Darwin's survival of the fittest theory. In order to survive, one must be fit, and to be fit, one must understand the environment in which he or she operates and the forces driving change in that environment—and then adapt accordingly. Thus, the essence of strategy focuses on the environment in which a firm competes and one's understanding of that environment, any changes taking place, and what needs to be done to adapt and stay fit (that is, out in front of the competition). Strategy takes a future orientation and looks to developing a game plan and competitive posture to successfully compete and build competitive advantage. In the words of Hamel and Prahalad (1994, p. 64):

> The vital first step in competing for the future is the quest for industry foresight. This is the race to gain an understanding deeper than competitors, of the trends and discontinuities—technological, demographic, regulatory, or lifestyle—that can be used to transform industry boundaries and create new competitive space.
>
> Industry foresight gives a company the potential to get to the future first and stake out a leadership position. It informs corporate direction and lets a company control the evolution of its industry and, thereby its own destiny. The trick is to see the future before it arrives.

As Hamel and Prahalad (1994) so eloquently articulated, many business failures are a direct result of an organization's inability to properly see or forecast the future. Hamel and Prahalad believe it is impossible for any company to succeed without a clear view of the opportunities and challenges lurking on the horizon that will shape the future. For these reasons, the co-alignment principle takes on such importance in a firm's quest for competitive advantage.

The co-alignment principle, depicted in Figure 2-3, simply states that in order for a firm to be successful, it must be well aligned, both internally and externally, with the forces driving change in its business environment. After identifying opportunities and threats in the external

The Path to Firm Profitability

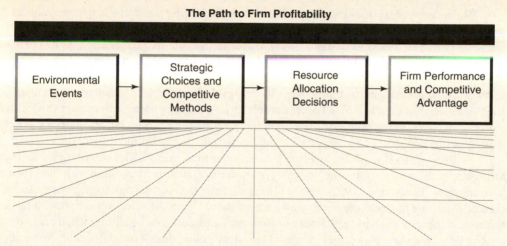

FIGURE 2-3 The Co-Alignment Principle

environment, a firm can then plan, formulate, and execute strategies so as to exploit these environmental opportunities and minimize any potential or actual threats. These strategies and strategic choices should focus on the development and investment in a portfolio of products and services, competitive methods, resources, and core competencies that will competitively position the firm within the environment, while accounting for the forces driving change. This investment requires consistent allocation of resources to these initiatives over extended periods of time. If done well, a firm should achieve profitability and generate competitive advantage in its industry (Chandler, 1962; Thompson, 1967; Bourgeois, 1980; Venkatraman and Prescott, 1990; Venkatraman, Henderson, and Oldach, 1993; Murthy, 1994; Olsen, West, and Tse, 2008). In other words, if a firm can effectively identify opportunities and threats, develop the appropriate competitive methods (ways to compete), and consistently apply firm resources (which include people, capital, facilities, and IT), financial performance will improve and competitive advantage will result. Because technological change plays such an influential role in competition, being able to forecast technological developments, to select those most appropriate for a firm, and to implement them in a timely manner and in such a way that cannot be easily imitated by competitors become important skills and critical success factors for all firms (Porter, 1985).

Multiple measures of performance can be considered when determining the health of a company, its competitiveness, and its overall success in applying the co-alignment principle. Olsen et al. (2008) suggest that the best measure is **cash flow per share**, a measure of firm profitability. Their arguments supporting this metric state that while seeking a balance between long-term and short-term earnings requirements, cash flow per share can (1) reflect the cash flows generated by investments in a complex and dynamic environment; (2) illustrate management's effectiveness with environmental scanning, choice of competitive methods, and resource allocations, and, therefore, management's overall ability to compete; and (3) demonstrate how a business utilizes its assets to add value to the firm. Antonucci and Tucker (1998) also favored the use of cash flow over other accounting measures of profitability derived from the income statement because accounting practices sometimes mask cash flows with noncash expenses (e.g., depreciation, amortization, and write-offs) to create gains or losses reported on a firm's income statement. While all of these authors favor the use of cash flow over other profitability measures, they do concede that not all cash flows translate directly into earnings per share.

The most popular thinking and prolific theories regarding the strategic use and value of IT come from the Harvard Business School, which is dominated by the works of Michael Porter (Porter, 1980, 1985; Porter and Millar, 1985). Porter's works are frequently cited in the IT literature as the theoretical underpinnings for studying IT and its use to create competitive advantage. Applying this school of thought, the frameworks used to measure the strategic significance of IT and identify opportunities to apply IT are value chain analysis, Porter's industry and competitive analysis (ICA) framework or **Five Forces model** (which addresses barriers to market entry, intra-industry rivalries, buyer power, supplier power, and substitute products), and Porter's **generic strategies** (i.e., low-cost producer, product differentiation, or market niche focus).

Technology strategy refers to a firm's plans, intentions, and policies regarding current and future use of IT, information, and "softer" IT-related issues such as integration with the firm and its employees (Brady et al., 1992). Porter (1985) suggests that technology strategy must include choices regarding the technologies in which a firm should invest, the firm's position with respect to the technologies selected (e.g., leader or follower), and decisions regarding when and how to acquire or license the technologies. A firm's IT strategy guides decisions related to its technological architecture, infrastructure, applications, and services in accordance with that firm's business strategy and objectives. Yet, in today's context of rapid change and in a marketplace that is inundated with new technology products and offerings (hardware, software, and services), hospitality leaders find it difficult and even daunting at times to effectively evaluate these technological advancements and assimilate them into their organizations' strategies. As a result, they typically maintain short planning horizons. While it is clear they must be judicious as to their investments and select only those that will provide value to the firm, selecting and implementing those technologies are often difficult and risky tasks, since not all of the benefits will be tangible. Porter (1985) recommends concentrating on those technologies that will lead to the greatest sustainable impact on cost, product, or service differentiation. When choosing among technologies in which to invest, hospitality executives should base their decisions on a thorough understanding of each technological choice and its impact to the firm's value chain (Porter, 1985).

4. ACHIEVING COMPETITIVE ADVANTAGE

Competitive advantage sounds really awesome, but what does it mean? Understanding this concept is vital to the success of future hospitality leaders, especially given the competitive and volatile nature of the hospitality industry, the high stakes of competition, and the growing trend towards commoditization—where products blur and become indistinguishable from and, therefore, interchangeable with one another. In simplistic terms, competitive advantage is derived from one or more unique capabilities of the firm and brings value to the firm. These capabilities set one firm apart from others within the industry and within its competitive set. These single out the firm for some reason, making it *different* from others competing in the same space. Typically, this differentiation comes from the firm's resources and capabilities, is established as part of the firm's strategy, is reinforced by the firm's culture and mission statement, and is supported by the firm's budget. Competitive advantage results from doing things faster, better, cheaper, or different than anyone else. It can be measured in many ways; for example, in terms of product or service quality, market share, brand recognition, customer loyalty, employee loyalty, profitability, and cost structure.

Traditional sources of competitive advantage come from gaining leadership positions in one or more of four arenas: price and quality, timing and know-how, stronghold creation, and deep pockets (D'Aveni, 1994). To properly put things in perspective, consider that everyone (that is, employees, customers, investors, or franchisees) has a choice in today's competitive marketplace. Oftentimes, this choice can be made between multiple competing, yet similar, offerings.

With information being so readily available, these people can do their homework and make more informed choices. They can be picky and extremely demanding. Are you positioned well to win their attention and to get them to select your company's offerings? What makes your firm a better choice over other options in the market place? What is the deciding factor, the thing that really makes the difference? This is what competitive advantage is all about.

IT provides competitive advantage if it helps a firm reduce the firm's cost structure, generate profits, make better and faster decisions, or differentiate its products and services. Competitive advantage results when a firm gains an advantage (typically in the form of economic rents, increased market share, or information asymmetries) over its competitors by exploiting its strengths relative to those of its competitors (Ohmae, 1992). In this context, competitive advantage from IT results when the technology itself helps a firm in achieving economies of scale, reducing costs, differentiating the firm's products and services, creating barriers to entry, building **switching costs** (things that lock in or bind a consumer to a product or company), changing the basis of competition, adding customer value, altering the balance of power with suppliers, providing first-mover effects, or generating new products (see also Applegate, McFarlan, and McKenney, 1996; Hitt and Brynjolfsson, 1996; D'Aveni, 1994; Bakos and Treacy, 1986; Clemons and Kimbrough, 1986; Porter and Millar, 1985; Cash and Konsynski, 1985; McFarlan, 1984; Ives and Learmonth, 1984; Parsons, 1983).

Based on Porter's teachings, a series of questions can be raised (see Figure 2-4) to help evaluate the strategic potential and ultimate competitive advantage that can be derived from

---

- Can IT create entry barriers to keep out potential new competitors? If so, how?
- Can IT create switching costs to lock in customers and make it difficult or undesirable for them to seek out other alternatives?
- Can IT help the firm understand its customers better, use information to provide unique experiences and customer service, and build lasting relationships that lead to loyalty and more spending?
- Can IT be used to lower the firm's cost structure, streamline operations, or to create economies of scale?
- Can IT be used to create new business opportunities and revenue streams?
- Can IT be used to differentiate the firm's products and service offerings? If so, how?
- Can IT be used to improve product or service quality or ensure consistency?
- Can IT be used to build better alliances or strategic partnerships to help the firm gain access to new markets or access to resources and skills it does not presently have?
- Can IT be used to provide an edge in dealing with suppliers or enable better negotiating leverage?
- Can IT change the nature of competition and the dynamics within the industry, shifting them in the firm's favor?
- Can IT help the firm sustain its competitive advantage in the market place?
- Can IT better equip employees to be more productive and capable, perhaps by providing information to them or providing faster access to information to help them do a better job and outperform the competition?
- Can IT help to provide informational advantages, namely more and better information than what suppliers or competitors may have to make faster decisions, negotiate better prices, and so on?
- Can IT help a firm do more with less?
- Can IT help to create a "wow" experience that is memorable and will be recounted to others?
- Is IT aligned with the strategic objectives of the firm?
- How can IT be better used to help the firm achieve the firm's strategies?

FIGURE 2-4   Key Questions to Ask of All IT Projects

a technology-based initiative. This list is not exhaustive, but it is representative of the types of considerations one should have. It is suggested that these questions be raised often when defining strategy and setting priorities involving IT.

Resource-Based View of the Firm

The assessment of competitive advantage is an important step in the IT investment decision-making process, and internal efficiency can provide one source of competitive advantage (Sethi and King, 1994). According to Sethi and King (1994), the two prevailing approaches to assessing competitive advantage are the following:

1. **Outcome Approach**—This approach places great emphasis on competitive efficiency, business value, and management productivity, and uses such measures as revenue growth rate, ROI, return on assets, profits, and net worth. It takes a macro-level perspective by focusing on aggregate measures that address performance of the firm.
2. **Trait Approach**—This approach identifies specific attributes of an IT application that are known to contribute to competitive advantage. These are reflected in concepts like competitive forces, strategic thrusts, value activities, and the customer resource life cycle. This approach takes on a more micro-level view since the focus is on an individual IT application and the role it plays in enhancing the firm's competitive advantage.

To assess competitive advantage derived from a single IT application, Sethi and King (1994) define a construct called Competitive Advantage Provided by an Information Technology Application (CAPITA). **CAPITA** is defined by five dimensions: efficiency (the extent to which an IT application allows a firm to produce products and services at prices lower than its competitors), functionality (the extent to which an IT application provides the functions and capabilities required by users), threat (the impact of an IT application on the balance of power between suppliers and buyers), preemptiveness (early adoption of an IT application to usurp the market), and synergy (the degree of integration between an IT application and the firm's goals, strategies, and environment).

Because of the commodity-like nature of IT, Cho (1996) presented an alternative view of competitive advantage grounded in theory pertaining to the **resource-based view** of the firm as studied by Clemons and Row (1991) and Mata, Fuerst, and Barney (1995). Using this framework, Cho suggested that a company achieves competitive advantage through the culmination and convergence of a series of events, resources, experiences, and underlying management processes. Alternatively stated, competitive advantage is the result of not only how a firm competes (or plays the game) but also the assets it has in which to play or compete. The competitive advantage is derived collectively from a variety of firm assets that make up its resources and capabilities. These include its people (and their skills and expertise), financial assets, IT portfolio and infrastructure, corporate culture, portfolio of products and services, competitive methods, strategic alliances, and so on. There is no one contributing factor but a series of ingredients or idiosyncratic resources that when combined provide a competitive edge in the marketplace. Plimpton (1990) termed this hidden or **tacit** competitive edge as the *X Factor*. It's like a secret ingredient in a recipe. For many organizations, the integration of software applications and IT with the organizational structure and its staff provides the source of competitive advantage (Adcock et al., 1993). Because of its tacit nature, the competitive advantage and its contributing factors are difficult to identify and, therefore, hard to duplicate. The resulting competitive advantage can then be sustained for as long as it remains inimitable and not obsolete, a period that is becoming shorter all the time in today's hypercompetitive marketplace.

Finding sources of competitive advantage that are unique and inimitable is important, especially in the service industry where barriers to entry tend to be relatively low and because service concepts can be easily copied. One of the reasons so many Internet firms failed in the Dot.Com era is because many Internet entrepreneurs underestimated the ease and speed in which their concepts could be copied. Thus, their concepts became undifferentiated and indistinguishable among their competitors, and competition grew at a much faster rate than what was anticipated. A small customer base at the time (recall that Internet access was not as prevalent and that the number of users was a much smaller percentage of the overall population as it is today) was diluted. Customers spent their time shopping for the best price, causing everyone's profitability to fall. Therefore, barriers should be erected whenever possible, and sources of competitive advantage should be embedded in the organization and should be comprised of the firm's unique factors (or what is known as idiosyncratic resources). This will create tacit competitive advantage. Lastly, firms should protect their competitive advantage and discourage employees from talking with outsiders regarding the sources of competitive advantage. Doing these things will make it harder for others to copy, and allow firms to prolong their advantages.

Examples of Competitive Advantage Derived from IT

Throughout the hospitality industry, there are many examples where firms are creatively using IT to create competitive advantage. The following are some examples seen across the hotel industry in the context of global distribution systems (GDSs) but whose reach goes beyond to include service delivery and customer relationship management (CRM). Although described in the context of GDS, the examples of competitive advantage derived through (1) economies of scale, (2) functionality, (3) accuracy of information, and (4) proprietary technology are readily transferable to other technology applications and areas of the hospitality industry.

1. **Economies of scale** have been among the most significant sources of competitive advantage derived from GDSs. Building a GDS is a costly, time-consuming, and difficult venture. It requires great expertise, both technical and operational. Not all companies have the resources, expertise, and wherewithal to develop a GDS. Moreover, the costs have exceeded the reach of many organizations. In chains and affiliate organizations that provide reservation systems technology and services to their member hotels, the incremental cost to add new hotels is pretty minimal relative to the core investment required to build the system. As such, the initial investment and fixed costs can be allocated over a wider base, thereby providing greater economic efficiencies and decreasing the participation cost for each hotel in the network. These efficiencies appeal to franchisees that seek access to global distribution channels but lack the capital and expertise to develop their own. Efficiencies and economies of scale lead to lower deployment costs, operating costs, and transaction fees. Hence, a GDS is a primary selection criterion for companies interested in affiliating with a franchisor or a management firm. As the franchise network and number of hotels under a single umbrella grow, so do market penetration and market share. Size then becomes an important factor that can be leveraged to gain additional economies and clout with external entities.

2. Another source of competitive advantage comes from the functionality of the GDS, its links to external systems, and its flexibility to adapt to an ever-changing business environment. For the hospitality industry in particular, this means having the ability to

control inventory and rates (including booking rules, restrictions, and selling strategies), to distribute this information seamlessly and in real time to a multitude of access points (e.g., travel agents, airline GDSs, reservation call centers, sister properties or products, other member hotels), and to generate instant confirmations continues to separate the capabilities of competing hotels. Access and links to external systems extends the reach of the hotel GDS, thereby attracting a broader audience from all over the world.

Functional advantages also include ease of use and the GDSs' role in supporting the selling process (i.e., the conversion of inquiries to bookings at the best possible rates). These advantages are typically measured in terms of the number of room-nights or revenue generated by the GDS, occupancy, REVPAR (revenue per available room), REVPOR (revenue per occupied room), and guest loyalty. An example of a temporary competitive advantage resulting from GDS functionality is Marriott International. At a time when the industry was in recession, Marriott turned to strategic and disciplined discounting as a means to increase occupancy. Borrowing pricing strategies from the airline industry, Marriott created a twenty-one-day advance purchase promotion. In order to receive these low rates, a guest was required to meet certain conditions and comply with certain rules or restrictions (called "fences") (Hanks, Noland, and Cross, 1992). In order to enforce these fences, Marriott's Automated Reservation System for Hotel Accommodations (MARSHA) needed to contain sophisticated functionality to manage room inventory and to monitor customer purchase patterns. Since many competing chains lacked similar functionality at the time, they had difficulty in copying Marriott's promotion. Thus, Marriott enjoyed a competitive advantage until such time that other chains could modify their reservations systems to accommodate the same type of practice. Recognizing the short-lived nature of its competitive advantage, Marriott continued to develop its MARSHA reservation system and enhance its integration with its hotel property management and demand forecasting revenue management systems to develop more sophisticated pricing strategies that allowed higher rate premiums and occupancy percentages than industry competitors. Thus, Marriott managed to stay ahead and outperform its competition. A key lesson for all to take away is the need to continue to improve or develop new competitive advantages because they seldom last. More than likely, they will be short lived before someone figures out how to copy or build a better solution.

Flexibility is another important consideration. GDSs must be able to effectively adapt to changing market needs at a moment's notice. Cycle times are too short to tolerate long lead times. Because of the systemic nature of a GDS environment, a change in one area (which could be either functional or technical) will most likely constitute a domino effect. For example, many hotel companies are looking to deploy mobile applications (mobile apps) to support reservation inquiries and bookings, guest profiles, loyalty account balances, online check-in, keyless room entry, and more for guests on the go via their smart phones. The development and implementation of mobile applications require a great deal of thought to systems enhancements to many core systems (including GDS, PMS, the hotel's Web site), usability (i.e., user interface design), platform considerations (i.e., hardware and operating systems), system interfaces, security, the guest experience, and the overall service delivery process. Mobile apps represent just one of many areas that could be used to illustrate the need for flexibility in design and programmability of the information systems and interfaces comprising the GDS to accommodate new business needs and guest expectations. In a hypercompetitive environment, changes like this will become more common, more frequent, and more necessary for one's competitiveness. They will be driven by new consumer trends, more capable technologies, advances in mobility and the

Internet, and competitor moves. Like in the Marriott example previously cited, companies that can capitalize on these functional advantages can gain competitive advantage as long as other firms cannot easily copy or acquire the functionality.

3. A third source of competitive advantage is less tangible. It relates to the accuracy of the information (i.e., content) and the hotel's ability to track the guest. From a guest's perspective, a hotel's ability to meet his or her expectations and provide the correct room type, features, amenities, and services requested at the time of reservation distinguishes the hotel from its competitors. Regardless of what channels are used to book a reservation, each guest should find convenience, hassle-free service, and reliable information. The distribution channel should convey a sense of confidence to the guest that the information being shared is indeed accurate and current and that all of his or her requests for services (i.e., location, room type, features, amenities, etc.) will be honored upon arrival. This confidence and convenience, in turn, builds guest loyalty. From the hotel's perspective, tracking the guest plays an important role in guest recognition and delivering customized services. Since each guest interaction represents an opportunity to learn more about a guest, data collection, storage, and retrieval are critical to building strong relationships, creating unique and personalized experiences, and developing customer switching costs. Being able to mine the reservations database will be a new source of value and advantage.

4. Another form of competitive advantage comes as the result of proprietary technologies or patents, which create barriers to entry or duplicate capabilities. Although patents present challenges, patents are common throughout the software industry, because they represent intellectual capital. Their presence in hotel GDSs is less common. Hyatt Hotels and Radisson Hotels are two companies that currently enjoy patents for functional features contained in their GDSs. Hyatt (U.S. Patent 5,404,291) patented an inventory control process and revenue maximization routine used by its SPIRIT CRS. Radisson's patent (U.S. Patent 5,483,444) protects the company's innovative "Look to Book" program and "World of Winners" sweepstakes program, which provide incentives to travel agents and others who provide electronic bookings at Radisson hotels. Under the "Look to Book" program, agents are awarded points or credits, which can later be redeemed for prizes, for each reservation booked. The "World of Winners" sweepstakes program randomly provides prizes or rewards to booking agents. The technology implemented by Radisson administers this program over a diverse network, where multiple computer systems and travel agencies are involved.

Although these sources of competitive advantage continue to remain viable, they are not sufficient in today's hypercompetitive world, especially since hotel products are becoming more commodity-like. In the future, as the concept of branding erodes, hotels will need to find new sources of competitive advantage.

5. SUSTAINABILITY?

There is great debate as to whether or not competitive advantage—from IT or some other source—can be sustained. In other words, how long can a firm enjoy competitive advantage? What is its life expectancy? While there are no easy answers to these questions and while the answers would be context-dependent, there is general consensus among management gurus and industry leaders that competitive advantage is not, by itself, sustainable for long periods of time. Some forms of competitive advantage (for example, ones that involve patents or steep learning curves) can provide periods of sustainability. However, in all cases, competitive advantage can be lost or become obsolete with time. This is especially true with IT since it becomes obsolete so quickly. Moreover, as IT becomes more affordable, more standardized, and more easily copied, what once only the big chains could afford is now accessible by small chains and independents, albeit at slightly higher costs. Just consider how software as a service (SaaS) and cloud computing (where browser-based computers access computer programs housed remotely via the Internet) are making software functionality available and affordable to the masses.

It is possible that, in some cases, competitive advantage can be sustained over periods of time, particularly if it is not easily copied, if it alters industry structure, or if it has some protective parameters such as a noncompete contract or a patent, but in most cases, competitive advantage will be short lived. Therefore, hospitality leaders should always be thinking about their next competitive move or next big thing. Porter (1985, p. 171–172) suggests four tests of desirable technological change that can lead to periods of **sustainable competitive advantage**:

1. The technological change lowers costs or enhances differentiation and provides a sustainable (i.e., inimitable) technological advantage.
2. The technological change shifts cost or uniqueness drivers in favor of a firm.
3. Pioneering the technological change translates into first-mover advantages besides those inherent in the technology itself.
4. The technological change improves overall industry structure.

Copeland and McKenney (1988) noted that economies of scale and experience (i.e., the learning-curve phenomenon) are important but insufficient in establishing long-term success and competitive advantage; management foresight and attitudes also play vital roles and are necessary to building lasting advantages. Hopper (1990) agreed that sustainability of competitive advantage from IT is difficult, if not impossible, to achieve. He further observed that once the competitive advantage is lost, the industry's sophistication (i.e., the minimum stakes needed to compete and maintain competitive parity) becomes greater. This, in turn, increases the costs of doing business and the complexity of competition for all players in the entire industry (Weill, 1991). We see this today. The hospitality industry is capital intensive due in part to the sophistication of technology and the number of systems required to operate a business to maintain parity with competitors.

For illustrative purposes, consider property management and point-of-sale systems. At one time, the earlier adopters of these technologies enjoyed competitive advantages. Over time, however, as these systems became more affordable and commonplace, the advantages were minimized, and these systems changed from ones that provided strategic advantage to ones of competitive parity. Today, if an operation does not have these core systems, it is at a noticeable competitive disadvantage.

To prolong competitive advantage, Hopper (1990) recommended shifting the focus of IT to *how* IT is used rather than on the tools themselves. Assume that whatever technology is being used, it can be easily acquired and implemented by a competitor. Therefore, the competitive advantage will come, not from the technology itself, but how the technology is used, what it can do, and how it enables employees to perform their jobs. Hopper (1990) predicted that competitive advantage will be derived from the information collected and shared throughout the organization. Technology can always be purchased, but this is not necessarily the case when referring to knowledge (Copeland and McKenney, 1988). Therefore, competitive advantage will be a function of the ability of a firm's workforce to creatively exploit the capabilities of IT to create new products and services that sell well, to personalize products and services, and to create memorable experiences that wow guests while charging premium prices. Competitive advantage will come in the form of (1) innovations that result from a firm's ability to effectively leverage its unique resources, (2) competitive asymmetry or differences between firms as a result of their unique resources, and (3) the ability to preempt competitive responses and, thereby, maintain technological superiority (Cho, 1996; Segars and Grover, 1995; Clemons and Row, 1991; Feeny and Ives, 1990).

To achieve sustainable competitive advantage, most scholars and industry leaders agree that a firm must continuously invest in its resources and capabilities to build core competencies and a culture that encourage learning, innovation, and risk taking so that new advantages can be created. Deep pockets, know-how, and technology are not enough to ensure long-lasting advantages. In fact, D'Aveni (1994) advised firms to continually seek ways to destroy their competitive advantages (creative destruction) and create new ones before the competition does this for them. He even recommended multipronged approaches (sequential thrusts) to make it more difficult for competitors to react with counter responses. Successful firms continuously innovate and reinvent themselves. In doing so, these leaders stay out in front while others are several steps behind trying to play catch up with some previous initiative.

6. SUMMARY

The industry is headed for exciting but turbulent times. For the foreseeable future, the trends towards greater technological sophistication and usage will continue to dominate executive boardrooms and business strategy throughout the hospitality industry worldwide as IT continues to bring about fast-paced, continuous, and radical changes. Within the hospitality industry, many of these changes can be seen in the fundamental structure of the industry, the methods of interaction and shifts in the balance of power between buyers and sellers, and the pricing and distribution models used to sell products and services. Although industry executives may not agree as to whether digital economy represents opportunities or threats for their organizations, few would deny that the ramifications of IT are breathtaking in their pervasiveness and capital intensity.

It is no longer fruitful to resist IT and or to take a "wait-and-see" approach. The hospitality industry must overcome its reluctance to invest in new ideas and technologies that transform the organization, drive the bottom line, and generate value. In doing so, executives must formulate strategies for the development, adoption, and implementation of IT consistent with their business strategies. They must then prepare and defend compelling business cases that clearly demonstrate financial ROI through reduced costs and/or increased revenues and IT's strategic

potential (e.g., IT's ability to create differentiation, enhance guest service, or build lasting loyalty among customers, employees, franchisees, and suppliers). Arguments that suggest the use of technology merely to remain state of the art are insufficient for winning firm resources, especially under situations involving capital rationing and internal competition for resources.

Because the impact of IT stretches across the entire hospitality enterprise, it is becoming an increasingly important component of management decisions. For most hospitality firms, IT now ranks among the largest capital expense items and will continue to remain so as these firms seek new and creative ways to exploit the growing capabilities of IT through the Internet (and sister technologies, intranets, and extranets), telephony, networking, wireless communications, and portable computing devices. To succeed, companies must transition their business models, processes, and systems to the new digital economy and the world of electronic commerce. Additionally, all employees (from top executives to frontline staff) must become technologically proficient to ensure the long-term viability of the enterprise.

Hospitality companies should actively seek ways to gain competitive advantage through IT. It is not enough to be first to market. For example, Marriott International was the first hotel company to implement in-room check-out in conjunction with the now defunct Spectradyne. Unfortunately, it failed to develop this technological amenity under terms of exclusivity with its vendor. Consequently, it was not long before this functionality started to appear in its competitors. Now, it is an industry standard. Alternatively, Carlson Hospitality, parent of Radisson, has sought patents to protect some of its technology initiatives and give the company some time advantages, however slight. Everything that can be done to create an uneven playing field in your favor (so long as it is legal and ethical) should be actively explored. Think differently!

Please remember that IT itself is seldom the source of competitive advantage because it can be easily acquired and copied. Rather, it is how IT is implemented and used within a firm (i.e., what people do with it) that leads to competitive advantage. The degree to which competitive advantage can be attained will be a function of how well IT is integrated within the firm, from the culture to the business processes to the systems themselves. The specific competitive advantages derived will be based on how a firm chooses to allocate its resources to implement IT, its overall effectiveness in doing so (e.g., its ability to cost-effectively harness the capabilities provided by the IT tools and applications), its portfolio of resources and capabilities, and the employees' willingness to embrace the technology itself.

7. Case Study and Learning Activity

Case Study

IT, when used effectively, can truly transform an organization and extend the organization's reach and capabilities. What follows is an example of how one company is using IT to leverage its resources and create unparalleled advantages across the company. Its continuous investment in IT and innovativeness are providing sources of sustainable competitive advantage. The case is based on an actual company, but some of the names and facts have been changed to protect the identity of the company.

Today's marketplace is filled with tumult, new development, increased market segmentation, and merger mania. In other words, the environment is hypercompetitive, and in such an atmosphere, companies must continually refine their strategies and develop new competitive methods in order to survive. With more sophisticated and demanding consumers, investors seeking better ROIs, and a transient work force, companies cannot rely on their traditional methods or rest on their laurels because there are no sustainable advantages and because the competition is becoming increasingly more formidable. The only constant in such an environment is change. Therefore, companies must continuously seek new methods and IT to compete and stay ahead of the competition. They must break the rules and create new ones.

One such company leading this wave of innovation is the Paris-based Hospitality Extraordinaire International. Hospitality Extraordinaire is highly revered in the hospitality industry. Often a pioneer, its operating philosophy is simple: to be the best. The company is constantly seeking new ways to apply IT to streamline its operations, increase revenue, attract and retain guests, and create competitive advantage. With over 1,200 properties and 165,000 rooms spread across major international cities in forty-five-plus countries, Hospitality Extraordinaire has a property to meet almost any guest's needs. As a global industry leader, it is exemplar in its ability to provide consistent service and maintain high service standards across its entire portfolio of products, which runs the gamut from select service to luxury hotels, not to mention time shares and short-term apartment rentals. At the heart of the company's success are its employees (including a corporate IT support team of over seven hundred people), a seasoned management team, a great set of products, a tight franchise network,

- Technology infrastructure and IT portfolio
- Human capital (skills and expertise)
- Corporate structure and culture
- Financial capital (deep pockets)
- Size (critical mass) and industry clout
- Market penetration
- Geographic dispersion
- Brand recognition and reputation
- Customer loyalty
- Franchisee relationships and contracts
- Operating standards and practices
- Service delivery
- Product quality
- Value-adding programs (to customers, owners, and franchisees)
- Negotiating power with suppliers

FIGURE 2-5   Factors Contributing to Hospitality Extraordinaire's Competitive Advantage

a sophisticated portfolio of IT applications, and a very capable technology infrastructure. Each of these items and those listed in Figure 2-5 are, in and of themselves, impressive, but when combined, they create many competitive advantages, both explicit and tacit, for Hospitality Extraordinaire that are hard to duplicate, and help to explain why the company is the envy of the industry.

With such impressive results, one might ask the question, "How does Hospitality Extraordinaire do it?" With industry maturation and performance tied to the economy, a company like this must be creative yet cautious regarding the technology initiatives it pursues. There is no simple answer to the company's success story, but a strong commitment, a dedicated and unrelenting focus, and a culture that supports quality service and the use of IT to accomplish its strategic objectives play important roles. The company's ability to leverage its workforce and its IT are also instrumental in creating success. IT and business strategy are carefully aligned. IT projects must be customer-centric, leverage the firm's core competencies, and focus on delivering value to the bottom line. If an IT initiative cannot demonstrate enhanced customer service or loyalty, improved employee productivity and

capabilities, reduced costs, increased revenues, new business opportunities, and/or increased shareholder value, the project is not funded. For every business decision, the company's executives will do their homework to understand the competitive landscape and consumer trends. Once they understand the opportunities, competitive threats, and consumer needs, they will take calculated risks and consistently invest in the initiative to make it a success. Based on the company's performance to date, its model works—with very few exceptions.

Hospitality Extraordinaire has long led the industry in technology initiatives. It was among the first hotel chains to implement and standardize PMSs. Its ROOMSnet reservation system has led the industry in functionality and booking capabilities and set the trend for two-way interfacing with PMS. Its RevMax Revenue management system also leads the industry in terms of capability and sophistication. With these systems, Hospitality Extraordinaire has been able to achieve rate and occupancy premiums over its competitors. Its Thank You Rewards loyalty/frequent travel program is one of the largest in the industry and has among the most loyal following of any hotel company. Even the company's centralized payroll system provides advantages that its rivals envy. It processes payroll for employees around the world at a cost per check that others wish they could match.

Hospitality Extraordinaire's success comes largely as a result of the company's ability to redefine itself and effectively use its resources in response to changing business conditions and market needs. Pushing new limits, the company is aggressively working to create an uneven playing field that will lead to a prolonged period of unmatched competitive advantage. Over the years, the company has expanded its lodging portfolio to include Extraordinary Hotels and Resorts, Humble Inns, Simplicity Inns and Suites, Xtra-Night Stay, Efficient Inns, Corporate Touch Apartments, and Outstanding Vacation Villas. With such a diverse and complementary portfolio, the company has sought ways to eliminate duplication. Rather than have each hotel brand operate as a separate entity (or strategic business unit, in Hospitality Extraordinaire's parlance) competing with one another, the company decided to embark on a strategy that would unify its lodging initiatives to leverage its resources and capabilities and create a stronger presence in the market place.

To explore Hospitality Extraordinaire's new focus for competitive advantage, we will turn to a concept referred to as *cluster management*. The company borrowed a page from the strategy handbooks of retail marketing giants like Proctor and Gamble, Coca-Cola, and PepsiCo, each of which owns a number of competing products or brands within their respective markets. While stressing brand equity, these companies cluster their "families" of products on the same shelf in a grocery store or within geographic proximity in a market to build associations that drive market positions and opportunities and ward off competition. The premise behind this approach is to deflect consumer attention away from price competition and focus it on product or concept differentiation for products that have achieved commodity status.

Hospitality Extraordinaire has come to realize that in order to continue growth and prosperity, each product line (or lodging brand) must

collaborate rather than compete with the company's other brands. Today, the company simply recognizes that each brand represents a player on the same (Hospitality Extraordinaire) team, not opposing teams. With this revelation, the idea is that, in highly competitive markets, it is better for a Hospitality Extraordinaire product to win business rather than to forfeit that business to a non-Hospitality Extraordinaire brand. Accordingly, the orientation shifts from optimizing individual hotel occupancies and revenues, which could lead to suboptimization for the company, to optimizing an entire cluster (or market) of Hospitality Extraordinaire hotels by managing each hotel as part of a larger entity for the benefit of the entire extended organization (including the corporate entity, franchise partners, owners, etc.). The company's reservation system (ROOMSnet), revenue management system, PMSs, and INN Touch executive information system are all integrated to support this initiative.

The fundamental principle behind Hospitality Extraordinaire's large-scale organizational change effort is leveraging resources and using teamwork and technology to gain economies of scale and new-found market efficiencies. This philosophy is essential for the company's survival because it cannot hire enough resources to fuel its growth. It needs more resources and must find other ways to achieve its aggressive growth strategy without compromising service, quality, and consistency standards. Plus, things must be done faster, cheaper, different, and better than before. The mantra, especially in a tight economy, is doing more with less.

For years, Hospitality Extraordinaire has shared resources across multiple facilities in several areas including reservations, marketing, advertising, procurement, laundry, and transportation, among others, but its technology capabilities are fostering new, creative approaches to collaboration, resource sharing, efficiencies, and economies of scale. Using IT, not only are resources and costs shared across product lines but so are expertise and information. In turn, these equate to better, more consistent services across properties, a better cost structure, and new sources of revenue.

By using technology effectively, Hospitality Extraordinaire can track and segment its customers, maintain brand integrity, reduce its operating overhead, and find new business opportunities. Helping to make the logistics of this possible is Project Connect, a companywide initiative as part of its PeopleSoft implementation to track the sharing of resources across all of the company's entities and bill the appropriate parties (e.g., properties and owners) for the services rendered and for their fair share of the resources consumed. This is an important initiative because Hospitality Extraordinaire is comprised of a complex ownership structure. Many of its hotels are franchised or owned by others but managed by Hospitality Extraordinaire. Since these contracts typically assess fees for services, it is important to keep an accurate accounting of these. As a result, the company can expand its management services to include consulting on a wide variety of topics and best practices and share its cost structure across all who benefit to keep individual property costs down. This provides Hospitality Extraordinaire's properties with a cost advantage over competing brands.

At the field level, total integration is the desired goal with shared data, systems, and other resources (e.g., laundry facilities, van service). Because Hospitality Extraordinaire equips its corporate, regional, and field staff with laptops and smart phones and corporate Web-based applications, an executive information system with a scorecard of measures, and the company's data warehouse (which culls data from such core systems as accounting, property management, guest history, central reservations, and the company's Thank You Rewards loyalty/frequent traveler database), Hospitality Extraordinaire's employees are equipped with up-to-the-minute operating results, company policies and news, and the latest in consumer trends analysis—anytime and anywhere they need such access. Armed with such sophisticated IT tools, decision makers can quickly "slice and dice" data to compare, analyze, and troubleshoot performance at a particular property, in a given market, across a specific brand, or throughout the entire chain. Using these IT tools

and the company's technology infrastructure (including its ubiquitous high-speed corporate network and wireless capabilities) to gain access to key systems, management in the field and at corporate can oversee multiple departments, properties, and markets at a time; share best practices; and keep better tabs on the business. Real-time alerts and red flags notify management of pending problems so they can intervene and seek resolutions before they get out of control. They are never out of touch, regardless of where they are and what they are doing. Clearly, these systems enhance Hospitality Extraordinaire's resources and capabilities, and because many of the benefits are behind the scenes, it is difficult for competitors to identify the contributing factors to the company's success and copy them, thus extending Hospitality Extraordinaire's competitive advantage. Cluster management provides the company with unprecedented opportunities through economies of scale and resource sharing to create competitive advantages that other hotel providers will have great difficulty matching or countering because they lack the structure, technology, and wherewithal to make it happen.

One example is revenue analysts who are responsible for monitoring supply and demand patterns within markets and for adjusting sales strategies and room inventory controls when appropriate. Revenue management is a sophisticated science that requires powerful systems and a high degree of expertise. This knowledge can now be easily shared across multiple hotels—complete with the booking patterns for each hotel in the area—so that all hotels within the cluster can more effectively manage their room inventory, rate structures, and selling strategies to avoid lost market share. Perhaps upscale hotels will be less inclined to discount their rates if they know that their sibling hotels in the economy or midscale sector are still projecting room availability.

Sales associates are also responsible for multiple brands. The sharing of resources here goes well beyond lead generation, referrals, and overflow business. Instead of having several sales representatives call upon the same clients in what may have appeared as a disjointed and disorganized sales strategy from the customer's perspective, one sales associate or a team of sales agents is assigned to clients or geographic region to sell a complete portfolio of products covering all of their lodging needs: budget, extended stay, full service, meeting and conventions, or luxury. No longer are multiple properties competing for the same business and confusing the customers with multiple requests for proposal (RFPs) from the same company. Equipped with desktop and wireless sales force automation tools, these agents have instant access to rate and availability information for any hotel in the system—from almost anywhere, including the client's office. This information can then be shared through the sales system to other hotels seeking to bid on conferences that travel from year to year. Having such historical data readily at hand, sales associates can submit more accurate bids, ones that take into account actual versus projected business in prior cities, pick-up rates, special needs, and so on. The system is not only a great booking resource but also a great client relationship building tool. Reservation agents are also shared across hotels in a given geographic area. Because these "mini" reservation centers are located within a given market, the agents are more qualified to answer questions regarding hotel facilities, local attractions, and upcoming events than a person sitting in a remote office trying to locate the information on a computer screen in the central reservation system. The information which they provide and the efficiency with which they provide it enhances the customer service and favorably sets a guest's initial impression for his or her upcoming stay in the area.

Just as reservations and sales staff can be shared across properties, so too can accounting and human resources staff. This allows better access to specialized resources and expertise. By sharing these resources, individual hotels no longer need to have their own accounting or human resources departments. Cluster offices, located at one of the larger hotels in the region, can provide accounting services, budgetary oversight, recruiting services, benefits administration, and other human resource functions for all properties within a cluster. The company's accounting information system provides detailed access to company expenditures. This information can then be used to tighten cost controls and negotiate better discounts with suppliers. Human resource systems aid not only in the recruitment but also in retaining employees. Capable of career tracking and progression and succession planning for the entire company, the system helps identify candidates ready for promotion—those who have completed the requisite training classes for a given position, held prior positions that serve as stepping stones, and completed stints in other product lines or functional disciplines to ensure a truly cross-functional workforce.

The examples cited previously are only a small sampling. There are many others and the potential is even greater. The number of collaborative efforts such as these can only increase as groupware applications, such as Lotus Notes, become more commonplace. Furthermore, few hotel companies can match the diversity, consistency, and quality that Hospitality Extraordinaire exemplifies. It is the company's core informational technologies like ROOMSnet, revenue management, PMS, Thank You Rewards, accounting, payroll, and human resources and the company's common hardware, software, and communications platforms that support data exchange and afford Hospitality Extraordinaire the opportunity to manage across product lines.

For Hospitality Extraordinaire, the competitive advantage is created by its resources (i.e., employees, capital, and technology). Complementing these resources are the relationships forged with the company's franchisees and the company's commitment to quality and product consistency (e.g., service delivery, cleanliness of facilities, amenities, program implementation and execution). In the end, the competitive advantage is a structural and cultural one created by innovative leadership and complementary resources and processes. Because it is difficult to duplicate, it provides Hospitality Extraordinaire with a decided and lasting advantage.

Although many leading lodging providers enjoy heavily segmented lodging portfolios, their zeal for growth and market share has resulted in loose contracts, lax standards, and blurred distinctions between their concepts by overlapping product positioning, so much so that customers cannot easily distinguish the advantages of one product over another. Confounded by low switching costs and inconsistent product quality, amenities, and service delivery within a product line, the problem of brand identity is exacerbated. Consequently, the barriers to implementing cluster management for competing chains are high should these organizations consider following or copying Hospitality Extraordinaire's lead.

For Hospitality Extraordinaire, a blurring of product lines is not much of an issue—at least not yet, though this could change as the result of recent additions to its product offerings. At present, the company maintains a unique identity for each of its brands in order to build customer loyalty and prevent such blurring from occurring. Since each brand has a distinct identity and target market, Hospitality Extraordinaire is able to uniquely position itself in any given market without the risk of cannibalization prevalent in other companies. Hospitality Extraordinaire's use of technology and market data allows it to select appropriate sites and determine the *right* product for that site. This is an important benefit that contributes to the success of cluster management and the acceptance by many of the company's franchise partners and outside owners.

The unsung hero of Hospitality Extraordinaire's technology capabilities that makes the cluster management concept possible and affordable is the infrastructure, which is somewhat transparent—especially to those outside. The company's use of standardized systems (which are defined in management and franchisee contracts), common technology architecture, and a pervasive communications network makes connectivity and integration possible.

Hospitality Extraordinaire is an exciting, dynamic company. It has its act together and is well aligned with the external environment. Its IT usage is state of the art and well aligned with its business strategy. Together, these create the many successes Hospitality Extraordinaire has enjoyed over the years. They will continue to create the basis of success for years to come. If Hospitality Extraordinaire is not a company you carefully track, you should be sure to put it on your radar screen. It is one to watch!

Learning Activity

1. Define Hospitality Extraordinaire's strategy. How does IT factor into this strategy to support or enable it?
2. Identify the core technologies being used by Hospitality Extraordinaire. Discuss the value each contributes and any competitive advantage derived.
3. If you worked for a competing hotel company, what traits would you find most admirable in Hospitality Extraordinaire and why? What would you do to compete?
4. If you worked for Hospitality Extraordinaire's IT department, what challenges might you face? What recommendations would you have for new technology initiatives or directions?
5. What are the key teaching points in this case? Why are they important, and how will you apply them in your professional career?

8. Key Terms

Asset Optimization
CAPITA
Cash Flow per Share
Co-Alignment Principle
Competitive Advantage
Competitive Method

Digital Convergence
Economies of Scale
Five Forces Model
Generic Strategies
Outcome Approach
Preemptive

Resource-Based View
Sustainable Competitive
   Advantage
Switching Costs
Tacit
Trait Approach

9. Chapter Questions

1. How do you define value in the eyes of key stake-holders, namely customers, investors, franchisees, and employees? How can IT contribute to value for each? What opportunities exist?

2. What is competitive advantage? How is it created? How can it be sustained? Be sure to consider the roles of corporate culture, firm resources and capabilities, and core competencies.

3. Define the co-alignment model. How is co-alignment achieved, and why, for a hospitality manager, is this so important to understand?

4. Can IT provide competitive advantage? If so, how? Provide some specific examples.

5. Can IT create sustainable competitive advantage? Support your answer.

6. Select some leading hospitality firms. Compare and contrast their uses of IT. What advantages does IT provide to them? How does IT limit or constrain these firms?

7. Conduct a brief literature search on the works of Harvard University Professor Michael Porter. What contributions has he made to our understanding of strategy and IT? How can these be applied in a hospitality industry context?

10. References

Adcock, Ken, Helms, Marilyn M., and Jih, Wen-Jang Kenny. (1993, Spring). Information technology: Can it provide a sustainable competitive advantage? *Information Strategy: The Executive's Journal*, 10–15.

Antonucci, Yvonne Lederer and Tucker, James J., III. (1998, Spring). Responding to earnings-related pressure to reduce IT operating and capital expenditures. *Information Strategy: The Executive's Journal*, 6–14.

Applegate, Lynda M., McFarlan, F. Warren, and McKenney, James L. (1996). *Corporate information systems management: The issues facing senior executives* (4th ed.). Chicago: Irwin.

Bakos, J. Yannis and Treacy, Michael E. (1986, June). Information technology and corporate strategy: A research perspective. *MIS Quarterly, 10* (2), 107–119.

Bourgeois, L. J., III. (1980). Strategy and environment: A conceptual integration. *Academy of Management Review, 5* (1), 25–39.

Brady, Tim, Cameron, Ross, Targett, David, and Beaumont, Chris. (1992). Strategic IT issues: The views of some major IT investors. *Journal of Strategic Information Systems, 1* (4), 183–189.

Burrus, Daniel (with Gittines, Roger). (1993). *Technotrends: How to use technology and go beyond your competition.* New York: HarperBusiness.

Cash, James I., Jr. and Konsynski, Benn R. (1985, March–April). IS redraws competitive boundaries. *Harvard Business Review*, 134–142.

Chandler, Alfred D. (1962). Strategy and structure: Chapters in the history of industrial enterprise. Cambridge, MA: MIT Press.

Cho, Wonae. (1996). A case study: Creating and sustaining competitive advantage through an information technology application in the lodging industry. Unpublished doctoral dissertation, Virginia Polytechnic Institute and State University.

Clemons, Eric K. and Kimbrough, Steven O. (1986, December). Information systems, telecommunications and their effects on industrial organizations. Proceedings of the Seventh International Conference on Information Systems, San Diego, CA, 99–108.

Clemons, Eric K. and Row, Michael C. (1991, September). Sustaining IT advantage: The role of structural differences. MIS Quarterly, 15 (3), 275–291.

Cline, Roger S. and Blatt, Louis A. (1998, Winter). Creating enterprise value around the customer . . . Leveraging the customer asset in today's hospitality industry. Arthur Andersen Hospitality and Leisure Executive Report, 5 (1), 2–11.

Copeland, Duncan G. and McKenney, James L. (1988, September). Airline reservations systems: Lessons from history. MIS Quarterly, 12 (3), 353–370.

D'Aveni, Richard A. (with Gunther, Robert). (1994). Hyper-competition: Managing the dynamics of strategic maneuvering. New York: The Free Press.

Feeny, David F. and Ives, Blake. (1990, Summer). In search of sustainability: Reaping long-term advantage from investments in information technology. *Journal of Management Information Systems,* 7 (1), 27–46.

Hamel, Gary and Prahalad, C. K. (1994, September 5). Seeing the future first. Fortune, 64, 66–68.

Hanks, Richard D., Noland, R. Paul, and Cross, Robert G. (1992, February). Discounting in the hotel industry: A new approach. Cornell Hotel and Restaurant Administration Quarterly, 15–23.

Hensdill, Cherie. (1998, February). Hotels technology survey. Hotels, 51–76.

Hitt, Lorin M. and Brynjolfsson, Erik. (1996, June). Productivity, business profitability, and consumer surplus: Three different measures of information technology value. MIS Quarterly, 20 (2), 121–143.

Hopper, Max D. (1990, May–June). Rattling SABRE—New ways to compete on information. *Harvard Business Review,* 118–125.

Ives, Blake and Learmonth (1984, December). The information system as a competitive weapon. Communications of the ACM, 27 (12), 1193–1201.

Mata, Francisco J., Fuerst, William L., and Barney, Jay B. (1995, December). Information technology and sustained competitive advantage: A resource-based analysis. MIS Quarterly, 19 (4), 487–505.

McFarlan, F. Warren. (1984, May–June). Information technology changes the way you compete. Harvard Business Review, 98–103.

Murthy, Bvsan. (1994). Measurement of the strategy construct in the lodging industry, and the strategy–performance relationship. Unpublished doctoral dissertation, Virginia Polytechnic Institute and State University.

Negroponte, Nicholas. (1995). Being digital. New York: Vintage Books.

Ohmae, Kenichi. (1992). *The mind of the strategist: Business planning for competitive advantage.* New York: Penguin Books.

Olsen, Michael D. (1996). Into the new millennium: A white paper on the global hospitality industry. Paris: International Hotel Association.

Olsen, Michael D., West, Joseph J., and Tse, Eliza C. (2008). Strategic management in the hospitality industry (3rd ed.). Upper Saddle River, NJ: Pearson Prentice Hall.

Palmer, Colin. (1988, December). Using IT for competitive advantage at Thomson Holidays. Long Range Planning, 21 (6), 26–29.

Parsons, Gregory L. (1983, Fall). Information technology: A new competitive weapon. Sloan Management Review, 3–14.

Plimpton, George. (1990). The X Factor. Knoxville, TN: Whittle Direct Books.

Porter, Michael E. (1980). Competitive strategy: Techniques for analyzing industries and competitors. New York: The Free Press.

Porter, Michael E. (1985). Competitive advantage: Creating and sustaining superior performance. New York: The Free Press.

Porter, Michael E. and Millar, Victor E. (1985, July–August). How information gives you competitive advantage. Harvard Business Review, 149–160.

Post, Gerald V., Kagan, Albert, and Lau, Kin-Nam. (1995, Fall). A modeling approach to evaluating strategic uses of information technology. *Journal of Management Information Systems, 12* (2), 161–187.

Quinn, James Brian. (1988). Service technology and manufacturing: Cornerstones of the U. S. economy. In Bruce R. Guile and James Brian Quinn (Eds.), Managing innovation: Cases from the service industries (pp. 9–35). Washington, DC: National Academy Press.

Segars, Albert H. and Grover, Varun. (1995, May–June). The industry-level impact of information technology: An empirical analysis of three industries. *Decision Sciences, 26* (3), 337–368.

Sethi, Vijay and King, William R. (1994, December). Development of measures to assess the extent to which an information technology application provides competitive advantage. Management Science, 40 (12), 1601–1626.

Tapscott, Don. (1996). The digital economy: Promise and peril in the age of networked intelligence. New York: McGraw-Hill.

Thompson, James D. (1967). Organizations in action. New York: McGraw-Hill.

Venkatraman, N., Henderson, John C., and Oldach, Scott. (1993, June). Continuous strategic alignment: Exploiting information technology capabilities for competitive success. European Management Journal, 11 (2), 139–149.

Venkatraman, N. and Prescott, John E. (1990, January). Environment-strategy coalignment: An empirical test of its performance implications. Strategic Management Journal, 11 (1), 1–23.

Weill, Peter. (1991). The information technology payoff: Implications for investment appraisal. Australian Accounting Review, 2–11.

Computing Essentials

Chapter Contents

Rob Grimes, Chairman of Accuvia

INTERVIEW

Q: Hi, Rob. You are well known in the field of hospitality technology. Would you share a little bit about your background?

A: I am basically a restaurant manager who found his way into technology. I was involved in technology projects in Bob's Big Boy and Marriott Hotels as an Assistant Restaurant Manager and then found my way to the Marriott Corporate Headquarters for some systems projects. This is how I got my initial start in systems. After this, I created an "Intrapreneurship" within Marriott to sell IT services to the various divisions in the 80s. Later, this became the nucleus of Cyntergy, the company I started after leaving Marriott, to provide implementation, training, and help desk services to the hospitality, foodservice, and retail industries. From there, the events, publishing, and consulting businesses were formed which continue today under the name of Accuvia.

Q: Great. What are some general skills that you see as essential in order to succeed in our industry.

A: I have always believed that a person has to understand operations and have an aptitude for technology. Technology needs to be an area of interest and something the individual understands—but you really cannot teach the operations side of the hospitality industry to a technology person. One must work within the industry on the front lines to get to really know the industry and really understand how it works. The key here is to understand how the systems will be used and what the outcome for the user is—then to understand systems and technology well enough to figure out the best way to apply it for use by operators. Being able to see and understand both sides of the equation is critical—but at the end of the day, technology is an "enabler" and is not the end-all solution to great operations and service.

Q: What are some specific technology skills for the current or future hospitality manager?

A: One really needs to understand the core systems for any operation. In the hotel segment this might be the property management system (PMS) and then all the other systems that need to integrate with this. In a foodservice operation, it would not only be the point-of-sale (POS) system but also the back office. In fact, POS is really just one component of a complete foodservice management system.

The important thing is to understand the systems and technologies that are used in each business area. The other thing that is important is to know where these technologies will be used in relation to the guest and how, if at all, they may also need to be part of the use of the applications.

Q: Have you seen any changes in profitability in hotels or restaurants due to technology?

A: Absolutely—but in two different areas. Obviously, most people might think about expense containment and cost reduction but more recently, the focus has shifted to enhancing revenues. Today the way to increase the average rate per room in a hotel may be the additional products and services offered in the hotel room. In a foodservice operation it may be in speed of service technologies—especially in the quick service segment and drive-thrus. Online ordering is key but with all operations, getting connected to the guest is a big deal. On the expense reduction or efficiency side, using less labor is one area—or increasing the productivity of the labor is the other.

Q: Looking into your crystal ball, do you have any predictions on what technology we might see in the future in our industry?

A: We will see much more "hosted" applications. Much of this will continue to come around by more secure and available bandwidth and high-speed access. This will allow easier integration of applications, training, and the access to data anywhere and anytime. Additionally, we will continue to see the growth of systems and applications that connect the guest before, during, and after their experiences in hospitality operations. We will see more guest-driven technologies being used such as mobile phones and tablet computers.

On the employee side, the same will be true for the utilization of personal technologies, but we will also see more applications requiring employees to have instant access to information in order to perform their jobs.

1. INTRODUCTION

Rob has provided a great overview of the importance of technology in our industry. Now you need to establish a technological knowledge foundation. This chapter will cover the basics of computing.

Before you can make accurate and timely decisions, you first need to know and understand the foundation. What is a computer? What are some different types? How does it work? Does it think as I do? What's under that cover? These and others are questions that anyone new to computing may have. From a review of systems and binary code, to system hardware and software, to the operating system and programming languages, this chapter provides you with the necessary foundation.

2. SYSTEM

Before you learn about computing devices, you must first understand the system behind them. Just what is a system? You see this word all the time with regard to computing: management information systems, systems analysis, the systems department, and so on. Simply put, a **system** is a way of doing things. Right now you may be writing notes about what you are reading in the margin of the book or highlighting your text on your e-reader. Perhaps you read a definition twice, or say it out loud to help you remember it. Whatever the case, you have your own system. One of the first endeavors hotel managers make when they start a new job is to evaluate the old system of their particular department (how was it done before?) and to adopt their own system (i.e., having more front desk clerks on duty at certain hours). That is how they handle busy periods, which is "a way of doing things." So in order to take the fear out of the word system, and hopefully computers as a whole, think of computers as a part of *your* way of doing things.

You might already have an ideal way of doing things, so how does a computer fit into your system? First off, a computer needs data, which is simply raw facts made up of words, numbers, etc. Data is input into the system, processed, and transformed, by you, into information (Figure 3-1). Here is a simple example: Assume you bought a stock for $10 and sold it for $15, generating a profit of $5 or a 50 percent return. A computer can do the operation 15–10 or 5/10 and give you an answer, but it is up to you to interpret the answer as good or bad. For example, you might ask, "How does this compare to other stocks?" Information is simply data to which people have given meaning and shape. An expanded definition of information can be found in Chapter 11.

How does this apply to someone in hospitality management? Well, besides the obvious systems, such as managing rooms or seats and food and beverage consumption (which will be covered later), managers often use computers to handle their budgets. You input all the numbers, tell the computer what to add, subtract, divide, and so on, and the computer supplies a number. It is the manager's duty to interpret that number. In other words, you give the data shape and meaning, turning it into information. Maybe the number will tell the manager that she or he is over budget when it comes to labor and, therefore, needs to schedule fewer people during certain shifts. The manager is using the data and the system and, with a computer application, is getting information to make a managerial decision. This is a prime example of how computers are used in the hospitality industry to help managers make accurate and timely decisions.

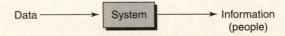

Data ⟶ System ⟶ Information (people)

FIGURE 3-1

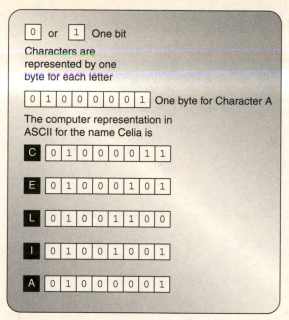

FIGURE 3-2 Bits can either be a 1 or a 0. Eight bits make up a byte or a standard character. The word *CELIA* is made up of the depicted bytes.

The raw facts in the definition of data come in a specific form. This form is known as **binary code**. *Bi* comes from the Latin word for two. In binary code, the data can be presented in two options: a 1 or a 0. It makes words or letters by stringing together these 0s and 1s in a particular order. The order 01000001 represents the character A in Figure 3-2. This binary code is how a computer counts, whereas our own counting system is in base 10 (see Table 3-1).

In the decimal system, you go up to ten digits and start over. Binary counting is a little different. Look at Table 3-1. Can you see the pattern? Start with a 0, and from the left, each new number is where a 0 from the previous number is replaced with a 1. Can you see how the 1s seem to be moving to the left? When all 1s have replaced the 0s, a new number is started with a 1 in the beginning and more 0s than in the last set. These 0s and 1s are known as bits.

Bits, short for binary digits, make up the smallest form of data storage. Put eight of them together and you get what is known as a **byte**. A byte represents one standard character or number. Again, the letter A is represented by the following bits: 01000001. The next vowel, E, is represented by its unique combination of 1s and 0s: 01000101.

Bits and bytes make up the beginning of data storage and measurement. They are followed by **kilobytes**, **megabytes**, **gigabytes**, **terabytes**, and **petabytes**. Remember that eight bits make up a byte.

1024 bytes = 1 kilobyte

1024 kilobytes = 1 megabyte

1024 megabytes = 1 gigabyte

1024 gigabytes = 1 terabyte

1024 terabytes = 1 petabyte

| Table 3-1 | Base 10 Versus Binary Counting | | | |

Base 10				
1	11	21	91	101
2	12	22	92	102
3	13	23	93	103
4	14	24	94	104
5	15	25	95	105
6	16	26	96	106
7	17	27	97	107
8	18	28	98	108
9	19	29	99	109
10	20	30	100	110

Binary
0
1
10
11
100
101
111
1000
1001
1011
1111
100000

The number 1024 is the one to remember. You can make up your own mnemonic device for the letters *K* for kilobyte, *M* for megabyte, *G* for gigabyte, *T* for terabyte, and *P* for petabyte (a common one is *Keep My Giant Tree Peter*).

To understand how a computer "sees" whether a bit is a 1 or a 0, you must first understand how a bit travels. Remember electricity and Ben Franklin? Electricity is actually defined as "the class of physical phenomena arising from the existence and interactions of electronic charge." Therefore **electricity** is a phenomenon and **voltage** measures its potential. If you vary these two in a consistent manner, then you have a **signal**.

A signal can travel down a wire or even through the air. Signals come in two general categories: analog and digital. **Analog** signals travel as a wave that has many points or states as seen in Figure 3-3.

It has a high point in B and a low point in D with points A, C, and E in between. A **digital** signal does not have points in between such as A, C, and E. It only has high and low points and varies instantaneously with no points in between. These high and low points are called high states and low states, which are just voltage levels. Look at Figure 3-4.

In a digital signal there are only two states. The high voltage level represents a 1 and a low voltage level represents a 0, which is precisely how a computer identifies bits.

Remember when the television signals went digital? Chances are that you used cable which is already digital and were not affected. However, many still used the old "rabbit ear antennas" that received analog signals, and had to replace them with new equipment that received digital

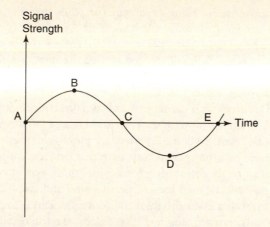

FIGURE 3-3   Sine waves have many levels. Here the sine wave has a high point B, a low point D, and points A, C, and E at the beginning, middle, and end.

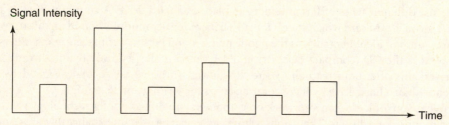

FIGURE 3-4   In contrast to sine waves, digital signals have just a high and a low point.

signals. Analog signals are older than the digital signals that computing devices use. Analog lines are found today in phone lines generally running from your house to the nearest phone company building. From there, the majority of carriers use digital signals. Other types of connections will be discussed in Chapter 4. It is important to know that analog signals are used for data requiring continuous states such as voice and video and that the two types of signals can be used in conjunction with one another for greater efficiency. In daily usage, an analog signal can be converted into a data signal whereby it can be "cleaned up" and then converted back into an analog signal with no background noise. In Chapter 4, you will also see how signals can be converted.

3. HARDWARE

Hardware is something physical you can touch and feel such as your computer screen. If you take off a cover of a computer, you would see a green board with circuitry and extensions. This is known as a printed circuit board (PCB) or a motherboard. This is the foundation of the computer where all of the connections take place. On this foundation sits the **central processing unit** (**CPU**). This is the brain of the computer and will be discussed later. Laptop and netbook manufacturers continue to shrink the motherboard for advanced portability. Attached to the motherboard is memory. There are two kinds of memory: **RAM** and **ROM**. RAM stands for *random access memory* and is where your applications such as word processing or solitaire run when they are used. RAM is temporary, meaning that once you turn your computer off, it is erased like a blackboard. That is why you need to save your work. When people add more memory (RAM) to their computers, they are able to have more applications open at once. Today, RAM, more often than not, is DRAM, short for dynamic random access memory, which means that the CPU can access exactly which part it needs without having to go through the parts it does not (known as sequential). ROM, on the other hand, stands for *read only memory*. This memory is permanent and contains basic instructions for the computer to follow upon start-up. When the power is shut off, ROM retains what is in it. Also attached to the motherboard are expansion slots. When computers are purchased, they do not necessarily come with printers and scanners or other **peripherals** (external devices connected to the computer). Expansion slots provide a ready connection for devices that need to communicate with your computer. These slots may also be used for additional sound and graphic cards if and upgrade is desired. The **hard drive** is sealed in an airtight metal container. This is to prevent any dirt or other particles from entering and corrupting the data. This disk drive is where data is stored and retrieved. Disks are divided into sectors and tracks, with the **operating system (OS)**, which will be discussed shortly, keeping track of which sector contains what data. The hard disk also contains an area that is used for memory known as a **cache**. This part of the disk works with RAM in storing and retrieving frequently used data such as Web pages or files. For the most part, smart phones and other handheld devices use different types of flash memory in place of a hard drive. A common term in the cell phone lexicon is **SIM card** which stands for **subscriber identity module**. Found on this transferable card are common identifiers such as the phone number and personal contacts among others.

Next is the **CD** (compact disc) drive: older versions allowed only reading from CDs but newer versions offer both read and write capabilities and blue ray format. A CD drive works differently than a hard drive by incorporating lasers for writing and listening.

What you look at when you work on computers or with computer technology is known as either a **monitor** or a **display**. These units, whose names can be used interchangeably, are responsible for projecting images. The image can be projected by a cathode ray tube (CRT), a liquid crystal display (LCD), or gas plasma, among others. Monitors, which are separate from the CPU, use a CRT. This technology requires a set amount of distance from the projecting source to the screen, which is one of the reasons it is so big compared to a laptop, which uses an LCD. LCD technology uses liquid crystals and less power than CRTs but LCD is difficult to view at angles other than straight on. Plasma is quickly becoming the display of choice for many televisions in hotel rooms, if not your own.

Next is the CPU.

The CPU is divided into four main parts:

1. *Register.* Temporarily stores the pieces of information being processed
2. *Arithmetic Logic Unit (ALU).* Carries out math and logic functions
3. *Control Unit.* Coordinates the work of the register and ALU
4. *Data Storage.* Stores the results

These four parts of the CPU correspond *roughly* to the four steps of computer operation. Everyone does things in a certain order. For instance, before you drive a car, you open the door, start the car, put it in gear, and then go. When computing devices operate, they follow these four basic steps:

1. Get instructions
2. Decode instructions
3. Execute instructions
4. Store results

How fast a computer can go through these steps over and over again in one second determines its processor speed, which is measured in megahertz. For example a 3-gigahertz processor can go through the preceding four steps three *billion* times in one second! So, the higher the number of the processor, the higher its computational speed. Processors operate so fast that a cooling unit is needed to reduce the heat produced. On top of the processor sit either cooling rods or a fan to disperse the heat the processors generate from working so hard and fast. That humming you hear is often from the cooling unit.

4. SMART PHONES AND TABLETS

A **smart phone** is a mobile phone that can access the Internet and is increasingly incorporating more PC-like features. **Tablet PCs** are flat computing devices that use touch screens. With our many customers and employees using these devices in place of computers or laptops, understanding some basics is needed. Smart phones are offered by many different vendors such as Apple (iPhone), Blackberry, and Google (Android), in very similar sizes. Their Size is obviously a big selling point but also a liability for such tasks as spreadsheet usage. Nevertheless, more applications are being written for the main types with Apple having the largest offering. Tablet PCs are being offered from many different vendors as well with fuller or dedicated functionality such as e-readers, which some people label in a different category altogether.

Interaction with tablets and newer smart phones involves a touch screen which utilizes either *capacitive* or *resistive* screens. Capacitive touch screens, such as in the iPhone, have a common amount of voltage flowing through the device. When touched, voltage is disrupted and reduced and the OS, which uses a gesture interpreting software, interprets the gesture made (e.g., finger tapping, using thumb and first finger to enlarge a picture). Resistive touch screens are made up of two thin layers of indium tin oxide (ITO). The plastic layers keep the tin layers apart. When pressed together, by say a pencil, the tin layers touch. Then, an electric charge is engaged at the location, and the component registers what letter, picture, sound, etc., is represented by that location.

5. SOFTWARE

Software is the detailed instructions that control the operation of a computer system. "A software program is a series of statements or instructions to the computer. The process of writing or coding programs is termed programming, and the individuals who specialize in this task are called programmers" (Laudon and Laudon 2009 p. 75). Software comes in two basic categories: application software and system software. "Application software, or applications, are the programs written for or by users to apply a computer to a specific task" (Laudon and Laudon 2009 p. 173). The "off-the-shelf" productivity software such as word processing, spreadsheets, or specific programs written in languages such as C++, Pearl, and Javascript are examples of application software. Application software is needed because the hardware understands only its own "machine language," or binary numbers. Application software is written in words and then translated into machine language by a compiler or interpreter. Putting it together, a programmer writes words of code; the code is sent through a compiler or interpreter that translates it into machine code—those 1s and 0s that computers understand—as illustrated in Figure 3-5.

Other examples of common "out-of-the-box" application software include database, multimedia presentation, contact management and e-mail, instant messaging, browsers, publishing, and so on. Think of an industry, and chances are it has software that is standard to it. Out-of-the-box software is convenient because thousands of common tasks have already been automated and

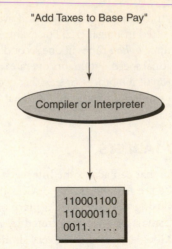

FIGURE 3-5 Through the use of a compiler or interpreter, familiar words are translated into machine code.

can be accessed by pointing and clicking. The two main versions in our industry are the property management system (PMS) and the point-of-sale (POS) system that will be covered later. Today, independent software vendors (ISV) such as Microsoft and Oracle, or more specific to our industry, Micros and PAR, spend lots of money on research and development (R&D) to develop what is known as "a killer app" for computers, tablets, smart phones, and whatever comes along next that requires software, and will lead to a high volume in sales.

6. OPERATING SYSTEMS AND MORE

Between the application software and the hardware sits the system software, one major part of which is the operating system (OS). By definition, the OS is "the system software that manages and controls the activities of the computer" (Laudon and Laudon 2009 p. 173). Further, it serves as the "middle person" between the application software and the hardware components. OS manages the computer hardware and software while making sure that all tasks are executed correctly. It is the boss.

A PC OS has seven main functions:

1. It starts the computer. Here, the OS works in conjunction with the system **BIOS** (basic input output system) found in ROM. BIOS is a lower-level OS found in personal computers that contain basic start-up functions. It is at this stage where a power-on self-test, POST, is performed in which the OS reaches out and tests the computer hardware and all its peripherals.

2. It insulates the user from direct hardware contact. Instead of lifting the cover and messing around with all the various components, we are able to make the hardware accomplish tasks via the OS.

3. It provides a **graphical user interface (GUI)** to the user. Those icons, folders, files, and words that you are able to point and click on are the points of interaction provided by the OS.

4. It manages the processing of programs efficiently. Every time an application is opened, it uses a certain amount of RAM. Other system software likewise requires memory. Some

applications use more memory than others. Computing devices have a finite supply of memory. It is up to the OS to allocate each application or system software the memory it needs. It is also up to the OS to allocate and track the memory assigned to each application.

5. It provides advanced processing features. The OS provides both multitasking and multiprocessing features. Multitasking is just what it sounds like: one user performing a variety of tasks. The computer does not actually do all the things at once. In reality, the OS assigns processor time to each event in a rotating fashion. It rotates so fast that it appears to be doing many things at once. Multiprocessing is simply the management of more than one CPU. The supercomputers you may have heard of are moving away from the gigantic units of the past to the linking of many processors under the control of one OS.

6. It manages input and output devices effectively. From keyboards to printers and the like, the OS is in control.

7. It manages filing operations and storage. Moving, copying, and storing all fall under its auspices. It is also the OS that formats a disk for file storage.

Smart phones "roughly" provide the same core features as PC OSs. Common PC and smart phone OSs are shown in Table 3-2.

When the OS communicates with an application or an application communicates with another application, it is done through an application program interface (API). This little-known part of a computing environment is important to hospitality managers since different software programs are used that often must communicate with one another.

With all of the benefits of software comes a downside that warrants further discussion:

Viruses. A virus is an unwelcome piece of software that has unknowingly been introduced into your computing environment. Most often, it is introduced via the Internet or another network, as an e-mail attachment, or in some other creative way. What makes viruses so dangerous is their often destructive nature. Some viruses are harmless and do little more than display a character that wishes you a happy birthday and disappears. This is an example of a macro virus most often found in word processing programs or other application software. Other viruses hide by attaching themselves to system or boot software until a specific date and time have been

Table 3-2   Sample of Popular Operating Systems

Operating System	Description
Windows 7	Latest offering from Microsoft with multiuser capabilities and improved Web integration
Unix	Nonproprietary OS popular in the scientific community, among others
Linux	Nonproprietary OS with available code allowing modification
Mac OS X	Macintosh OS favored by desktop publishers

Smart Phone Operating Systems	Description
iPhone	With a virtual keyboard and many third-party applications, the iPhone is quickly gaining market share.
Google	Android
Blackberry	From RIM with a big business user following
Windows Mobile	Yes, from Microsoft
Symbian	With nearly half the market (it powers Nokia)

reached and then cause havoc. Damage is usually defined by corrupted files or overwhelmed RAM. More common today are viruses that spread over networks. Knowing the source of files received and having up-to-date antivirus software have been common practice since the U.S. Department of Defense fell victim to a computer virus in 1987, and continue to this day.

Today, the computers you typically use are smart computers, meaning they have a CPU and are able to perform their own processing. It was not always this way. In the past, "dumb" terminals, which lacked a CPU, were used to communicate with mainframe computers that did all of the processing and then outputted the results to the dumb terminals. Dumb terminals are all but gone; however, the mainframe has remained and is still being used. This is an example of a legacy system, which is simply antiquated hardware or software that is still in use mainly because the cost of replacing it is too prohibitive. The newer technology of **virtualization** (there are many types) where, generally speaking, an application or OS may in fact not reside on your computer but is distributed over a network (Chapter 4) is seeing increased adaptation in our industry due to its cost-saving implications.

7. Summary

Management, in any form, requires understanding. Since technology plays such an active role in daily operations and future planning, understanding technology is critical. On this road to discovery, you have found out that computers work much the way that other things do—via a system. Data goes into a system, which (and with the aid of people) turns it into useable information. When data moves in digital signals, a computing device will read the high and low points of this signal, giving you a binary code. From the motherboard to DVD players, you have seen where these binary digits travel and are stored. In conjunction with this hardware, different software is used to manipulate the data and generate information without having to understand machine code. Whether a generic smart phone application or an industry application, it is quality software that provides the value in the management of information. One type of software, the OS, coordinates the many different interactions of all the hardware and software devices. With computing becoming more complex over time, more has been required of OSs. However, even as new components are introduced in the industry, older ones, or legacy systems, are still in use. This chapter has introduced you to some computing essentials that any hospitality manager must understand. With this knowledge, you're ready for Chapter 4 on networks, where technology is studied in a wider context.

8. Case Study and Learning Activity

Case Study

Mike is a new front office manager who has inherited computers with different ages. Some were bought recently with all of the latest features, while others were over three years old. His four computers at the front desk were the newer ones that were required to run the many applications used in the running of the hotel. His computer in his office was older and was used primarily for managerial tasks involving spreadsheets and word processing applications in addition to e-mail and other Internet functions. In addition to the front desk staff, Mike managed the concierge department and van drivers. Each of these outlets contained two old computers. Mike was also in charge of the hotel's business center near the front desk with five older computers in addition to a printer and scanner. In total Mike had fourteen computers under his management.

Guests who frequented Mike's hotel were primarily business travelers who tended to bring their own laptop computers and smart phones. Some traveled with just their cell phones and needed access to a desktop computer for a short period of time. One thing they all had in common is that more often than not, they needed to print something.

Vague of Windows was the OS for the computer and was the required one for the hotel system at the front desk, concierge stations, and the van drivers. In six months, Mike's limited budget will allow him to purchase only three new computers. Mike knows a little bit more than the average person about technology and is thinking of possibly moving away from computers to other computing devices.

Learning Activity

1. What should Mike purchase?
2. Who should get these new purchases and why?
3. Who comes first, second, and third?
4. What would you do differently if anything?

9. Key Terms

Analog	Graphical User Interface	RAM
Binary Code	(GUI)	ROM
BIOS	Gigabyte	Signal
Bit	Hard Drive	Smart Phone
Byte	Hardware	Subscriber Identity Module
Cache	Kilobyte	System
CD	Megabyte	Tablet PC
CPU	Monitor	Terabyte
Digital	Operating System	Virus
Display	Peripherals	Virtualization
Electricity	Petabyte	Voltage

10. Chapter Questions

1. How do people fit into the definition of information?
2. How is data counted?
3. What is a virus?
4. What are some examples of smart phone OSs?
5. What is binary code?

11. References

Laudon, Kenneth, and Laudon, Jane. 2009. *Management information systems* (8th ed.) Upper Saddle River, NJ: Prentice Hall.

Long, Larry, and Long, Nancy. 1998. *Computers* (5th ed.) Upper Saddle River, NJ: Prentice Hall.

Networks

Chapter Contents

Kathy Misunas

INTERVIEW

Q: Hi Kathy, would you mind telling us a little bit about your background?

A: I have spent much of my professional career in the travel and tourism industry—with a focus on marketing, distribution, and technology. My former roles include CEO of Sabre, the Global Distribution System (GDS) used by professional travel agents and OTAs, and CIO of American Airlines during my tenure at AMR Corporation; CEO of Reed Travel Group, the global travel media giant; and CEO of brandwise, a nontravel start-up supporting comparison shopping of home durable products. I currently have my own advisory business and am fortunate to assist entrepreneurial and traditional companies with both online and offline distribution challenges, as well as strategy, general business issues, technology, and marketing initiatives.

Additionally, I serve as a director on a variety of public and private company boards; speak at company or association functions; and, in addition to providing volunteer support for various charitable causes, I assist education programs as lecturer and through curriculum analysis.

Q: Airlines are heavy network users. What are some main points that any new manager should know about networks?

A: First of all, there are various types of networks that a new manager must deal with. Although in today's environment everyone sees the Internet as the "key" network, any manager must insure they are knowledgeable about voice networks, and non-Web data networks as well. There are networks within individual companies for desktop interoperability and other connectivity throughout the enterprise, and there are various external networks that the internal systems connect to for either product extension, shared data with customers, electronic billing and payments, etc. Since each of these business network requirements includes its own set of software, the overall topic of networks is quite complex.

A most critical aspect associated with networks is that of security. In today's open environments, any manager must be knowledgeable about system architecture and associated security of the connectivity and interfaces of their own business needs, as well as the inbound and outbound messages they handle on behalf of the enterprise.

Additionally, in the business environment "time is money," therefore new managers must recognize their responsibility to create and support networks that are cost-effective. This includes analysis of various solutions so as to choose the best value for monies spent, as well as considering the ongoing maintenance involved with a solid operating environment. These metrics can include 7×24 uptime, quick response times, back up capabilities in case of disaster or outages, and scalability if the company is growing.

Q: From your past experience, any do's and don'ts?

A: Do consider *all* your constituents as clients. Although most employees consider the primarily deliverable to be requests of their internal "boss," I would caution that the needs of the end customer are what you must understand in order to deliver the optimal solution.

Do keep informed about current technology solutions and be flexible to adapt appropriate solutions into your architecture.

Do create the best organization structure vis-à-vis what the technical team is tasked to do.

Do hire the best talent.

Do have a good project management process so projects are tracked end to end from inception of the concept to implementation and training.

Do insure you create an environment for upward, downward, and cross-communication both within the technology arena and across the enterprise—or even with external clients if the business requires it.

Do create a training and support mechanism so your tech team stays state of the art.

Do make sure your system documentation is current.

As far as the don'ts, it is really the flip side of the above. For example, don't operate without a project management process, or with untrained tech staff, or without constantly updated documentation.

Q: How about security?

A: Similar to the networks themselves, security of them is also complex and can be addressed at many different levels and through various solutions. Usually identifying what you are trying to secure and to what degree is a first step by analyzing the various layers of the system architecture.

As noted previously, in any network, data security is critical and is often protected as a hierarchy. It must be evaluated related to internal security needs, as well as external access. Additionally, even internal access will differ as developer access versus end-user access is identified and addressed. Who can change data versus merely look at it is an easy example of what developers should be building into their application on a regular basis.

Having said that, although technology systems should be designed to control security access to the highest degree possible, it is important that cooperation and accountability in the business unit(s) among those responsible for gathering and using the data is part of any business culture.

And, as a final point, there should be a clear disaster recovery plan in case security is breeched. For example, securing personal data associated with employees or billing information related to clients comes to mind.

Quickly addressing a breech often requires a technology solution whereby access to up-to-date system documentation is needed—and a communication plan is in place—especially if the security breech caused risk to the company and where external communication is necessary to inform others of the problem.

Q: Looking into your crystal ball, what do you see coming down the road in technology in the tourism industry?

A: There are so many ways to address this topic. There is technology created within the travel sector that is often proprietary to the suppliers like airlines, hospitality companies, cruise lines, etc., and there is more generic technology that is adapted by the sector. The "technology" can be hardware, software or networks. The Internet comes to mind as an example of the later, whereby the Web was not created by the travel industry, but the travel sector became one of it earliest adaptors in the mid-90s. I think perfection of some of the recent introductions like remote hotel or cruise check-in will occur, and I hope the ability to easily create a customized trip itinerary will be forthcoming versus having to go from site to site so as to cobble together how you get there, where you are staying, what you are doing, etc.

Also, only time will tell whether travelers will rely on professionals for their restaurant reviews or destination information—or simply depend on blogs or other social network feedback to assist with decision making. At any rate, all these solutions will involve technology.

As far as my crystal ball, overall, in the next months and years I think mobile technology will demand a good bit of attention in the travel sector as each constituency attempts to determine how to put connected PDAs of one type or another to good use. It is a rather broad issue for the industry since internal company and external user needs vary greatly around the globe, and adaptation rates differ significantly from country to country. The need for "mobile Web sites" is already apparent and there will be development required to offer efficient yet engaging experiences for travelers during all phases of trip planning and while en route.

I also believe that search capabilities will become more important as the Internet becomes more and more a part of everyone's daily life. Whereas the technology focus by Google and others until now may have been more on the robustness of the data associated with the search inquiry, I hope the future focus will be on the quality of the response and its appropriateness to what the user is requesting. Also, as mentioned above, mobile capabilities will need to be perfected—especially for providing effective search results on a small screen.

I think the GDS will undergo technology transformation, and I believe video conferencing will continue to gain momentum as prices of the high-end systems are reduced.

But probably the biggest change will be that in a few years, all consumer-related devices will be "unplugged." We will be online all the time and be able to access and store data versus the more inquiry–response metaphor still used today. The devices will have long battery life, and wireless will allow businesses and consumers to operate anywhere at any time. These are ideal capabilities for travel since a user can easily have end-to-end data and functionality while planning a trip, during travel, and also upon return home. And, it will also allow suppliers to stay in touch with their key customers and push appropriate products to them along the way.

There are so many other possibilities for travel as IDs and payment systems are all online (versus having credit cards and IDs), as tablets become more commonplace, etc. Even health issues will be tied into travel as medical travel proliferates.

Technology will make it all possible.

1. INTRODUCTION

The prevalence of networks in the hospitality industry may surprise you. A guest making a room reservation on the Internet, a meeting planner virtually touring a potential property for a large meeting, or simply using your cell phone are all examples of networks in use in the industry today. How often you interact with networks, when studied in detail, demonstrates not only their ubiquity as pointed out by Kathy in our interview but also their importance in communication as well as in revenue generation.

Additionally, with the ever-increasing availability of real-time information to management and staff, not to mention customer expectations of communication at the property level, network knowledge is vital to remain competitive.

The terms **networks** and **networking** refer to the broad subject of managing computer networks and the information on them. "A network is a transmission system that connects two or more applications running on different computers" (Panko, 2007, p. 1). Networking is a detailed subject matter. To management, however, there are three primary interest areas.

SECURITY, PERFORMANCE, AND RELIABILITY   Is it safe, fast, and running are three questions that beg for the answer "yes." Ensuring that the network is protected from unauthorized users while available to authorized users seems logical. In reality, it is a daily challenge. Hacking of a company's Web page or theft of customer data are often nightly news items. New regulations by the credit card companies actually mandate a certain level of security to thwart any such occurrences. Speed is also important. Slow networks not only lessen communication ability but can also drive guests towards your competitors. If you encounter a Web page that is loading slowly, how long does it take you before you move on to another page? There are just too many options, and "fast" is what the customer expects regarding technology. Finally, any system that doesn't function properly or "goes down" is not an option. It has become too much of a worldwide lifeline. How upset you are when you can't get your e-mail, or a cell phone signal? This chapter will help answer those and other questions as well as acquaint you with networks within the hospitality industry.

2. SMALL NETWORKS

Remember the definition of a data bus path where data moved from one point to another inside the computer? If this is expanded to include data moving to another device such as a printer in the next room, then you have networking. If you operate in an office or school setting and your computer can communicate with other computers or computing devices, you are most likely using a **local area network (LAN)**. Like all advances in technology, LANs provide a business need. Specifically they do the following:

1. Allow resources to be shared. For example, instead of everyone having a printer, which would be cost-prohibitive, the resource is shared by multiple end-users.
2. Allow data and information to be shared. Through networks, and unrestricted by geography, all managers can have access to "real-time" company information.

Obviously networks are all about sharing. On the back of a computer you will find openings with multiple pins or sockets. These are known as ports. "A **port** is the combination of a connector plug and internal electronics . . ." (Panko 2001, p. 39). Ports include serial, parallel, and the newer more interoperable, united serial bus (USB). Ports are used mostly for local communication with peripherals such as scanners. In networks, computers need another important device. All stations on a network, such as computers, printers, and kiosks, which are ease-of-use touch screens, are known in networking terms as nodes. In order for nodes to join a network, a network interface card is needed. **Network interface cards (NICs)** provide network access and addressing information. An expansion slot can be seen on the rear or side of most computers. This is where a NIC can be inserted. Each and every NIC has a unique 48-bit address (known as the MAC address) that the manufacturer assigns. This unique addressing allows for efficient sending and receiving of data. With a NIC, your computer is given a new name and joins a larger community.

Just as storage has its own measurement in bytes, data transfer rates have their own form of measurement in bits per second (bps). These bits are the same as found in binary code. Remember that storage is measured in bytes and data transfer rate, or speed, is measured in bits. Measurement is similar to data storage and comes in the form of kilobits (kbps), roughly 1 thousand bits per second; megabits (mbps), 1 million bits per second; gigabits (gbps), 1 billion bits per second; and finally, terabits (tbps), traveling at 1 trillion bits per second.

What these fast-moving bits travel through from computing device to computing device are known as mediums. Currently, there are four main medium options:

1. **Twisted pair copper wires.** Copper is a great material for signals to travel on. The phone line in an average house (if not using cable or fiber) contains two pairs of copper wires (four wires in total) twisted together and known in networking terms as RJ-11. Each pair represents a line. When you request a second "land" phone line from the phone company, the company simply activates and assigns a number to this second line. In many LANs, a larger form of twisted pair is used. It is known as RJ-45 (often known as Ethernet) and contains four pairs of twisted copper wires. The wires are twisted in such a manner that points on the twist can block interference from the other pairs of wires. RJ-45 comes in categories with the common CAT5 and offers speeds up to 1 gbps.
2. **Coaxial cable.** If you have cable television, this is the medium involved. LANs can also utilize this copper core medium with speeds also up to 1 gbps. Coaxial cable contains one heavy copper wire that is heavily insulated by three different layers to prevent interference.
3. **Fiber optics.** This is a medium consisting of very thin (think of a strand of your hair) and expensive glass fibers covered by a protective layer. Here, instead of an electromagnetic signal, pulses of light are used. A flash of light indicates the 1 bit. Absence of light indicates the 0 bit. Fiber optic technology is very reliable and unsusceptible to electromagnetic interference. Fiber optic cable has been around enough that it is being seen more at the local business and residential level. Its speed (increasing amounts of terabits, however megabits at the local level) and reliability makes it ideal for the larger networks discussed in the next section.

4. **Wireless.** To be fair, wireless is not a medium but rather a broadcast technology. It is not bound by wires in between points. At the LAN level, wireless technology enables users to operate digitally without being tied to a desk. It is not perfect. Brick walls can be a major obstacle. For that reason, multiple access points, which transmit and receive data for the nodes on the network, are used. Access points at the local level vary in appearance from small cones to plates and are in charge of moving the data across the wireless spectrum. Advancement in wireless local area networks (WLANs) has speeds approaching the 100 mbps range.

5. Other wireless technologies found at the local level include **bluetooth** and **near field communication (NFC).** Bluetooth is used at the very local level (10 meters or less typically) and can aid in such tasks of wirelessly syncing your smart phone calendar with the one on your computer. Near field communication is even closer (very close or touching) where synching (i.e., photos) is also often the purpose. We will continue our discussion of wireless in the section, "Large Wireless Networks."

Choosing a medium can be both tricky and costly. In addition, certain expertise and knowledge may be required. At the local level, CAT5 and wireless continue to dominate; however, the cost of fiber optics is declining. There are many different variations of each medium with their own characteristics and speeds. Whatever the choice, selection of mediums must take into account the distance and number of nodes to be served. In fact, the standard setting organization, the *Institute for Electric and Electronic Engineers, Inc. (IEEE),* has set capabilities and limitations for each medium and its various subsets. This organization has thoroughly tested, studied, and, even more crucial, *certified* network mediums among other network technologies. Before any network installation or adoption, you should understand the applicable IEEE standard. An example of what expertise IEEE provides deals with attenuation. **Attenuation** is the weakening of a signal. Signals, like all things moving, eventually tire. They can be cleaned up and strengthened by repeaters and sent back on their way. Signal regenerators in an analog environment are called amplifiers. Amplifiers are unable to clean signals and often amplify noise, making digital transmission more attractive across hard wire mediums. IEEE has researched and standardized distances and many other factors for networks through their many workgroups. IEEE is the Zagats (the famed restaurant reviewers) of the networking world, and its legwork and knowledge are respected by vendors and managers alike. To prevent any possible bottlenecks, it is vital to follow IEEE specifications in network purchase and implementation.

A **bottleneck** is a device or application that significantly degrades network performance. Bottlenecks are named, oddly enough, from the thin neck of a glass bottle through which the thicker contents from below must pass. A state-of-the-art computer with a fast CPU, abundant memory, and hard disk space accessing a network with an inadequate or slow network card is an example of a network card bottleneck.

Two important components of LAN hardware connectivity are switches and routers. Data travels within the network through **switches**. Ethernet uses an addressing system known as MAC address. MAC addresses are found in the NICs of the various nodes (remember—not just computers) and aid the switches in data transfer at the local level. When your network communicates with another network such as the Internet, a **router** is used which routes the data.

Networks are not just hardware. Just as the operating system runs the show of a desktop computer, another system software is the boss here. A **network operating system (NOS)** is a system software that routes communications on the network and manages network resources. A NOS commonly resides on a server. A **server** from a hardware perspective is simply a more expensive computer with lots of memory, hard disk space, and a fast CPU (to name a few items) that provides shared resources to the network. The NOS is the boss of the LAN with switches quickly maturing and offering many of their capabilities challenging their authority in the future. Because network outage can result in lost revenue and decreased employee productivity and because security is always a concern, often a redundant or backup NOS server is used in case the primary server fails. Additionally, a backup power supply such as a generator or off-site power supply arrangements made with a third party are a good idea in case the electricity should fail. This is of particular concern for international properties, where infrastructure can be unreliable.

A network server is just one example of a server. Servers can be dedicated to specific tasks in large organizations. Three other servers play a crucial role in LANs and networks at large.

1. A file server is a computer and a storage device dedicated to storing files. Any authorized person on the network can store files on the server. File servers often contain commonly used templates and data for day-to-day activities. An expense report used by management is an example of a file stored in a file server.
2. A print server is a computer that manages one or more printers. Hospitality organizations may use a large number of printers as well as make them available to guests. A large number of printers in use requires a dedicated server.
3. A database server is a system that processes database queries. Most hotel systems are server based where a search engine is integrated into the system to handle simple and complex queries. We will look at databases more closely in Chapter 10.

Today, hospitality organizations predominantly operate in this **client/server (C/S)** architecture with the client being a computing device on the network that requests resources from the server such as files, records, or services. In C/S architecture the processing is distributed, meaning that both the client and server possess a CPU; however, the server's CPU does the bulk of the work. Another architecture making a comeback is peer to peer. In a **peer to peer** architecture, processing is evenly distributed among individual computers, and communication is more direct between these computers or peers. By definition, components in a peer to peer environment possess the same potential communications capabilities and initiatives. A LAN can operate without a server.

In the hospitality world one common piece of networking equipment is also found— the **private branch exchange (PBX)**. The PBX has long been a part of the hotel industry. For example, a hotel with five hundred rooms that all contain phones needs a connection to the phone company. However, purchasing or leasing five hundred phone lines plus staff lines would be cost-prohibitive, particularly since at any one time only 30 percent or less of the phone lines are utilized. Enter the PBX. The PBX is used to direct incoming calls to the larger organizational setting. An incoming call goes to the PBX, with say fifty ports, and is directed to the specific location such as a hotel room. An outgoing call is done in reverse. With phone lines already in place in many organizations, PBXs can also be used in lieu of LANs although this is less and less the case. Older analog PBX systems are being replaced with newer digital ones. The PBX's interface with the telephone network introduces our next network topic, large networks.

3. LARGE NETWORKS

To understand large networks as well as the evolution of small networks, you need to understand telecommunications. **Telecommunications** is simply long-distance communications. This long-distance communication involves a network you already use, the telephone system.

Alexander Graham Bell accomplished the first voice transmission in 1876. Many years later a nationwide phone network was established and controlled by one company, American Telephone and Telegraph (AT&T) until its breakup in 1984. From there, other companies such as MCI and Sprint entered the picture in competition with AT&T for the long-distance telephone market. Since a 1996 deregulation act, in theory, companies from different industries such as cable companies, broadcasters, and phone companies have been allowed to compete in each other's markets. In addition, state-by-state regulation has increased the competition between your local phone carrier or "baby bells" (the regional bell operating companies resulting from the AT&T breakup and merging over the years with the current makeup of Verizon, Quest, and yes AT&T and the long-distance carriers in their respective markets). The bigger battle today is between the phone and cable industries. Think of an advertisement that you have recently seen or heard for one or the other. It used to be that you got your phone network from the traditional phone companies and your cable television from the cable company. Soon both industries began offering high-speed Internet access and now both offer all three: voice, video, and data. It all has to do with convergence.

With digital signals replacing and working with analog signals, this ideal of convergence has been realized. **Convergence** is the combining of voice, video, and data into one experience and is also known as media streams. If all the signals are digital, then the vast phone network can communicate with LANs and PBXs in new and exciting global ways.

The efficiency of digital signals can be seen when contrasted to analog signals. As noted earlier, analog signals are still important and utilized in such forms as sound. However, in digital mediums using copper or glass, the digital signal takes up less space, enabling other media streams to use the channel. A **channel** is an instrument through which nodes on a network communicate. Think of it as part of a medium.

The "last mile" or "local loop" of the majority of the telecommunications network still uses analog technology with newer construction or changes adopting fiber from the phone company or cable from the cable company, and even wireless. Competition for this space is fierce, which explains the advertising from the two competing elements. For instance, if the phone in your house uses RJ-11 wires, it uses an analog signal that is converted to digital at the first phone company's building. Conversion to data signals locally is often necessary, as done when accessing the Internet, which will be described shortly. Remember the modem? A **modem** *mo*dulates a digital signal, converting it to an analog, or *dem*odulates an analog signal back into digital form. While digital is more efficient for transmission, analog is more fluid, which is why digital signals may be converted to analog at the hand level for sound in your cell phone or iPod.

A modem is a type of connectivity device that generally aids in network transmission. Other connectivity devices include multiplexers, which allow a channel to carry multiple media streams, and concentrators, which collect multiple signals until enough signals are ready to be sent.

With the adoption of digital signals, large networks can reap the benefits. The first type of larger networks is the **wide area network (WAN)**. A WAN is a network of larger geography than a LAN, ranging from a couple of miles to the entire world. An emerging network is the metropolitan area network (MAN) for a metropolitan area or in and around a city network. With hospitality organizations having multiple sites or properties, connectivity and collaboration are needed. This functionality was first enabled by WANs.

Different network services are available in WAN utilization on the mediums discussed earlier. Basically these services or technologies speed up data transmission over long distances. Their transfer rate is dependent on bandwidth. **Bandwidth** is the difference between the highest and lowest point of a signal. It is this available area in between where the data flows on a channel.

Remember a channel is part of a medium, and channels and mediums have specific bandwidths that can be improved upon by newer technologies presented in the next section.

4. TRANSMISSION TECHNOLOGIES

DSLs (digital subscriber lines) operate over existing phone lines but require special local hardware to digitize the signal. Transmission can reach 9 mbps or even greater over shorter distances. This technology is the phone company's first venture into the broadband or high-speed market. With many of the existing DSL "pipes" already installed, the existing phone companies are increasing the speed of DSL constantly.

Cable modems use existing cable lines and can transmit up to 10 mbps, with speeds due to increase. Take heed, oftentimes cable bandwidth is shared among other cable subscribers in your area. Both cable modems and DSL currently cost $60–140 per month depending on the package.

A **T1** connection is a dedicated phone connection with twenty-four of those RJ-11 phone lines. These are often referred to as *trunk lines* due to the number of channels, and they move data at 1.54 mbps. Current pricing is about $350 per month. With bandwidth needs quickly exceeding the capability of T1, more organizations are adding other transmission technologies. The equivalent E1 in Europe operates at roughly 2 mbps. In the five-hundred-room hotel example with a fifty-port PBX, that hotel would most likely have two T1 lines. From here we have the higher level T3 with approximately 44 mbps and again in Europe the similar E3 operating at approximately 34 mbps.

UTILITIES FIBER NETWORK The utility companies (i.e., natural gas and electric) are also getting into the game by providing fiber networks. From here your company's data is handed off to mainly the Public Switch Telephone Network (PSTN) called "the telephone network," or the Public Switch Data Network (PSDN), a newer network for data.

With all of these advances a new technology has emerged called a **link load balancer** (or WAN switch or even a router switch) which can operate multiple mediums in a cost-efficient manner.

Long-distance and international communication can be expensive to create and maintain. For that reason, many in need of cross boundary connectivity turn to the major telecommunication carriers and lease their existing networks. There are a whole host of companies that provide these services.

5. THE INTERNET

Perhaps the most well-known network is the Internet. Internet access, particularly wireless, is almost totally expected from guests, with pricing always an issue. From smart phones to laptops, the Internet is used by many devices and in different ways. The Internet, a network that no one owns outright, links multiple networks and users around the globe. Currently, the Internet primarily uses C/S technology where servers process and provide data to clients. Please see Table 4-1 for some examples of clients on the Internet.

As in LANs, peer to peer networking is seen on the Internet as well. Examples of such networks include music-sharing programs such as BitTorrent or Morpheus.

Like anything else, in understanding the Internet, you first need to understand the rules. In networks, communications between nodes require certain procedures and regulations known as protocols. When you send a letter by standard mail, you follow certain protocols. You place the address of the recipient in the center of the envelope, your return address in the upper left or

Table 4-1	Examples of Internet Clients
Device	**Description**
Smart Phones	Cell phones with data services
Laptop/PC/Tablets	General-use computers
IP Telephones	Internet protocol telephones that are being used more frequently
Game Machine	Game box with Internet access and specific controls
Kiosks	Self-ordering/communication systems
Paging/e-mail devices	Devices such as BlackBerry which facilitate e-mail on the go

rear, and the postage in the upper right. This protocol for standard mail is used the world over and facilitates communication. Specifically, network protocols are concerned with four main objectives:

1. The type of error-checking to be used
2. Data compression method, if any, utilized
3. How the sending device will indicate that it has finished sending a message
4. How the receiving device will indicate that it has received a message

The Internet has its own protocol that is quickly becoming the dominant small and large network protocol worldwide. This protocol, known as **TCP/IP** (**transmission control protocol/Internet protocol**), was established by the department of defense in the 1970s. The Internet's foundations lie with the U.S. military. The thought process is that a decentralized network would make any nuclear attack upon the network less significant because network control and storage are not in one place. If the server at your location goes down, it has almost no impact on the Internet at large. With this spread out network in mind, the military came up with the TCP/IP protocol to ensure common practices in communication. TCP/IP has layers that govern data flow through the software and hardware of the sending and receiving computing devices.

TCP/IP is not the only network protocol in use today. Different network protocols such as Internetwork Packet Exchange (IPX) are still used. For that reason, hardware devices known as gateways are needed. **Gateways** bridge networks using different protocols.

Today the Internet has been embraced by multiple organizations, with quasi-governmental organizations overseeing its operation and address allocation. When you use the Internet, you access it through an Internet service provider (ISP), which has its own servers and IP addresses (provided to them) to be given to customers. IP addresses provide the location of a node or network. An IP address is a static address. For example, 198.4.159.10 is the IP address of *www.prenhall.com*, the publishers of this book. In contrast, a dynamic address may be assigned by an ISP to a user accessing the Internet via an ISP for a short time. It is the ISP through a **domain name server (DNS)** that assigns letters—which are easier to remember (e.g., Prenhall.com)—to numerical IP addresses, although both may be used. Just as the hub and switch controlled the traffic in LANs, a director is needed on the Internet. Communication between nodes on the internet is managed in part by routers. As you remember from our earlier discussion, routers are used when your network communicates with another network. In Internet usage, routers, the traffic cops of the Internet, are used to move or route data from one node to another based on these IP addresses.

The Internet offers many communication tools available to management. Three major ones are the following:

- E-mail
- Instant messaging
- File transfer protocol

Electronic mail (e-mail) has all but surpassed standard mail in communicating with guests, coworkers, and suppliers. E-mail uses software on a client that accesses an e-mail server. A DNS server is likewise used here for mapping IP addresses to domain names. For example, the e-mail address of the president of Penn State in State College, PA, President@psu.edu, begins with a name identifier, President, followed by the host name psu, and finally its function .edu, signifying an educational institution. Other functions include .gov for government agencies, .com for business, .net for network carriers, and .org for organizations. New functions such as .shop have been approved and may see larger adaptation in the future. E-mail addresses outside the United States end in location identifiers such as .it for Italy and .uk for the United Kingdom. Newer plans involve .travel or .nyc for, yes, New York City, to name a few that are being put forward. Soon, if approved by the organization in charge of naming on the Internet, Internet Corporation for Assigned Names and Numbers (ICANN), many other identifiers will follow.

Instant messaging (IM) usage on the Internet is increasing every day. IM is a form of chatting where two or more persons simultaneously connected to the Internet with IM software can engage in live conversations. Text messaging (i.e., SMS, which stands for short message service) on cell phones is quickly rivaling desktop instant messaging.

File transfer protocol (FTP) is used in both data transmission and retrieval of large amounts of data between two nodes (most likely computers) on the Internet. FTP requires password authentication since a computer is to be accessed by another computer. FTP is often unknown to hospitality managers but could be quite useful if a large amount of customer data is needed by a soon-to-open property on the fly.

Newer to the Internet are smart phones with stand-alone applications that partition and utilize networks without a browser, which will be discussed in detail later.

6. THE WORLD WIDE WEB

The **World Wide Web** is the most recognizable communication tool on the Internet. The *Web* and the *Internet* are terms often used interchangeably, which is incorrect. The Web is *part of* the Internet. The Web likewise uses the TCP/IP protocol. A **uniform resource locator (URL)** uses the aforementioned DNS server to point to Web resources and addresses such as *www.psu.edu*. A URL is a Web address. The Web also uses specific formats. **Hypertext markup language (HTML)** is one format of the Web that provides formatting and presentation functionality as well as navigation and search capabilities. Hypertext signifies that the text when clicked will take you to another location on the Web. **Extensible markup language (XML)** is a newer form of formatting and presentation on the Web with greater emphasis on the meaning of the data. XML allows businesses to interact via the Web with a common understanding of what the data represents. Incorporating these and other functionalities is the vital piece of software used to surf the net. Applications such as Internet Explorer, Firefox, or Safari, which are known as browsers, open the door to browser-based Internet communication.

Finding what you need can often be a daunting task on the Web. For this reason, search capabilities on the Web are enabled by search engines that may be part of your browser's functionality or may be located on specific Web pages. Oftentimes, these Web pages are called portals, from the name of windows on a ship. It is through this portal that the Internet experience begins although smart phone applications are quickly rivaling them. Popular portals include *Yahoo.com* or even a social networking site such as Facebook. We will look at more Web offerings in greater detail in Chapter 5.

7. INTERNET LAYOUT

Rounding out the earlier discussion of servers is the **Web server**. A Web server is a server in a C/S architecture that contains organizational Web pages and services and is detailed in Chapter 5. How much of a company's Web or Internet resources are to be made available is a managerial decision. Oftentimes, private information such as credit card numbers needs to be kept in house.

We have discussed a number of different types of servers so far. Any business with a large amount of these servers may consider a new technology named **virtualization** where servers are combined into a virtual environment where this new collective is managed by what is known as a **hypervisor**. Virtualization enables a more cost-effective and efficient use of multiple servers.

8. LARGE WIRELESS NETWORKS

Because of their mobile nature, wireless networks are on the rise. Wireless transmissions are electromagnetic signals sent through the air. Common wireless transmissions include satellites, and cellular and personal communication services (PCS).

The word *microwave* causes most to think of the type of oven. When an electromagnetic signal passes through water it is disrupted and generates heat as a by-product. The good-microwave ovens send electromagnetic signals that end up heating water molecules, giving us warm food and drink. The bad-satellite television in rainy Seattle can be problematic since water droplets can upset reception. Microwave usage in networks is highly efficient. In conjunction with satellites that redirect the data to a new location, wireless transmission can move large amounts of data over remote places such as oceans and deserts, making it ideal for distant sites.

Cellular technology uses geographic areas that are divided into "cells." Each cell has an antenna or tower to receive a signal transmitted by a cell phone that passes it off to an available channel in the next cell all the way to the end point. Because many antennas and towers are needed to hand off the phone call, coverage can be scarce in remote areas. Additionally, unlike most of the rest of the world, U.S. cellular technology uses different wireless protocols, hampering connectivity. The two dominant protocols in use today are **code division multiple access (CDMA)** used by such companies as Verizon and **global system for mobile communication (GSM)** used by such U.S. companies as AT&T and much of the rest of the world, making GSM the dominant wireless protocol. A third offering named **worldwide operability for microwave access** *(WiMax)* is a technology offered by Sprint Nextel and Clearwire. WiMax has the backing of other major companies such as Google and Intel to compete with both CDMA and GSM. Current development includes GSM and CDMA moving to a fourth-generation technology (4G from today's 3G) named **long-term evolution (LTE)** with WiMax as a separate offering.

For obvious reasons, the Web has embraced wireless technology as well. Specifically for the hospitality industry, the technology can be used to pinpoint a potential customer's location and provide that customer information about nearby restaurants, hotels, stadiums, and so on.

From a managerial perspective, executives are no longer dependent on being at their desks to access information. The wireless Web in the United States that does not access the Internet via a browser uses the **wireless markup language (WML)**, which is part of the larger protocol suite **wireless application protocol (WAP)**. Through a microbrowser or minibrowser on a PDA, cell phone, or other wireless Web-enabled device, the World Wide Web can be accessed in a scaled-down version. Advances in cell phone messaging include multimedia messaging service (MMS), which incorporates pictures and of course smart phones. Smart phones are "smart" if they can access the Internet. Smart phone applications access the Web without a browser and are quickly gaining in popularity with many companies offering their own applications for their customers. Next time you are using a smart phone, take a look at the different hospitality applications.

9. OTHER NETWORK USAGE IN THE ENTERPRISE

Information access, communication and collaboration, and e-commerce are all vital components of networks. E-commerce is discussed in detail in Chapter 5. Apart from the aforementioned benefits, networks also provide organizations with standard communication services such as faxes, voice mail, and **electronic data interchange (EDI)**. EDI technology came before the Web and still enables companies to electronically conduct business over networks, resulting in lower transaction costs and paperwork. Currently, much of the bulk purchasing and aggregate financial transactions in hospitality use EDI. EDI provides a structure that the parties involved understand and is used primarily over private networks due to the sensitivity of the financial transactions. With the advances and common structure of such Web technologies as XML, EDI is moving to the Internet platform.

10. FORWARD-LOOKING ISSUES IN HOSPITALITY

With the many advances in technology, guests are expecting an increasing amount of network technology before, during, and after their travel, stay, or meal. In all hospitality entities wireless access and smart phones are gaining in importance and can differentiate one location from another. In hotels, Internet access is a must, with wireless almost expected. As we will discuss in Chapter 7, due to convergence, we are now seeing IP television and Internet phone service (**VOIP—voice over Internet protocol**) as well. With more self-service options via a kiosk or personal cell phone in hotels and restaurants, guests are able to take advantage of location-based technology by which their location is pinpointed and services provided by the nearest team members, if not by the guest themselves. Smart phones can store a boarding pass, be given permission to act as a room key during a stay, and of course order a pizza. While these advances are in their earlier stages, and most guests do not have a smart phone, wider adaptation is almost certain. This will be expanded upon in Chapter 5.

From a management perspective, and to some degree from a guest perspective, new uses of the Internet are giving hospitality organizations more options. **Cloud computing** is one such offering where companies such as Amazon, IBM, Google, and Microsoft are providing processing power, storage, and applications on their servers which can be accessed via the Internet. Hospitality technology-specific vendors are also increasing in offering their applications over the Internet rather than on-site. What was once known as an application service provider (ASP) where generic software was made available over the Internet has developed into a more customized application tailored to a specific company's needs by the vendor but likewise stored and managed by the vendor on their servers and accessed over the Internet. This is known as **software as a service (SaaS)**. Lastly, businesses are able to harness some new advanced technology in communication known as **unified communication** in which various forms of communication (voice, IM, fax, etc.) can be managed in one mailbox which facilitates communication in our fast-moving industry.

11. SECURITY

Security issues are a great concern when using networks and the Internet. Current mandates regarding credit card security will be looked at in Chapters 5 and 6. Virtualization, as one example, can open up your network to malicious software spreading much faster than older networks. Meeting this need, newer classes of networks using Internet technology have sprung up, providing businesses with a secure way of conducting transactions in such a public environment. Currently, ISPs and organizations utilize **virtual private networks** (**VPNs**). A VPN provides a secure connection to different sites of an enterprise over the Internet. Specific protocols are used that wrap data transfer, inhibiting penetration from unauthorized users. With innovations such as this, secure transmissions are further enabled. Now companies can offer telecommuting options to their workers. This allows off-site workers comparable access to the same data and network speeds while at home or away from the office. VPN's effectiveness has led to it also becoming a standard for internal or company networks.

The degree of access, if at all, given to others using a network calls for difficult decisions. Granting and restricting access to Internet resources is done by software known as a firewall. **Firewalls** prohibit unauthorized users from accessing Internet resources through user verification and passwords. Advanced firewalls also monitor Internet intrusions and attacks. A popular form of attack is a *denial of service attack* where routers and other devices on the Internet are co-opted and form what is known as a **botnet** and are directed to a specific Web site. The volume overwhelms a Web server and prohibits other users from accessing its resources, rendering it useless. Botnets may also spread viruses, **worms**, **Trojan horses**, and **spyware**. Recalling from Chapter 3 that viruses are malicious pieces of software, worms, Trojan horses, and spyware work a little differently. While a virus needs an end-user to activate it (unknowingly), say opening an attachment which ends in .exe (Don't do it!), a worm does not. Worms exploit information on your computer (e.g., e-mail addresses) and spread themselves without human interaction. Trojan horses are phony software that appear to do one thing but once installed do another, such as deleting files, whereas spyware can record passwords and key strokes. Be careful what you install and click online!

Due to the Internet's designed public nature, oftentimes the Web server is put out in front and separated from other network resources. The area between the Web server and the rest of the network is given a military-sounding name, the demilitarized zone (DMZ). Use of firewalls and placement of servers often dictate how remote workers can and cannot access company resources such as files and e-mails.

Firewalls play an important role in network protection. Good network administrators will update their firewalls daily against the malicious pieces of software. Smaller hospitality organizations with network connections provided by DSL or cable modems do not realize that their connection is continuous, making their computer more vulnerable to malicious software. To prevent this, firewalls must be used. It is often surprising to organizations that use advanced firewalls with monitoring capabilities how often an attempted or successful intrusion happens on their network. Larger organizations can see thousands of attempts daily, yes daily.

Communication between different networks has its own security issues, particularly when the Internet is used for such privileged data as credit card numbers. In addition to the methods used by VPNs, scrambling of messages, known as **encryption**, is often necessary to keep transmissions private. Encryption involves a mathematical operation that assigns different values to a key. Given the discussion of 8 bits representing a specific key, encryption assigns more 1s and 0s algorithmically to each key to mask the actual keys used, and thereby the entire message. The number of additional 1s and 0s used represents the strength of the encryption method used. Common cost-effective encryption methods used today are 128 bits. Luckily, there comes a point where it is cost-prohibitive to attempt to crack higher encryption methods. It simply takes too much processing power and time. Unfortunately, technological advances in encryption are also taking place in the nefarious encryption cracking software realm.

Security issues are more local than one might think. Studies show that most breaches or thefts of company data are done internally. A locked door and restricted access can solve many problems. On the other hand, external threats are often at a lower level than you may think. They are enabled by telephone tricks where one party calls another and tricks that party into giving access information. This is an example of **social engineering**. Oftentimes, hackers, or those who penetrate a network, use social engineering methods to get in the door of a network and wreak havoc on Web sites or illegally obtain data. For these reasons, network administrators concern themselves daily with a host of issues. The first issue deals with user authentication. Currently, user identifications and passwords are commonly used. Other tools include rights and permissions of data. For example, a housekeeper is not given access to sales data, nor is a member of the wait staff given client home phone numbers. By restricting who has access, many problems can be avoided. Having proper policies in place can also aid in network security. Letting employees know about current phishing e-mails is a common one. **Phishing** is broadly defined as fake e-mails that trick the user into providing information such as social security or bank account numbers. In the age of employee empowerment, data access must be studied constantly by all levels of management. Advanced network software development has created **network behavior analysis (NBA)** software which analyzes a network for irregularities.

Advanced identification technology such as iris (eye) and fingerprint scanning along with facial recognition take away many of the vulnerabilities of password and user IDs. Costs have dropped to a degree that fingerprint technology is becoming more common as a password replacement.

While smart phones have enabled much more personalized access by both management and the guest, security must be applied here as well. Proprietary corporate property may reside on many smart phones, so passwords at a minimum are needed. Aside from the aforementioned content regarding security, smart phone security software is available, giving the administrator many options on what can be done with both the corporate phone and guest access.

12. Summary

Network understanding is now a required tool for any hospitality manager. We use it daily and so do our guests. From small networks, found in a restaurant, to larger global hotel communication systems, network knowledge is a must. When a network goes down or is not used properly, lost revenue and unhappy customers can result. Executives meet this challenge by first applying the right combination of network topography, mediums, transmission technologies, and smart phone integration into their organization. With the proper foundation in place, network offerings such as wireless access, IP TV, and VOIP can be used to their fullest potential. Other networks, such as telephone, electronic data interchange, wireless systems, and cloud computing are equally important, and can be used to benefit the organization and guest alike. Growing in importance by the day is network security. Up-to-date firewall software and data encryption are a good start, particularly when considering that customers' personal information and credit card numbers make up much of the network data. A true security strategy including employee policy and procedures, which is tested often, serves as a true complement to any hardware or software. No matter what organization you are in, networks require constant attention.

13. Case Study and Learning Activity

Case Study

Julie is the assistant general manager for a local independent hotel. She was recently hired due to her technological expertise. The owners of the hotel wished to increase their property's network security. Other hotels in the area were the victims of security breaches, and the owners feared that they would be next.

Julie knew from her training and past experience that what needed first was a situational analysis to find points of vulnerability. She wanted to handle the major problem spots first before she dug into the more technical matters and relatively quickly identified some potential hazards. She compiled a list of the first ten vulnerable points she encountered and turned it over to the owners that morning.

Vulnerabilities

1. Front desk staff is giving out too much information over the telephone
2. The room holding the network servers is unlocked
3. The computer system does not require users to change their passwords often enough
4. Both guests and employees use the same network
5. Employee and guest cell phones can access the hotel's wireless network
6. Firewall software requires manual updates
7. No employee network policy currently exists
8. Software installation is allowed on all computers
9. Business center computers do not require passwords
10. She was able to access the hotel's wireless from across the street

After receiving the list, the owners told Julie that a competing hotel a couple of blocks away just had their network hacked and were unsure of the damage. Since this was the fifth hotel in their area to be breached this week, they were worried that they might be next. They wanted her to act fast. Julie was by no means done with her audit and was sure that she would find many more points of vulnerability, but she believed that these were most of the "big ones." She knew that network security was both an art and a science, but she needed to start somewhere to secure the operation.

Learning Activity

1. What should Julie do first?
2. Why should she do this first?
3. List in order your next nine priorities and justify your answers.
4. Apart from these ten, can you think of other possible vulnerable points?

14. Key Terms

Attenuation
Bandwidth
Bluetooth

Botnet
Bottleneck
Cable Modems

Cellular
Channel
Client/Server (C/S)

Cloud Computing
Coaxial cable
Code Division Multiple Access
   (CDMA)
Convergence
Domain Name Server (DNS)
digital subscriber lines (DSL)
Electronic Data interchange
   (EDI)
Encryption
Extensible Markup Language
   (XML)
Firewall
Fiber Optics
File Transfer Protocol (FTP)
Gateway
Global Systems for Mobile
   communications (GSM)
Hypervisor
Link Load Balancer
Local Area Network (LAN)
Long-Term Evolution (LTE)

Modem
Near Field Communication
   (NFC)
Network Interface Card (NIC)
Network Operating System (NOS)
Network
Networking
Network Behavior Analysis
   (NBA)
Personal Communication
   Services (PCS)
Peer to Peer
Phishing
Port
Private Branch Exchange (PBX)
Router
Server
Social Engineering
Software as a Service (SaaS)
Spyware
Switch
T1

TCP/IP
Telecommunications
Trojan Horse
Twisted Pair
Utilities Fiber Network
Unified Communication
Uniform Resource Locator
   (URL)
Virtualization
Virtual Private Network (VPN)
Voice Over Internet protocol
   (VOIP)
Wireless Application Protocol
   (WAP)
Web Server
Wide Area Network (WAN)
WiMax
Wireless
Wireless Markup Language
   (WML)
World Wide Web
Worm

15. Chapter Questions

1. What is the difference between a router and a server?
2. Describe the different mediums used in data transmission.
3. What is the main difference between client/server and peer to peer networks?
4. What is an extranet and how can it be used advantageously in hospitality?
5. How is FTP used?
6. What is social engineering?
7. How can management make a network secure?
8. What is cloud computing?
9. What network issues should small organizations consider?
10. How is network understanding related to hospitality management?

16. References

Davidson, Johnathan, and Peters, James. (2000). *Voice over IP fundamentals.* Indianapolis: Cisco Press.

Laudon, Kenneth, and Laudon, Jane. 2009. *Management information systems* (8th ed.). Upper Saddle River, NJ: Prentice Hall.

Panko, Raymond R. 2007. *Business data networks and telecommunication* (6th ed.). Upper Saddle River, NJ: Prentice Hall.

Weisman, Carl J. 2000. *The essential guide to RF and wireless.* Upper Saddle River, NJ: Prentice Hall.

E-Commerce

Cindy Estis Green

INTERVIEW

Q: Hi Cindy, could you tell us a little bit about your back ground?

A: I have spent thirty years in hospitality and travel marketing. Most of the time was spent at the intersection of marketing and technology ranging from sales automation, reservation systems, distribution, online marketing, revenue management, data mining, and CRM. I worked for Hilton International for seven years heading up a new marketing information systems department and then moved into operations where I ended as a general manager for a four-hundred room full-service Hilton International hotel. I started my consulting practice in 1990 built on the marketing technology techniques I had developed, and in 1998 sold the business Driving Revenue to

Pegasus Solutions. I have since conducted research on an industry level examining best practices in distribution and online marketing for many sectors of the travel industry.

Q: How would you define e-commerce and online marketing?

A: E-commerce is a subset of the online marketing discipline that focuses on the booking component of the online experience. The travel marketer is now charged with a more comprehensive requirement for outreach so they can find and communicate to their consumers wherever they are browsing, gathering information, conversing, or buying online. The e-commerce piece is more directly related to the shopping and buying function.

Q: You know a lot about social networking. What are some of the keys to success for businesses engaging their customers through this medium?

A: Social networking is increasingly the way consumers are spending a portion of their time online. While some is purely social in nature where friends keep up with friends and family, much of it involves a method used for information collection. Typically, a consumer interested in a travel industry purchase would spend some time gathering information about options, pricing, and other factors depending on the nature of the purchase. There is a large percentage of consumers who will include one or more social networking sites as part of this process. They may use sites to read other consumers' reviews and to look at photos and videos of others' experience in a similar destination.

In terms of success in the use of social media and networks, a travel marketer needs to become immersed in the world in which his consumers reside. This will include reading the reviews they write, the blogs they respond to, and the commentary they make about different travel products and services. When there is a dialogue between consumers, there is a lot to gain for the astute marketer who wants to understand what drives the purchase and use of his products.

The main opportunities for the travel marketer are to listen, respond as needed and to provide and/or participate in forums to stimulate discussion on the topics about which the marketer wants to gain more intelligence or garner more attention.

Q: How about keys to success for Online Marketing in general?

A: Online marketing in general requires a shift in direction away from a focus on the marketer's own Web site with a push toward distributing content to all the Web sites where a consumer would go to find information about the marketer's products and services. It's not just getting things right on your Web site, which is still important, but the relevant content has to find its way to all the places consumers are browsing, info gathering, and shopping. "Distribution" is evolving from its original emphasis on reservations to a blend between message and booking distribution. It is incumbent upon the travel marketer to have an online presence at each point of contact with the consumer, and many of these points will not be on the marketer's own Web site. Learning how to manage this widespread presence is challenging because it is a complex network to master, and also because it is a dynamic environment that requires constant vigilance to know well enough to manage effectively.

Q: Looking into your crystal ball, any predictions as to how online marketing will continue to affect the hospitality industry?

A: The dominance of online marketing in the hospitality revenue toolkit will continue for some time. The marketer's drive to facilitate customer engagement will become the overarching strategic theme with the techniques for building traffic and bookings as the main part of the tactical plan.

1. INTRODUCTION

E-commerce transactions are merely adopting the latest and greatest communication tool—the Internet. Just as the invention of movable type and the telephone revolutionized the way people communicated and conducted business, so too does the world's network. In fact the Internet is quickly transforming (some say killing) the moveable type (i.e., newspapers) and telephone industries. Some companies and organizations utilize e-commerce more than others. Think of the different Web sites that you have visited recently. Certain outlets just provide information such as a menu while others allow for intense interaction to spur a purchase such as virtual tours of a hotel property.

From room nights to restaurant equipment, corporate buyers and consumers will concentrate their spending on where they can find what they want and need in the most efficient and satisfying ways. Along with the logic and systems behind e-commerce, this chapter will detail how to satisfy the wants and needs of any customer successfully on the Internet.

From a management perspective, the newness of the Internet presents a challenge. Its speed, reach, and operability can be both confusing and intimidating. Basically, **e-commerce** is doing business over the Internet. Generally speaking its scope increases day by day. It is now a management tool, and you are required not only to understand it but also to apply it to your daily worklife.

An often-used business term is **business model**, which is simply how you make your money (i.e., selling food or renting hotel rooms). E-Commerce has some different models with some easy-to-remember names. When a company sells something online such as an article of clothing or a room reservation to a customer, this is known as **business to consumer (B2C)** e-commerce. Company and guest interaction has increased where the purchasing aspect is only one part of the entire e-commerce hospitality cycle. Currently e-commerce of all types is more prevalent on the hotel side of our industry (this will also be covered in Chapter 7), so we will focus on a lodging example. Figure 5-1 shows that hotel-specific customer and company interaction takes place during more than just the shopping and booking (making the reservation) stages giving e-commerce greater scope.

B2C is joined by two other types of general e-commerce. First, if two businesses exchange goods or services over the Internet, this type of e-commerce is known as **business to business (B2B)**. Think of your university or company buying bulk from another company online. Business to business e-commerce is also known as e-procurement. B2B e-commerce is seeing increased growth due to efficiencies found in conducting transactions online. Second, two individuals doing business with each other directly is known as **consumer to consumer (C2C)** e-commerce. More specific business models and variations on these three main themes (B2C, B2B, and C2C) are detailed in the next section.

Advertising

Perhaps the most obvious, if not distracting, aspect of e-commerce and Web sites in general is advertising. Everyday usage of the Internet yields a barrage of advertisements for a great number of products and services. Ads are presented in many ways, such as those that move and blink or

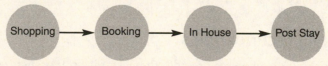

FIGURE 5-1 Hotel E-Commerce Guest Cycle. It is hoped that during the poststay the guest can be engaged properly to start the cycle anew.

those that are stationary with colorful backgrounds and logos. Often the end-user is forced to acknowledge these advertisements by "clicking to clear." This form of forced engagement is not new. You must still turn past advertisements that you do not wish to see in newspapers and magazines, and even some credit card companies force you to listen to advertisements before accessing account information over the telephone. Newer online attempts are the many videos which are preceded by an advertisement that cannot be skipped, or in another example, sound and video which suddenly turn on if your mouse should brush over it. Whatever your view of advertising online, companies in the advertising business are financially dependent on making sure that their advertisements are being seen.

Currently, advertising revenues are suffering, with some estimates stating that only some 2 percent of online ads are actually clicked on. With advertising-blocking software becoming more available, this particular business model has many challenges ahead.

Auctioning

The Internet created a market that brings sellers and buyers together instantly. The auction format of e-commerce is likely to become increasingly popular. Sites like *Expedia.com* continue to grow exponentially since they enhance efficiency while maximizing the return for the buyer and seller. Many companies that conduct auctions take a percentage of the revenues from auction-driven transactions. These third parties, or clearing companies, usually charge the seller a commission fee based on a percentage of the total revenue generated at auction. This is exactly what e-Bay does.

Subscriptions

Just as you may have or once had a magazine subscription, obviously the same thing can be done online. One term you may have heard before is **blog**, which is short for *Web log*, which is simply an online entry that is updated frequently. Blogs, videos, and other online offerings are threatening the traditional newspapers and magazine companies who offer subscriptions. Subscribing to something on the Internet is an everchanging business model. The corporate fear is that if you charge for information, your customers will flee for the free information provided somewhere else online. This is just now beginning to be tested with major companies starting to charge for some content. The debate over subscription continues.

Mobile Commerce

Mobile Commerce is making a purchase with your portable electronic device, most often a cell or smart phone. Smart phones have the added capability of using **global positioning system (GPS)**, a satellite-based technology used for finding a location, to allow the consumer to see what's nearby. In addition to GPS, **short message service (SMS)**, an almost umbrella term for cell phone text messaging, has shortened the communication between our coworkers to, more importantly, our guests.

2. E-COMMERCE TECHNOLOGIES

The technology behind e-commerce provides the necessary infrastructure and systems to properly enable online initiatives. At its heart is the application software. Let's discuss the key aspects.

Servers

In e-commerce, servers (not your waiter or waitress, but computer) play an important role. The first type is the **Web server**, which primarily stores Web pages, tracks usage known as "hits," and provides the requested Web pages to the end user. It is the server software and additional functionality of the server (faster processor, more memory and hard disk space, etc.) that enable the server to perform its many tasks. Dictating the size of the server is the amount of expected traffic it is to handle. In high-traffic organizations, redundant servers are employed. For business transactions, **e-commerce server** software is used to handle everything from online reservations to purchasing. It is this software running on the server that provides links to payment systems such as credit card interfaces and includes storefront listings such as availability, price, and shipping information. Additionally, this software links to other systems and provides the user with the shopping cart utility seen on many Web sites.

Content Management and Performance

In the fast-moving world of the Information Age, keeping a Web site current, particularly if it contains thousands of dynamic pages, can be a daunting task. Fortunately, content management software helps keep businesses up to date. **Content management software** gives companies the tools to manage and update their Web material. Changes can be made to the entire site through single entries rather than changing the content page by page. Other software functions include **performance monitoring software,** which is primarily concerned with how quickly a Web page is downloaded and makes sure that all links to other Web sites are active.

Consumer and Business Tracking

E-commerce technology is also concerned with tracking customers' trends and behavior before, during, and after their visits. With this business intelligence, companies can adjust and personalize their offerings to each user. Popular technologies used include **collaborative filtering**, where a customer's purchases and behaviors are compared to other customers' interests to predict further purchases. Amazon.com's "Customers who bought this also enjoy . . ." is an example of collaborative filtering. Other technologies include **clickstream tracking**, which records exactly where and when a customer clicks on a Web site and what Web sites he or she visited before and after. Clickstream tracking has come under much controversy due to its secretive and intrusive nature. If used ethically and correctly, proper monitoring can help businesses further understand their customers' spending habits and behavior.

Within these server technologies are some other important e-commerce technologies. You may have heard the very friendly term *cookies* in an Internet context. **Cookies** are nothing more than small bits of text that are written to your hard drive by someone else during a Web site visit. If a Web site welcomes you back and knows who you are, it has located a cookie that it left before on your hard drive. Since cookies are written by someone else without the user's permission, browsers have an option which allow them to be blocked. Cookies are supposed to make things easier, as are widgets. **Widgets** come in different categories, but are mainly instances that can be changed or manipulated by the user, such as text boxes on a Web page where you can enter a zip code for the local weather, or even a clock. Combining different applications such as a calendar program which accepts and places the weather outlook, from another piece of software (again, a weather program), for a specific day (or type of weather, i.e., sunshine) is known as a **Mashup**. Both widgets and mashups are seen more and more in the e-commerce realm. The next two technologies involve the word *syndication*. When you think of syndication think of an original work that is seen or received by multiple end points. When a television program goes into syndication (re-runs), it is no longer the property of just one network but can now be broadcast to other channels. Now, one can also set their computing device to accept constant updates or live feeds using **real simple syndication (RSS)**. Examples of RSS feeds include news and blog updates. Another type of syndication where many can see the original work online is known as **podcasting**. While both contain data streams, RSS is real time while podcasting is more like a recording, in this case a link, which can be accessed when convenient. Finally, remember how hotels are extending the stay? An e-concierge does exactly that. An *e-concierge* is a Web site that hotel guests may use to interact with the hotel (i.e., info, reservations) before, during, and after their stay.

3. E-MARKETING

Search Engines and Strategy

E-marketing plays an important role in hospitality organizations using the Internet for business. Simply having a Web site is not enough with the thousands of new pages created every week. The goal is to have customers and others *find* your property online with ease, using the common Internet tools we use daily. Think Google.

These agents used in finding information are known as **search engines.** Search engines use **crawlers**, sometimes called spiders, which are software-based searching tools that crawl the Internet constantly and add new sites and updates to their indexes as needed. Crawler technology utilizes proprietary algorithms that rank each site as to its relevance to the topic searched. Search engines can also be complemented by human interaction in the rankings. Search engines also accept **paid listings**, which use different business models focused mainly on charging by the number of hits a page receives. These are the listings that often appear on the top and side of the search result page with a heading indicating that they are advertisements. Combination offerings also exist here as payment is all too important in any e-marketing strategy and since all high-traffic search engine companies highly profit from paid listings.

Web site design and implementation use HTML and XML tags to display information and describe their subject matter. In an e-marketing initiative, how a specific component is utilized can aid in high placement on the list of a search result. This item is known as a **meta-tag**, which serves as a summary of your Web site's *description* and *keywords* read by those crawlers. Other meta-tags do exist; however, these two types (description and keywords) are the most important in searches. It is important to note that crawlers read and analyze much more than just this part. The whole Web page is scanned for relevant words as are links to other Web sites. If your content and links are not consistent with the subject matter of your page, your ranking may suffer. With these components and the sacred proprietary algorithms, crawlers size up a Web site and rank it accordingly.

Getting found online utilizes **Search Engine Optimization** (SEO) techniques. SEO is defined as the set of Internet tools used to increase one's page ranking in search engines' results. If your business does not show up on the first couple of pages when someone enters the keywords "Philadelphia Barbeque Restaurant" you may never be found by that potential customer. SEO companies exist and charge for getting your Web site found. Three SEO tricks that you can do yourself are the following: (1) make sure that potential keywords that a user might type into Google or Bing appear on your actual Web page, even more than once, with the more common ones in bold (i.e., *Philadelphia Barbeque*), (2) putting all the keywords in the meta-tags, (3) placing those relevant links (i.e., other well-known barbeque-related sites) on your page. We are seeing increased usage of the third trick between two companies who may have reciprocal links which are nothing more than links set up on each other's Web page and commissions paid in resulting sales. In our example, imagine the barbeque restaurant having a link to a barbeque sauce Web site which in turn has a link on its Web site back to the Philadelphia Barbeque Restaurant. Finally, if nothing else, any hospitality entity should utilize the various alert functionalities provided by a search engine Web site such as Google and Bing. Simply plug in your search terms and your e-mail and the search engine will do the work for you and send you an e-mail when you want it with the results.

4. HOSPITALITY WEB 2.0

Web 2.0 refers to user-generated content. Today in e-commerce, we are seeing an increased usage of **social networking** which is defined as people or organizations linked together through a network. Facebook is a very recognizable example where users can send messages, browse profiles, upload pictures and videos, and form and join groups, among other offerings. Another company, Twitter, offers its users to upload up to 140 characters at a time, which is known as microblogging. Users may request to follow other users and see their updates, also known as "tweets." From a service standpoint, Airlines, hotels, and, to a lesser degree, restaurants are handling guest requests and complaints via social networking sites, with marketing efforts coming in a close second. Presently, most of the features of social networking sites are free to the users or organizations using them, and these sites are managed "above property" by someone else (i.e., Facebook's technical team). Its free price is not expected to last much longer.

Our conversation on blogs is more specific to our industry. While search engines can be used to search blogs, certain Web sites are dedicated to searching them directly. Two such examples are Technorati and Icerocket. It would be wise to search these and other such listings for any possible mention of your property.

5. SECURITY

Security of Your Electronic Transactions

In any e-commerce transaction, data security must be a prime concern. Consumers have come to accept the risks of using credit cards in places like hotel lobbies and restaurants because they can see, touch, or consume certain products and make judgments about that specific environment. On the Internet, without those physical cues, it is much more difficult to assess the safety of a business. Also, because serious security threats have emerged, becoming aware of the risks of **Internet-based transactions (IBT)** and acquiring the proper technology solutions (cell and smart phones too!) that overcome those risks is imperative. The major risks associated with e-commerce and its security include the following:

1. **Spoofing**—The low cost associated with Web site design and ease of copying existing pages make it all too easy to create illegitimate sites that appear to be published by established organizations. These sites set up professional-looking storefronts that mimic legitimate businesses in an effort to obtain credit card and other information.
2. **Unauthorized Action**—A competitor or disgruntled customer can alter your Web site so that it refuses service to potential clients or malfunctions.
3. **Unauthorized Disclosure**—When transaction information is transmitted, hackers can intercept the transmissions to obtain your customers' sensitive information.

4. **Data Alteration**—The content of a transaction can be intercepted and altered en route, either maliciously or accidentally. User names, credit card numbers, and dollar amounts sent are all vulnerable to such alteration. (VeriSign 2001, p. 3)

From an end-user or customer perspective, we find that they have four main concerns when doing business online:

- 73 percent of online shoppers cite identity theft as a major concern
- 97 percent of online shoppers are concerned about others illegally accessing their transactional info or online accounts
- 95 percent of online shoppers are concerned about phishing
- 83 percent of consumers want more assurance that their information is secure

(*Sources:* Synovate/GMI Research, September 2008; Javelin Strategy and Research, March 2009.)

Securing Your Web Site

A secure online transaction is the goal of every consumer. A proven, low-cost solution to secure online transactions is a **server ID**. Server ID technology is used by virtually all of the Fortune 500 companies on the Web and all of the top forty e-commerce sites. Server IDs work to make online transactions secure.

A server ID, also known as a digital certificate, is the electronic equivalent of a business license. Server IDs are issued by a trusted third party, called a **certification authority (CA)**. The CA that issues a server ID is vouching for your right to use your company name and Web address.

Before issuing a server ID, a CA reviews your credentials, such as your organization's Dun & Bradstreet number or articles of incorporation, and completes a thorough background checking process to ensure that your organization is what it claims to be and is not claiming a false identity. Only then will a CA issue your organization a server ID. This ID provides the ultimate in credibility for your online business, which is so critical for users of hospitality resources.

Message Security

Another security concern is the actual message or content being transmitted. Message security is handled by a high-layer protocol and is aided by encryption. This technology is known as SSL. **Secure sockets layer (SSL)** technology is the industry-standard protocol for secure, Web-based communications. Web servers are now configured to work with a server ID, with the server automatically activating SSL. The result is the creation of a secure communications channel between your server and your customer's browser. Any hospitality-based Web site can communicate securely with any customer who uses Firefox, Microsoft Internet Explorer, or most popular e-mail programs. Once activated by, and in conjunction with your server ID, SSL immediately begins providing you with the following components of secure online transactions:

- **Authentication.** Your customers can verify that the Web site belongs to you and not an impostor. This bolsters their confidence in submitting confidential information.
- **Message privacy.** SSL encrypts all information exchanged between your Web server and customers, such as credit card numbers and other personal data, using a unique session key.

To securely transmit the session key to the consumer, your server encrypts it, with each session key used only once during a single session.

- **Message integrity.** When a message is sent, the sending and receiving computers each generate a code based on the message content. If even a single character in the message content is altered en route, the receiving computer will generate a different code, and then alert the recipient that the message is not legitimate. With message integrity, both parties involved in the transaction know that what they are seeing is exactly what the other party has sent. (VeriSign, 2001, p. 6)

These and other features provided by SSL are no longer sufficient to many customers, who are often put at ease by seeing an actual logo of a well-known certification authority such as VeriSign or Thawte. We will look at other data security measures for on-site credit card transactions in Chapter 6.

Hospitality units that can manage and process e-commerce transactions gain a competitive edge by reaching a worldwide audience, at very low cost. But the Web poses a unique set of trust issues that hotel, restaurant, and travel groups must address at the outset to minimize risk. Customers submit information and purchase goods or services via the Web only when they are confident that their personal information, such as credit card numbers and financial data, is secure. The solution for hospitality companies that are serious about e-commerce is to implement a complete e-commerce trust infrastructure for all endpoints, and not just computers.

6. Summary

Proper e-commerce strategy and usage are quickly becoming a *must have* tool in any manager's skill set. Both B2B and B2C concepts must be understood since you will be dealing with both customers and other businesses online. Posting a Web site on the Internet and hoping that "customers will come" is far from an efficient plan and will not result in any cost savings or revenue increases. Only proper knowledge, study, and implementation of an e-commerce rollout will make it a successful one. Particular attention must be paid to e-commerce technology and marketing. Although software capabilities such as clickstream tracking may be great, ethical and privacy issues may cause your customer to feel uncomfortable about using your site. Additionally, security issues must be understood to prevent unauthorized breaches and data theft. With these components in place and a thorough understanding of e-marketing differentiating you from the rest, an e-commerce initiative can be a successful one.

7. Case Study and Learning Activity

Case Study

With Web 2.0, businesses small and large are finding new ways to interact with their current and potential customers. Brian was hired by a large restaurant chain to help it with its Web 2.0 strategy. Brian was fresh out of college with a hospitality management degree and found that his youth worked to his advantage. The problem that the company had was that Web 2.0 was new and unknown to many of the senior executives who were the decision makers and they did not completely trust the ideas they were hearing from their consultants who were also senior-level people. It very much seemed a younger person's game. Brian remembered the last thing his boss said to him before he accepted the offer,

"I didn't have Facebook in college." He knew Web 2.0 was much more than Facebook and was actually the general term covering all user-generated content on the Internet. What an opportunity! He was in charge of Web 2.0 strategy.

He remembered from his hospitality management classes that he needed to think broadly at first, then target his initiatives. He also had heard many times that there is a point where customers feel that a company can overdo it (constant e-mails, texts, etc.) and disengage. His new company was a quickly growing fast casual chain with a wide menu that attracted customers of all types. Each restaurant's marketing was done at corporate headquarters which supported fifty restaurants on the east coast. On average, each restaurant served three hundred people a day and provided both lunch and dinner. Only 10 percent of the customers belonged to the company's loyalty program which entitled them to certain discounts. A fair amount of data was captured, including e-mail addresses of these customers. Many did not join for privacy concerns. Anecdotal evidence from the on-site managers estimated that well over half of their customers frequented the restaurants more than once a week. Brian began to wander off thinking of all of the many Web 2.0 outlets he could utilize, such as Facebook, Twitter, Google alerts, smart phones, and YouTube.

Learning Activity

1. What parts of Web 2.0 should Brian use and how?
2. In your mind, which is the most effective and why?
3. Which is the least effective and why?
4. How can Web 2.0 be used effectively internally for employees?
5. What problems could one encounter in any Web 2.0 endeavor?

8. Key Terms

Authentication
Blog
Business to Business (B2B)
Business to Consumer (B2C)
Business Model
Certification Authority
Clickstream Tracking
Consumer to Consumer (C2C)
Content Management Software
Cookie
Crawlers
Data Alteration

E-Commerce
E-Commerce Server
Global Positioning System (GPS)
Internet-Based Transactions (IBT)
Mashup
Message Integrity
Message Privacy
Meta-tag
Paid Listings
Performance Monitoring Software

Podcasting
Real Simple Syndication (RSS)
Search Engines
Search Engine Optimization
Secure Sockets Layer
Server ID
Short Message Service (SMS)
Social Networking
Spoofing
Unauthorized Action
Unauthorized Disclosure
Widget

9. Chapter Questions

1. What is a business model?
2. Describe the difference between B2B and B2C e-commerce.
3. What are some other e-commerce business models?
4. What is a blog?

5. How is a Web server used in e-commerce?
6. How is an e-commerce server used?
7. What does collaborative filtering software do?

8. What are cookies?
9. What is search engine optimization?
10. How is SSL used in e-commerce security?

10. Reference

VeriSign. (2001). "Secure your website with a VeriSign server," white paper.

CHAPTER 6

Restaurant Management Systems

Chapter Contents

INTERVIEW

Mark Hamilton is Vice President of Operations for RealTime Intelligence.

Q: Hi Mark! Would you mind telling us a little bit about your company?

A: RealTime Intelligence is a software company that specializes in helping retail and hospitality operators become more productive, reduce expenses, and increase profitability. RealTime Intelligence's technology is installed in over five thousand locations across the United States.

Recent studies estimate that loss resulting directly from waste and fraud equates to between 1.5 and 1.7 percent of gross revenue for retail and hospitality operations. For a five-billion dollar retailer that represents 75 million dollars per year. Additionally, it is estimated that 60 percent of this loss is generated by employees, equaling 45 million dollars per year. Of the employee shrink (theft) generated annually, research shows that 95 percent or almost 43 million (for the same retailer) can be tied to some form of electronic transaction. This is the primary area that RealTime addresses with the CatchPoint software suite.

RealTime Intelligence's CatchPoint product line enables retailers to redeploy existing loss prevention (LP) tools to have a much greater impact on the organization. CatchPoint integrates with existing hardware and software tools to deliver monitoring information in real-time, along with recommendations generated by a rules-based intelligence system. When exception situations or patterns are detected, a message is delivered to ensure that the correct person is immediately working the solution.

CatchPoint continually monitors in-store systems and notifies associates or management of issues in time to resolve them, including escalation processes for ensuring rapid response. Associates can be notified via phone, text message, e-mail, POS terminal display, or through the CatchPoint Control Panel.

Q: Aside from solutions such as yours, are there other steps that a restaurant can take to enhance security/loss prevention?

A: While considering all aspects of the operation, reducing loss and increasing profitability by monitoring key performance indicators amounts to basic operational controls. In the perfect world, strong training programs, attentive management, and good hiring processes always lead to reduced issues with theft, and facility security. It's about managers being educated and prudent in how they hire, train, and manage their employees. In poorly run operations the overall numbers will show that the operation is not performing up to standard in area. There will be inventory issues, sales issues, cash overage issues; these issues will be reflected in some measurement that, when reviewed by a trained manager, will prompt a response that will in turn bring the issue back into a controlled state.

Managers that are well trained in operational controls can play a large role in stemming the tide of loss in any operation. The primary challenge with this in large organizations with hundreds or thousands of sites is the effort that it takes to maintain that cadre of trained managers across the individual operations to ensure that standards are upheld. There are examples of organizations that have been somewhat successful in this area (McDonald's, Brinker, and some others). However, the majority of multiunit operations see this as a major challenge and are then faced with implementing technology that helps to ensure a measure of standardization across all managers at the unit level.

In smaller organizations, control measures center around reports that are generated from some combination of the POS, labor, and inventory systems at the store level. Additional information may be generated above the store through the review of consolidated data from these systems. Larger operations may add exception reporting and data analytics that are applied to consolidated data or data warehouses to produce targeted reports that may reveal areas of control that need attention across the organization.

If an organization has the benefit of a defined loss prevention function, additional measures and systems may be employed for added benefit. Digital video systems that have the ability to synchronize transaction detail from the POS system to the video imagery of the operation are strong forensic tools in loss prevention. Other tools such as case management and operational dashboards are often employed to assist in managing the loss prevention function.

In most organizations, however, the burden of control rests in the hands of the unit manager. It is challenging to implement control systems across such organizations that are consistently effective when so many managers are involved in applying the systems. Companies continually seek ways to make managers more effective overall while minimizing their need to perform analysis and giving them more immediate insight into emerging or existing control issues.

Q: In your view, what are some common mistakes that are made by the owner or operator?

A: Even in well-run operations, oversights occur. Call it what you will, but people make mistakes. Additionally, even though most would hope differently, some percentage of employees are dishonest. This is a proven statistical fact. Shrink happens.

Possibly the most common mistake of managers in operations of any size is that of overconfidence. The majority of successful people that are good at their job believe that they understand their business so well that there is no possible way that controllable shrink exists in their business. These managers simply need to become aware, through training and education, to help them understand where to look and what to look for to improve their profitability by better controlling shrink.

Another common oversight of owners and operators is that of dismissing small daily anomalies. What I mean by this is when operators dismiss transactions or events that individually equate to a small dollar amount. Small voids, over-rings, refunds, etc. that do not amass a large dollar amount on any given day will add up over time. If an operator had the ability to view these patterns and look at the total amount over a longer period of time, many would find that there exists in these transactions the opportunity for large amounts of lost revenue. Attention to the insignificant can sometimes reveal larger control issues in an organization.

Finally, we often find companies that have strong controls and effective ways to eliminate shrink often do not apply these methods consistently over time across the operation. In these cases, operators will focus on a particular issue or controllable for a period of time, bring it back into standard and then move on to the next issue, only to find that some period of time later, the issue has arisen again. In these cases, if operators were able to continually monitor and manage all the possible areas that arise over time, they would avoid the peaks and valleys of control that happen otherwise. Implementation of a focused effort is a good thing, continuing that effort over time is sometimes difficult to achieve and leads to future losses.

Q: Looking into your crystal ball, what do you see coming down the road?

A: I would like to say that society will evolve, dishonesty will be eliminated, and there will be no need for stringent operational controls and control systems. But, I know better. The future is a difficult thing to forecast, especially when one deals with technology. I risk either being too optimistic or too conservative and lose every time. But since you ask, here is my best guess at how operational controls, loss prevention, and real-time data analysis will evolve over the next few years.

Personal communications or personal kiosks are becoming more powerful than ever. We commonly call these devices mobile phones, PDAs, or something similar. The current leading multiuse devices in this space are very powerful computers that have become affordable to most any individual and or company. Employing such devices in the operation to do things other than take orders or settle transactions is quickly becoming a real option. It is now affordable and desirable for unit-level managers to receive store telemetry right on their mobile device, drill down into detail, and receive suggestions on how to address any issue that might arise. This technology, when pushed directly to the person in the operation that can affect immediate change, will improve consistency of standards of control across large organizations, and improve profitability before the results of a weekly exception report can be distributed to the same in-store manager. The technology to do this is available now. Implementation is a matter of time to assemble technologies into a solution and demonstrate that the return on investment is attractive to operators.

Outsourcing real-time controls in loss prevention and security is changing rapidly through technical innovation and will become an attractive alternative to organizations of any size. Until recently the idea of central station monitoring was relegated to monitoring burglar and fire alarms. These stations, although very sophisticated, had very little ability to offer much more to an operator than dispatch of police or fire to a location if an issue occurred. Moving forward, using technology, new types of central stations will emerge. These monitoring stations will have the ability to view operations live, view live transaction detail, receive exception advisories on transaction trends, and communicate with stores live, in real time. These stations will capitalize on the well-known economies of scale realized in the traditional central station (alarm) model, but will be able to provide complete loss prevention, controls, and possible IT support services in an effective and economical way that will extend enormous benefit to operators.

Finally, although I have mentioned little about this in this interview, I believe we will start to see convergence of technologies in transaction monitoring in stores with similar monitoring of online transactions. This convergence will begin to benefit retailers of all kinds in creating customer profiles that can then be used to focus improvements in both online and in-store operations. I am not referring to profiles that breach privacy and perhaps create credit card security issues. I am referring to the ability to group transaction detail into generic customer profiles that allow marketers to focus efforts on improving the experience for those in specific profiles. In restaurant operations, this could change the way operators manage menu items and add a new dimension to the menu mix paradigm. In retail, it could influence product mix and merchandising. In operations that cannot engage in mainstream e-commerce, the benefit will be realized in their ability to know more about customers' online experiences and use that to enhance how they address these customers when they come into the operation. This is the new focus of marketing and holds promise for retail and hospitality in the near future.

1. INTRODUCTION

In the interview Mark spoke about his company's security software offering. Newer software such as this needs to work with and access the data from some common systems found in foodservice. **Restaurant management systems (RMSs)** are the crucial technology components that enable a single outlet or enterprise to better serve its customers and aid employees with food and beverage transactions and controls. Everyday examples of their application range from quick food to fine dining. When you place an order in a fast-food restaurant, the machine being used by the person in front of you is part of the RMS. The same is true when you make a reservation online for a five-star restaurant. These are just two instances of RMSs in use today. This chapter's objective is to acquaint you with the many elements of an RMS and show how, through its use, current and future restaurant technology can enable management to operate a more profitable and efficient business. Restaurants are fast-moving and dynamic environments with many parts that do not play well with the digital age. Technology is only a tool that can aid management in operating within this environment.

2. RESTAURANT MANAGEMENT SYSTEM (RMS) COMPONENTS

The size and scope of RMSs vary among organizations. There are five main offerings:

- The point-of-sale (POS) system
- The kitchen management system
- Inventory and menu management systems
- Reservations and table management
- Back office applications and interfaces

Restaurant operators are constantly looking for ways to better understand their customers in order to serve them better. They also need a centralized system to carry out the business at hand. Many now use the POS system. By definition, a POS is either a stand-alone machine or a network of input and output devices used by restaurant employees to accomplish their daily activities including food and beverage orders, transmission of tasks to the kitchen and other remote areas, guest-check settlement, credit card transaction processing, and charge posting to folios (Figure 6-1). As mentioned earlier, a POS system looks much like an **electronic cash register (ECR)**. In fact, earlier POS systems were known as ECRs. Many restaurants have just a POS system in their technology solution. Others utilize handhelds and other advancements. Whichever the case, it is these systems that collect and disseminate information about the guest and guest orders for the establishment. The POS is the main component in restaurant management systems.

Other POS Functionality

Aside from its basic task of order handling, a POS system also provides additional functionality.

DECREASED SERVICE TIME   One of the benefits of technology is the increased speed found in communication. In a restaurant setting, both dine in and take out, a POS system allows for quicker communication among all points involved. If set up correctly, an order placed at a POS station or

FIGURE 6-1 Point-of-sale systems such as this from the MICROS Corporation aid servers and managers in a growing number of ways. Because of their proximity to food and beverages, POS systems are often built to be more resistant to spills and other mistreatment than other pieces of technology. *(Source: Courtesy of Micros, Inc.)*

a handheld component will also be seen in the kitchen, the bar, offices, the host stand, and any other necessary areas. In other words, everyone has the needed information. Newer advancements in handheld technology allow quicker order processing, with each order being transmitted in real time to the applicable area. Imagine a large table with ten customers. With handheld technology each order is seen, by say, the kitchen, as it is taken in real time without having to wait for the whole table's order to be completed and then inputted afterwards at a POS station, allowing the kitchen more lead time. For this and other reasons, operators are embracing handhelds.

Recalling from Chapter 4, the concept of software as a service (SaaS) is being embraced by some in the food service sector as well. POS transactions and data can be remotely hosted by a vendor and provided to scaled-down POS terminals (known as thin clients), when needed, usually over a wide area network. While some see efficiencies and cost savings in this model, others see problems in security and potential down networks. Expect more debate and advancements in this arena. Another example of operators embracing SaaS is through their enterprise management, where POS data from various outlets can be accessed through online browser-based software in almost real time. Actual transactions are not handled here. Rather, this online software offered by a number of vendors provides crucial management data, such as sales of a specific food or sales made by a server, by poling the various POS data, again in almost real time. With this data, accessed from anywhere where the Internet is available, and the ever-expanding offerings of these enterprise systems, management is capable of making more timely decisions.

ORDER ACCURACY   With a POS system, miscommunications are minimized. Each order has a specific field assigned to it that is used by all. For example, a hamburger may have the field "HMBGR" or simply "Hamburger." Rather than input the field, a server chooses from a list of fields provided by the POS system. With this common language, all involved in the service of food and beverage are communicating with the same vocabulary and presentation methods, thereby eliminating common handwritten and oral miscommunications. Advancements in conversational ordering, where the specific words of the customer's order (Can I get my hamburger bun lightly toasted?) is also being accepted by newer POS systems.

SECURITY OF CASH TRANSACTIONS AND INTERNAL AUDITING FUNCTIONS   As we saw in the interview with Mark Hamilton, theft is a concern in food and beverage settings. Many restaurants are temporarily responsible for handling cash and credit cards, and maybe even checks. To minimize risk and help coordinate with other security software or video, a POS system records all orders and transactions, including gift cards, to each employee's assigned identification number on the POS system. It is up to the employee to make sure that his or her financial totals match those recorded by the POS. If a discrepancy occurs, a POS system utilizes an auditing function that allows management, through report generation, to dissect and backtrack a particular employee's transactions during the shift(s) in question.

REDUCED TRAINING BURDEN   The hospitality industry has a great deal of employee turnover. Training can become difficult with so much staff coming and going. POS design takes this factor into account. With familiar graphical user interfaces, touch-screen function buttons, and help commands, a waitperson is not left in the dark.

LABOR SCHEDULING AND PERFORMANCE CONTROL   Newer POSs may offer a labor-scheduling function replacing spreadsheet planning. However more efficient labor scheduling is accomplished through separate software with advanced versions containing Web and cell phone interfaces. Additionally, through report generation, a proper POS can aid management in employee performance appraisals. How much product is sold by each server and when along with other performance controls are controlled and accessed via this function.

ANALYTICS   Lastly, what are the most profitable items? When are they being sold? Which items are not selling? How are customers paying? How has the weather affected our sales? These and many other questions can be answered by the sales reporting functionality of the POS. Due to the importance of understanding sales, other third-party vendors have targeted this aspect of the POS in their product offerings. Now, there are numerous software options for the manager who desires better food and beverage sales intelligence including Web 2.0 monitoring.

The Kitchen Management System

KITCHEN MANAGEMENT SYSTEM (KMS)   The kitchen management system (KMS) is concerned with displaying and tracking food orders. Think of a computer monitor in a kitchen which displays the orders and type (eat in vs. take out or delivery), it's assigned server, and the time elapsed, among other details. With a KMS, a kitchen can become more efficient and quicker with paging systems incorporated which alert a server when an order is ready—to make sure that the soup is served hot! A KMS also allows back-of-the-house management access to data to be used for staff-training purposes, such as turn-out times or order of production.

Inventory and Menu Management

To remain competitive, management can no longer reevaluate inventory and menu items on a monthly basis. Through known technologies such as bar codes and tags, inventory can be tracked. How establishments use technology to manage their inventory and menu items differs among locations. In some, the POS is used. In others, it is tracked by a system that may or may not connect to the POS. Whatever the case, inventory and menu systems are primarily concerned with three themes:

- Inventory levels and consumption
- Purchasing
- Theft

Inventory Levels and Consumption

In assuming a new role in food and beverage, a new manager is given (it is hoped) a detailed report of how much inventory of each product is to be kept on hand. This level is known as *par stock*. With a networked RMS, item removal and action can be tracked. From there, the RMS can also track consumption volume, rate, and sales price. Common inventory-level functions also include the crucial "snapshot by day" operation summarizing all inventory actions for that period.

Purchasing

Restaurants are also concerned with a number of factors surrounding the purchasing of products for their site(s). Dates of purchases and delivery, quantity, and purchase price must be logged and tracked for safety and business reasons. From there, alerts may be set up to prevent dated food and beverage products from being served. However, people determine the final outcome since some items, such as fish and vegetables, are not easily tracked and managed by technology.

As with the sales report generation in the POS, business intelligence plays a major role as well. Those food costs are just too important to the bottom line and promotions not to be tracked and managed by the advancements in RMS technology.

Theft

As detailed in the interview, a major problem facing restaurants today is employee theft—often called shrinkage. Controlling shrinkage significantly adds to a restaurant's bottom line and is an important cost-control measure.

Inventory control operations handle this task through ID association with every item removed. Item removal may occur only when an employee assigns his or her ID or pin to the product. As with possible food spoilage, the human factor plays a crucial role here.

Newer inventory and menu management systems also serve as a managerial monitoring tool and data record of food and beverage's critical control points for spoilage. With much of the inventory in our industry being perishable, close scrutiny is needed.

Benefits of Inventory and Menu Management

Some may view the use of technology in inventory management as disruptive. Taking the time to input user IDs and access codes can be perceived as a burden when a customer may be waiting. Aside from the aforementioned business intelligence aspects, the inventory and menu management component of an RMS help in other ways. Nutritional aspects may be improved. In an age where demographics prove that the number of elderly will increase dramatically, nutritional aspects must be considered. Additionally, some inventory and menu management systems also have the ability to monitor the actual nutritional aspects of a particular dish—from sodium to cholesterol. More often than not, this is accomplished through third-party culinary and nutrition software such as Mastercook™. Software such as this, which may run on just a few computers in the restaurant (the chef's or the food and beverage manager's), can provide additional information including predictive modeling and variable analysis. If you want to know, for example, how much you may need of a certain food item given the average age and number of expected covers, this software outputs the answer.

Reservations and Table Management

An RMS may also contain an electronic software module for reservations. This may be software that is part of, or separate from, the POS. It is simplistic in nature. The name, number in party, date, time, and so on, are inputted here. With many restaurants still using a handwritten reservation book, model usage here is limited, although is expected to increase dramatically.

Those who incorporate technology into their reservation operations and procedures may widen their potential business by moving online. Due to the increasing level of reservations that are being made online, restaurateurs are starting to purchase monthly services from Internet companies such as OpenTable for their solutions. OpenTable is the Expedia of the restaurant world, taking reservations for many restaurants in different locations (see Figure 6-2).

The Web site *www.OpenTable.com* is a great example of a portal specific to the hospitality industry. When its reservations are interfaced with the on-site system, which may or may not be made by OpenTable, significant volume increases may be seen. Data can also be captured from the reservation management system, as they can from the POS for future marketing or customer loyalty efforts.

| Sheet | Lunch | Tmw | ◄ | 05/31/2000 | ► | 1:00 PM | Total count / Seated count | 39 | 02:56 | Add | Change | Status |

Time	Name	#	Tbl	N	Time	Name	#	Tbl	N	Time	Name	#	Tbl	N
11:30	Blocked	0			12:00	Aberg, Roland	5			12:30		6		
11:30	Blocked	0			12:00	Sokal, Kent				12:30		6		
11:30	Blocked	0			12:00		2			1:00	Abington, Rol	2		
11:30	Blocked	0			12:00		2			1:00	Naito, Adoobl	6		
11:30	Blocked	0			12:00		4			1:00		2		
11:30		2			12:00		4			1:00		2		
11:45	Abizad, Charl	4	65		12:15	Slusky, Alex	2			1:00		4		
11:45		2			12:15		2			1:00		4		
11:45		2			12:15		4			1:00		6		
11:45		2			12:30	Jonson, Nels	3			1:15	Kahn, Liz	2		
11:45		4			12:30		2			1:15		2		
11:45		4			12:30		2			1:15		4		
12:00	Blocked	0			12:30		4			1:30	Gale, Janelle	2		
12:00	Blum, Richard	2			12:30		4			1:30		2		
12:00	Falkenberg, P	2			12:30		4			1:30		2		
12:00	Blocked	0			12:30		4			1:30		4		
12:00	Takaga, Yosh	4			12:30		4			1:30		4		

FIGURE 6-2 Restaurants with computerized reservations systems have more options for handling current and future business. Current information is just a mouse-click away. *(Source: OpenTable, Inc.)*

After reservations comes table management. **Table management software (TMS)** is designed to allocate the reservation/wait/walk-in list with appropriate tables or locations and services within the establishment. TMS is the matchmaker between a dining party and a table with its assigned server and may take the form of an application on a computer or even a kiosk. TMS is considered standard on large-scale RMS systems and as an add-on for smaller POS systems. TMS standard functionality includes the following:

- A map view of the entire front-of-the-house seating
- Alerts on open, long-duration, and dirty tables
- Reservation assignment to tables
- Track covers for more efficient kitchen and server management
- Record and view shift notes for each day

Look at Figure 6-3, a sample TMS screen from OpenTable.

With table management systems, operational staff can better control and manage the flow of customers within a restaurant and offer timely service to the benefit of both the client and the business.

Interfaces

An RMS, particularly its POS component, often needs to interface with other systems. If the restaurant is in a hotel environment, the system must be incorporated into the larger hotel system. Interfaces will be discussed in more detail in Chapter 7.

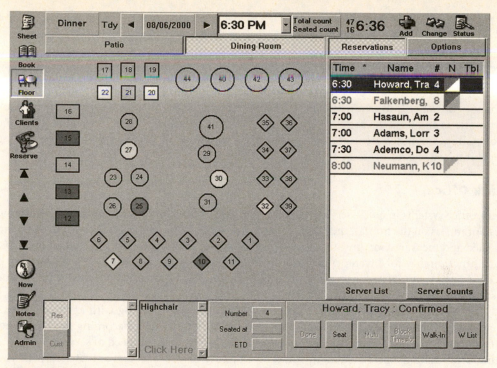

FIGURE 6-3 Table management systems such as this from OpenTable provide a bird's eye view of an establishment as well as specific details of each table. Armed with this information, management can better serve its occupied tables and have access to past table history. *(Source: OpenTable, Inc.)*

Since an RMS is geared towards day-to-day restaurant operations, any back office components such as human resource and accounting software may require an additional interface. Certain technology vendors are actually offering restaurant solutions that take into account all offices within a restaurant—widening the definition of an RMS. You may see more of these offerings in the future.

3. OTHER RESTAURANT MANAGEMENT SYSTEMS

Fast-food restaurants use a special type of an RMS, a DRMS. The **delivery restaurant management system (DRMS)** is a software and hardware package that works with the POS and other systems with an emphasis on the delivery of orders. Since orders are not brought to you by a server, but rather delivered to you at the counter or drive-through window, the establishment's use of technology has a different scope. The DRMS was designed a little differently than the RMS and is divided into three major components:

- Storefront operations
- System functions
- Back office

Storefront Operations

Storefront operations in the DRMS world look much like the POS. Orders are inputted and total amounts are given. The DRMS also transmits those orders to a display system both in the kitchen and drive-through window. Aside from the order contents, approximate time of order processing is the most important item displayed here. If a manager sees an order on one of the displays over a certain amount of time allowed, action may be required.

System Functions

System functions are primarily concerned with facilitating the changes and optimizing the functionality of the DRMS as a whole. Fast-food restaurants face constant change in offerings and promotions and need the ability to change their systems as fast as possible. Specific system functions allow for quick item and price changes, control of all peripherals involved, backup capability, self-diagnostic tests, and training programs.

Back Office

Back office systems in quick-service establishments are small. Most of the emphasis, as with most restaurants, is on the front of the house. However, at a minimum, certain tasks need to be accomplished and measured for any business wishing to remain competitive. DRMS contain the necessary functionality for inventory control, financial transactions, and sales data. These may be accessed and manipulated from a computer in the manager's office or with a managerial ID from a storefront POS.

In certain fast-food environments, the person you are speaking with at the drive-thru may not be in the restaurant but in a centralized call center. This is becoming more common among large franchisees who can obtain cost savings and increased speed of service by centralizing order-taking where validation could be a picture of your car that is matched with your order at the pick-up window. Another advancement in the DRMS is the addition of predictive algorithm software which compares past data to aid in current preparation questions. Data could include yesterday's popular orders, the number of cars currently in line, and the weather report, to name a few. This software predicts what may be purchased and enables staff to get a jump on the orders.

4. SELF-ORDERING

Although management has many options in taking and handling customer food and beverage orders, diners are seeing increased self-ordering options at their disposal. The success of online ordering has led to further advancements. With more and more consumers possessing GPS-enabled smart phones, applications from multiple vendors such as Yelp or Urbanspoon can find the nearest cuisine option(s) based upon location. Even restaurants are now creating their own applications that sense when a smart phone enters their premise and launch (with the customer's permission) their own software on the consumer's phone to proceed with any searches or orders among other features. Digital signage is also becoming more sophisticated and interactive (see Figure 6-4). In fact some cell phones using near-field communication (Chapter 4) can obtain everything from coupons to nutritional information from some signage by merely pointing their phone towards it.

For certain food and beverage segments, kiosks are seeing increased usage. **Self-ordering kiosks** are stand-alone or networked devices that mainly allow for order-taking in food and beverage settings. In other settings, they may provide currency, tickets, or even room keys. In the hospitality industry, kiosks are seen as a labor-saving device. Like all technology, the delivery of customer service should be taken into account. While technology such as kiosks may replace or free up labor, sometimes our customers would rather be served by a person.

FIGURE 6-4 Menu boards are becoming more digital, allowing for easier changes and customer interactions. (*Source: Courtesy Micros Systems, Inc.*)

Table ordering systems take different forms. Some offerings include touch screen battery-operated computing devices with wireless connections while others rely on tablet PCs or even electronic readers (e-readers). If table ordering systems are Internet enabled, customers have a world of information at their fingertips to aid them in such decisions as food and wine pairing. In conjunction with table ordering systems, server paging systems can be incorporated where your server wears an alert that is activated by a button at your table should you need his or her services.

Finally, we close the self-ordering loop and come back to the personal computer and discuss widgets. Remember, a **widget** (chapter 5) is a small application dedicated to some specific tasks. Common examples of widgets are live weather applications or stock tickers. In the food and beverage industry we see widgets used by different pizza companies in Web 2.0 applications such as Facebook, where one can place an order within the social networking environment or in a small screen on your desktop.

5. PROPRIETARY VERSUS NONPROPRIETARY RMS

Proprietary is synonymous with *private*. Proprietary systems come from a single source. Mixing and matching software and hardware from other vendors with these components can be troublesome, if not impossible. Purchasing from a single source has both advantages and disadvantages. You may know whom to call if something breaks, but you only have that one company and its service providers as a resource. Further, imagine if a solution comes out tomorrow from a competing company. It may not be possible to integrate the new product with your system. Decisions such as these are common in technology. In the hospitality industry, they are most applicable to POS systems. There are some superior proprietary vendors. It is up to the restaurateur to weigh the good with the bad in making a purchase.

6. SECURITY AND COMPLIANCE

With the many advances in both on- and off-premise technological offerings, security and compliance are gaining in importance. With the restaurant industry highly vulnerable to credit card breaches, the major card carriers (Visa, MasterCard, etc.) have mandated that certain steps be adhered to for outlets that wish to accept credit cards. These steps are contained in the **Payment Card Industry Data Security Standard (PCI DSS)**. They are summarized here:

1. Maintain a firewall
2. Change vendor-supplied passwords
3. Protect customer data
4. Use encryption
5. Use and update antivirus software
6. Develop and maintain secure systems and applications
7. Reduce access to data by a need-to-know basis
8. Assign a unique user ID to each computer user
9. Restrict physical access to cardholder data
10. Track and monitor access to all card holder data
11. Regularly test security systems
12. Maintain a policy that addresses information security

Another layer of security can be added if the credit card never leaves the customer's sight. The restaurant business is one of the few industries where the credit card is removed from the cardholder's sight to complete the transaction. Payment-at-the-table options are addressing this concern. Payment at the table can take many forms, from a networked device that sits at your table, to a portable payment solution worn by your server. European security options known as Chip and PIN are gaining more attention in the United States and elsewhere. **Chip and PIN** replaces the magnetic stripe (on the back of your card) and signature verification with a microchip in the card which is verified with the user entering a PIN, much as one does in debit transaction to an external database over a network. In Chip and PIN technology, the PIN is checked against the PIN of the microchip in the actual card in front of you.

Finally, going back to the chapter interview, we see that many restaurateurs are using the advanced capabilities in digital video surveillance and exception-monitoring software to keep a closer eye on their business. If an exception is noticed, say a minimum number of comps have been surpassed, management can now "go the tape" for that exact transaction and see visually what exactly happened. We will look at video surveillance in more detail in Chapter 11.

7. Summary

Restaurant management systems (RMSs) are a critical tool used by management in restaurant sales and operations. If studied and used properly, RMSs will enable different locations and employees to join together in a more profitable business. Their importance, however, must be placed in a wider management setting. An RMS is a tool used by people. While this is true of technology in general, it is even more applicable here. A study of any restaurant will reveal numerous items that are not, and need not be, touched by technology. Sometimes in hospitality, more art than science is needed. In restaurants, this is particularly true. Nevertheless, an RMS, with its primary components, can give management more control over spending and sales. With these controls, owners must also reevaluate customers' tastes and expectations regarding technology. If your clientele expects a certain amount of technology, it must be provided. This rings true for the future. Of particular note is the increase of payment at the table and self-ordering options. Credit card security is not only important, but mandated. Additionally, the online medium is being used for restaurant research and bookings. Any restaurateur must incorporate this foresight into his or her operations. With proper knowledge and application of the various RMSs, along with a keen eye to the future, RMS technology can help grow the single site or enterprise business.

8. Case Study and Learning Activity

Case Study

Mr. Johnson has owned his own casual dining restaurant chain for over twenty years. He still remembers graduating from college and taking over the family business. With ten restaurants in Florida, business was steady and the customers seemed loyal. One major concern was that his customers were the same ones. While this was a sign of success in the hospitality industry, newer customers were not really coming in to eat. He reached out to a local marketing organization, which advised him that his restaurants had an older feel to them and recommended that he update his technology to reach and dialogue with younger customers. Mr. Johnson knew next to nothing about technology, although he did learn some in a chain-wide upgrade two years prior. He decided to hire a new manager who could evaluate what he needed. The new manager, Sue, was a newly minted graduated of a local hospitality program and was charged with visiting all ten locations and reporting back to Mr. Johnson, who operated out of a small corporate office with three employees (two accountants, one assistant).

Sue found all ten locations very similar as would be expected in a chain restaurant. Therefore, she was able to apply her report on the different processes and how technology was used in each to the organization as a whole. Mr. Johnson, the experienced restaurateur, ran a lean operation with a full-time staff consisting of a GM, three managers, and a staff of fifteen in each of his one hundred-seat restaurants.

Host Stand/Reservations

A table management system was purchased along with many other pieces of technology two years prior for PCI DSS compliance issues. Mostly it sat idle while the hosts continued with the old white board and dry erase marker system. Reservations were kept by hand in the large reservation book and input into a database weekly after the fact.

Kitchen

A new KMS was also in use and part of the two-year-old upgrade. Chefs, while reluctant at first, have grown to like it. It is mainly used during the operation to track preparation times and task assignments.

Front of House

While the newly updated POS system had the standard touch screen features, the servers saw little difference in putting in orders and in closing out their shifts. Time spent at the POS stations by each server seemed about the same.

Bar

The bar's POS was also updated, as was the printer.

Back Office

The accounting department, which consisted of one part-time accountant, since many of the managers had accounting-type duties incorporated into their job descriptions (namely inventory and scheduling), used newer reporting software to communicate with the main office.

Learning Activity

1. Are all the departments up to date? Why or Why not?
2. How can the various departments improve their technology or usage?
3. Are any other additions necessary?
4. What Web 2.0 endeavors should be considered?

9. Key Terms

Chip and PIN
Conversational Ordering
Delivery Restaurant
    Management System (DRMS)

Electronic Cash Register (ECR)
Point-of-Sale (POS) System
Restaurant Management System
    (RMS)

Self-Ordering Kiosks
Table Management Software
    (TMS)
Table Ordering Systems

10. Chapter Questions

1. What are the five main components of an RMS?
2. Why is integration so important among the various RMSs?
3. Explain proprietary versus nonproprietary purchasing decisions.
4. Which self-ordering technology do you see as the most important and why?
5. What is Chip and PIN?

11. References

Laudon, Kenneth, and Laudon, Jane. 2009. *Management information systems* (8th ed.). Upper Saddle River, NJ: Prentice Hall.

Panko, Raymond R. 2007. *Business data networks and telecommunication* (6th ed.). Upper Saddle River, NJ: Prentice Hall.

CHAPTER 7

Hotel and Resort Technology

Chapter Contents

INTERVIEW

Mark Haley, CHTP* is a partner with The Prism Partnership, LLC., a Boston-based consultancy firm. Mark manages the firm's hospitality technology practice, which provides services that include strategy development, needs analysis, system selection, specification development, and more. Some of the many technologies with which he works include customer relationship management, Internet applications, property management, central reservations and global distribution systems, and all aspects of hotel voice and data communications.

---

*CHTP refers to Certified Hospitality Technology Professional. It is a professional certification awarded by the professional trade association Hospitality Financial and Technology Professionals (HFTP) based upon successfully passing an exam and industry work experience. This is something worth exploring for those interested in pursuing a career related to hospitality information technology. For further information, please consult HFTP's web site (www.hftp.org).

Q: Mark, please share a brief overview of your background in terms of your education, work experience, current role, and responsibilities in working with hotel technology.

A: After graduating with a psychology degree from the University of Virginia and a business degree from the University of Denver's hospitality management program, I began my career in the front office at the Sheraton in Steamboat, a ski resort hotel. This was the beginning of a fifteen-year career with ITT Sheraton, which included a stint as a systems management trainee at the (then) Sheraton Centre-New York Hotel in New York City. I then was promoted to the Sheraton Boston Hotel, followed by numerous positions in the corporate information technology (IT) organization. During my time in the corporate IT organization, I helped to deploy a new worldwide central reservation system (CRS), a new integrated property management system (PMS), a proprietary revenue management system (RMS), and many other industry firsts. My last position there was director of property technology.

I left ITT Sheraton when I was asked to relocate, shortly before Starwood acquired ITT in 1998. That led to founding High Touch Technologies, a boutique consultancy. Sheraton and Starwood were my first clients, a launch pad for which I remain grateful. High Touch prospered, and then in 2000, I took a career detour with a dot.com company providing procurement services to hotels called hsupply.com. Like most dot.coms, hsupply flamed out, and I was back in the consulting business. Then, in 2001, Bill Watson, a Sheraton colleague also turned consultant, suggested we combine practices. Also joining us in founding The Prism Partnership was Gary Leopold of a firm called ISM. Our newly created firm had a decidedly marketing bent to it compared to High Touch, given Bill and Gary's backgrounds as marketing heavyweights and my interests in customer relationship management (CRM) and travel distribution technology. Today, The Prism Partnership has six partners and a global client roster any consultant would be proud to claim.

Q: With respect to IT, what are the hospitality industry's biggest opportunities and needs?

A: Opportunities include leveraging guest information to improve service delivery. Today, it is all about the guest experience and how personalized it is. Needs include finding and keeping qualified people and developing a funding mechanism that gets past the inherent conflicts of owner-funded capital expenses versus manager-funded operating expenses.

Q: What trends do you see emerging, particularly in the areas of (a) guest expectations and needs, (b) service delivery methods, and (c) technology developments and innovations?

A: Guest expectations are becoming more sophisticated. Guests now expect lodging service providers to know everything about them and to service them as though this is true. They also expect all of the creature comforts of home and work and the ability to quickly and easily transact business whenever and wherever they want. This is a stark contrast to the past, when a quiet room and comfortable bed were the extent of guest expectations.

Service delivery methods have moved online; the battle between high touch and high tech is over. Without question, technology is a core enabler of service delivery and is opening up new ways to deliver services. Mobile technologies, the Internet, and kiosks are just a few of the technologies that are changing the face of service delivery and empowering guests to serve themselves.

Technology innovation is diffusing through the industry much more rapidly than before. IT allows better, more reliable, and faster service to be delivered with fewer people and in a more personal manner. CRM and rapid response tools have really changed the game. I see hotel and resort companies actively seeking out technology as a competitive edge or differentiator. This is a big change from the past, when IT was often considered to be something to avoid like the plague.

Q: What are the most critical systems needed to run a hotel and the top technology priorities?

A: Well, you really have to start with the PMS, which has been morphing into more of a hospitality management system (HMS), with endpoints for distribution and CRM applications as well. If the PMS/HMS is running well, you have happy guests and happy employees. If it isn't, you will be out of business pretty quickly.

Q: Should technology be located at the property or above the property using cloud computing or virtualization?

A: The trend is moving towards the cloud. One should note that for branded properties, large-scale CRS and other corporate systems have been above the property for a long time; this is nothing new. To the extent that a hotel or resort can move technology above the property, it can reduce and simplify the IT footprint, the need for IT talent, and the amount of capital tied up in IT at the property level. These are all compelling reasons to move towards cloud computing.

Q: Who at the property level should be responsible for IT, and in your estimation, what does a hotel or resort general manager need to know about lodging technology? Where should his or her focus be to ensure a property is getting the best possible results and maximizing the benefits realized from technology?

A: The real answer to the question regarding responsibility is "It depends." The industry default has been and will likely remain the controller. In truth, IT is pervasive in a hotel or resort. Therefore, everyone needs to be involved and proficient in using technology, including the general manager.

General managers need to understand technology, especially regarding distribution and other aspects of marketing. They don't need to know all of the technical aspects of how technology works, but the more knowledge they have, the better off they will be in managing technology. To be great in business, one should know as much as possible about his or her business. Because of the many ways technology is impacting, enabling, and reshaping the business, general managers need to have a strong understanding of technology. What they need to know is often big picture stuff like what can technology do, what are its limitations, what issues and considerations should be taken into account, what costs are involved, etc. Ultimately for general managers, it is about being able to ask the right questions, selecting the right people, and holding them accountable.

Q: What are the key considerations and questions to ask when selecting and implementing a new system or technology-enabled change in a hotel or resort environment?

A: Will the vendor still be in business next year and the year after? Is the technology platform already obsolete? Does the solution really work? Can the staff work with it?

Q: What are the common hotel or resort IT issues or problems you see, and what can be done to avoid these from occurring in the future?

A: Poor project management and lack of expectation setting or scope management are two big issues. Many IT projects are often implemented late, over budget, and/or lacking some of the required or expected functionality. To avoid these problems, one must ensure that the project team has the right training and expertise, that there is disciplined management, that communications are open and frequent, and that the organization continues to attract and retain high-caliber people.

Q: What parting words of advice can you share with current and aspiring hospitality business professionals?

A: The hotel industry is a great business and a great career choice. My advice is to find a great company with an interesting culture and get on a career track for the long term. Great companies will find a way to help talented and energetic individuals grow and mature to become managers.

1. INTRODUCTION

Hotels and resorts, especially large ones, are extremely complex businesses. In fact, they are made up of a collection of businesses (or **profit centers**). These profit centers include lodging operations, food and beverage outlets, retail stores, meeting rooms and banquets, spa, parking, and more. To run such complex businesses requires a strong reliance on IT applications and a sophisticated IT portfolio. Figure 7-1 provides an illustration of the breadth of the IT portfolio for a typical full-service hotel. The number of systems and their heterogeneity increase the complexity of a hotel/resort business. According to Hotel Technology—Next Generation (2010), a typical hotel may use between 50 and 100 different technology applications to run its business. Systems integration (or the ability to exchange data between systems in real-time) is one of the greatest IT challenges facing hotels and resorts. In totality, the costs for IT are high, adding to the capital intensity of a hotel or resort property. Today, practically every department and business process relies on one or more technology applications. Some of this technology is guest-facing (i.e., **front-of-the-house**) and directly relates to guest services (e.g., PMS, Web site, and point-of-sale [POS]), whereas other technologies (e.g., accounting, human resources, and security systems) play supporting roles behind the scenes (i.e., **back-of-the-house or heart-of-the-house**). Finally, there are infrastructural technologies that are absolutely critical in empowering the property's IT portfolio and ensuring its integrity and reliability. These technologies provide the foundation and backbone upon which all applications run. They include things like the operating systems, security applications, network monitoring, communications hardware, back-up software, and cabling.

The application of technology in business should be done purposefully, with the business priorities and strategic objectives driving technology choice and adoption. Technology should be serving, supporting, and enabling the business. The principal areas of focus include customers (revenue, service, and retention), employees (attracting, training, retaining, and equipping employees to perform their jobs), and owners (growing value). With these in mind, a simple formula used by companies like Marriott and Southwest Airlines is to take care of the employees. If they are happy, they will, in turn, take care of the customers, and if customers are happy, profits will come and satisfy the owners or shareholders. In the hospitality industry, major brands often suggest, if not dictate, what systems and technologies to use to ensure service consistency and enable consolidated reporting across properties. Regardless of brand affiliation or independent status, hotels and resorts turn to technology solutions for a variety of reasons. Some of these include:

- To improve profitability by driving revenues and/or reducing operating costs.
- To enhance and personalize service to wow guests and build loyalty.
- To extend marketing reach (especially globally) to new and existing guests in a cost-effective manner.
- To address labor shortages and labor quality issues so that services can be delivered in a consistent manner.
- To collect, analyze, and communicate data.

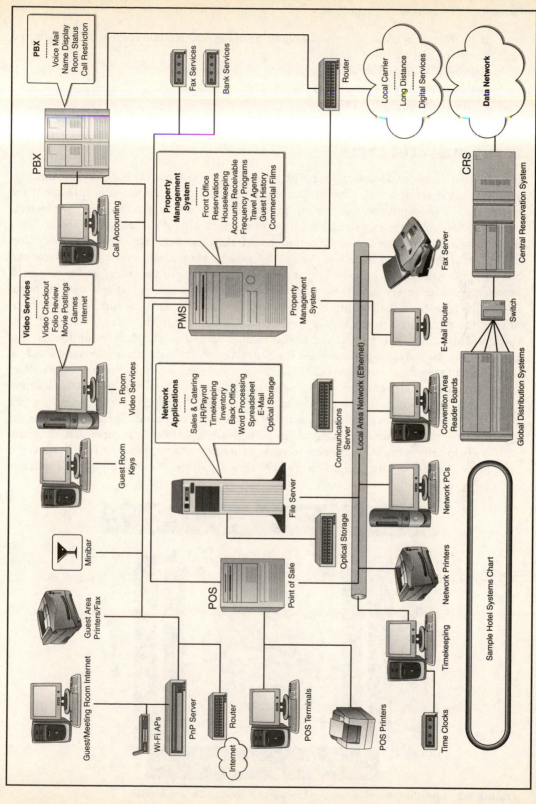

FIGURE 7-1 Hotel Technology Schematic for a Typical Full-Service Hotel

- To provide managerial controls and reporting needed to maintain the health, strength, and integrity of the business.
- To provide a safe and secure environment.
- To differentiate and create strategic competitive advantage.
- To maintain competitive parity.
- To assist with legal and regulatory compliance.

2. THE GUEST LIFECYCLE

Hospitality is not about discrete transactions; it's about relationships. It's all about providing personalized guest services that meet or exceed guest expectations. In the end, it is about the experience and pleasantly surprising or wowing guests. Hotels and resorts that can create incredible and memorable guest experiences that wow their guests will have a definite advantage in the market place. Therefore, technology adoption should take a **guest-centric** approach in every facet of the organization's value chain (see Figure 7-2), looking at value-add in terms of services and amenities from the guest's perspective that ultimately contribute to the overall and lasting guest experience. Because every guest is different and has different needs, expectations, and situational factors, the notion of what constitutes great service or incredible experiences can vary widely. In essence, the quality (or perceived quality) of service delivery rests in the eyes of each guest. It is, therefore, incumbent upon hotels and resorts to offer various service delivery options so that guests can choose the appropriate delivery method or channel suited to their needs and situation at the time of the service interaction. Since hospitality managers are in the business of manufacturing these outstanding, memorable, and personalized guest experiences, they must think strategically about guest needs and how to architect the service delivery processes to appropriately take advantage of technology and ensure that the human touch and personalization as well as the appropriate internal or managerial controls are properly designed into the implemented solutions.

To help determine how and where to apply technology in a hotel or resort environment, it is helpful to understand the role and services of each department (e.g., front office, concierge,

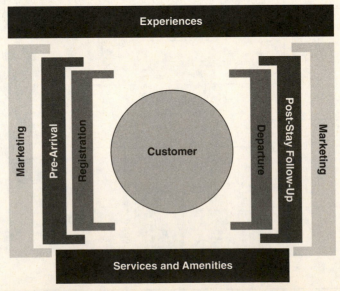

FIGURE 7-2 Everything Revolves around the Guest in a Guest-Centric Model

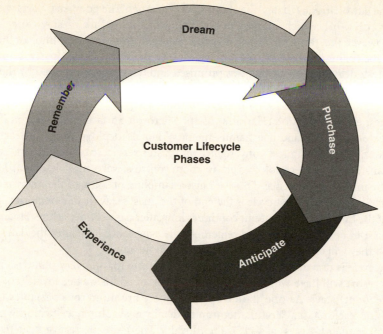

FIGURE 7-3 Guest Lifecycle

sales and marketing, accounting, housekeeping, and engineering) in the organization and the guest lifecycle (see Figure 7-3). It is important to realize that the guest experience begins long before a guest checks in, and it should continue long after bill settlement at check-out. The goals are to delight guests at every stage of their lifecycle so that they will be convinced to return again and again. Increasingly, hotels and resorts are turning to technology to enhance the guest experience. Every guest interaction (or service dyad)—whether it be in person, over the phone, or via technology (e.g., a Web site, kiosk, or mobile device)—is an impressionable moment or what is called a **moment of truth**. These service moments or interactions help to define a guest's overall level of satisfaction and influence one's intent to return.

The guest lifecycle starts with someone having an interest or need to travel overnight. This travel could be an exotic vacation, a trip to visit friends and relatives, a simple getaway, or a business trip. In the case of leisure travel, once the travel bug has hit, people typically research travel destinations, lodging providers, and activities in the area. This research helps to build excitement and establish guest expectations. Because of the many rich media tools on the Internet, the power of social networks, and the abundance of travel reviews, guests tend to be well informed and, as a result, pretty demanding. They know what they want and what they should expect and won't be satisfied unless their needs and expectations are met or exceeded. Business travelers will likely do some research as well, but their purchase decisions will be guided by company travel guidelines and policies.

Once a destination has been selected, it is time to book (purchase) lodging accommodations and begin preparing for the trip. The time between booking and the arrival date is called an anticipatory phase. In industry parlance, this is termed lead time to booking or **booking lead time**. This could be months in advance, or it could be last minute, say the day of or the day before arrival. Regardless of how long or short this lead time is, it is important to maintain the guest's level of excitement and address any questions or needs that might arise, such as questions about property location or amenities, activities and events, sights to see, driving directions, weather, and so on.

Eventually, the day of arrival (that is, the check-in date) comes. The guest stay starts with guest registration (or check-in), which marks the beginning of the on-site or stay experience. Please remember, however, that the actual experience really started at the very beginning of the cycle when the guest first began his or her search for lodging accommodations. The property is now faced with the ultimate test: delivering on all that was promised and has become expected by the guest up to this point. Some innovative applications include Courtyard by Marriott's interactive digital signage (Go Boards) for information and way-finding, Starwood's deployment of Microsoft's Surface computers for guest enjoyment, Rio's (Harrah's) use of Microsoft Surface computing in its lounges to promote social interactions and guest amusement, W Hotels' deployment of interactive poolside ordering systems for added guest convenience and faster service, and Mandarin Oriental's and MGM's Aria in-room guest technologies like in-room controls, wake-up calls, digital TV, and music to enhance the in-room experience. These are just a sampling of some of the many recent innovations. The final stage in the guest cycle is the end of the guest's stay or the memories. This phase is established at the time of check-out but continues long after a guest's departure. Hotels and resorts want each guest to be able to relive and remember the experience long after the dates of stay have passed so that they will return often and tell others to do the same.

The lifecycle is drawn in a circular fashion to indicate that if every phase is executed well, the hotel or resort will have won over the guest and earned his or her loyalty for future (and hopefully frequent) stays. As one should surmise, there are numerous variables that must be managed within each phase. Careful attention to details is absolutely critical in winning guests over and earning their business as well as their loyalty. Therefore, perfect or near-flawless execution is a must. Otherwise, hotel or resort risks losing a guest for life—and, thanks to the Internet and social media, will likely lose countless more as word spreads quickly like wildfire.

To be effective, service processes must be carefully designed and planned from a guest's perspective. They need to account for the intended users' mind sets and technical abilities, the service work flow, company branding, aesthetics, and placement of the technology. Both form and function matter. As described previously, guests have specific needs and wants during each lifecycle phase. They select service providers that make it easy for them to do business and ones that provide great benefits at an appropriate price–value relationship. If a hospitality manager understands guests' needs and wants, he or she can then determine how best to meet them and determine ways in which technology can serve to support, enhance, or enable the service delivery process while also looking for ways to build in **switching costs** (i.e., barriers to change service providers) so that guests will remain loyal. By drilling down into each phase, we can develop a **guest interaction map**. This map looks at the various guest interactions, transactions, or moments of truth within each phase of the guest lifecycle and illustrates ways in which the interaction can be aided by technology. This tool helps to ensure that the right technologies are being matched with the right business processes at the right times and points of guest interaction. To be successful in delivering outstanding service, there must be a goodness of fit between people, business processes, and technology. An example of walking through the guest lifecycle to create a simple guest interaction map is presented in Figure 7-4.

3. THE PROPERTY MANAGEMENT SYSTEM

At the heart of any hotel or resort technology portfolio is the **property management system (PMS)**. This system is essentially the nervous system that runs the hotel or resort and the system with which most other property-based systems must connect or interface to exchange data (such as guest charges from the property's restaurant, bar, and retail outlets and other areas in which guests can make purchases). It was initially given this name because of its role in managing the

Guest Phase	Dream (Research & Plan)	Purchase (Book)	Anticipate (Prepare)	Experience (Enjoy)	Remember (Relive & Share)
Property Goals	*Inform & Entice*	*Convert & Monetize*	*Excite & Sell*	*Delight & Build Loyalty*	*Re-Engage & Win Back*
Service Delivery Methods	• Virtual tours & rich media • Guest blogs • Guest reviews • Trip planning tools • Powerful search capabilities • Interactive maps • Collaborative shopping tools • Robust Web site • Language translation • Push-to-talk/live Web chat	• Online, real-time booking engine • Promotional pop-ups • Cross/up sell • CRM • E-mail confirmations • Currency conversion	• Personalized push messages with cross/up sell offers • Driving directions • Activity planner • Weather alerts and travel advisories • Destination guides & event calendars • Pre-blocking rooms • Advance check-in	• Mobile commerce • Check-in kiosks • POS • Concierge services • Itinerary management • In-room technology amenities • Guest safety & security • Guestroom climate controls • Rapid response system • Digital signage • Location-based services • Business center • Wake-up calls	• Guest satisfaction surveys • Photo galleries • Guest reviews & blogs • Guest profile updates • Loyalty points & statements • E-folios • E-newsletters

FIGURE 7-4 Sample Guest Interaction Map

property's room inventory and revenue; that is, keeping track of room availability and statuses, the guests who occupy each room, and the payments or revenues for rooms sold. Its original function was primarily administrative. Over the years as both the business and technology have changed, so has the role of the PMS. Its role expanded to revenue and sales lead generation as well as business reporting. Now, the PMS is integral to managing everything about a hotel's or resort's guests and their experiences, including their profiles and preferences, loyalty points, and CRM. It is hard to imagine running a hotel or resort today without the aid of a PMS. Many industry professionals (for example, Mark Haley in the introductory interview to this chapter) suggest that the term PMS has become outdated, especially since these system functions are moving off property and heading to the cloud; instead, the term hospitality management system (HMS) seems more appropriate and rightly puts the primary emphasis on the guest experience (the reason for existence) rather than the administrative running of the property. For now, we will continue to use the term PMS in this chapter in order to remain consistent with industry standard terminology.

A PMS is a sophisticated management tool comprised of many modules. PMS vendors are continuously expanding their solutions to provide more robust application suites that can support more aspects of hotels and resorts and the guest lifecycle. The modules and specific functionality can vary by software vendor, but generally speaking, all PMSs will include (or have options to include) the categories depicted in Figure 7-5. Which options are purchased will depend upon the type or segment of hotel (e.g., full-service, mid-priced, economy, extended-stay) and services offered, what functions are performed at the property level versus at a regional or corporate level, corporate or brand requirements if affiliated with a lodging company, and one's preference towards an integrated solution and one-stop shopping versus purchasing best-of-breed applications (i.e., finding the best available application to perform each function). Cost may also be a factor.

While it is easy to underestimate the complexity and detailed functionality of today's PMS, it is just as easy to get bogged down in a detailed discussion of specific functionality and method- ologies at the cost of "not seeing the forest through the trees." Simply stated, a PMS is a room in- ventory management tool, a sales tool, and an accounting/billing tool. In its most basic form, a PMS must be able to perform six basic functions:

FIGURE 7-5 Property Management System Functionality

1. Enable guests to make reservations.
2. Enable guests to check-in/register when they arrive and check-out/pay when they leave.
3. Enable staff to maintain guest facilities.
4. Account for guests' financial transactions.
5. Track guests' activities for use in future sales efforts
6. Interface with other systems.

Each of these important functions will be discussed in the following sections. Where necessary, details will be included so that you can fully appreciate how PMSs perform certain functions.

Enable Guests to Make Reservations

The **property management system (PMS)** works in tandem with the **central reservation system (CRS)** and the **revenue management system (RMS)** to manage, price, and sell guestroom inventory and ensure that the appropriate rates, availability, and selling rules and restrictions are made available as appropriate to all of the various distribution channels (i.e., sales outlets) used by the property. Additionally, the PMS must work with the guest loyalty program system to be able to access guest profiles, track guest history, and accrue loyalty points. While there are a myriad of ways in which a guest can book his or her lodging accommodations (e.g., online, via travel agent, through a group block, over the phone with a central reservations agent, or directly with the property itself), the reservation record must find its way to the PMS to create the guest record or guest account.

Enable Guests to Check In/Register When They Arrive and Check Out/Pay When They Leave

Whether a guest has a reservation or not, this essential function of the PMS includes not only check-in upon arrival at the property but also the ability to interface with any self-service check-in kiosk and Internet or smart phone applications enabling check-in. Figure 7-6 provides an example of a guest registration screen and illustrates the type of information captured in the Opera, a PMS from MICROS Inc.

Enable Staff to Maintain Guest Facilities

The housekeeping functions of a PMS provide hotel or resort staff and management the ability to access some basic necessities when managing rooms:

1. Room type, room number—king, double, 101, 201, and so on.
2. Room status—clean, dirty, departing today, and so on.
3. Information about the occupant of each room—name, guest preferences (e.g., likes extra pillows), and so on.
4. Internal operational information—inspections, maintenance issues, history, and so on.
5. Report generation, for example, the departures report listing guests due to check-out on a given date and the housekeeping breakout report detailing work assignments per housekeeper.

Discrepancies occur when the housekeeping department's definition of the status of a room differs with the front desk's status. This can result from many things. An example is a guest checks out a day early without going to the front desk. A housekeeper will clean the room and report it

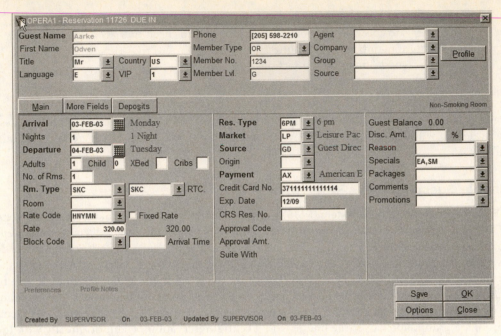

FIGURE 7-6 This reservation screen of the MICROS Corporation Opera property management system contains many necessary pieces of guest information for various hotel departments. *(Source: MICROS/Fidelio, Inc.)*

as vacant or clean. However, since the room has not been checked out by the front desk, that department will display it as occupied. Managing discrepancies is a daily ritual in hotels. The PMS generates reports such as these to aid management in solving such problems. Figure 7-7 is a screen shot, again from the MICROS Opera system, of a housekeeping screen and a field that displays the front office (FO) status. If the two differ, there is a discrepancy.

Account for Guests' Financial Transactions

Billing information such as credit card number, home and/or business address, and the specific type of room rate are accounted for here. Typically, a front office is divided into three eight-hour shifts with the overnight shift (generally 11 PM to 7 AM) left to complete the night audit. The night audit function involves generating a series of daily reports, monitoring internal controls, reconciling accounts and the day's business transactions, posting room and tax charges to each guest folio, balancing the books for the day, and rolling the computer date to the new business day.

Track Guests' Activities for Use in Future Sales Efforts

It is important that the PMS capture any and all information about a guest that is relevant and beneficial to future sales efforts. This information can also be accessed by the CRS and any CRM applications (see Chapters 8 & 9) for sales and marketing initiatives. Figure 7-5 of the PMS is important. If staff members (or guest service associates) fail to capture all of the information requested on this screen, data needed for downstream services (i.e., service encounters or touch points such as the restaurant, concierge, or guest services that occur after check-in) will be incomplete. This could impede service or even cause service failures.

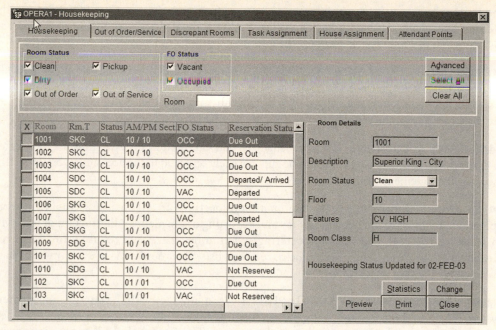

FIGURE 7-7 The management of hotel rooms can be a daunting task. With many different and constantly changing characteristics, organizations can benefit from department-specific modules of a property management system such as housekeeping from MICROS.   *(Source: MICROS/Fidelio, Inc.)*

Interface with Other Systems

Effective systems implementation and seamless guest service around the property can only be achieved if the PMS is interfaced with other core systems and applications used throughout the property (refer back to Figure 7-1). Some examples systems that must be interfaced with the PMS and why these interfaces are necessary are described in the following.

CENTRAL RESERVATION SYSTEM (CRS)   Real-time integration between the PMS and the CRS is necessary to ensure that all available rooms are listed as such so that they can be sold under the rules set and at the rates for which they are meant to be sold. Poor systems integration can result in undersold or oversold situations, both of which are undesirable situations, and hurt overall revenues. Consistent information regarding rates and availability in the CRS and PMS is important to guest service and to building trust with guests. If they receive different answers at different points of service, they begin to wonder what to believe, if they are receiving honest answers to their questions, and if they are being treated fairly.

POINT-OF-SALE SYSTEM (FOOD AND BEVERAGE POS)   As the main system on the food and beverage side, the importance of this interface cannot be understated. In the past, the lack of an interface resulted in lost revenue and poor service due to the fact that these two systems did not communicate directly. Guest charges were sometimes processed *after* the guests checked out, which resulted in lost revenue, or guests were made to wait while a charge was manually added to a folio. Secondly, if a guest wished to dispute a restaurant charge and no data appeared on the front desk screen, the front office was at a loss and often deleted the charge at check-out to speed things along. Through a two-way interface, restaurant services and bartenders can verify that a guest is in-house (i.e., registered) prior to serving and posting charges. Both the total guest charge and the detailed guest check detail can be transferred from the restaurant/bar POS system to the PMS for guest billing. If questioned by the guest at the time of check-out, a front desk clerk can easily retrieve the guest check detail for the guest.

HOTEL RETAIL POINT-OF-SALE SYSTEMS   If a hotel contains other retail shops such as gift shops, pro shops, spa, recreation rentals, parking, and so on that allow room charges, these POS systems, just like the restaurant/bar POS system must interface with the PMS to ensure that purchases appear on the room bill.

BACK-OFFICE ACCOUNTING   All of the financial data captured by the PMS must be transferred to the back-office accounting system to be appropriately reported in the accounting books so that the financial statements will all be up to date.

SALES AND CATERING SYSTEM   Banquets and meetings are all part of a hotel or resort's operation and must be included in any revenue reporting of the night audit function of the PMS. In addition, the PMS and sales and catering system must share data required for the group business such as forecasting, room blocks, rooming lists, and room pick-ups (rooms that have been reserved within a group block).

ENERGY MANAGEMENT SYSTEM   The PMS needs to interface with the **energy management system (EMS)** to control energy costs and maintain room climate controls at predefined temperature set points when guestrooms are not occupied. The PMS can send instructions to an in-room thermostat to change the temperature setting or speed of the blower or simply turn on or off the heating or air conditioning.

IN-ROOM AMENITIES   Guestrooms have gone high tech offering guests a number of for-fee services. These may include high-speed Internet access, in-room movies, mini bars, and in-room safes. If there is a charge for usage, there needs to be an interface with the PMS to ensure proper and timely guest billing. These charges must be posted to the guest account prior to his or her check-out to ensure collection of payment. An interface to the guest television system can enhance guest services by enabling a customized guest welcome message upon entry into a guestroom.

SECURITY   Most hotels and resorts use electronic guest locking systems. At the time of check-in, key is activated and authorized for the dates of the guest stay. On the date of departure, the key is deactivated.

THE CALL ACCOUNTING SYSTEM   Calls placed from in-room guest phones may result in local or long-distance charges. The costs of these calls are tracked by a property's telephone system (PBX or private branch exchange) and the **call accounting system**. Charges are then posted via the PMS to the guest folio.

TELEPHONE SERVICE AND GUEST MESSAGING   The PMS must interface with the telephone system and voice messaging system to activate outbound phone and voicemail services upon check-in and to deactivate them and delete voicemail messages upon check-out. If a hotel does not have voice mail, the PMS must allow for messages to be taken and applied to individual rooms.

4. FOUR KEY INTERFACES

While all of the interfaces described in the earlier section are important, there are four interfaces that warrant more in-depth discussion. These include:

- Real-time interface with the global distribution system (GDS)/CRS
- The activities management systems
- Built-in revenue and yield management tools
- The enterprise

Real-Time Interface with the GDS/CRS

While the integration between PMSs and GDSs/CRSs is rapidly evolving, this interface has traditionally been the single most important element in multiunit operators' and brands' decision about which PMS and/or CRS to implement. While brands, owners, and agents all have the same general goal—to generate as much revenue as possible from the sale of as many room nights as possible—the different business models and the varying relationships between these entities have historically made the integration of GDS/CRS and PMS data complicated in many ways.

In short, most hotels want to sell as many of their own room nights as possible so they do not have to pay commissions or booking fees, but the hotel does not want to leave any room empty that could have been otherwise filled by any booking source. Almost everyone else wants to sell as many of a hotel's room nights as possible in order to collect commissions or booking fees. Oftentimes, hoteliers must decide in advance how many rooms are to be allocated to various third-party booking agents, particularly if set prices are pre-negotiated under a merchant model type agreement.

In a situation where there is no real-time integration between systems, rooms allocated to third-party booking agents, known as "blocks of rooms," are essentially removed from the hotel's inventory. As a result, the hotel cannot sell those rooms to potential guests, even if those guests would be willing to pay a higher rate per room than was given the third-party booking agent for the block. This situation may or may not benefit the third party depending on the circumstances, but it always acts to limit the hotel's ability to manage or maximize its own revenue. In recent times, with the development of large, Internet-based third-party booking agents, there is even some concern that such situations may result in a single third party having the ability to negatively affect average room rates for an entire geographic area by controlling too large a percentage of the available inventory.

Real-time integration between the PMS and the GDS/CRS (and other booking engines), provides hoteliers and brands with much greater ability to manage their room inventory in real time in addition to providing a number of benefits relative to revenue management (discussed in a following section).

Because many GDSs and CRSs in use today rely on the collection of room inventory data aggregated from the local PMS at each participating property, a PMS must have sophisticated and reliable interfaces with the CRS and GDS used by the hotel brand. Many of the major hotel chains have invested significantly in these systems and interfaces in order to maximize sales opportunities and reduce the risk of unsold inventory. Chapter 8 will provide greater detail regarding global distribution.

Integration with Activities Management Systems

A number of lodging properties are comprised of fewer than one-hundred rooms and do not offer many additional activities or services beyond the basics that need to be managed within a PMS. On the other hand, larger hotels and resort properties generally feature a myriad of nonroom facilities and services such as restaurants, banquet rooms, meeting rooms, spa, golf courses, and tennis courts. Additionally, guests in these properties may desire to reserve specific services at predetermined times, many of which require preplanning such as spa treatments, golf tee times, and tennis lessons.

Many times, these properties will have entirely separate systems for managing nonroom services and resources. These systems often include golf tee time management, spa management, sales and catering, and other systems. It is not uncommon for some hotels and resorts with older or non-integrated systems to require guests to schedule their various recreational activities and personal services in multiple reservation transactions with different staff members serving each area and with access to the appropriate booking system. When this happens, guests are often asked to resupply all of the same information provided at the time the room was reserved or at the time of registration. Having to repeatedly ask guests for their personal information is a sign of poor guest service, as is the inability to produce a comprehensive guest itinerary confirming all activities and services booked.

Guest service issues aside, using separate and nonintegrated systems for this purpose decreases revenues and increases expenses. Hotels and resorts can experience significant potential revenue loss when reservation agents fail to sell all available hotel services to guests when they call to book their rooms. Additionally, hotels lose even more potential revenue when guests cancel room reservations in a PMS that is not integrated with other property systems because the cancelled room reservation does not automatically result in cancellation of the spa treatment, restaurant reservation, or athletic facility use. Staff may be scheduled or other guests denied reservations for various hotel amenities and resources based on false availability information in spa, tee time, and other systems because they are not integrated with the PMS.

Modern PMSs designed for use in large hotels and resort properties have integrated functionality that allows users, staff, or guests to reserve multiple hotel resources either in conjunction with or independent from an actual room reservation. Thus, each reservation provides an opportunity to easily and effortlessly (i.e., without a lot of data entry) upsell or cross-sell guests on additional services and amenities, helping to increase revenues per each guest. Also, when a guest cancels a room reservation, the staff member providing the cancellation is prompted to ask the guest if he or she would also like to cancel other activities at the hotel.

Integration of the PMS with other activities management systems, therefore, drives additional (nonroom) revenue and saves the hotel money by decreasing the incidents of "false no-shows" for various hotel resources.

Built-In Revenue Management Tools

In general, a hotel or resort's goal (relative to rooms) is to maximize revenue. To do this, one must carefully manage rates and occupancy levels. Contrary to what you might instinctively believe, maximizing room revenue does not necessarily mean selling as many rooms as possible. Since *Total Room Revenue = Average Dollars per Room-Night × Room-Nights Sold*, maximizing revenue requires hoteliers to consider both the number of rooms they sell and the price at which they sell those rooms. Most PMSs provide hoteliers with some revenue management tools for managing room sales so as to maximize revenue and profits by helping to track key hotel performance measures such as **occupancy rate** (number of guestrooms sold or occupied as a percentage of the total number of rooms available or the hotel's capacity) **average daily rate** (ADR—total guestroom revenue divided by the number of guestrooms sold), and **revenue per available room** (REVPAR—total guestroom revenue divided by the number of rooms available for sale [that is, total hotel capacity] or hotel occupancy rate times the hotel's average daily rate).

Just like airlines, retail stores, and financial firms, hoteliers must continually calculate and recalculate potential revenue models based on a number of variables affecting their businesses. Although a completely accurate projection of potential maximum revenue requires the development and processing of complicated equations with many variables, statistical data, historical business data, and assumptions about the future, basic calculations can be performed using historic sales and pricing data in conjunction with information that one can reasonably predict (such as major convention bookings, sports events, special groups, holidays, etc.). Most PMSs provide this basic functionality.

PMSs typically use a weighted historic average determined by the user along with the systems calendar (for holidays) and any additional information supplied by the user to set rates and predict availability for future room nights. While the functionality supplied by most vendors in this regard is currently not extremely complicated, it is fast and easy to use compared with stand-alone yield management systems that generally require a significant financial and labor investment that is often not realistic for a small property.

The Enterprise

An **enterprise** refers to the entire business operation; that is, all of the various departments, operating units, and corporate and regional offices. You need to look at the development of the PMS within the hotel computing environment as a whole. Other important systems with which the PMS needs to interface are the applications used by other departments such as finance and human resources. These applications are sometimes referred to as the **back office** since they are behind the scenes. Whereas the PMS is involved with the day-to-day guest-facing operations of the hotel, back office systems handle other actions such as payroll or purchasing. The *enterprise* refers to all the systems throughout the entire organization used in both the front-of-the-house (guest-facing) and in the back-of-the-house (behind the scenes). As stated earlier, a hotel or resort organization is a complex organization with many different systems used throughout the entire operation. Figure 7-8 shows an example of an enterprise view of the information technology portfolio that supports a hotel or resort organization. **Enterprise application integration (EAI)** is part of the enterprise system's evolution. EAI involves the incorporation of this technology at the application level with an end goal of fewer redundancies and an increase in collaborative synergy among staff members and knowledge workers. This collaboration is all too important in understanding the enterprise. With this collaboration, everyone is using the same data. EAI is the next step of its predecessor, enterprise resource planning (ERP), on the road to what has become somewhat of a Holy Grail for business people and technologists everywhere, **business process integration (BPI)**. Figure 7-9 shows an enterprise-wide view of property availability at multiple properties during a guest reservation inquiry.

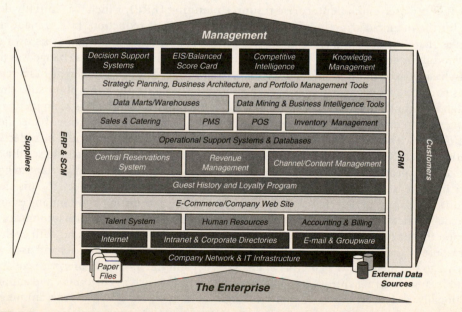

FIGURE 7-8 An Enterprise View of the IT Portfolio for a Hotel or Resort Business

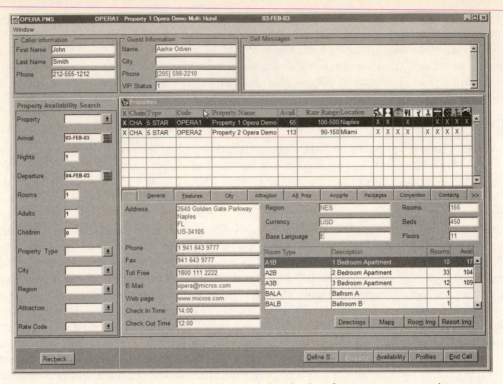

FIGURE 7-9   Within a brand, there may be numerous hotels; therefore, systems are used to manage multiple properties and each a customer across the entire company. This MICROS screen shows how chains are moving towards more global systems in customer service. Here, different customer criteria may be applied to specific member hotels around the world.   *(Source: MICROS/Fidelio, Inc.)*

Take a closer look at **enterprise resource planning (ERP)**, which was initially developed for the manufacturing industry for the purpose of cost reduction. ERP is made up of modules that represent and are used by specific departments. Accounting has its own software module as does human resources, sales, and so on. In the past, when a change was made in purchasing, accounting would not see that change on its computer screen or in its reports unless someone from the purchasing department let accounting know about the change through traditional channels (phone, e-mail, etc.). ERP companies saw this as an inefficiency waiting to be remedied. This led to the development of modules or department-specific applications which were made to *work together*. Any change in one system would be reflected in the other systems as well. For example, if sales were increased, operations would see the need to make more products in real time and adapt accordingly. So how is this important to hospitality? Imagine a banquet doubling in size and going on longer than expected. This change would immediately be reflected in all modules, including accounting and human resources. These departments could then use this timely and identical information to account for and act upon these new costs in both food and beverage and labor. Over time and with evolution and real use of the Internet for e-commerce, *EAI* was the new term introduced and used when referring to the theme of the enterprise. EAI goes beyond the in-house enterprise collaboration to include external entities involved with the company such as customers and suppliers. Additionally, EAI incorporates newer technologies such as object-oriented programming and

XML, among others. The hospitality industry is unique in that its front-of-the-house system, the PMS (or POS in a restaurant scenario), often stands alone or contains a thicker seam in integrating with other systems such as the back office. Integration between the two is taking place; however, obstacles still remain.

BPI is more complicated than the previous two. Remember what a system is—a way of doing things. The definition of a process is "a systematic series of actions directed to some end." For example, think of a department using a system to complete specific departmental tasks. The controller balances the books, the housekeeping manager inspects the rooms, and the sales person entertains a client. Organizations as a whole and hotels in particular have many different departments and therefore many types of processes. This is the coveted next step of the back office or computer systems in general where such processes of sales, operations, and project management can share and benefit from a common system and information once hidden–is unearthed. This ideal currently resides in theory and not in practice. The key is that if processes from different departments can somehow share the same system, then more can be gained. BPI is by definition the real-time integration of information, processes, and projects in a real-time setting. In another example, imagine a hotel being built, a new management team being formed, supplies ordered, payments made, reservations taken, and so on. Today different systems handle these different actions and are integrating through such initiatives beginning with ERPs and now EAIs to what is hoped is something much more efficient and intelligent—business process integration. Why is this so important? In the future, the PMS will be one piece of a larger BPI system. BPI may not happen overnight, but the further integration and tightening up of data collaboration at a minimum will be highlighted. With this improved internal communication, multilevel properties can share customer and business data among other locations, expanding the enterprise.

In this example, a clerk or manager can get a companywide view of a chain or multi-property hotel to further serve guests and obtain business intelligence. Through this screen, questions such as "does your Miami property have a golf course?" can be answered and cross-property business improved. Study the enterprise-wide screen shot in Figure 7-9.

5. GRAPHICAL USER INTERFACE

You have probably never used anything but an intuitive graphical user interface (GUI). In addition, as college students, you probably have a higher level of literacy and cognitive capabilities than the general population. As a result, many of you probably take the concept of being able to "point and click" your way through any application for granted. The screen shots already presented in this chapter provide examples of the user interfaced for one commonly used PMS.

You probably never bothered to look at the user manual or instructions for the vast majority of computer applications you use on a daily basis. This is because almost all consumer-based technology applications from Google to iPhone apps have been developed with inherently user-friendly or intuitive GUIs. It is important to remember, though, that consumer-based information systems have been designed by large companies that derive billions of dollars in revenue from the widespread use of these systems. On the other hand, specific business-based applications, such as PMSs, have been developed by much smaller companies (with fewer resources) and are required in many cases to perform much more complicated tasks than their consumer-based cousins. So it should come as no surprise that the development and implementation of intuitive user interfaces for business-based applications such as PMSs have taken much longer than they did for consumer-based applications.

For hospitality professionals employing a PMS, however, there may be no single element of the system more important than the user interface. Not only must modern PMSs' user interfaces support the rapid training of a workforce that historically turns over almost two to three times per year, but going forward, the PMSs' interfaces will also have to support direct guest usage without the assistance of hotel staff. Whenever a choice is made regarding which PMS to use, study the interfaces. Are there other fields you wish to see? Can someone be trained on the system in a short period of time?

Modern PMSs' user interfaces must be almost training free. People have to be able to ascertain how to use them as easily as they would a popular Web site. From an internal staff perspective, the issues are easy to understand. Every time an employee quits, a new employee must be trained to use the system. During the new employee's training period, the hotel must pay for additional labor (the trainee and the trainer). During the first several days of an employee "working the system solo," there are customer service slowdowns and decreased worker productivity. As a result, by the time you calculate the average number of people a typical hotel must hire and train during any given three- to seven-year period (the life of a typical PMS), it will inevitably cost more to train new staff in the use of a PMS then it does to purchase and install the system itself.

People (i.e., guests) have grown accustomed to self-service, and many guests will prefer to enter their own reservation information via a browser or self-register and make their own reservations, as opposed to relaying information through a hotel operator. Consumers have grown to expect business applications to have the same type of easy to use GUIs they are accustomed to in consumer products and Web sites. Direct guest interface also means much more than just accepting room reservations from computer literate people with sophisticated educational backgrounds. Educated consumers are not the only people in the world who have money and stay in hotels, so user interfaces must be intuitive even for guests who are not computer literate or lack high-end cognitive capabilities.

Direct guest interface in a rapidly shrinking world also means much more than just accepting room reservations from computer literate people who all speak the same language. Thanks to many advances in translation technologies during the past several years, people have become accustomed to viewing Web pages in their native language. Both guests and staff now expect to be able to use a PMS in multiple languages.

As a result, newer PMSs must have robust user interfaces that are extremely intuitive and user friendly. Luckily, most do. However, many still do not and telling the difference between the two is almost impossible for the average person sitting through a sales demonstration. There is an entire field of endeavor referred to as human factors engineering and a science associated with the development and testing of all those intuitive interfaces people take for granted in their favorite consumer applications. In a sales demonstration of a system, a professional salesperson can make almost any GUI look easy to use. To actually determine the difference in levels of intuitiveness between two systems, however, requires somewhat extensive testing that generally is only affordable at the brand, chain, or multiproperty level.

You should understand, however, that the intuitive nature of a PMS's user interface is probably one of the most critical elements there is relative to the system's ability to enable a guest to make reservations. If potential guests, either via hotel staff or directly, cannot make reservations in the system quickly, efficiently, and easily, they will ultimately find a different hotel where they can. Hence, the intuitive nature of a PMS's user interface is a critical success factor relative to a hotel's obtainment of its gross revenue goals.

Security concerns around the world have called attention to security practices within hotels and resorts and various technologies that can help provide safer, more secure environments. Possible new interfaces may include biometrics such as retina scanning, fingerprint reading, and facial recognition software for individual identification.

6. Summary

Hotels and resorts are complex businesses requiring numerous systems to manage all facets of the business and guest details. Because of the competitive dynamics of the industry, hospitality managers must have a solid command of both the business and the technology used to support and enable the business. At the heart of all hotel and resort technology is the property management system (PMS), which could be located on property or above property through cloud computing. When looking to apply technology to guest services, it is helpful to understand the guest lifecycle and the specific guest needs within each phase of this lifecycle. It is also important to make sure that the things guests value most are being provided and not lost in a property's quest to be high tech. It is all too easy to get caught up in trying to offer the latest technologies while losing sight of the basic elements of guest service. For example, several hotels and resorts have recently upgraded their in-room technology amenities with room controllers that can adjust the room's environment and ambiance, from climate control to lighting, music, and position of the window curtains. While guests find these technology advances to be impressive and contribute to novel guest experiences, they are left wondering why these hotels and resorts have gone to such an expense to wow them when what they are really seeking is reliable, fast, and free Internet access. Thus, the focus must be on value-adding technologies—those that enhance the guest experiences, garner guest loyalty, drive revenue, and reduce operating costs.

Another key consideration to keep in mind is the goodness of fit between people, business processes, and technology. Service delivery must be carefully planned and designed. One cannot simply buy and install technology and then expect results. For example, many hotels have turned to kiosk technology to shorten check-in and check-out lines and reduce labor costs. The technology is very adept at handling routine check-in and check-out transactions, but at many properties, guest usage rates have been disappointing and much lower than anticipated. In these situations, things were overlooked. One must consider a host of factors, especially since this technology serves as a face of the organization and is tasked with delivering a very important moment of truth. The corporate personality and culture must be embodied in the user interface. As well, the device must be well integrated with the CRS system (see Chapter 8) to provide on-screen personalization and relevant offers and room upgrade recommendations. Furthermore, just because technology is enabling the service interaction and facilitating the transaction does not mean that technology should completely replace people. One must find new ways to diffuse people into the overall guest experience to ensure that the human touch is not lost. Finally, the lobby design must be addressed to ensure that the kiosks fit in aesthetically and are placed appropriately for traffic flow patterns, visibility, power and network access, and security.

Because service quality (or perception of service quality) rests with the guest, hotels and resorts should offer multiple service delivery options to account for different situations and comfort levels. By doing so, guests can choose the methods best suited for their needs. In the end, technology coupled with people can contribute to superior guest service and memorable guest experiences, thereby driving differentiation and competitive advantage.

7 Case Study and Learning Activity

Case Study

The Union League of Philadelphia

Challenges and Solutions

The Union League of Philadelphia is one of the oldest clubs in the nation with 67 guest rooms, 12 meeting rooms, and a staff of 150. Clubs can provide a great example of the challenges faced in technology and its evolution, since oftentimes they are found in very old buildings that make major changes difficult. In going behind the scenes, you can appreciate the knowledge and energy needed in working with technology in the hospitality industry. Under the general management of Jeff McFadden, Robert Hencinski, the MIS manager, was faced with the task of bringing the club into the future. Upon his arrival four years prior, and bringing over sixteen years of experience to the job, Robert faced numerous challenges. An environment with multiple brand personal-based computers running with an antiquated DOS-based operating system on a dated club management system (a PMS particular to clubs), with different departments using proprietary software and hardware was only the tip of the iceberg of his challenges. The staff was using different systems that did not communicate and the building was full of mysterious data and analog wires with no way of allocating costs to any phone calls made. Lastly, a look in the files revealed unnecessary and costly service and purchase agreements.

Encounters such as these are all too common in the industry. With ownership or management of the fixed assets, such as the building itself, changing many times over, continuity is lost or forgotten. The result is a building with disparate, outdated systems that is not administered properly. A tour of the property shows a setup all too common in large holdings today. The phone system switch and interface is in one part of the building, the data network and servers centralized in another, and the cable and entertainment systems on another floor. With each system requiring its own dedicated space and possessing its own product evolution and life cycle, integration and consolidation are an obvious challenge. Cost considerations and building structure often hamper solutions and only allow for stopgap measures to be implemented. Further, with back-of-the-house space always losing out to front-of-the-house space, an MIS director's job is always a battle.

Besides staying current and solving any technology issues arriving hourly, the Union League faces the task of dealing with a number of outside vendors and service providers. A brief list of some of its technology dealings—an Internet service provider, a Web page management company, a company managing the pay phones, a different company providing local and long-distance calling, a high-speed (two T1s and DSL) hardware company, and of course the multitude of software vendors—exemplifies how many different entities (and their related costs) can be involved in any operation utilizing the latest technology.

The leadership of the league through Robert has met these challenges head-on. Due to the historic nature of the building and the need for more meeting space, major systems have stayed in their dedicated places; however, their operational efficiency has been streamlined. Outdated wires and interfaces have been removed while the infrastructure has been updated to Category V cable for standard Ethernet network architecture. The PC of choice is now coming from one vendor—Dell, and the printers from Hewlett Packard, resulting in bulk discounts and easier to maintain hardware. A state-of-the-art club management system from Gary Jonas Ltd. was purchased for use in the restaurant, hotel, and back offices, allowing for staff and management to share and retrieve information from the different departments in real time. The League Web page has been outsourced to a specialty vendor, allowing the staff to concentrate more on daily operations. Finally, the operating system was moved to Windows XP and the productivity software to Microsoft Office, enabling knowledge workers to operate within the same framework and aid in software training.

Current projects in the works include upgrading to digital cable and the purchase of another T1 for additional phone lines. Additionally, September 11th has resulted in increased security concerns. Some possible new ventures include the purchase of member identifier cards small enough to fit on a key chain that could track members' interaction with the club and allow for secured access. The cards would be aided by the installation of additional cameras to confirm that the person in possession of the card is indeed the proper one.

With the proper system now in place, the Union League is now moving towards becoming a truly digital club.

Learning Activity

1. With all the different problems faced by the League, how do you think it did? Why?
2. Of the major changes made, which one should have taken first priority? Why?
3. List the next four priorities in order. Justify your answer.
4. Given all the new improvements in the League, what demands or improvements are needed in its club management system?
5. Can you think of any aspects unique to clubs that may make their property (club) management system unique?

8. Key Terms

Average daily rate (ADR)
Back-of-the-house
Back office
Booking lead time
Business Process Integration (BPI)
Call accounting system
Central reservation system (CRS)
Energy management system (EMS)

Enterprise
Enterprise Application Integration (EAI)
Front-of-the-house
Guest-centric
Guest interaction map
Guest lifecycle
Moment of truth
Occupancy rate

Profit center
Property management system (PMS)
Revenue management
Revenue per available room (REVPAR)
Security
Switching costs

9. Chapter Questions

1. What are the broad areas of functionality that a PMS must provide?
2. Since PMS is so critical to hotel and resort operations and guest services, what key considerations should one have when considering the selection and implementation of a PMS? Hint: Think about service delivery, operational issues, staffing and training, management needs, and so on.
3. What is an intuitive user interface, and why is it important to a PMS?
4. Why is it important to integrate a PMS to spa management, golf tee time, and other activity management systems?
5. What other hotel information systems rely on the PMS for information?
6. What is an ERP?
7. Why is business process integration so important?
8. When purchasing a PMS, what are some major considerations?
9. Aside from the chapter content, can you think of any other future PMS requirements?
10. Who on your staff should be trained on PMS usage?

10. Reference

Hotel Technology—Next Generation. (2010, May). Vision and first steps for shared technology services for hospitality: A position paper. Available: http://htng.org/mediacenter/htng_shared_services_position_paper_1.0.pdf.

CHAPTER 8

Global Distribution Systems and Channels

Chapter Contents

INTERVIEW

William (Bill) Peters is Vice President of Reservation Services and Market Development for Outrigger Enterprises Group, the parent organization for Outrigger Hotels and Resorts and OHANA Hotels and Resorts. In this capacity, Bill is responsible for overseeing the reservation sales and distribution functions for the company's 47 properties or nearly 12,000 rooms located in Hawaii, Asia Pacific, and the Oceania regions. Using voice-over-IP (VOIP) technology, Bill and his Outrigger team recently converted the company's centralized reservations center to a home-based agent model. Having worked for a variety of hospitality companies such as Loews Hotels, Playboy Resorts and Country Clubs, Helmsley Hotels, Forte Hotels International, and the Timeshare Vacation Club of Four Seasons Hotels and Resorts, Bill is a true industry veteran.

Q: Please share a brief overview of your background in terms of your education, work experience, and current role and responsibilities in working with hotel and resort distribution.

A: For much of my career, my focus has been on distribution.

In my current position, I am responsible for the electronic integration of all customer touch points for both the consumer and wholesale channels. The customer touch points include all voice, Internet, live Internet text chat, Internet call back, e-mail, fax, and Internet video chat. Consolidating the management and oversight of all of these touch points under one umbrella gives Outrigger Enterprises the ability to service and track the effectiveness and importance of online marketing.

To stay abreast of industry trends and contribute to the hospitality industry's advancement through technology, I actively participate in numerous industry groups; including HEDNA (Hotel Electronic Distribution Network Association), AH&LA (American Hotel and Lodging Association), IARE (International Association of Reservation Executives), HSMAI (Hotel Sales and Marketing Association), HTNG (Hotel Technology Next Generation), and HFTP (Hospitality Financial and Technology Professionals). I am a graduate of the New York City Technology University where I received a degree in Hotel and Restaurant Management.

Q: Distribution is one of the most complex yet critical aspects of the hotel and resort business. Why is this? What are the key challenges and opportunities?

A: Distribution can be boiled down to being able to reach your customers with bold statements and rates as to why they should make a reservation and stay at your hotel or resort verses a competitor. In today's marketplace where information concerning your property is available at the touch of an iPod, personal computer, and also most mobile networks, it is both a challenge and a great opportunity to put your best features forward so your future guest can make an intelligent decision.

Q: How can hotels and resorts win in the distribution arms race? What are the most important concepts and technologies for people to know about distribution in order to be successful hotel/resort managers?

A: Hotels and resorts need to keep all means of guest interactions available and open to guests at all times. These interactions need to include all Web-based online travel agency (OTA) sites, wholesaler sites, property direct Web sites, social media sites, global distribution sites, property-based voice reservation offices, hotel/resort front desks, and central reservation offices.

Q: What is the relationship between reservations, sales, revenue management, and channel management?

A: There should be a voice of one augmented by well-integrated systems to support the information flow between each area and ensure that rates, room availabilities, selling rules, and restrictions are in sync across distribution channels. Room rates and availability of those rates should be coordinated in advance of the up and coming seasons. The relationship also needs to be flexible depending on the state of the economy. In other words, room rates and room availability need to be changed on the fly if necessary for hotels and resorts to be successful. It is the responsibility of reservations, sales, and revenue management to communicate on a weekly basis of the up and coming rate and availability strategies that will be needed to make the hotel/resort successful and meet budgetary requirements for the next rolling 30 days. It is important that these strategies are evaluated weekly by all concerned. If not, the business will miss opportunities in both rate and occupancy levels as its competitors react to the market.

Q: Today, there are so many different options to distribute hotel/resort products and accept reservations. How can a hotelier determine which channels to use and which to pass over? Is more "shelf space" better, or should hotels and resorts follow the example of Southwest Airlines and be more selective? What evaluation techniques and measures do you suggest?

A: In my opinion, the lodging industry is very different from the airline industry. Air travel competition is defined by a few air carriers with very limited amenities, depending on where you need to travel. Air travel is also controlled in many ways by the expensive frequent traveler clubs that the airlines started many years ago. Hotels and resorts, on the other hand, have extensive competition ranging from limited-service hotels and full-service hotels and resorts to condo rentals and time shares. The different distribution areas in which a hotel/resort needs to have shelf space depends on the market place or market places in which the hotel/resort needs to conduct business. These can vary for the commercial business traveler, the individual leisure traveler, group business, convention business, military business, and also the incentive meeting business. These factors are all part of evaluating the overall business and budget needs of the hotel/resort to insure that it and the distribution channels used are profitable.

Q: There are different fees associated with the various distribution channels, impacting overhead and overall guest acquisition costs. These fees can have a significant impact on overall profitability. How do you propose managing them? Is outsourcing or cloud computing a viable option to pursue? Given the vast difference in channel costs, is it wise to offer rate parity across all channels or to vary rates by channel to account for the various fees incurred?

A: Rate parity needs to be offered in comparable channels. For example, OTAs on the Internet should list comparable rates to the leisure traveler, the global distribution services, and the hotel's property's Web site. The majority of today's leisure travelers are quite sophisticated when it comes to product offerings and researching travel. A property that has rate parity in different market channels stands the best chance of winning over the leisure traveler and capturing his or her business, especially if the quality of the hotel/resort and its services are confirmed on the social media sites. The same stands true for all sources that are offering wholesale and group business services. Independent properties, those that are not associated with a particular flag or brand, should definitely consider using an outsourced reservation service. This provides these properties an affiliation with similar types of properties and increases their visibility in the market place in order to compete with branded or chain-affiliated properties.

Q: How do consumer reviews, social media, and mobile technologies fit into the distribution ecosystem? How can these be exploited and managed?

A: Social media and consumer reviews are now commonplace and frequently used by travelers as a resource to support their decision making. As noted before, today's traveling public is very sophisticated and discerning when evaluating destinations and lodging accommodations. There are many new electronic tools on the market place that will allow customers the ability to quickly and easily to review the major social media sites for comments from other travelers who have made purchases from the service providers under consideration and share these reviews with members of their traveling parties to help in making their purchase selections. To service providers, these social media sites provide valuable listening posts; they allow the collection of important guest feedback and, in some cases, the opportunity to response to unsatisfied guests. Mining these sites will give properties information so that they can correct any shortcomings and show the public how they are being responsive to consumer complaints. Guest satisfaction is and always has been one of the top goals within the hospitality industry.

Q: What do you see as the top distribution trends to watch and the key priorities for hoteliers to be well positioned for the next three to five years?

A: One of the most important initiatives in most lodging companies is to improve electronic distribution integration with their property management systems. I also see social media programs continuing to evolve such that they can be easily addressed directly by hotels and resorts on a daily basis. Mobile distribution of product offerings will be essential as well as having a complete database on all previous customers. E-mail marketing will need to be stepped up by offering free points, gifts not just special offers. Most customers are starting to shy away from e-mail marketing, just as they are fast forwarding through television commercials using Tivo or other digital video recorders (DVRs).

Q: Where do you look for emerging trends, new developments, and innovations in distribution? Who is leading the way?

A: Emerging trends and innovations can be found in all existing distribution companies. Distribution companies are coming up with new and profound customer response systems just to make it much easier and quicker for the customer to attain information for which they are seeking. Live robotic chat will lead the way, answering most of the customers' questions using a knowledge-based database interfaced both with chat and live voice. New emerging air travel technology will open up additional market places around the country and world. Being able to communicate in the language of the customer will become more and more important.

Q: Going forward, what role(s) do you think travel intermediaries, especially travel agents and wholesalers, will play? Do you see further disintermediation and/or consolidation?

A: OTAs and travel agents, especially the ones dealing with the wholesalers are here to stay. There will be constant consolidation of wholesalers in the future, but there will also be a new type of OTA emerging. It will be one with the hottest frequent traveler program that has the best free offerings. This will reward frequent travelers with choices between many participating lodging companies, not just one. This will provide travelers with greater flexibility and fewer blackout dates when redeeming points. It will be like the American Express credit card point system. Using those points, one can buy miles in several different airlines and hotels or resorts. Once the OTAs establish themselves as a club that move points into many different companies for purchase, they will definitely hold onto their own customers.

Q: What is the role of discount services like *Priceline.com*, *Hotwire.com*, and auction Web sites? How do they work, and how can hotel/resort companies take full advantage of them? Do these companies create the risk that competition will be based on price rather than demand?

A: The opaque (i.e., brand-shielded discounts) sites are very important to last-minute bookings and to offloading distressed inventory. They should be treated as a separate pipeline. The hotel/resort revenue manager should be making last-minute deals to sell inventory that has not yet been sold. This can be adjusted on the fly and should be managed daily for at least a rolling 30 days. There are always risks that competition will be based on price and not demand. This is where the sophisticated managers have to make their decisions. Electronic systems are excellent tools, but it still takes a good manager to understand the underlying trend of the business state and determine how to react accordingly.

Q: What parting words of advice can you share with current and aspiring hospitality business professionals?

A: Stay on top of your game. Continue to learn. Evaluate what has been done prior, and understand the results. A winning business is a business that is run by a team. Do not dismiss any ideas. Never settle for technology that just works. Expect and always require technology companies to bring their best finished products to the table. Technology companies need to be familiar with your business needs and not trying to learn your business in order to create programs to sell to you. There are many off-the-shelf technology companies that can add to the success of your business immediately without recreating the world. Seek and you will find.

1. INTRODUCTION

Since the early stages of commerce, merchants have wrestled with determining the *best* approach to delivering their products and services to the marketplace for purchase and consumption. The area of global distribution is one of the most complex aspects of the hospitality business and an area that has been greatly impacted by technology change with the rise of new channels or sales outlets. The term **global distribution** can be defined in this case as attaining the broadest possible reach to the largest available audience meeting a company's target market segments at the most affordable cost and with the highest potential for winning conversion (i.e., generating bookings). It is all about selling the right products and services to the right guests at the right times and prices under the right set of circumstances in ways that are convenient to guests (Stein and Sweat, 1998). When booking hotel and resort accommodations, consumers have many choices, both in terms of product selection and in terms of the tools they use to search for, research, and purchase their accommodations (see Figure 8-1). While clearly a marketing function, global

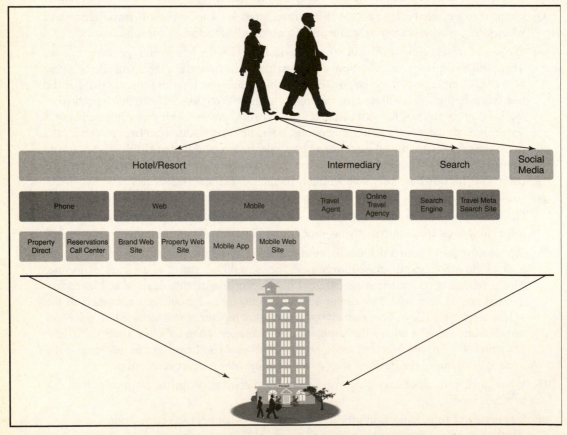

FIGURE 8-1   Common Channels Used When Booking Lodging Accommodations

distribution is completely reliant upon sophisticated information technology (IT) and is continuously being reshaped as new technologies, Internet developments, and mobile applications emerge. The marketing and IT teams need to work in tandem to deploy technologies that will aid the business in growing and capturing more market share. With new channels come new ways for customers to shop for and book their lodging accommodations and, hence, new ways for marketers to reach, interact with, and serve customers or guests. Because there are a series of tradeoffs among reach, richness, cost, and effectiveness or conversion (Evans and Wurster, 1999), it is challenging to determine the best distribution methods for each targeted customer segment. What a difference there is in today's distribution process and global economy from those our forefathers experienced when the concept of commerce first emerged! Thus, distribution is an area with some of the greatest opportunities to develop strategic advantages and drive revenues.

Until recently, hotel and resort distribution was characterized by philosophies like "location, location, location" or "if you build it, they will come." Unfortunately, these tend to overshadow more rational approaches to selecting distribution channels and applying IT to broaden visibility and win market share. Moreover, these traditional philosophies, by themselves, are no longer sufficient in attracting today's sophisticated and demanding consumers. Within the lodging industry, the area of distribution has become far too complex and costly to be treated with such simplicity. Because distribution costs can be as high as 35 percent of room revenue (Estis Green, 2008), it makes sense for organizations to pay attention, develop effective distribution strategies, and manage their channels carefully to maximize results. In some cases (often in larger chains), we see a new position emerging called **channel manager**. This person, working closely with the revenue manager or revenue management team, oversees all of the different distribution channels used; makes sure content, rates, availability information, and selling rules and restrictions are up to date in each channel; and verifies whether each channel is properly representing his or her portfolio of properties.

The thrusts of distribution are market reach and penetration, branding, merchandising, and revenue generation. Supporting the global distribution function is a **global distribution system** (**GDS**), that, in effect, has become the circulatory system of the lodging organization (Estis Green, 2008). For the purposes of this chapter, we define GDS in the broadest possible sense. It is the entire network of people, systems, technology, and distribution channels that are used to help lodging providers sell their products and services. Given this scope, the GDS can be considered to be an ecosystem of sorts (see Figure 8-2). The primary focus has been on guestroom sales or reservations

FIGURE 8-2 The GDS Ecosystem

for individual and group travel, but attention is expanding into other areas such as meeting rooms, restaurant reservations, spa treatments, golf tee times, and more. A company's GDS must support two primary objectives. First, it must provide distribution channels that allow customers the ability to easily and quickly search for products and services they are willing to purchase with full (i.e., transparent) disclosure of rates and availability (what is often termed seamless, **single-image inventory**), and second, it must provide a means to conveniently conduct the transaction on the spot, with immediate confirmation that the transaction has been successfully completed.

To achieve these objectives, a GDS requires a clear strategy, dedicated resources, effective management, and a sound IT infrastructure. These are necessary in order to provide competitive advantage—and it can with access to new customers, better and faster service, sophisticated rate and inventory management, economies of scale, reduced overhead, lower transaction costs, enhanced buyer and supplier relationships, **cross-selling** (selling complementary products such as spa, golf tee times, restaurant reservations) and **up-selling** (room upgrades and packages), unique capabilities, and superior channel performance.

Generally, a GDS (or some part of a GDS) is the first point of all guest contact; it is also the initial and oftentimes primary source of data collection. Important guest data regarding one's stay (e.g., dates of stay, room preferences, payment information) are then used in downstream services and guest interactions (e.g., guest registration). Therefore, it is one of the most important technologies in a lodging company's IT portfolio. Remember, it is all about the guest experience and relationships with guests. Hotels and resorts must own these interaction points to collect the necessary data needed to create exemplary and memorable service experiences and build brand loyalty. A GDS is also one of the most complex components of a hotel or resort company's IT portfolio due to its technological sophistication, the complicated business logic and rules embedded in its applications, the numerous interfaces that must be supported to connect heterogeneous systems together to share data (both within the company and with the outside world), the volume of transactions and speed by which they must be processed, the uniqueness of room inventory and attributes across a lodging chain, individual guest needs, and the sophistication of the underlying database and search engine that powers it.

Within the lodging industry, distribution channels are being reshaped as the result of technological advancements, new and emerging players, and a shift in the balance of power among suppliers, buyers, and intermediaries. At the same time, the corresponding costs associated with technological investment and transaction processing are rising due to the complex networks and technological infrastructure (e.g., two-way interfaces) required and the sophisticated applications that must be in place to support seamless, single-image inventory across the spectrum of distribution channels that exist today and that will soon exist in the future. Complicating matters, executives have few tools and little guidance to help them determine when to invest, how much to invest, and how to assess or gauge the business value to be gained from the investment. Consequently, this is an important area of study requiring shrewd and decisive decision making due to the strategic positioning implications and the high costs of doing business in today's competitive industry environment.

It is important for hoteliers to consider the strategic implications of using certain distribution channels while avoiding others. Consider, for example, discount airline company Southwest Airlines and how it has intentionally chosen to limit the number of distribution channels used to sell its tickets to keep costs low and pass along savings to its customers. The company educates its customers on how and where to book its flights in order to get the best available fares. In doing so, it is actively seeking to drive consumers to its Web site, the least distribution channel with the lowest overhead. Southwest Airlines' approach seems bold and is vastly different from the strategies employed by many hotel and resort companies, but it works well and contributes greatly to the success of the company. For hotels and resorts, a broad net is often cast in efforts to be everywhere the competition is and everywhere they are likely to find their target customers. Distribution channels are considered to be like retail store shelf space. Using this metaphor, the prevailing philosophy by many hoteliers is that more is better; more shelves carrying one's products will result in more purchases. While this seems logical on the surface, the corresponding costs associated with technological investment and transaction processing necessitate greater focus on better, proactive distribution channel selection, management, and assessment. Thus, it is important to use a disciplined approach to channel selection and have a strong measurement program in place to measure effectiveness of each channel used. Measurement should include traffic and conversion rates, volume of reservations booked, distribution and customer acquisition costs, revenue, profitability, and repeat usage. Marketing and distribution strategies and measurement programs will help to determine how best to target one's distribution channel selection. The sections that follow will discuss the strategic significance of hotel/resort GDS. It will explore the many components of GDS, developments and trends in the distribution arena, and the importance of developing a **distribution strategy** to create competitive advantage.

2. IMPORTANCE OF GDS

As previously stated, the objective of a GDS is to distribute a company's products (in this case, hotel/resort guestroom inventory or meeting space) to as broad an audience as possible but in the most effective and cost-efficient means available so that they can be purchased. More specifically, the roles played by a GDS have evolved over time—from one of transaction-based emphasis to one of strategic value—but at any one point in time, a GDS fulfills five important roles, as illustrated in Figure 8-3 and described in the following.

The first role of a GDS is one of simple utility: transaction processing and maintaining, controlling, and reporting room inventory levels and hotel/resort rates. Initially, a GDS provided

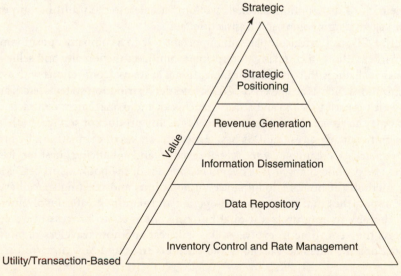

FIGURE 8-3 The Many Roles of a GDS

a simple accounting of rooms available versus rooms sold at predetermined rates, generally set by each hotel/resort for some defined period of time (e.g., seasonal rates). Over time, this function has expanded in complexity and strategic importance as more emphasis has been placed on yield management to maximize a property's total revenue. Now, this function is responsible for the definition of room pools and rate categories, the allocation of rooms, and the rules and restrictions that govern the sale of these rooms. The system must support all decision-making regarding the setting of rates, the allocation of rooms, and the rules and restrictions. The system must then communicate this information to all points of distribution in real time, enforcing all the rules when a room is reserved or cancelled.

In its second role, a GDS plays an important function as a data repository and a learning system for guest history, preference, profiles, and buying patterns. This system is one of the primary collection points of valuable guest-related information and preferences. The value of the stored data increases with each subsequent guest encounter[1] and from data mining used to help a company in developing, positioning, and marketing its products and services. Because of the data collected, this system becomes an important feed to other core systems, including a company's property management system and data warehouse which then enable a company to improve guest recognition, the customization of guest experiences, product positioning, and new service developments and product offerings.

Its third function is that of a communications vehicle. It disseminates vital information regarding inventory availability, rates (including rules and restrictions), and hotel property information as well as guest profile data to various points of distribution and service delivery in real time for access by all service associates to allow them to better perform their jobs, recognize their guests, and personalize the guest experience.

Fourth, a GDS represents a source of revenue, not just in terms of room-nights or meeting sales generated and revenue maximization through yield management but also through fees charged for participation and for transactions processed. An effective GDS and skilled channel management will be key success factors, provide competitive advantage, and influence firm profitability. Since the cost of distribution can easily reach 35 percent of a room's daily rate (Estis Green, 2008), effective management is essential to containing overhead. Mismanagement of distribution channels will only accelerate the profit margin erosion that results from agent commissions and transaction fees.

Finally, a GDS is strategic. It plays an important role in a company's positioning, provides access to markets, allows a company to implement unique functionality and selling strategies, builds strategic alliances through **interorganizational systems** (connections with systems from other organizations such as airline GDSs, OTAs, Internet distribution systems, etc.), and provides a product which is used to sell to and attract franchisees and management contracts.

GDSs play a critical role in the sales process of any product or service. In the hospitality industry, significant advances in GDSs have raised the stakes of competition by providing access to more markets, creating new sources of revenue, and enhancing guest service (Connolly and Moore, 1995) while changing the overall economics of the booking process. More importantly, the methods of booking lodging accommodations and meeting space have shifted to alternative approaches that are cheaper to operate and require greater involvement from the customer, thereby freeing up traditional booking channels to process more complicated scenarios. As they continue to evolve, GDSs will reshape how travelers plan and arrange accommodations for personal vacations and business trips and how hotel/resort companies

---

[1] Kirsner (1999) terms this interactive, iterative learning process *progressive profiling*.

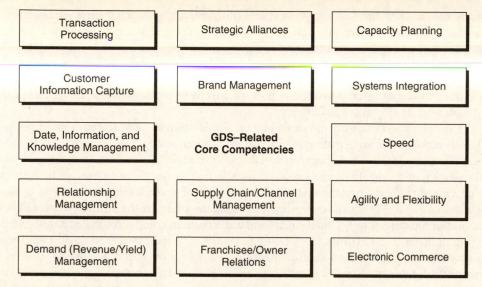

FIGURE 8-4 GDS-Related Core Competencies Essential for Competitive Advantage

interact with their customers. Without question, a GDS is a mission-critical application, and quite possibly, the lifeline of the organization. Any disruptions in service can severely inconvenience, if not cripple, a hotel or entire lodging company.

It can be said that a GDS is the cornerstone for the service delivery process in a hotel or resort and for all property-based technology. Yet, one should not consider a GDS as a single system or entity. Rather, it is a collection of systems, technologies, telecommunications, people, and strategies, that, when coupled, provide an effective means of marketing and selling a hotel's guestrooms, meeting space, and other facilities. In most cases, it is the initial and principal data collection point that, in turn, feeds information to all other aspects of the organization and all subsequent processes in the guest lifecycle (namely, registration, in-house services, guest history, post-stay follow-up, and ongoing marketing efforts). Without a well-integrated GDS, functions like marketing, customer relationship building, data mining, revenue (yield) management, and labor forecasting, to name a few, would be severely handicapped—if not impossible to do.

The world of GDS is highly complex and requires that hospitality organizations master a number of competencies if they are to be successful in this arena. Hamel and Prahalad (1994) stress the strategic importance of **core competencies** and competency-building to achieve competitive advantage. The core competencies required of hotel and resort companies with respect to distribution channels and GDS are included in Figure 8-4. Essentially, competitive advantage stems from excellence in and mastery of several key areas, including technology development and deployment, supply chain management, customer relationship building, knowledge management, electronic commerce, speed, agility, and flexibility.

3. DEVELOPING A DISTRIBUTION CHANNEL STRATEGY

Being able to successfully manage something and invest in it requires complete understanding of precisely what it is one is trying to manage and how best to allocate firm resources to it. Alternatively stated, one must fully comprehend the concept of global distribution channels in today's context and have the ability to forecast where they are headed in order to select the appropriate channels and technologies to build competitive methods. Effective management of, investment in, and resource allocations to GDSs and their ensuing channels will result in improvements to a hotel's or resort's profitability on two fronts: decreased costs and improved revenues. The fundamental principle at work here is that if a property or lodging company can effectively exploit its distribution channels, it can gain market share through increased sales while simultaneously reducing overhead. Both go directly to the bottom line, thereby improving profitability and competitive advantage.

A distribution strategy does not require participation in all channels but should be able to articulate rationale for participating in those that are chosen and for electing not to participate in others (Dombey, 1997). The rising costs and the sheer number of distribution channels available make participation in all channels prohibitive and unnecessary due to overlap in customers served. One of the best illustrations in the travel industry of strategic choices and resource allocations related to GDS is Southwest Airlines, mentioned earlier. In the airline industry, it is not uncommon for airlines to list their flights and availability in competitor systems. Just as in the lodging industry, these airlines pay a booking fee for each reservation booked in addition to ongoing fees for participation and flight listings. To reduce overhead, Southwest Airlines has consciously decided not to participate in all airline GDSs and available travel distribution channels. Southwest is able to make these types of decisions because it understands its customer base and knows how best to reach its targeted audience. Perhaps this is why Southwest Airlines remains one of the most profitable airlines in the industry. These are precisely the same kinds of decisions hotels and lodging companies must make—but only after customer booking habits, market share, and other variables are better understood.

As transactional costs continue to rise, hotels and resorts will need to determine which channels are most profitable for them and how they can yield the best results using these channels. This may mean discontinuing channels that are less productive or ones that cost more to maintain in favor of channels that yield greater room revenue and require less overhead to operate. The focus will be placed on distribution share per channel (i.e., the marketing mix or the amount of volume and revenue generated by each channel in the GDS network in comparison with the others to which an organization subscribes or in which it participates). More does not necessarily mean better. Another focus will be on how the winning systems match customers with lodging providers (Olsen, 1996). With a growing number of hotel and resort products and suitable alternatives, it becomes increasingly difficult to discern one property from the next. It also becomes harder to get the consumer's attention, since he or she is bombarded with an array of options, many of which may seemingly appear to be equally attractive. Therefore, it will be incumbent upon leading systems and GDS providers to find ways to rise above the noise and convert lookers into bookers.

Finding and Competing for Electronic Shelf Space

Gaining a presence in multiple points of distribution is analogous to finding shelf space in a grocery or retail store. More is generally considered better because it improves visibility, customer access, and convenience. Yet, this is not always the best strategy due to the cost implications and support issues associated with maintaining multiple channels. When applying the principles of organizational economics theory, it is easier to see that more is not always better. Each distribution channel has associated with it certain fixed costs, which may include hardware, software, and interface development. Depending upon the channel, these fixed costs may be quite high. To achieve transactional economies of scale, the volume of transactions (reservations) must increase if the average cost per reservation is to decrease. Hence, adding a new distribution channel may destroy this relationship. It has two effects. First, it requires a fixed investment in order to make the channel operational, and second, it will likely reduce the volume of reservations processed via the other, established channels. Both consequences increase average costs and prolong the amount of time it takes to recover the initial investment (Clemons, Reddi, and Row, 1993). This is only desirable if (1) the new distribution channel is more cost-effective than other channels and can shift enough volume to recoup the initial investment, and (2) the new distribution channel attracts untapped markets and generates new demand. Otherwise, it may be more advantageous to have fewer distribution channels. What is difficult to measure in this scenario, however, is the degree to which a channel influences the booking decision even though it may not be the actual source of the booking.

Lodging firms must make a strategic commitment to GDSs. This implies defining, developing, and implementing a strategy as well as investing in the corresponding technology to support this strategy. No longer can one afford to gratuitously spend money on marketing or distribution channels without knowing the appropriate target markets and anticipating the expected returns. To help hoteliers develop a global distribution strategy and evaluate various distribution channel options, a list of criteria has been provided in Figure 8-5.

Cost Implications

For lodging companies, connectivity to airline GDSs has been costly and problematic but necessary if they want to take advantage of the travel agent market, worldwide. The challenges of displaying detailed property information in an easy-to-use format and synchronizing databases in real time add to the administrative burdens of managing a GDS. In particular, the delays in transmission between airline GDSs and a hotel/resort GDS, the batching of transactions, and the processing of error messages that result from incompatibilities between different systems create a cumbersome queuing process that must be closely monitored to avoid overbooking and to ensure that reservations are received at the property level before guests arrive. Manual and semi-automated processes also rely extensively on queues. Oftentimes, dedicated staffs are required to manage these queues. While improvements in airline GDS/lodging GDS interfaces help to alleviate the situation, they unfortunately do not completely eliminate the problems from occurring; and hence the queuing process still exists. Despite these shortcomings, hotels and resorts are dependent upon the airline GDSs because of their extensive market reach, not only to travel agents but also to Internet booking channels. Airlines recognized early on the value of the travel agent network (see Copeland and McKenney, 1988). To maximize travel agent bookings, airlines helped automate travel agents by providing easy access to their mainframe-based reservation systems. These relationships proved fruitful for the airlines and quickly became a source of competitive advantage. For lodging companies to realize some of the same benefits as airlines in terms of access to the travel agency networks, they needed to list their properties in each of the major airline GDSs. Today, these GDSs help to further distribute lodging accommodations to various online channels. However, with advances in technology, new solutions have been coming to market, weakening the stronghold airline GDSs have enjoyed heretofore. These technology advances, while welcome, add to the complexity of the distribution landscape and make this a dynamic and exciting space.

To participate in this listing service is a costly endeavor. Hotels and resorts must pay listing fees and transaction costs for every reservation booked. Additionally, hotels and resorts are responsible for the information displayed about their facilities, rates, and availability. To maintain this information, the large lodging chains invested heavily in the development of interfaces between their GDSs and the airline GDSs. These interfaces are not only costly to develop but also

Can the new distribution channel:

- Gain access to new markets and new customers to drive top-line revenues?
- Strengthen customer relations and build lasting loyalty?
- Provide incremental bookings and revenue?
- Improve yield through rate lift or increases in average daily rate (ADR), occupancy rate, and revenue per available room (REVPAR)?
- Create switching costs?
- Build barriers to entry?
- Offer unique and sustainable advantages?
- Merchandise the property and adequately and appropriately convey its best features and value?
- Yield better information that can be used for competitive advantage or for creating or enhancing products and services?
- Provide easy and convenient access to single-image inventory and last-room availability?
- Be easily updated with rate changes, selling rules, restrictions, etc.?
- Be easily integrated into the company's global distribution network and managed on an ongoing basis?
- Streamline or simplify the technological complexity or management of existing distribution channels?
- Reduce the number distribution channels required?
- Eliminate potential points of failure and third-party intermediaries?
- Provide economies of scale?
- Reduce customer acquisition costs?
- Reduce operating costs or transaction fees and shift traffic to a channel of lower cost?
- Eliminate duplication?
- Change the balance of power in customer or supplier relationships?
- Alter the basis of competition or change the nature of intra-industry competitive rivalries?
- Enable new business opportunities?
- Track sources of origination for each reservation?
- Protect customer data and ensure privacy?
- Allow the hotel/resort to maintain the locus of control over room inventory and rates?
- Support multiple formats of content (i.e., text, graphics, sound, video, etc.)?

FIGURE 8-5 Distribution Channel Evaluation Criteria

costly to maintain. They require constant updating due to the dynamism of the airline GDS market and recent changes in the lodging industry. For example, the implementation of revenue management systems in many of the large chains resulted in thousands of price updates each day to the airline GDSs. Needless to say, the high costs and complexity of these interfaces put them out of reach of many smaller chains and independent hotels and resorts. This resulted in a definite disadvantage with respect to their representation in the marketplace by external sales agents (e.g., travel agents). The gap between the technology haves and the have-nots became evident. The Internet and the rise of alternative distribution systems (ADSs) have helped to give smaller entities and independents some of the same capabilities enjoyed by chains, thereby leveling the playing field.

Hoteliers should consider the role IT can play in building and supporting distribution channels and the subsequent economics of these channels, which include the total cost of ownership (TCO), operation, and maintenance for each point of distribution. Understanding and controlling this cost structure can be a valuable source of competitive advantage. Many of the interfaces between systems are costly to develop, maintain, and operate—especially for small properties and lodging companies, which cannot achieve the same economies of scale of their larger competitors. Because larger companies can share or leverage costs over more properties or rooms, they tend to achieve cost advantages more easily than smaller properties and independents. Initial interface development can cost as low as a few thousand dollars to as much as tens of thousands of U.S. dollars per interface, depending on the systems architecture, complexity of the interface, and the functionality. Although organizations like the OpenTravel Alliance (*www.opentravel.org*) and the Hotel Electronic Distribution Network Association (*www.hedna.org*) along with open systems and better standards have helped to improve connectivity between many of the technologies involved in distribution, the costs remain high. Therefore, hoteliers must estimate the value and strategic importance of each interface before embarking on its development. The ongoing support and maintenance costs must also be factored into the decision. Because the core technologies comprising the GDS environment are subject to frequent modification to keep up with market demands, these interfaces require constant monitoring and updating. Many properties and small lodging companies cannot afford the dedicated resources and lack the technical knowledge base to make these enhancements and modifications. Instead, they either choose not to participate in certain distribution channels, compromise the degree of integration, or outsource these services and become subject to the terms and service levels of their contractual arrangements with a chosen vendor. All of these decisions have strategic consequences.

The costs assigned to each channel vary and are typically based on prenegotiated volumes. Some channels require fixed fees in addition to transaction fees. Transaction fees are generally based on net bookings (i.e., reservations booked less cancellations), but in some rare cases, a transaction may be defined as any database query or inquiry (i.e., availability check or address look-up). Approximate average costs (in U.S. dollars) for a single reservation are as follows:

- Travel agent or intermediary commission: 10 to 15 percent of the total room revenue
- Airline GDS fee: $10 to $15
- Universal switch: $1 to $3
- Hotel/resort CRS: $10 to $15
- Hotel/resort Web site: $2 to $5

As mentioned before, these costs quickly accumulate and can represent reportedly as much as 35 percent of a hotel or resort's daily room rate (Estis Green, 2008). Consider a simple example in which a guestroom sells for U.S. $200. If the reservation is made through a travel agent accessing an airline GDS that transfers the reservation to the hotel/resort CRS via a universal switch, the cost of the transaction could be as high as U.S. $75. Demonstrably, the profit margin erosion is real. Therefore, it behooves a hotel or resort to direct reservations traffic to those channels that are able to meet its distribution needs but at lower operating costs. Offering special incentives such as price breaks, room upgrades, lowest price guarantees, and frequent travel bonus points can and often does influence consumer behavior. Any time a cost can be avoided, the bottom line performance can be improved. Because not all organizations operate on the same level of efficiency, opportunities exist to gain competitive advantage for those hotels or lodging companies that can optimize their distribution channels by reducing overhead. Remember, it's not just about revenue. It's about profitability—what gets converted to the bottom line counts.

The reservations booking process is just one type of exchange or transaction in the guest lifecycle. The costs in the process are a direct result of the channels and technology used, the relationship a hotel or lodging company has with each channel provider, the support structure of the organization, and the volume of transactions. Using this paradigm, it becomes possible to rethink the booking channels using a new set of lenses. A whole new set of possibilities and implications can result. For example, in the future, an interesting dimension to the revenue management equation may emerge: how to yield by distribution channel or by profitability versus yielding by revenue. Which channel or channels of distribution used by guests will depend on a number of factors including, but not limited to, familiarity and comfort level with the channel and service provider, complexity of the reservation, perceived risk, travel policies imposed by an employer, and so on. If hotels and resorts can segment their customer base by channels, they can potentially eliminate channels that are unnecessary. They can also work to enhance the functionality of lower-cost channels to meet the needs of their guests.

Understanding Share of Distribution

It is important for practitioners to consider which distribution channels will be most advantageous to them and subscribe or participate in only those channels. One of the common questions raised is "To which channels should a company subscribe?" A commonly held belief is that more channels lead to higher visibility, which, in turn, generates more demand. This may not always be the case. The quality of these channels and their links to the GDS must also be considered. The question regarding which channels to offer is becoming more prevalent in light of the many new distribution channels that are forming as a result of the Internet. The answer to this question is likely to vary from company to company and market to market. Each company must understand the sources of its business and the cost to acquire business through each of the distribution channels. Each channel has distinct costs; some are easily measurable such as transaction costs. Others are more intangible; for example, the cost to provide information to answer a guest inquiry that may or may not lead to a guest booking. To gain an advantage in this competitive marketplace, one must think intelligently about how resources are allocated so as to achieve an appropriate economic return. With respect to global distribution channels, this can be achieved only if a property or lodging company understands from where its business comes, how its distribution channels are used, how they contribute to the bottom line (this includes occupancy as well as profitability), and what the costs are to operate each channel.

When marketing professionals select media or places in which to advertise, they are advised to consider the medium and its targeted audience and compare them with the profiles of their customer base. The same must be done when considering investment in distribution channels. In addition, when selecting distribution channels, one should determine what reach the channel has, its visibility, the level of marketing provided by the channel operator, and the services that front-end this channel. This equates to broader distribution and visibility. For example, being part of an airline GDS has a profound reach. An airline GDS provides product representation to anyone or any service with access to that GDS, thus extending the potential audience for a given hotel or resort. When determining which distribution channels to subscribe and in which databases to market their product(s), hoteliers cannot ignore the reach of each channel and the popularity of its database. If the database is front-ended by a number of services, such as those found on the Internet, there is no need to join each service independently. Services such as Expedia and Travelocity provide access to numerous products and extend that access to numerous service providers. As these services promote their own Web sites, they indirectly promote the products they sell and thus, increase the likelihood that consumers will find a given hotel/resort without that property incurring additional marketing costs for such publicity. In summary, when selecting distribution channels, one should select them carefully and choose those that will provide the most value for the investment.

The advantage of distribution channels versus traditional advertising is that more information can be captured regarding its impact and use via booking statistics, call volumes, and other traffic or usage monitoring. These statistics are not always available for unidirectional forms of media. It is important to note that not all channels provide equal value and that some consumers use multiple channels when researching and purchasing lodging accommodations. In some cases, distribution channels may be redundant, in other cases, they may complement one another. As such, one cannot ignore the **look-to-book ratio** (i.e., the number of people who shop versus the number of people who actually make or book reservations). It is also important to consider the fact that channel usage can vary by market segment, accommodations needed, purpose of travel, or comfort level.

Maintaining Inventory Control: A Daunting Challenge

The challenge for hotels and resorts will be to manage and control the multiple entities that make up their GDS network, even when they do not fall under the current domain of control. In a virtual world, organizations must be willing to relinquish some of their control or sovereignty in favor of a shared destiny with other organizations comprising the Internet-worked enterprise (Davidow and Malone, 1992; Tapscott and Caston, 1993). Working in a virtual world requires trust among the partners. Chesbrough and Teece (1996) offer an interesting discussion regarding the management of virtual organizations. In particular, they suggest understanding the relationships between each entity in the network and how it impacts change and innovation. Underestimation of systemic versus autonomous innovation could stifle an organization and prevent it from making desirable changes to gain new market advantages. In cases of systemic change, hotels and resorts must maintain strategic leverage and coordination over the participating partners in their distribution network. Otherwise, the change will fail to come to fruition as planned.

According to research sponsored by the International Hotel and Restaurant Association (IH&RA), a property's loss of control over its guestroom inventory was cited as a major concern by industry executives (Olsen, 1996). Some control has shifted from lodging suppliers to those that own or manage the distribution channels and to those that can aggregate volume to negotiate and secure substantial discounts. With the rise in social media and online consumer reviews, consumers are finding and using their voices to gain control. Many hoteliers feel helpless because of the speed by which these reviews travel, the number of people that read them, and the potential impact that they can have. Anecdotal comments from interviews with hospitality executives suggest eight additional reasons why hoteliers feel the loss of control over their own inventory. These include (1) inadequate GDS technology infrastructure, (2) inventory and rate management issues, (3) commissions and transaction fees erode profit margins, (4) the rise in number of electronic intermediaries, (5) a shift in balance of power from supplier to customer, (6) new models of distribution and pricing, (7) accelerated rates of change, and (8) relinquished control of the customer relationship. Each of these factors is discussed next.

Inadequate GDS Technology Infrastructure

The first reason relates to the GDS technology infrastructure. Quite frankly, many hotels and resorts do not have the necessary technology and information systems in place to support the selling process from multiple locations via different channels and systems. Lacking last-room availability and seamless access to the property's rates and availability create hardships and add to the overall level of frustration. Those that are considered more advanced are still not state of the art. The industry's software and systems lack many of the functions required to support the industry's future directions. It is as if the software has put a stranglehold on the industry and given rise to a host of opportunities for outside players.

Inventory and Rate Management Issues

The second explanation is somewhat related to the first. It has to do with a hotel's/resort's ability to control its rates and availability using the principles of revenue (yield) management. Many properties accept commissionable or discounted reservations when it is possible for them to fill these rooms with higher-rated and/or noncommissionable business. Because many hotels and resorts lack the systems to set the appropriate restrictions and the technology to communicate these restrictions to each distribution channel, they find themselves taking business that they would otherwise consider turning down. This business is displacing more desirable, profitable opportunities.

Commissions and Transaction Fees Erode Profit Margins

The third interpretation as to why hoteliers feel a sense of lost control is the rise in new booking channels that require commissions and subscription fees from hotels and resorts. In many cases, hoteliers are not even familiar with these channels, and as the result of onward distribution (where airline GDSs pass on property rates and availability information to third-party booking entities typically found on the Internet), they cannot always track the source of origination of a reservation (Dombey, 1997). A hotel or resort selects a channel to help represent its products and service offerings. That channel then subscribes to a wider network of its own, giving the products and services it represents broader distribution and visibility; thereby creating a much broader, virtual network for the hotel or resort. When a reservation is booked in this broader network, a hotel or resort cannot always tell from where the booking initiated and all of the entities that had a hand in the process.

Typical payment models used in the distribution process include the following:

- *Commission-based agency model*—The agent or booking entity receives a commission (typically 10 to 15 percent of the daily room rate) or flat fee for rooms booked.
- *Merchant or wholesale model*—A booking service negotiates room rates with a hotel or resort in advance of sale. These are called **net rates**. It is then free to mark up the rates. The difference between what it charges and what it must pay the hotel or resort is its payment for service.
- *Opaque pricing model*—This approach is used by services like *Priceline.com* and *Hotwire.com*. It allows hotels and resorts to discount rates while shielding their brand identities and maintain rate integrity. Guests make purchase decisions based primarily on price and location without knowing the service provider until after completing the booking transaction and committing to the purchase. This is a common way for hotels and resorts to sell distressed inventory at the last minute.
- *Auctions*—There are a number of Web sites that sell hotel and resort accommodations using a traditional auction model in which guests bid on rooms or a reverse auction model in which rates gradually decline until someone makes a purchase.
- *Pay per click*—A referral fee is commonly charged by travel meta search sites like Kayak.com, Hipmunk, and Mobissimo, which generate leads and connects them with travel suppliers' Web sites to complete their booking transactions. Some prefer to use the term cost per click instead of pay per click.

Rise in Number of Electronic Intermediaries

The fourth possible explanation results from the rise in number of intermediaries in the selling process, especially as seen on the Internet. While it is a commonly held belief that **disintermediation** will result as new electronic paths are built between the customer and supplier to create a more direct link, this thinking only applies to travel agents. The reality is that, in this digital age, the number of electronic intermediaries is increasing with greater seamlessness to both the customer and the supplier. Consider, for example, travel **meta search** engines like Kayak, Hipmunk, and Mobissimo. These search engine Web sites search and compare multiple travel sites to help consumers find the lowest rates and fares. On the surface, they look might look or sound like an online travel agency, but they don't actually transact or fulfill the booking. They provide comparison-shopping services that then electronically link consumers with online providers who can transact the business. When a customer clicks on a link, he or she is redirected to a landing page within the booking process for the entity offering the product and price selected. These new electronic intermediaries match customer demand with products and services available for purchase. They are the information brokers operating on a pay per click compensation model; they earn revenue every time a consumer clicks on a listing. They can also earn revenue through sponsorship and advertising.

It is important to remember that each node in the distribution process, human or electronic, represents a potential point of service failure and a potential expense, typically a charge per transaction. Therefore, knowledge of and management of these players is critical. However, since intermediaries fall outside the traditional span of control of a lodging provider and since they are further removed from the primary source of information, it is difficult to motivate these resources to sell a particular brand or product and to educate them on how best to sell that brand or product. There is also greater potential for service delivery errors and misinforming guests due to incomplete information or general lack of knowledge. This is especially true when these intermediaries are less familiar with the products (i.e., lodging accommodations, facilities, and destinations) they are selling. The quality and timeliness of service delivered by these intermediaries can impact a guest's overall perception of the destination hotel or resort, either positively or negatively. It is that latter situation that worries hoteliers most.

Shift in Balance of Power from Supplier to Customer

The fifth explanation for the feeling of lost capacity control by hoteliers relates to a shift in the balance of power between the consumer and the lodging supplier. The balance of power is moving away from the supplier in favor of the consumer. Consumers, armed with knowledge easily obtained from the Internet, develop greater expectations and now demand higher price–value relationships than ever before of any property in which they stay. The tools available via the Internet allow consumers to quickly and effortlessly shop and compare products and services from one company to the next before making a buying decision. They can instantly tap into the many comments (good or bad) of prior visitors and factor this feedback into the selection and decision-making processes. Their efforts are expedited by push technology and smart agents which help to filter out irrelevant or unwanted information, find the best travel bargains, and bring material of interest directly to the consumer's desktop in a manner that is easy to process and digest. This means consumers are now in charge; therefore, lodging properties must create, package, price, and deliver the perfect experience every time. In a digital world, there is no room or forgiveness for error.

New Models of Distribution and Pricing

Another important and related consideration resulting in the feeling of lost capacity control is that many of the newer forms of distribution are changing the model for how guestrooms are bought and sold. As a result, the sales, marketing, and distribution models are being turned on end, creating a new set of dynamics and a playing field. For example, consider smart phone apps (e.g., iPhone and Google Android phones) and Facebook as two emerging booking sources as well as the influence of social media (e.g., consumer reviews) on the booking process. Consequently, hoteliers are uncomfortable because these new tools are ones in which they have little or no experience and ones in which they are slow to embrace. They have also come to realize that they cannot control all of the content or the brand image being communicated. Consumers, on the other hand, love and embrace the new model because it is consumer-centric and affords them control of their own destiny.

Accelerated Rates of Change

The seventh factor is the pace of change. The industry has had a tendency to fear and resist change. This is especially true when the changes being introduced are coming from unfamiliar or unknown sources. As a result, it is difficult to forecast the many changes on the horizon since industry leaders may not be looking in the right places or at the right indicators. By now, the business environment is characterized by the need to do more with less, faster and cheaper than ever before. The cycle time for getting products to market and the number of competitors has heightened the complexity of competition. With technology in general and the Internet in particular growing at phenomenal rates, industry players cannot possibly keep abreast of the latest indicators or determinants of their business. The rules of the game are changing, introducing uncertainty, lack of familiarity, and even fear of the unknown. The resulting anxiety creates that sense of lost control.

Relinquished Control of the Customer Relationship

The final explanation relates less to a property's inventory and more to the customer relationship. In an age of digital distribution, lodging providers are increasingly concerned about losing control over the customer relationship. At a time where one-to-one marketing is paramount to success and winning customers over, lodging providers cannot afford to relinquish any control in the sales process or in customer relationship building. Because of the many distribution channels and intermediaries available and onward distribution, it is often difficult to track consumers, their identity and patterns, and the originating source of the booking. The problem is even more pronounced if the guest is part of a meeting or convention.

Control and management of the customer relationship are being involuntarily relinquished in favor of outside forces such as Google and alternative distribution systems that are now emerging. Hoteliers, in general, seem to lack a vision of where the GDS market is headed and the role technology is having in determining that vision. Hamel and Prahalad (1994) made a similar observation in their research and consulting efforts to help multinational organizations prepare for the future. In the absence of such a long-range view, others, they cautioned, from outside the industry step in and take advantage of an explosive opportunity. The result is less control over inventory, more transaction fees, and higher overhead—not to mention a new set of rules dictated by unfamiliar sources. Early indicators suggest that Google has bigger plans for travel with its recent acquisition of ITA software.

4. TRENDS IN HOTEL AND RESORT GDS

Disintermediation and Reintermediation

Until recently, travel agents had near-exclusive access to information, thus creating an appropriate niche in which to operate. However, the value they provide is diminishing as new, user-friendly tools become available to the general public that offer many of the same capabilities of travel agents. These new tools are providing the general public with full access to information and capabilities that, in years prior, only professional travel agents had enjoyed. At one time, travel booking systems were complex and difficult to use. Users required special training to operate them and interpret the screens and cryptic codes. Today, this is no longer the case. Graphical user interfaces and easy look-up tables have negated the need for specialized knowledge, making it possible for consumers to book their own reservations without relying on travel agents.

Automation of the GDS enterprise gives rise to the notion of disintermediation (i.e., the elimination of middlemen) and the thought that a flatter, less complex network could exist. Disintermediation reduces the value chain to its most efficient state (Davis, 1987). Do-it-yourself technologies are making the elimination of middlemen possible and are bringing consumers and service providers closer together.

For the hospitality and travel industries, more specifically, the focus has been on the elimination of travel agents and the role that they play as intermediaries. Instead, these services can be replaced by IT. Although it is true that automation can eliminate the role of middlemen, in many cases, sometimes, these middlemen provide invaluable services and provide them cheaper than can be done internally. This is why outsourcing many functions has become so popular.

The Internet, as vast as it is, is creating just as many intermediaries as it displaces. For example, buyers need help in finding sellers and wading through the vast amount of information available. Search engines came to the rescue to provide this service. Through increased competition and greater consumer needs, these engines will be refined and become more focused and more powerful. As markets become more segmented and specialized, new players emerge to fill in and bridge gaps. Future intermediaries will add value and save time through their adeptness at transforming information into usable knowledge and subsequently providing services and convenience as a result of the knowledge gained. In an information world, it will be this new knowledge that will provide the currency of tomorrow. Mega portals formed through intra- and inter-industry alliances for one-stop shopping and aggregators will provide value through brand recognition, trust, convenience, and access to specially discounted rates that can only be provided through them.

Digital Divide

Because of the many facets of GDS and the complexities involved, hoteliers must consider GDS as more than just the reservations booking process or the company's CRS. It is much broader in scope with far-reaching implications. Competitive advantage will be derived less from the gap between the technology haves and the have-nots and more from the bipolarization that results between those who know-how versus those who know-not. This distinction is far less subtle than might appear. It is about who can effectively manage its distribution channels to yield the best results.

True, there will be gaps in what one company can afford versus another, with economies of scale favoring the larger chains. However, with many facets of the GDS technology readily available on the open market at affordable prices or accessible via outsourcing, the gap between the technology haves and the have-nots becomes very small. Therefore, the advantage will be in knowing how best to make use of this technology. This includes finding cost-effective uses as well as creating new ways to grow market share and build customer loyalty. The ultimate value will be in converting information into knowledge that then results in improved business performance, as demonstrated by the company's financials and market statistics. This can be realized only if the *right* GDS infrastructure is in place. What is right is subjective and variable by organization because each organization fills unique market needs and sets different goals. There is no one right answer, but there are some definite wrong ones. Furthermore, what is right today will likely change tomorrow, so hoteliers must be flexible and ready to adapt to meet the demands of tomorrow.

Transparency: A Hope for the Future

Many consumers love to shop and love to travel, but increasingly, they don't like to shop for travel. On average, travelers consult at least three, if not more, sources when shopping for lodging accommodations. In doing so, they are often quoted different rates for the same accommodations and dates being shopped. As one can suspect, this is frustrating to the consumer and needlessly consumes his or her time as well as resources for the hotel or resort with booking searches that don't result in converted sales. Therefore, it behooves hotels and resorts to provide seamless integration and single-image inventory with last-room availability and rate parity across distribution channels so the same availability and rate information will be quoted under the same set of travel circumstances. These are service issues and issues of trust. Hotels and resorts should want to discourage their guests from shopping around because in the process of doing so, they might find a better offer from a competitor. Therefore, hoteliers should strive to simplify things and make it easy and convenient for guests to book accommodations with a high degree of trust.

There may come a point in time when focus on the individual components of a GDS is less important. For example, when a person uses the telephone to place a call, he or she does not consider the many linkages and systems that are required in order for that call to be completed with an acceptable level of voice quality. The behind-the-scenes components are completely transparent during the course of the conversation. Within the lodging industry, the service levels and reliability are not to a point in which the various components can be treated as transparent as in the telephone example. Complicating the situation is the number of customer interface options. Since each customer interface represents a critical incident, hotels and resorts must fully understand how to safeguard these opportunities and guarantee unblemished service delivery. Failure to do so will result in a tainted experience for the customer and a blemished image for the organization. The transactional economics of the GDS and its various components and linkages provide another reason that this level of attention and detail is warranted. As long as middlemen are involved, require remuneration for services rendered, and influence or control the process, the components will remain the subject of interest.

Bypassing Airline GDSs

Bypassing traditional airline GDSs during the electronic booking process is becoming more appealing due to the cost-savings that can result. The technology linking travelers directly with suppliers without always having to go through a GDS now exists. Additionally, Internet distribution systems and alternative distribution systems are replacing the need to rely on airline GDSs and providing lodging companies with more cost-effective options to distribute their products and services.

Leveraging Technology to Reduce Overhead

The Internet provides hotels and resorts with many ways to service guests in a more cost-effective way than via the telephone or in person. As a result, hotels and resorts promote self-service and use of the Internet to help guests transact their business needs. There are also other technologies that can be used to help lower overhead. Outrigger Hotels and Resorts and JetBlue turned to the Internet and voice-over-IP (VOIP) technology to enable a home-based agency model rather than a centralized agency/office model. The result has been a lower overhead costs by not having to tie up money in real estate or office rental, power consumption, and so on. Employees also love the flexibility of working from home and their own savings of no commute costs.

United Airlines provides another example of a company deploying voice recognition systems that allow customers to make reservations by speaking in a normal conversational tone to computers. Using this technology, United Airlines is reducing transaction costs per reservation and boosting reservations productivity. The quality of voice recognition systems is improving and the prices of the hardware and software required to support them are declining, making them attractive and viable alternatives for the travel industry and others (e.g., financial services).

Mobile Apps (Applications)

The proliferation of smart phones with broadband access makes mobile apps one of the hottest new development areas. Many travel companies (including lodging providers, OTAs, and meta search engines) have entered this arena with their first wave of applications. As the technology gets better and faster, so will these applications. Companies will continue to seek ways to provide convenience and value-adding services to guests to make it easier to do business with them and to win their loyalty.

Shopping Bots

As technology becomes more advanced, smarter and more user-friendly shopping tools will become available. Many of these tools will function as shopping bots (that is, robotic, computerized agents that will carry out tasks for people) , which will be powered by smart agent technology. Travel meta search engines provide the first wave of these tools. In the future, these tools will have the capability to read a traveler's profile and shop for available travel services and accommodations that match a person's needs and preferences with little to no involvement from a user—and all within a fraction of a second. They will then present a short list of options to the traveler or, if authorized, proceed directly with the booking process. Developments such as these will drastically reshape marketing and how hotels and resorts reach consumers. After all, how can one sell to a robot, a device with no emotion or human feeling? It cannot appreciate the unique attributes and sensual qualities that are presently sold by many hotels and resorts. As these robots catch on, Web site traffic will increase at a faster rate than conversions, creating less favorable look-to-book ratios. The challenge will be to attract these devices, appeal to the criteria they are seeking, create matches, and win the business.

Robotic type of technology can also be deployed by lodging providers. As Bill Peters alluded to in the opening interview, live robotic chat will lead the way, answering most of the customers' questions using a knowledge-based database interfaced both with chat and live voice.

5. Summary

A GDS is one of the most important strategic applications in a lodging firm's IT portfolio due to its revenue-producing potential, role in building customer relationships and serving customers, and the need to focus on reducing costs. It is the cornerstone on which most other hotel/resort applications and services depend. Therefore, lodging executives must focus on this technology, monitor the emerging trends, and carefully chart an appropriate course of action. The rapid change of technology, the capital intensity of IT required to support a GDS, and the number of new distribution options being introduced to the marketplace make managing in this environment difficult, confusing, and seemingly in a constant state of flux.

With tomorrow's leaders aggressively jockeying for position, the GDS arena is clearly in transition. The landscape is vastly changing as a result of consolidation, new technologies, distribution paths, and attempts to restructure the existing channels of distribution (e.g., bypass theories) to reduce the high fixed and variable costs associated with distribution. The future is likely to see major paradigm shifts for the lodging industry, such as revenue management programs that seek to implement dynamic or real-time pricing models (Davis and Meyer, 1998) and optimize by profit rather than by revenue, as is the case today. If hotels and resorts can channel reservations through services that allow them to yield greater contribution margins, they can improve their operating results and enjoy a competitive advantage over those unable to effectively manage their distribution channels.

With rising distribution costs, new channels entering the marketplace, and additional intermediaries gaining access to important customer information, hotel/resort companies must carefully evaluate distribution options, select appropriate partners and channels, and measure and monitor effectiveness (i.e., contributions in terms of *incremental* room-nights and revenues). Where possible, the number of channels should be simplified to ease the management and maintenance of them, to reduce the overlaps, and to reduce overhead costs associated with them.

Hospitality firms must begin to develop a comprehensive distribution strategy. The marketplace is getting too complex with its distribution channel offerings and too costly for companies to serendipitously choose which channels to subscribe. Likewise, it cannot leave these decisions to chance or defensive responses to competitors' moves. Gaining representation in as many channels as possible is a noble goal, but at what cost and at what value?

The dynamics of distribution have changed drastically over the years as a result of segmentation, greater competition, more demanding customers, and now, newer forms of technology. How a hotel/resort company uses a GDS to win sales and marketing advantages, to gain access to new markets, and to build and strengthen customer relationships and how a company ensures effective representation (i.e., presentation of rates, availability, product amenities, etc.) in each channel using the prevailing technologies should become top priorities. The ultimate goal of a GDS strategy should be to fully automate the entire booking process to create a cost-effective, streamlined, and hassle-free guest service that cannot be duplicated by anyone else.

6. Case Study and Learning Activity

Case Study

Understanding distribution—knowing the channels and technology in which to invest and how to effectively use and manage them—is critical to a hotel/resort organization's competitive positioning. This is a complex undertaking that requires constant management and oversight. What follows in an example of how one company is using IT and its distribution channels to gain market advantages. The case is based on an actual company, but some of the names and facts have been changed to protect the identity of the company.

Company Overview

Hotel Eleganté is a global leader and technology innovator in the lodging industry. Its success and reputation, revered by all, are widely chronicled

throughout the industry and in the trade literature. Hotel Eleganté has received numerous accolades for its programs, operations, and facilities, including high industry rankings for its use of and investment in IT. The company enjoys a strong brand image. To many, its name is synonymous with quality, consistency, and attention to detail. Moreover, its employees' commitment to service has become a hallmark of the company's culture and core values, providing a distinct competitive advantage. These tributes notwithstanding, Hotel Eleganté's market position and distribution—in terms of globalization, location, breadth, and size—are esteemed by its competitors.

Hotel Eleganté's customers exhibit a high degree of brand loyalty, due in part to the company's highly successful, multibrand frequent travel (guest loyalty) program. Through an aggressive segmentation strategy, Hotel Eleganté's lodging portfolio spans the entire gamut of the lodging industry's segmentation (i.e., from luxury to limited service) and, with more than a dozen brands, is one of the broadest in the industry. The company likes to think it has the right product for any market location in the world, although some critics would accuse the company of over segmenting the market to the point where brands converge and confuse consumers. Hotel Eleganté's portfolio consists of over 2,000 hotels with more than 330,000 rooms in 55 countries. The company's products typically rank top in their segments in industry surveys, and its growth in earnings per share surpass the industry. In almost all of the segments in which Hotel Eleganté competes, it outperforms the industry when it comes to sales, occupancy rates, and customer preference. The rate premiums the company commands allow its properties to earn higher REVPAR and ADR than industry averages and to outpace inflation rates.

Distribution Strategy

Hotel Eleganté was one of the early players in the industry to embark on electronic distribution. Today, Hotel Eleganté's hotels rank among the most booked properties in each of the major airline GDSs. Since the company introduced its first centralized reservation system in the early 1970s, it has witnessed many changes over the years in electronic distribution and in how hotel companies deliver their products and services to the marketplace. The industry is quite different in terms of the dynamics, competitive threats, and industry cost structure as the result of computers and GDSs. Reminiscing about Hotel Eleganté's original strategy, one company executive remarked of its genuine simplicity and intuitiveness: "In the early days, the goal was obvious: to put inventory in front of as many people as possible to sell it." At the time, an open and close approach to inventory management worked well for managing room inventory in multiple distribution channels, with little need for sophisticated interfaces. Last-room availability and

single-image inventories were not even imagined then, but over time, these concepts have evolved as the company grew and as the logistics became more complex for managing room inventory across multiple properties around the world. They are now critical in today's competitive marketplace and require complex, sophisticated, and costly interfaces.

Several years ago, Hotel Eleganté developed interfaces to SABRE and Galileo, two of the largest airline GDSs. Through the years, these interfaces provided Hotel Eleganté with competitive advantage through first-mover advantages based on evidence collected by the company's marketing department. Over time, however, other hotel companies began copying Hotel Eleganté's moves. This required Hotel Eleganté to invest more to stay ahead of the competition and protect its lead. As the functionality of these interfaces become more complex and as airline GDSs and the company's CRS changed with time, maintaining these interfaces became more challenging and costly.

Hotel Eleganté's philosophy concerning distribution has always been to provide methods or channels that people want to use to book rooms and to provide a set of choices or options so that customers can select the channel best suited to their needs or convenience. In other words, Hotel Eleganté takes a consumer-centric approach. According to one marketing executive at Hotel Eleganté: "Distribution is all about making it easy for our customers to do business with us." In her mind, channel selection must be driven by two key considerations:

1. How customers want to book with Hotel Eleganté.
2. The revenue upside versus the costs of creating, maintaining, and using a distribution channel.

Thus, Hotel Eleganté will enter any distribution channel that is indicative of how its customers want to buy its products rather than try to dictate how its consumers buy its products and services. To this end, Hotel Eleganté will continue to fund distribution channels of higher cost so long as there is sufficient volume to justify their existence. For example, one executive at Hotel Eleganté indicated he would like to eliminate the company's toll-free reservation call centers because they are so costly to operate. However, since a significant number of people prefer this service and channel to others, Hotel Eleganté will continue to offer reservation call centers as a distribution channel, but it will make them as operationally effective as possible.

Over the years, Hotel Eleganté has successfully pursued a two-pronged distribution strategy that involved building relationships and developing loyalty with both consumers and travel agents (or other influencers such as secretaries/administrative assistants). Hotel Eleganté's competitive positioning today can largely be attributed to this strategy. Going forward, Hotel Eleganté's overarching distribution strategy continues to be: "To make it as easy as possible to do business with the company by putting its products and services on as many shelves as possible." It accomplishes this objective by offering:

- A customer-centric sales force capable of selling multiple brands.
- A strong loyalty program and detailed customer profiles to recognize repeat customers and speed the reservations process.
- Superior worldwide toll-free reservation services and event booking centers.
- Easy access to a fast, reliable reservation system through the highest level of connectivity presently available to each of the major airline GDSs.
- Real-time, two-way, seamless links to all its hotels, with single-image inventory and access to last-room availability.
- Cross-selling capabilities between properties and brands.
- A fully functional Web site and presence in most Internet booking sites.
- Help desks and special service counters offering support and assistance to customers and travel agents.

- Strong ties to the travel agent community.
- The company is also evaluating the development of a mobile application for smart phone users and participation in Kayak, a travel meta search engine, and social media applications through Facebook and Twitter.

The company's reservation technology and distribution channels, support infrastructure, and rational pricing strategy simplify the shopping process and add to the guest convenience. Through a simple menu of rates, Hotel Eleganté maintains that there is "a logical and rational reason for every rate offered at every hotel." This approach reduces rate haggling, improves rate integrity, and virtually guarantees that customers will be offered the best available rate given their qualifications, dates of travel, affiliations, and room requests. Rational pricing also ensures that the same rates are offered through any booking channel used by the company.

Protecting Relationships with the Travel Agent Community

Recognizing the important contributions of travel agents in influencing and stimulating travel, Hotel Eleganté has spent years developing and fostering good relationships with the travel agent community. Programs to boost travel agent relations include special service desks, centralized travel agent commissions, familiarization programs, double commission guarantees, access to single-image inventory, last-room availability, and more.

Travel intermediaries presently deliver about 25 percent of all of Hotel Eleganté's room-nights, chain wide. In 2010, Hotel Eleganté reported paying a company record high of U.S. $150 million in travel agent commissions. The company attributed this volume to its reservations and GDS capabilities, its commitment and strong ties to the travel agent community, the quality and breadth of its lodging portfolio, its strong customer service, and its single-image inventory with last-room availability. Because of the significant contributions from the travel agent community, Hotel Eleganté continues to foster relations and develop programs that include, rather than preclude, travel agents. As one executive put it:

> "Even if travel agents influence only 5% of the company's business, this is still a significant chunk of business that cannot be overlooked."

Therefore, Hotel Eleganté is overly cautious about doing anything that might jeopardize relationships or be perceived as a threat or an attempt to undercut travel agents out of fear of losing their business. While the Internet may threaten the role of travel agents, Hotel Eleganté does not see them disappearing—at least not any time soon. Moreover, Hotel Eleganté believes that further consolidation in the travel agency marketplace will create mega-agencies that will carry significant clout, especially in corporate travel where they help companies control travel and entertainment expenses. Thus, building and maintaining healthy travel agent relationships will continue to be important.

While Hotel Eleganté could benefit financially from steering customers away from travel agents in favor of cheaper distribution channels like its Web site, Hotel Eleganté will not promote its Web site in this way or do anything that could be construed as an overt attempt to direct bookings away from travel agents. Instead, it will assume the role of a cautious follower. It would prefer to see some other companies challenge travel agents much in the same way that Delta Air Lines has done in the airline industry. Its efforts, according to one executive, will be covert so as not to "put the mother load at risk." Hotel Eleganté will continue to monitor booking patterns, and as booking volumes shift over time with travel agents—or any other distribution channel, for that matter—Hotel Eleganté will reinvest its resources accordingly to optimize customer access, booking volumes, and revenue and work to facilitate bookings through channels of lower cost.

Future Developments

Moving forward, Hotel Eleganté will continue to explore innovative approaches that make it easier, faster, and cheaper for guests to book rooms at each of its brands. It will continue to look for ways to leverage its size and expertise to build unparalleled competitive advantages while maintaining an interminable commitment to its customers. It will also focus on exploiting Internet, intranet, and extranet technologies to lower costs of distribution and increase booking volumes.

Future developments for hotel GDS will concentrate on functional enhancements, advances in revenue management, content management systems to manage a consistent brand image across various distribution channels, mobile applications for smart phones, sales force automation, decision support tools, and further centralization of meeting space reservations and group reservations. Additionally, capabilities will be expanded to incorporate electronic requests for proposal, better group handling, Internet integration, geo-coding, and cross-selling of properties and brands. Ultimately, the growing number and complexity of distribution channels will require "one-button" rate loading and updating for ease of administration and management.

Learning Activity

1. Critically evaluate Hotel Eleganté's distribution strategy. Is it appropriate? Can you think of any other GDS strategies which Hotel Eleganté might embrace or should be considering in light of emerging technologies?
2. How customer centric is Hotel Eleganté's approach towards distribution?
3. How can Hotel Eleganté evaluate each distribution channel and measure its contribution to its bottom line? Create a measurement scorecard that can be used by company leaders to monitor the performance of each distribution channel.

4. Which distribution channel needs the most attention and why? Does Hotel Eleganté need to be concerned with channel conflict (i.e., one or more channels cannibalizing or taking business away from other channels)?

5. Are travel agents still important to Hotel Eleganté? Going forward, what type of relationship should Hotel Eleganté have with travel agents? What role should they play? Should Hotel Eleganté continue to pay travel agent commissions? Why or why not?

7. Key Terms

Auction

Channel manager

Commission-based agency model

Core competencies

Cross-selling

Disintermediation

Distribution strategy

Global distribution system (GDS)

Inter-organizational system

Look-to-book ratio

Meta search

Merchant or wholesale model

Net rate

Opaque pricing model

Single-image inventory

Up-selling

8. Chapter Questions

1. Discuss the many roles a GDS plays and why it is so important for a hotel company from strategic and marketing perspectives. How can it be used to achieve competitive advantage?

2. Why is a hotel/resort GDS considered to be a mission-critical application?

3. What core competencies must a hotel organization possess to excel in the distribution arena?

4. What are the key technologies and hospitality applications that comprise a hotel or resort's distribution system? Discuss the roles and importance of each.

5. How does distribution for hotel and resorts rooms differ from other types of products and services?

6. Should a lodging company strive for representation in any and all distribution channels? Describe and justify your response.

7. Why is the technology to support hotel and resort reservations so much more advanced than the technology used to support meeting space reservations?

8. How is the Internet reshaping lodging distribution and the ways in which hotels and resorts interact with their customers?

9. If a CEO of a major hotel or resort chain hired you as a consultant to help develop a distribution strategy for his or her company, how would you go about getting started? What sorts of advice would you provide?

10. What do you consider to be the weak links of today's hotel/resort GDS? How would you prioritize these, and how can these limitations be reduced?

11. What are the advantages and disadvantages of having hotel/resort guestroom inventory and meeting space sold by intermediaries?

12. Why do many lodging executives feel they are losing control over the distribution process and over their inventory? What can they do to win back control?

13. Is it a good idea to participate in discount services such as Hotwire.com and priceline.com? Why or why not?

14. Where should one turn to study future technology developments and innovations in hotel/resort distribution? Who are the leaders and innovators?

15. Discuss the latest trends shaping distribution. What do you consider to be the most important changes on the horizon and why? How will these reshape the way business is transacted in the hotel industry?

16. What do you consider to be the best practices in hotel/resort distribution?

17. What is seamless, single-image inventory? Why is it important?

18. How do you think guests will book lodging accommodations and meeting space ten years from now?

19. Select an individual hotel or resort and see how many different ways and in how many different places you can find it on the Web.

20. Select two or more hotel or resort companies to research. Compare and contrast their distribution strategies and Web strategies. What works and what doesn't and why?

9. References

Chesbrough, Henry W. and Teece, David J. (1996, January–February). When is virtual virtuous? Organizing for innovation. *Harvard Business Review*, 65–73.

Clemons, Eric K., Reddi, Sashidhar P., and Row, Michael C. (1993, Fall). The impact of information technology on the organization of economic activity: The "move to the middle" hypothesis. *Journal of Management Information Systems, 10* (2), 9–35.

Connolly, Daniel J. and Moore, Richard G. (1995). *Technology and its impact on global distribution channels in the hotel industry.* Proceedings of the Decision Sciences Institute, USA, 3, 1563–1565.

Copeland, Duncan G. and McKenney, James L. (1988, September). Airline reservations systems: Lessons from history. *MIS Quarterly, 12* (3), 353–370.

Davidow, William H. and Malone, Michael S. (1992). *The virtual corporation: structuring and revitalizing the corporation for the 21st century.* New York: HarperBusiness.

Davis, Stan M. (1987). *Future perfect.* Reading, Massachusetts: Addison-Welsey Publishing Company, Inc.

Davis, Stan M. and Meyer, Christopher. (1998). *Blur: The speed of change in the connected economy.* New York: Warner Books.

Dombey, Alyson. (1997). *Onward distribution of hotel information via the global distribution systems: The HEDNA White Paper.* Pittsburgh, PA: The Hotel Electronic Distribution Network Association.

Estis Green, Cindy. (2008). *Demystifying Distribution 2.0: A TIG Global special report.* Washington, DC: HSMAI Foundation.

Evans, Philip and Wurster, Thomas S. (1999). *Blown to bits: How the new economics of information transforms strategy.* Boston: Harvard Business School Press.

Hamel, Gary and Prahalad, C. K. (1994). *Competing for the future.* Boston: Harvard Business School Press.

Kirsner, Scott. (1999, November 1). Very truly yours. CIO Web Business (Section 2), 30, 32-33. Olsen, Michael D. (1996). *Into the new millennium: A white paper on the global hospitality industry.* Paris: International Hotel Association.

Stein, Tom and Sweat, Jeff. (1998, November 9). Killer supply chains. *InformationWeek*, 36–38, 42, 44, 46.

Tapscott, Don and Caston, Art. (1993). *Paradigm shift: The new promise of information technology.* New York: McGraw-Hill.

CHAPTER 9

Databases

Chapter Contents

INTERVIEW

Karen Sammon is a Vice President at PAR Technology Corporation.

Q: Hi Karen, your background in restaurants, law, and technology make you a great fit for this interview. First off, can you tell us what exactly data management is and why organizations need it?

A: All organizations depend on data, and good data management practices are critical to many organizational core business processes including enterprise resource planning such as inventory marketing programs, customer relationship management, investments (and divestments), new product introduction, promotions, and much more. Bad, incomplete, or inaccurate information can mislead management and impairs projects and/or organizations.

Data management is complex and includes such processes and functions as data governance, architecture management, development, security and master data management, data warehousing, and business intelligence to name a few. As a result of the breadth and scope of management, many organizations treat data as a cost rather than an asset.

In the restaurant and hospitality industries, technology solutions are prolific and are becoming increasingly more complex. Many restaurants operate point of sale, back office and kitchen management solutions at the store level. Other solutions, including order-taking and information kiosks, digital displays for menu boards and up-selling, and catering are also common. Enterprise content management systems are required to manage recipes, menu items, and pricing centrally across a wide geography with multiple users in dispersed locations. Web-based reporting must be accessible by many levels of management in real time, and systems need to communicate with food distributors, payroll, and financial packages. Even restaurant businesses are becoming more reliant on technology and with IT, the amount of data grows exponentially. Left unmanaged, the quality of the data degrades over time and therefore the overall ability to use the data to better manage the business operations and increase customer loyalty/intimacy cost of doing business increases.

In spite of the complexity of data management and the systems being used, information sharing, including the practical and effective approach to managing corporate data, improves communications and increases visibility to issues and opportunities within an organization. The positive impact of receiving good information supports an integrated and cost-effective approach to data and information management across an organization.

Q: Great. What would you say are some of the issues in restaurants and hospitality?

A: In both hospitality and restaurants, it is common to find multiple corporate system solutions operating within the organization. Need for timely and near real-time information is important for all business operations such as sales, marketing, distribution, finance, IT, operations, and managers.

Data management within the restaurant industry is complex by the nature of the franchising business model. Whereas franchising grows the business and increases the presence of a brand, most chains, especially in restaurants, do not have a standardized technology system throughout all restaurants. Furthermore and as explained above, there are typically multiple system solutions operating a single restaurant. Each system has its own data model. Add to that, data management is made more complex with aging systems, manual updates and lack of system visibility. As a result, executives at the corporate levels do not have one single system upon which to provide critical sales and product information upon which to operate their businesses.

In the hospitality industry, executives are challenged with the use of aging technology that does not seamlessly integrate the operations of the property. This lack of integration results in lower levels of inventory visibility and management, increased manual processes that are time and resource consuming, and an overall reduction of the property. Poor efficiency results in increased operational costs, lower customer satisfaction, and reduced profits. Lack of integration between applications and property management systems is the central source of pain (integration between property management systems and front office applications) and leaves the property unable to update sales and inventory in real time and reliant upon end-of-day batch uploads for critical data.

Establishing a method to interrelate the data from an ever-increasing number of sources is essential to provide the proper data for analysis and business decisions. There must be a single source of the truth to drive decisions from a proper perspective.

Q: Any thoughts on the how data flows through different processes, technology, and services?

A: Ensuring consistency across these many system solutions is a challenge for any organization and often there is not a process that determines the one point of truth. Companies that understand the power of their data and the changes that it can affect actively manage their data. Integration of disparate solutions coupled with a master data management process enables companies to make better decisions and positively impact business performance.

Increasingly, enterprise solutions are offering the opportunity to establish a centralized version of the data. Solutions providers, like PAR, are designing the database architecture around users' needs for information and reports empowering line of business executives to make real-time decision. Furthermore, we are increasing the amount of electronic transfers to reduce the required manual entry from POS to Enterprise applications. Optimization and prediction in business are key. Desktop and mobile dashboards with real-time information alerts assist managers in adjusting operations and can enhance the guest experience. To get to business intelligence, we need to focus on data management first. Nobody has time to sort through all the data, they just want a quick view of what they need to manage their business and do their job well.

Because information, from sales data to purchase orders, is becoming more relied upon for every level of owner/operator to everyday operations, organizations without large IT staffs, need support. For many organizations, managed services offerings are available to monitor data transport ensuring successful delivery or alerts via e-mail, text when they do not occur. Outsourcing data management is becoming much more prevalent and accepted.

In the hotel industry, HTNG (Hotel Technology Next Generation), the not-for-profit group, was established with the mission to foster collaboration among and between hoteliers, vendors, and consultants in the industry to specifically establish integration standards to more easily integrate product and services.

In retail, the larger industry that restaurants are a subset, there is a standards organization established by the NRF (National Retail Federation) a global industry organization called ARTS (Association for Retail Technology Standards) that shares the mission to foster collaboration among retailers, vendors, suppliers, and consultants to share a common data standard when sharing data across systems. This effort makes it easier for restaurants and retailers to establish the end-to-end system that best fits their organization. ARTS ensures that it supports standards of other industries and utilizes existing standards with extensions wherever practical. This helps to make sure there are not competing standards in place making it more challenging for adoption of a standards-based solution.

As standards become more prevalent, it is easier for an individual restaurant to leverage the various systems and data elements to create a single picture of their business to drive effective decisions to sustain and grow their operation.

1. INTRODUCTION

Karen introduced us to some complex themes. Let's see if we can break them down. Databases are playing an ever-increasingly important role in the Information Age. In the hospitality industry, their effective usage can help every department better manage assets, expenses, and sales. This chapter will acquaint you with client/server (C/S) databases and their usage in the hospitality industry.

2. DATABASE BASICS

From check-in, to food purchasing, to targeting customers, effective and efficient management of large quantities of data requires a database. You might keep a folder or notebook with different pages containing information. These papers have no apparent structure potentially linking them. When looking for specifics, you must go through each piece and extract it. In other words, they stand alone. Have you ever come across a written phone number and forgotten whose it was? You are almost forced to go through your cell phone name by name, or maybe recent calls. Companies that, even to this day, keep only paper records or noninterrelated computer systems face difficulties in data management. These are referred to as **flat files**. Flat files are usually text files that have no structured interrelationship. In the end, time and energy are wasted retrieving data with redundancies, while unseen relationships and potential couplings go undiscovered.

Today, hospitality organizations take advantage of the structural benefits provided by databases. A **database** is an organized, centralized collection of data serving applications. Databases are a key element of most mission-critical applications and represent the most common type of back-end software in C/S systems. A property's databases store data on such things as its transactions, products, employees, guests, and assets. Such databases must be efficiently organized and easy to access. They must also provide data integrity and ensure the reliability of stored data.

The database world is a large one and C/S databases are quickly replacing and interacting with mainframe databases. Mainframe databases are still used and are often superior to other databases due to their greater processing power. However, management, extraction, and display of the data are largely done via the platforms we use daily, be it C/S, the Web, or peer-to-peer. From here on, assume that a database is not in a mainframe platform. However do keep in mind that mainframe databases are very much still in existence.

The structure a database takes is important to later usage. Different databases were constructed by different people in different ways. There are four basic types of structured databases.

Hierarchical databases utilize parent/child relationships among data. A child cannot exist without a parent. This database looks like an inverted tree when depicted on paper, and it is hard to change this structure once you have begun. Hierarchical databases are useful for cost-effectively storing large amounts of data, but are less dynamic than some others.

Network databases have circular relationships defined by the user where new fields (which will be defined later) cannot be added later. As opposed to hierarchical databases, their structure on paper looks less orderly. Their usage is less and less common.

Relational databases are the most popular type of database and will be emphasized in this chapter. Relational databases organize data in tables consisting of rows (or records) much like graph paper. This form of organization allows flexible data organization and access and use of the **Structured Query Language (SQL)** database language.

Object-oriented databases are the newest type of structured databases and are in their infancy. It is believed that they will one day replace relational databases since they are better equipped to handle multimedia or graphics-based data commonly found on the Web. From guest pictures and movies to music, object-oriented databases will see more and more usage in our industry. Currently, object-oriented databases are manipulated through relational databases. In object-oriented databases, the data and methods (actions upon the data) are encapsulated into objects. Classes of objects are used and are capable of inheriting attributes of other objects. Think of combining a noun and a verb into one entity with the noun (there are more nouns than verbs) getting more attention than the verb. The end result is a more dynamic database since the data is the focus rather than the action upon it.

Database Management Systems (DBMSs)

Whichever structured database is used, an important software component is needed. A **database management system (DBMS)** is that critical piece of software that provides users and database administrators with the ability to access and manipulate data. It is through this piece of software, with all the common software features such as menus and places to click, that most managers will interact with the database. Therefore, this section also discusses commercial databases, especially those used by contemporary applications.

Many microcomputer and workstation DBMSs are available for prices comparable to word processing and spreadsheet packages. However, full-feature databases can cost half a million dollars just for enterprise software. DBMSs perform several key functions:

- Provide links between different files that are used together
- Allow the storage, updating, and retrieval of data in the database
- Apply data integrity, data security, and control constraints to the data
- Coordinate multiuser database access
- Support data reliability through backup and recovery features

The DBMS provides an intervening level of software between database users (and applications) and the data storage. Figure 9-1 shows where the DBMS works within a hospitality environment. The view of the database from the user's perspective is the **logical view**. There can be many logical views since different departments need to see data in different ways. The makeup and organization of the data on the storage device is the **physical view**. There is only one physical view. The DBMS takes the data from the physical view and presents it in the logical view.

The two views (logical and physical) of the data are used by the DBMS to provide data independence. This allows data models to be resistant to changes in the database's physical structure. This is convenient for system developers, who can easily change storage devices and data access methods.

Your knowledge of bits and bytes is expanded into more forms found in databases. Bytes form words and numbers that form fields. A **field** is a collection of bytes or data with specific

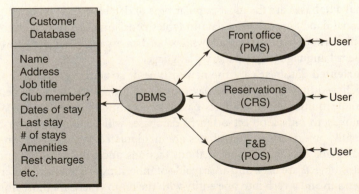

FIGURE 9-1   The DBMS serves as the link between departmental or user-specific requests and the database.

meaning such as "Last Name." Next is a **record**, which is a collection of fields such as a customer's "Last Name," "First Name," "Address," and "Credit Card Number." A collection of records is a **file** such as "Customers," "Vendors," and "Employees," and a database is a collection of those files.

Just what provides that structured linkage lacking in flat files? It is how the rows of data are identified and related to the other rows in other files (sometimes referred to as *tables*). Since a database is made up of files, something connecting all of the files to one another is needed. The key here is linking files that have a field in common. Let's use an example of a simple database with only three files—Reservations, Front Office, and Housekeeping. At times, each department may be concerned only with its data. At other times, data from the other departments in relation to its department may be needed. In reality, each file would contain many more fields. Look at Figure 9-2. Each file has one or two fields that *uniquely* identify a record. In the Reservation file, it is the reservation number. In the Front Office file it is the combination of the Last Name and Street Address. Two fields are used together here to uniquely identify a record in cases of guests with the same last name. Finally, in the Housekeeping file, the room number is the field that uniquely identifies that record since there are no rooms with the same number. These fields that uniquely identify a record are called **primary keys**. If two primary keys are used together as in the Front Office file, they are called a **composite key**. The files are linked together where a primary key from one file is linked to a like field in another file. This like field is called a **foreign key**, which is just a primary key in another relation. In Figure 9-2, reservation number is seen as a primary key in the Reservation file and as a foreign key in the Front Office file. When the Reservation file is linked with the Front Office file, which in turn is related to the Housekeeping file, all three files are linked, which allows the whole database to be utilized when needed.

Through the DBMS, an important language is utilized. Using a data manipulation language or DML, users can manipulate the data in a relational database in various ways. For example, rows in a relation may be inserted, deleted, updated, displayed, or printed. For example, an airline cancels a contract with your organization. Without having to search name by name in your active corporate client list, you can search the database via a query for the airline's name and delete the related last names in a block. Other relational operations are used to extract answers to

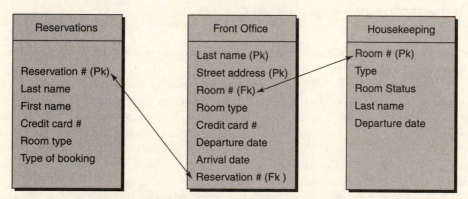

FIGURE 9-2 The valuable aspect of relational databases is the linkage of files. By connecting the files, you can make complex searches of the database as a whole rather than just the individual files. Here the three tables are joined by like fields—a primary key (pk) in one field and a foreign key (fk) in another. Primary keys uniquely identify a record. When two fields are used to uniquely identify a record, it is called a composite key. Foreign keys are primary keys in another relation.

a user's queries. One example is the "Select" operation, which returns a new relation with a subset of the relation's rows. You'll look more closely at the "select" query in use in the most widely used DML in the next section.

Functions of a DBMS

Both large and small DBMSs provide the same general features, although they vary in sophistication. They include the ability to create and manipulate new files and records using DBMS commands. For example, a DBMS should allow the user to set up a (relational) reservation database with RESERVATION # and ROOM TYPE relations by defining the fields and field types, as in Figure 9-2. Subsequently, it should allow the user to populate the files by typing in new records, or by importing or reading the data from another application (e.g., a word processed document or spreadsheet).

Another DBMS function minimizes redundancy among data elements to ensure database consistency. The fields shown in Figure 9-2 are stored just once. In a paper flat-file system, the reservation name may be found on many different documents. The ability of the DBMS to link and use files together eliminates this inefficiency and redundancy. DBMSs also support data independence, relieving the user of the need to know exactly how the data (e.g., supplier records) in the database is physically stored.

Data Extraction and Information Gathering

Once all the data is in place, you need to be able to extract it in a dynamic and structured way using a data language. While some DBMSs use their own proprietary DMLs, the data language of choice is *SQL*, the most widely used relational DML, originally developed by IBM. Queries allow a manager to extract specific data from a database. SQL, pronounced *sequel*, is used in products ranging from Access to Oracle. To find out which food items are at or below their reorder levels, for example, a food and beverage director might issue a SQL query:

SELECT ITEM_#, ITEM_NAME
FROM INVENTORY
WHERE ITEMS_IN_STOCK <=REORDER_LEVEL

This query uses the INVENTORY relation and returns item numbers and names for inventory items that should be reordered.

DBMSs also provide security features to protect files and records from unauthorized access or modification. Unauthorized access is a high-level concern since hackers may be able to use what are known as SQL injectors to open up a database. In conjunction with network security measures discussed in Chapter 4, through the DBMS, files can be protected by passwords to completely deny access to certain users, to provide read-only access, or to allow unlimited access. For example, the supplier file may have read-only access restrictions, protected by a password, to prevent possible fraud (e.g., rerouted payments).

DBMSs also allow users to create interactive programs that manipulate database data to support the user's business applications. For example, a program might be developed in PowerBuilder, a software building application, to present a set of packaged procedures through menus to the user. Each menu option could activate a group of DBMS commands that create, access, or print data from the database, or even perform analyses of this data. Sales and marketing departments are big users of custom applications created in conjunction with DBMS-manipulated data. Applications created here allow these departments to more definitively understand both current and future customers. This theme will be more thoroughly covered in the section "Database Usage" of this chapter and In Chapter 10.

Multiuser DBMSs are more sophisticated than the single-user variety and allow concurrent database access by tens or hundreds of users. If the inventory database described previously were implemented using a multiuser DBMS, two users on different terminals would be able to access multiple supplier records at the same time. However, problems occur in a multiuser context. The first is data integrity. For example, imagine a situation where two banquet managers retrieve an inventory record of fifty wine bottles, withdraw forty and thirty items each, and both end up with twenty bottles, potentially causing operational and security problems. Such problems are handled using file locks and record locks to restrict access to records in use. These locks are an important part of multiuser DBMSs.

Another problem multiuser DBMSs must handle is "deadly embrace," or deadlock, a situation that occurs when two processes require resources (e.g., records) held by the other. The result is that they would wait for each other, possibly indefinitely, if the ability to detect and break deadlock were not incorporated into multiuser DBMSs.

Database Servers and Distributed DBMSs

As computer networks have become more widespread, the need for database servers has grown. In non-C/S systems, requests for data from a central database in a multiuser setting would result in whole files sent by the DBMS to be processed at the user's terminal, creating heavy network traffic. For example, a request for suppliers in a certain city may result in the entire SUPPLIERS relation being sent to the user's terminal and the request processed there. Database servers process queries on the server, greatly reducing communications overhead and returning only the query results to the requesting terminal.

Distributed databases are becoming more and more common in this network age. The DBMS supports location transparency, relieving the user of the need to know where files are physically located. If, on the other hand, different properties use different databases, then problems can result. This is what is known as disparate databases. Ownership can be fragmented in the hospitality industry. Properties of the enterprise may be franchised and owned locally. Each property makes its own decisions regarding technology. A solution to this problem is **data-warehousing**, which is a collection of all the data from the entire enterprise centralized in one location. Its ultimate goal is "to integrate (this) enterprise-wide corporate data into a single repository from which users can easily run queries, produce reports, and perform analysis" (Connolly, Begg, and Strachan 1999). A subsection of a data-warehouse is a **data mart**, which is a departmental-specific section of a data-warehouse created to simplify tasks and improve processing time. Data marts were created so each department could analyze and query only its data.

3. DATABASE USAGE

You have already seen some of the uses of a database through queries and commands. Much of what has been covered detailed database usage in daily operations such as inventory management or customer loyalty programs. With a good number of data captured on customers, databases can also provide the foundation for forward-looking events such as sales and marketing initiatives.

Analysis

Companies with a database could find themselves with large amounts of data. At times it can be overwhelming. This stored data may have previously unseen relationships that could lead to future profit. For instance, after analyzing the data, it is uncovered that 80 percent of a hotel's weekend clientele comes from within a thirty-mile radius and has an annual income of over $75,000. Marketing initiatives could then be properly targeted to the records of a database with these same attributes and reevaluated at a later date as to effectiveness. This creates a profile that can be used to help target data for a sales campaign. A **profile** is a set of attributes and relationships that classify an entity, in this case a customer. Using this profile, the organization may then spend precious dollars more accurately in targeting potential like customers. This is an example of data mining. **Data mining** is analysis of data for potential relationships. Most data mining is statistical and can involve model formation such as **profiling**, **clustering**, and **cluster mapping**. Clustering and cluster mapping involve the plotting and mapping of data with like attributes. A newer data analytical technique is **online analytical processing** (**OLAP**). OLAP is "the dynamic synthesis, analysis, and consolidation of large volumes of multi-dimensional data" (Connolly et al. 1999). Whereas traditional queries and analytical tools output answers such as the average room rate for a specific property, OLAP can view a larger data set and output the average room rate for all properties. OLAP provides a wider view of queries and will be detailed in Chapter 10. In addition to database searches, whether done locally or over the Web, a newer form of search is evolving to search the enterprise's (company's) other resources in addition to databases, such as e-mails and documents. This new evolving search is known as an **enterprise search** and is aiding in capturing or finding out more information on a particular search.

Setting up an analytical function beforehand can help a property take preemptive measures in preventing losses. Consider a frequent customer, Mr. Morrell, who has not stayed with a hotel in some time. In data mining, a trigger could be set to alert management of loyal customers who are not recent ones. A **trigger** in database terms is something that sets off another event. In this case, an e-mail would be sent to the sales manager stating that Mr. Morrell is a loyal customer whose time between stays has lapsed and should be contacted. A sales representative may pick up the phone and gently state that much time has gone by since his last stay and offer a complementary amenity upon the next visit in order to retain Mr. Morrell as a customer. Customer retention is important in any industry, particularly hospitality. On the operations side, imagine a trigger set up to alert a restaurant vendor when a food or supply stock for one of the restaurants to which it sells dips below a certain level. A delivery could be initiated before the supply is depleted. Given the busy nature of the business, preemptive data management such as this can be a lifesaver. Aiding in this inventory management is a newer technology known as **Radio-frequency identification** (**RFID**). RFID is commonly used today in automobile toll passage (easy pass) and even in payment such as in gas stations. RFID is much more efficient than standard bar codes contained on packaging. RFID uses a tag that can be either passive or active that communicates through its embedded antennae with a reader which can then perform a number of actions such as raising a parking gate, to unlocking a door. RFID technology is quickly finding many uses in our industry.

Customer Relationship Management (CRM)

Databases are also helping the industry to serve and target customers in personalized ways. One such initiative is **customer relationship management** (**CRM**). The concept of CRM, sometimes referred to as *customer experience management* or other similar names, is defined by many different persons in many different ways. You will use two definitions. First, according to the respected marketing firm of Carlson Marketing Group, CRM is defined as "a comprehensive *process* in which a company fundamentally improves the quality of interaction with its customers and prospects through the use of relevant, timely, and actionable information resulting in improved profitability" (Carlson Marketing Group 2001, p. 4). Dan Connolly, a professor of Hospitality Technology and E-Commerce at the University of Denver, defines CRM this way:

> CRM is a complex and multifaceted phenomenon that involves taking a customer-centric view to every process, guest touch point, and department across the entire property (or chain, if applicable) to create rich, unique, and personalized guest experiences. It is as much a way of doing business as it is a *mindset* or *philosophy* that must be embodied by everyone in the organization to become an essential part of the organization's culture. It is enabled by information technology and a series of software tools and technology applications that facilitate data collection, storage, filtering, pattern recognition, guest profiling, modeling, mapping, and more. The goals are to develop a holistic, 360-degree view of each guest, to create a segment of one, and to own each guest—for life! (Connolly 2001, p. 15)

CRM in Operations

Databases are extremely important to CRM, incorporating all of the aforementioned functions. However, what these two definitions stress is the fact that CRM is not just a computer system tracking customer preferences. CRM is a *process, mindset,* and *philosophy.* Unless everyone and everything is on board with this initiative, it might not work. Applying knowledge from the chapter interview, we see that some CRM initiative "musts" include the following:

- All customer touch points (PMS, POS, CRS, etc.) must be engaged.
- All staff must be trained on its importance and gather data when *possible.*
- Access must be given to this data when and where appropriate.
- Staff must be empowered to react to data.
- The data must be centralized or warehoused at a minimum.

More often than not CRM is accomplished through specific software that accesses the database. Many CRM offerings today are Web based, which means they are accessed through a browser. Data input accuracy is a must. While the name Thomas Nyheim or Tom Nyheim may be the same person, it could result in two different records. Consistency is a must. Let's take a look at CRM at work today (Figure 9-3).

Starting with the bottom tabs, you see that, via this software from GuestWare, you have a number of different views of a guest. This particular screen shot shows the customer preferences from *room type* to *wine.* Armed with this kind of information, a hotel or restaurant is much better off anticipating a guest's needs. If the property is a chain, CRM can allow the organization to cater to the specific customer needs all over the world. In an industry where the guest is king, CRM can provide the data to make sure that a guest is treated like one. Figure 9-4 shows another screen shot of GuestWare's software, this time showing the follow-up

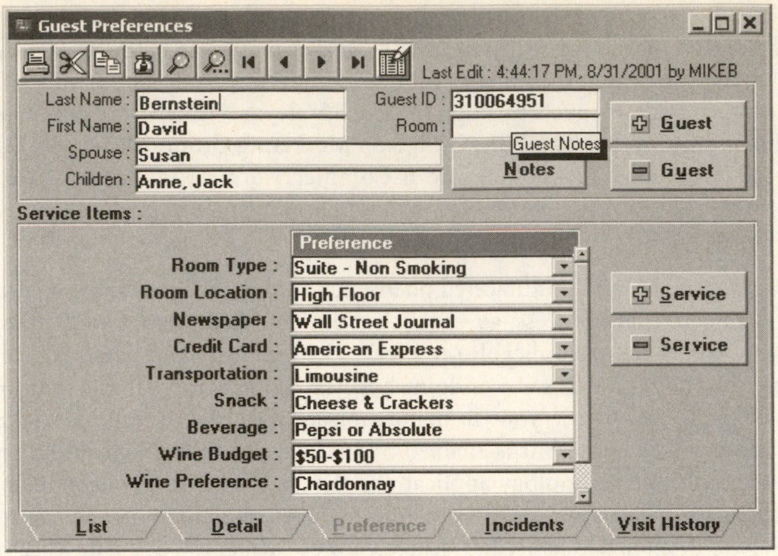

FIGURE 9-3 Software from companies such as GuestWare provides a user-friendly way to store and access unique guest preferences data.

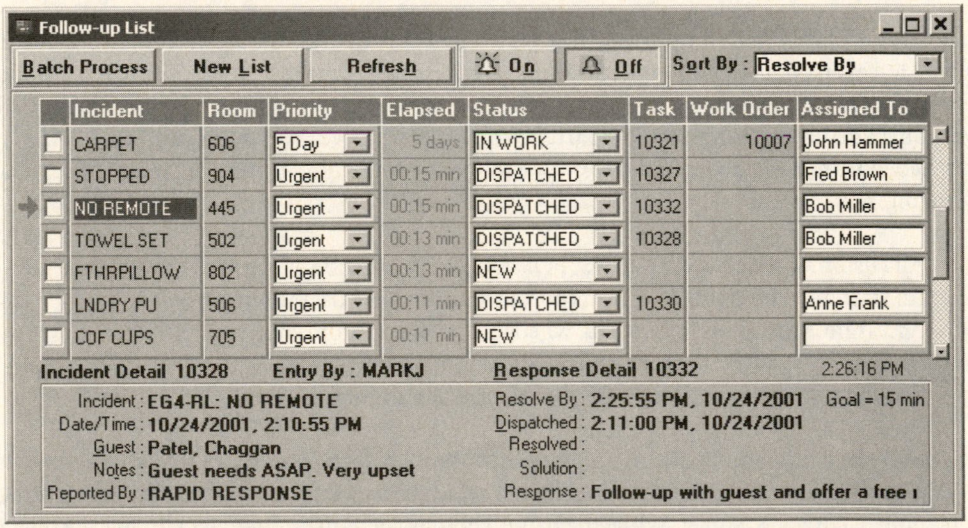

FIGURE 9.4 In the fast-moving hospitality industry, making sure that what was supposed to get done actually got done can be very time consuming. This GuestWare follow-up screen aids in such efforts.

list. With a click of a mouse, an employee or manager now has the potential to see what is and is not going on in the hotel and, more importantly, is able to react in real time. This software offering is quickly moving into a Web-based or software as a service (see Chapter 4) allowing companies a lower cost and accessed anywhere with an Internet connection capability.

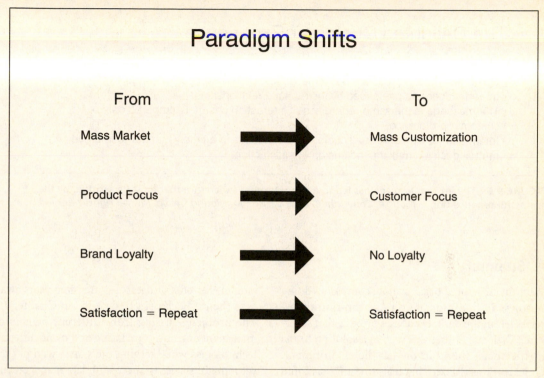

FIGURE 9-5 With the advances in technology, the individual has moved to the forefront in both marketing efforts and personal choices.   *(Source: Copyright © 2001 Carlson Marketing Group, Inc. All rights reserved.)*

CRM in Sales

Software such as GuestWare also aids in targeted sales and marketing efforts. Due to such new mediums as the World Wide Web, the field of marketing is undergoing a change. Figure 9-5 depicts this paradigm shift.

As this diagram shows, with CRM, marketing campaigns can now be targeted to the individual rather than to the masses. If you have ever logged on to a Web site and it personalizes a page just for you—this is an example of the paradigm shift. In hospitality, customization is needed for many types of guests. One of the most precious forms of data in a property's database is the *repeat customer list*. With the ability to purchase an item via the Internet, be it a room-night or an airline ticket, guests no longer are attached to a specific chain. Keeping them is a challenge. They are concerned with price and have less brand loyalty. If management is able to show them that they really know them and can cater to their every need, guests are less likely to choose another location. CRM is meeting this paradigm shift head on.

A management team will know whether it properly implemented and succeeded in CRM if the criteria listed in Figure 9-6 are met.

With these criteria met, the team can be certain that its CRM is working and should show up on the bottom line. Careful usage of data in any CRM initiative is needed since privacy laws differ from country to country. Europe having much stricter privacy laws than the United States in one example. From a database, to software, to people, successful CRM is quickly becoming a must do for properties wishing to stay competitive.

The Delighted Customer Experience

- The company interacts with its customers and prospects as a unified global entity.
- Customers and prospects receive messages, product/service offerings, and treatment/care as prescribed by their unique relationships.
- The message is the same regardless of interaction channel, tempered only by customer preference.
- Information is available at all customer touchpoints in a timely manner to improve mutual decision making and customer satisfaction.

FIGURE 9-6   The information age has led to a new customer experience that must be satisfied by the successful organization.   *(Source: Copyright © 2001 Carlson Marketing Group, Inc. All rights reserved.)*

4. Summary

Without structured organization, companies doing business in the Information Age can find themselves left in the dark. Databases provide that structure. Their use at first was seen as a solution to the inefficiencies found in the flat file environment. Quickly it was realized that real-time analysis could be done on data, and that initiatives such as CRM could actually help increase revenue and retention. However, moving to a database environment is not without difficulties. One of the largest impediments to organizations moving to a database is change. The old flat file environment allowed each department to control its own data. Political concerns are heightened at times when an organization is told to share its data. A database environment requires just that. Another problem is that the

tangible benefits of databases are often years away, as is the payback period, detailed in Chapter 13. The problems arising from different owners or management teams purchasing and using different technologies while serving the same customer are yet more obstacles to successful data management. Convincing management to purchase an expensive new system can be difficult. For that reason newer agreements and management contracts often stipulate the technology to be used and how the data is to be shared. The reason is simple: Shared data used effectively can increase revenue. Finally, with advancements in Web-based offering, management has even more options with less maintenance costs, enabling even small businesses to engage in effective data management.

5. Case Study and Learning Activity

Database Case Study—Loyalty

BY PAUL MANLEY, MS, PMP

Paul Manley, PMP, is a hospitality technology industry veteran who has worked for leading global hotel companies, systems vendors, and consultants. He is a project management consultant, educator, and an Officer of the International Hospitality Information Technology Association—an association of

educators and practitioners whose mission is to advance the use of IT in the hospitality industry through education and research.

The Situation

Hotel Company XYZ had multiple brands and was growing by acquisition, while organic growth was relatively stagnant. The challenge to achieve organic growth can be restated as three questions. How can XYZ maximize its marketing dollars to acquire and retain customers? How can it leverage its information-rich customer database containing tens of millions of unique customers across multiple brands while respecting individual hotel brand identities? What customer-facing initiative can it create to respond to competitors and to Wall Street analysts' questions? XYZ's current state of customer relationship management was where most of their brands had their own unique points-based or service-based brand loyalty program. The XYZ future state and answer to all three questions was a unified, points-based loyalty program across all hotel brands.

While there were many business implementation and technological challenges, none were greater than those involving data. This includes the data warehouse and transactional databases; the processes and technology rules that ensured data accuracy and integrity; and the business processes that captured and used the data. What follows is a brief description of the types of data XYZ kept, the various databases involved, and examples of the integration of business strategy and rules which impacted the databases.

The Creation of the Loyalty Database

Like many of its competitors, XYZ partnered with a loyalty system provider (LSP). They maintain the database of members which includes the member profile information, their member status, and their transaction history that includes points earnings, redemptions, and, a few years later, their wish list. In addition to the database, XYZ had to transmit the checked-out guest (including members) folio information, centralize it, clean and validate it, and then integrate that data into the LSP system. The LSP system maintained the summary transactions for hotel earnings and free night redemptions along with points earned and redeemed with program partners such as rental cars, online flower shops, merchandise, and so on. When a purchase was made with a program partner, the transaction details were received by LSP and points posted. When a member redeemed, the partner was electronically notified to ship the reward.

The additional database challenge to create the new, unified loyalty program was to take the data from several brand databases and merge them into the LSP database. Among the data questions XYZ asked and answered were:

- *How do we prevent duplicates from being created?*
  They added two of the existing program databases into a single database and then doing a match, using various rules that included credit card number, address, name, and phone number, developed a fresh database. In an iterative fashion, they added one current database at a time to the fresh database until all current program members were in the new loyalty database. It should be noted that part of the effort included the omission of longtime inactive members and members whose name or identity could not be recognized.

- *How do we respect brand identity?*
  The business requirement was to maintain existing hotel brand affinity when the old program was replaced with the new. To do this, the member's brand logo from their previous loyalty program was printed on the new loyalty program card. From a database perspective, this meant adding a field to the LSP database schema to store brand affiliation. From a business rules perspective it meant that any time a member enrolled, the channel through which he or she enrolled was captured so that the "brand affiliation" field could be populated.

- *How do we maintain an excellent customer experience during the transition?*
  There are several tactics involved including marketing communications and training for franchisees and call center agents. From a database perspective, XYZ needed to give call center customer service agents access to the old loyalty program data to investigate member queries around point balances,

redemptions, and earnings. Since only the point balance was transferred from the old program to the new (and not the supporting transactions behind them) the customer service agent needed access to the old data to answer questions.

Making the Loyalty Database Operational

There are actually several databases involved with supporting a loyalty program. In addition to the main member database, data marts are used to support the various marketing campaigns to acquire new members and activate existing members. These campaigns comprise seasonal promotions, e-mail campaigns, and direct mail. Hotel companies access a variety of databases which identify market segments, campaign success, and filter opt-outs and do-not-contact attributes. Combining, for analysis purposes, the loyalty database with the enterprise customer data warehouse can also provide additional insight into segmentation, behavior, trends, and other analytics.

Enhancing Database Capabilities

Once XYZ launched their new, unified loyalty program, many additional capabilities were added. These included:

- A credit card that earned points for any purchase and bonus points were given if the card was used to pay the hotel bill. The database challenge was to ensure that the loyalty program number was associated with the credit card. Due to banking regulations, the bank which issued the credit card had to allow anyone to apply for the card, so business processes were created to monitor new accounts and then update the credit card database with the member number.
- Real-time personalized offers through the customer service call center (and in the future, via the Web) were also added to the program. This entailed integrating the loyalty database, the call center system, and the offers database into a system that recognized the customer, scripted a relevant offer to the customer, and then stored the response back in the offers database so that it was either not offered again or offered at an appropriate time in a relevant context.

Learning Activity

1. What were XYZ's three questions that addressed growth?
2. In addition to a database, what are some other parts of a loyalty system?
3. What is brand identity?
4. How did XYZ prevent duplicate records from being formed?

6. Key Terms

Composite Key
Customer Relationship
    Management (CRM)
Clustering
Cluster Mapping
Data Mart
Data Mining
Data-Warehousing
Database
Database Management System
    (DBMS)

Enterprise Search
Field
File
Flat File
Foreign Key
Hierarchical Database
Logical View
Network Database
Object Oriented Database
Online Analytical Processing
    (OLAP)

Physical View
Primary Key
Profile
Radio-Frequency Identification
    (RFID)
Record
Relational Database
Structured Query Language
    (SQL)
Trigger

7. Chapter Questions

1. What is the difference between the logical and physical views?
2. What is a flat file?
3. What functions does the DBMS provide?
4. What is CRM and how do you know if it is successful?
5. What is an enterprise search?
6. What is a profile?
7. How is CRM using the Web?
8. What is SQL and what does it do?
9. What is a trigger and how can it be used effectively?

8. References

Carlson Marketing Group (2001), p. 4.

Connolly, Thomas, Carolyn Begg, and Anne Strachan. 1999. *Database systems* (2nd ed.). North Reading, MA: Addison-Wesley.

Laudon, Kenneth, and Jane Laudon. 2009. *Management information systems* (8th ed.). Upper Saddle River, NJ: Prentice Hall.

Martin, E. Wainright, Carol V. Brown, Daniel Dehayes, Jeffrey A. Hoffer, and William C. Perkins. 2002. *Managing information technology* (4th ed.). Upper Saddle River, NJ: Prentice Hall.

CHAPTER 10

Competing on Knowledge: How the Power of Information Can Enable Great Things

Chapter Contents

INTERVIEW

Dr. Kellie Keeling is an assistant professor at the University of Denver's Daniels College of Business in the Department of Business Information and Analytics. She holds a Ph.D. in Management Science from North Texas University. Her research and teaching interests are in the areas of statistics, business intelligence, and data mining.

Q: Please share a brief overview of your background in terms of your education, professional experience, and current work with business intelligence.

A: My education includes a BS in Mathematics, an MBA with a concentration in Management Information Systems, and a Ph.D. Management Science with a secondary focus on Business Computer Information Systems. I originally worked developing office automation support systems for the president's office at a small liberal arts college which morphed into a job as coordinator of institutional research. After spending time with the data generated by the university (retention rates, instructor teaching evaluations, fundraising tracking), I decided to pursue a Ph.D. in Management Science (or business statistics). I have taught a variety of courses ranging from business statistics, computer simulation, and data mining to sports statistics. I am currently exploring the area of data visualization.

Q: How do you define business intelligence, and how does it relate to or differ from concepts like knowledge management, executive information systems, customer analytics, data mining, customer relationship management, and competitive intelligence?

A: I use the definition from *Competing on Analytics* by Davenport and Harris (2007), where business intelligence is defined as "technologies and processes that use data to understand and analyze business performance." There are a number of techniques and subareas that fall under this category such as data mining and customer relationship management. Executive information systems were part of the first evolution of providing executive decision makers with access to real-time (or near real-time) business data with ad hoc query capabilities, scenario building, and drill-down analysis to help them make decisions. Knowledge management is a discipline to which organizations adher to capture the intellectual capital of the organization. This typically involves areas such as the competitive advantage, innovation, and continuous improvement of the organization.

Customer relationship management involves a system of business technologies that focus on building long-term relationships with the most profitable customers and making sure those customers have exactly the right information that they need at any time so that they continue to be customers. One subset of this is **customer analytics**, which uses customer behavior data to make business decisions such as direct marketing efforts and site selection using tools like market segmentation and predictive analytics.

Finally, competitive intelligence is a practice that focuses on gathering external business information (such as intelligence on products, customers, and competitors) and using the information to make strategic decisions for the organization.

Q: Why is business intelligence such a hot topic and business priority today? How can it contribute to an organization's competitive advantage?

A: There are many similar products on the market today; therefore, being able to optimize one's business processes is becoming critical to competition and differentiation. As a company moves from being able to report what is going on in its business (i.e., What happened? Where is the problem?) to using analytics to focus on the future (i.e., What will happen next if things continue as they are? What is the best outcome that we can expect? What additional products and services can be added to increase revenues?), a company increases its degree of intelligence and its competitive advantage. A 2010 survey by Gartner (www.gartner.com), a technology research firm, suggests that chief information officers (CIOs) consider business intelligence to be among the top five technology priorities for business organizations. Other priorities included networking, voice, and data communications; newer services-based technologies such as visualization and cloud computing; and Web 2.0 and social media.

Q: What should hospitality business students and professionals know about business intelligence? What are the key concepts, underlying technologies, and critical success factors required to make business intelligence work in an organization?

A: Davenport and Harris (2007) found that the most successful companies had analytics supporting a strategic, distinctive business capability. In these companies, the analytics were promoted by senior executives and implemented as an enterprise-wide approach. To be successful in the business intelligence arena, companies must provide full support from the top to bottom of the organization for analytics-based competition.

Q: Can you provide some examples in which companies have been successful with business intelligence and their best practices?

A: Marriott has a revenue management system in place called One Yield to automate its business processes for optimizing revenue (Overby, 2007). Marriott must determine how to price its hotel rooms in order to ensure the maximum profit while reducing the number of empty rooms each night. It uses an enterprise-wide statistical system that takes the guess-work out of setting rates by making recommendations to employees about what rate to offer at a property on any particular day. The Marriott hotels that use One Yield have seen leisure travel revenues increase by up to 2 percent, allowing them to achieve rate and occupancy premiums ahead of their competition.

Harrah's Entertainment, the world's largest gaming company, is another exemplar organization when it comes to business intelligence and customer analytics (Piliouras, 2006; Norton, 2009). It focuses on customer loyalty by segmenting its customers using a variety of behaviors, guest history, and spend patterns and then targets these specific customers based on this information to offer relevant promotional offers and services. Harrah's uses SAS predictive analytics technologies to analyze its loyalty card data, which has allowed the company to leverage its distribution advantage and engender loyalty across every key market. Its advanced technology and marketing expertise provide guest service associates with real-time information necessary to create highly personalized guest experiences at the time of service interaction. These moments of truth create a sense of wow and encourage guests to return frequently to Harrah's hotels, casinos, and race tracks. Because of its business intelligence and customer relationship management initiatives, Harrah's has outperformed its industry competitors in terms of overall profits as a percentage of revenue. In other words, for every dollar spent at Harrah's, a greater portion goes directly to its bottom line than what its competitors can achieve—a true competitive advantage. As a result, Harrah's Total Rewards is hailed as the industry's most sophisticated multi-brand loyalty program.

Q: How can an organization measure its success and return on investment from its business intelligence initiatives?

A: The approach for measuring business intelligence success can be divided into two dimensions: direct and indirect measures. In terms of direct measures, the effect of the business intelligence efforts on the key performance measures and comparisons to industry metrics and financial ratios can be examined as well as subjective assessments by managers. Indirectly, success can be measured by the utilization of the intelligence efforts in decision making by looking at data usage or by creating a survey to be distributed among users of the business intelligence process to get their impressions as to the quality and completeness of information, the ease and timeliness of decision making, satisfaction with decision outcomes, etc. (Lönnqvist and Pirttimäki, 2006).

Q: How can managers address the issue of information overload? Is technology adding to this problem or helping to solve it?

A: Managers must have good techniques in place to cull through the masses of information and find the nuggets of information that can help their businesses work more strategically. More and more data are being collected, which just points to more opportunities. Managers must make sure that the business analysts know the problems that their businesses are facing, and the capabilities, strategic business priorities, and focus are so that they can spend time studying and analyzing all of the relevant date in these areas.

Q: What parting words of advice can you share with current and aspiring hospitality business professionals?

A: In any organization, one key to success is realizing that many of the most important variables are related to humans. The human factors include doing what is right in your job so that you can enhance your organization and your boss, supporting your employees so that they are effective employees and citizens, and fostering relationships with your customers so that they return again and again.

1. INTRODUCTION

The present economy is often characterized as the information economy or digital economy. In such an economy, information is at the heart of all commerce, and knowledge is the basis of all competition. This is especially true in service industries like hospitality, where information becomes the essential ingredient to delivering unique, memorable, and unmatched service. Information also becomes a key competitive differentiator and can lead to competitive advantage. Differences in information, sometimes called **information asymmetry**, explain why firms respond differently and at different times to specific situations. They also explain how some firms can enter new markets or exit existing ones, launch new products and services, and respond more quickly to opportunities and threats than their chief competitors.

As seen in previous chapters, those who use information effectively can benefit. Thanks to information technology (IT), the good news is that managers now have better and timelier access to an abundance of data regarding business operations and how they are performing. Unfortunately, this also presents challenges, as there is an overabundance of data and insufficient time to wade through all of the reports to interpret them and apply what is useful. Understandably, it is easy for managers to be overcome by the volumes of data that bombard them each day. Therefore, today's managers must be extremely adept at gathering, analyzing, and using large quantities of data from a number of different sources about every facet of their businesses to see opportunities and patterns and to make smart business decisions in a timely and consistent manner. The business world is relatively unforgiving and intolerant of mistakes. As such, competitiveness and survivability depend upon one's ability to see and act upon opportunities that others don't see or before they see them.

This chapter's endeavor is to discuss how to effectively collect and use data to create information that can shape and guide managers' actions and decisions. It focuses on using IT to work smart, not hard. It will discuss how to funnel important information to managers to enhance their decision making, manage and control the business, guide the directions they set, and identify new opportunities for competitive posturing, positioning, and new product and service offerings. It will discuss the benefits of gathering usable information and applying it effectively and creatively to gain competitive advantage and to make it easier to manage the business.

To help frame this chapter and put things in context, consider the five questions presented in Figure 10-1. How readily you and others in your organization can provide consistent and agreed upon answers these questions will provide an initial and very rudimentary test to how intelligent your organization is and how in tune its management team is with the health of the organization and the business landscape—and this is just scratching the surface! As you will read, business intelligence and data analytics are quite complex and require a great deal of commitment from the organization and software resources. In essence, one wants to have the same type of detailed and sophisticated

What's Your Business IQ?

• Who are your top 10 customers, and what are they worth?
• Which of your products and services are the most (least) profitable?
• What are your guests' or employees' top 10 complaints?
• Who are the top 10 performing employees?
• What are your top competitors' major strengths and weaknesses?

FIGURE 10-1   A Quick Test of Your Firm's Informational Savviness

intelligence that the U.S. military and Central Intelligence Agency have, but focused on every facet of the business, its customers, competitors, suppliers, industry landscape, emerging trends, and so on.

2. DEFINING BUSINESS INTELLIGENCE

Over the past several decades, the hospitality business has steadily grown in complexity due to greater competition, more sophisticated customers, and more discriminating investors, not to mention rising costs and difficult economic conditions. While the craft elements of the business (i.e., personalized service) remain vital to the guest experience, a new sense of focus must be placed on the strategic use of resources and the hard numbers; that is, profitability and return on investment (ROI), topics which will be explored in greater detail in Chapter 11. Managing today's complex hospitality business requires effective use of information and a sophisticated **business intelligence** system that can gather, store, analyze, synthesize, share, and communicate information throughout the organization to those who need it, when and where they need it so that they may apply it in effective, value-creating ways (see Figure 10-2).

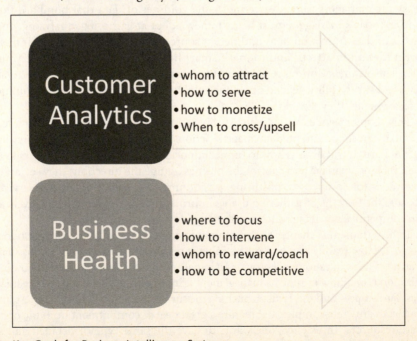

FIGURE 10-2   Key Goals for Business Intelligence Systems

A business intelligence system operates much like the nervous system of the human body, providing important and timely information to management, the equivalent of the organization's brain, so that managers, their employees, and the organization as a whole can sense and respond to changing business conditions and know how to apply resources and where management must intervene to stay out in front of competition and customers. The key is to **informationalize** every aspect of the business (Davenport and Harris, 2007); that is, keep and analyze information about everything related to one's business and use it to inform business decisions. To achieve this, organizations must leverage information and IT and treat them as strategic weapons rather than just support tools. In doing so, decision makers will be armed with the *best* evidence and tools to perform their jobs in timely and effective ways.

The business literature uses a number of terms to describe various aspects of knowledge or business data gathered by companies (e.g., business intelligence, knowledge management, customer analytics, data mining, decision support, and competitive intelligence). Sometimes, some of these terms are used interchangeably. Other times, they refer to different areas and different business processes and systems. For the purposes of this chapter, we will use the term *business intelligence* as the broad umbrella under which many different forms of intelligence gathering, knowledge management, information dissemination, and business technology fall.

Figure 10-3 shows how we have operationalized our definition for business intelligence and its ecosystem of corresponding applications or technologies.

Translating this view of business intelligence into a hotel or resort environment creates a much more complicated picture because a hotel or resort tends to be a fairly complex business entity run by a myriad of heterogeneous systems, many of which are discussed throughout this book. Simply put, each key area of the business—from the front desk, restaurant operations, and retail outlets to spa services, meetings and banquets, and other hotel/resort services—is powered

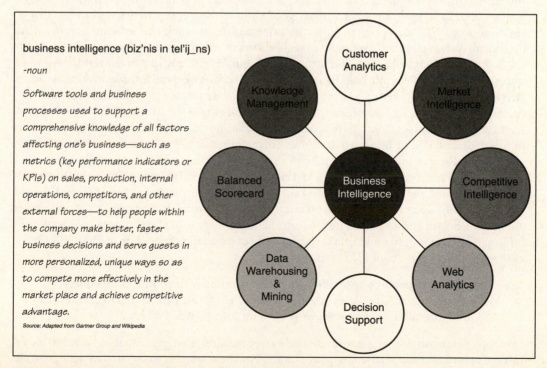

business intelligence (biz'nis in tel'ij_ns)

-noun

Software tools and business processes used to support a comprehensive knowledge of all factors affecting one's business—such as metrics (key performance indicators or KPIs) on sales, production, internal operations, competitors, and other external forces—to help people within the company make better, faster business decisions and serve guests in more personalized, unique ways so as to compete more effectively in the market place and achieve competitive advantage.

Source: Adapted from Gartner Group and Wikipedia

Customer Analytics

Knowledge Management

Market Intelligence

Balanced Scorecard

Business Intelligence

Competitive Intelligence

Data Warehousing & Mining

Decision Support

Web Analytics

FIGURE 10-3   A Proposed Textbook Definition for Business Intelligence

by a different system, often running on a different operating system (OS) and software environment with a different database system and data structure than other core systems used in the operation. These factors make it more difficult to collect, consolidate, and report data across an organization, causing challenges to answering simple operational questions such as "How much did the Jon Smith family spend at my resort during its most recent two-week ski vacation?" On the surface, this specific question seems to be straight-forward, but to find the answer, one must be able to identify every Smith family transaction involving an exchange of money across the resort operation—lodging, food and beverage, in-room services, spa services, ski rentals, and so on. This is difficult to do because of the many systems used to record these transactions (e.g., reservations system, Web site, property management system (PMS), restaurant and retail point-of-sale (POS) systems), the differences in how data are stored in each system, the time between each transaction, and the fact that the Smith family name might not be captured or uniformly captured with each transaction. For example, if there was a cash transaction or transactions under J. Smith, John Smith, Jon Smith, and Jonathan Smith, it would be hard to associate these transactions the right Smith party to gain a full understanding of the Smith family spending during this one trip, never mind over the course of multiple trips and properties in the case of loyal customer. To overcome some of these challenges, we propose the adoption of an integrated business intelligence framework (See Figure 7-8) that creates a unified systems infrastructure across the enterprise. While we recognize that challenges can still exist, this approach will go a long way to improving data quality and integrity across the entire hotel or resort enterprise to provide more accurate information and answers to important business questions.

Much of business success is determined by information and **knowledge management**— what is known, when, and by whom—and, then, how that information is put to use to outfox the competition. Good business decisions are a function of timely and accurate information in the hands of decision makers, knowledge of the context in which this information will be applied, appropriate and rigorous analysis, good common sense, experience, and speed (that is, the time to gather, interpret, and put the information to work and execute any resulting decisions). Moving forward, competition will continue to intensify in what appears to be a dog-eat-dog world. What will become important is how quickly companies can convert the reams of information they collect into knowledge that can be used for better decision making, product development, and marketing/pricing promotions. In essence, we are talking about how fast companies can learn, and as you know, continuous learning is the lifeline of any organization. As managers, it is important to have access to the *right* information at the *right* time to assist us in making fact-based or informed decisions. This requires us to (1) constantly be in the know, (2) always have our fingers on the pulse of the organization, and (3) continually know what information is necessary to do our jobs and run our businesses. It also requires us to be inquisitive, to know how and when to ask provocative questions that will lead to new information and answers. Finally, we must also possess an uncanny ability to sense and respond to opportunities and threats before anyone else in our industry. These are some of the many traits of leaders in information economy. In looking at the future state of business competition, perhaps Bill Gates, chairman and co-founder of Microsoft sums it up best:

> The most meaningful way to differentiate your company from your competition . . . is to do an outstanding job with information. How you gather, manage, and use information will determine whether you win or lose. (Gates, 1999, p. 3)

Leveraging information as a corporate-wide asset requires a strong, capable, and flexible **IT infrastructure** and supportive company culture. For these systems to be effective and generate value, hospitality companies must ensure that the infrastructure in place is capable of meeting a company's needs, both now and into the future. Critical components of an organization's information foundation include management's ability to monitor performance and enforce business rules (which should be programmed into all systems), query and reporting tools, proactive reporting, comparative reporting, and analytical tools that can help to find and identify hidden meanings in the data. The tools should be easy to use so that anyone can use them without first having to speak with the IT department.

To realize value requires alignment between people, technology, and business processes. The focus must clearly be enterprise-wide; that is on the entire organization. In many organizations, enterprise application integration (EAI) initiatives are underway to connect and integrate all systems so that data can be shared and leveraged across the entire organization. The company's systems should be viewed as knowledge capture, creation, sharing, and policy enforcing devices. Collectively, they create a knowledge bank that can be shared by all employees throughout the company. In effect, these systems represent the brain trust of the organization.

3. DATA VERSUS INFORMATION

Rounding out our discussion of **data** and **information** from Chapter 3, we now look at these from a decision and action perspective. The terms *data and information* are often used interchangeably, yet they are not the same. It is worth noting the distinction. There is actually a **data hierarchy**, which is illustrated in Figure 10-4.

At the lowest level are data, the very building blocks of information; they are the raw ingredients that comprise information. By themselves, they are relatively worthless, appear random and meaningless, and can contribute to noise or distraction, but when ordered, aggregated, and put into context, they begin to take shape, develop meaning, and have a purpose. Patterns begin to emerge, and as they do, information begins to form, but information is not enough. It provides the foundation for knowledge, especially when it is coupled with experience. The more knowledge one possesses, the smarter he or she becomes. Knowledge is used in the development of insights, foresight, and judgment, which collectively lead to **wisdom**, the sum of knowledge over

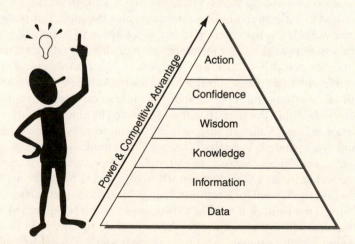

FIGURE 10-4 Data Hierarchy *(Source: Adapted from Professor Richard G. Moore (Emeritus), Cornell University's School of Hotel Administration.)*

time—combined with common sense, good judgment, a wise outlook, and plan of action. It is this wisdom that we, as managers, all seek in order to make informed decisions, act sensibly and responsibly, and outshine our colleagues. It is this wisdom that becomes our personal differentiator and helps to define our leadership capabilities.

As one ascends the hierarchy, more intelligence is gained, and with that intelligence comes confidence, power, and action—the ability to make informed decisions, pursue directions that others are incapable of, and gain the upper hand in negotiating. Confidence is a prerequisite to action because it reduces risk and builds trust within the organization. By truly understanding patterns and **cause-and-effect** relationships, we can better predict outcomes with greater certainty. The pinnacle of the pyramid is action because our ultimate goal should be to do something impactful with the newly acquired knowledge or wisdom. If no action is taken, one must ask, "So what's the point; why did we bother with all this analysis?" It is through the actions taken that will lead the firm to competitive advantage, so long as the actions taken are based on knowledge that no other firm has or the actions taken apply knowledge differently or create a different path than any other industry competitor. Through all of this analysis, it is important to try to weigh all of the factors involved, including risk and opportunity costs. If the business benefits don't outweigh or justify the risks and opportunity costs associated with taking a specific action, management is justified in taking no action or seeking to pursue alternative courses of action. It is also important to recognize in advance how accurate and precise information needs to be to make decisions. At times, ballpark estimates might be sufficient. However, at other times, pin-point accuracy may be required. Knowing how detailed and how precise one needs to be can help to determine the time spent on analytics, research, and diligence (i.e., thoroughness) and can lead to faster decisions and action or more scrutiny to make sure that right decisions and actions are taken while mitigating risk.

The keys to this ascent are capable systems, timely communications (powered by a great technology infrastructure), organizational efficiencies, and smart, inquisitive managers. Good managers ask good, tough questions and actively seek out their answers. For you to be effective as a manager, you must know how to ask the *right* questions, for that is the key to learning and being in the know, but keep in mind that not all questions have answers or ones that are easily obtainable, and you might not have as much time as you'd like to seek or develop answers. In a perfect world, we would always have complete, accurate, and timely information at our immediate disposal that is required to make sound business decisions and maximize our performance in our jobs. However, our world is less than perfect; in fact, it is often ambiguous and uncertain, sometimes making the wisdom state ideal but seemingly unattainable. Therefore, we must often make decisions with the *best* available data, however imperfect or incomplete, and as managers, we must be comfortable with this because this represents reality. At times, we are asked to fill in gaps in our data with assumptions and research and make inferences based on what knowledge is available while working within the given time frame provided by our boss, market conditions, or the specific situation at hand. Although analysis is important, we must balance this with the need to take action and avoid paralysis by analysis (i.e., too much thinking, studying, and assessing of situations and not enough timely action). To accomplish this, organizations must have in place an effective sense and response system that can tell what is and is not working. Many management consultants suggest the need for a culture within organizations that supports a bias towards action. If something is not working according to plan, intervention is required to fix it—but fix it quickly before the situation gets out of control. In order to do this, we need to have systems in place that can help us identify signals in a timely manner and correctly determine cause-and-effect relationships so that we can address the root causes of problems, not just their symptoms.

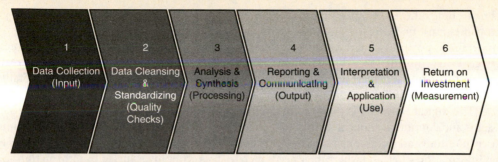

FIGURE 10-5 The Process of Refining and Making Sense of Data

It is worth mentioning this data hierarchy for two reasons. First, it calls attention to the importance of data and, in particular, the need to collect good, accurate data as close to the source of origination as possible. Second, it helps to explain the fundamental roles of all IT, which are to collect and organize data, process them while maintaining their integrity, and convert them from random bits to meaningful and usable information—as one progresses up the hierarchy—so that managers are well informed about the decisions they must make and the actions they must take in steering the business on a road to prosperity. All IT applications require data input as the raw ingredients. They then process these data and transform them into an intelligible output used to create the wisdom behind our thought processes. Ultimately, they become key repositories or the brain trust of the organization's collective knowledge or wisdom. The six stages of this process are represented pictorially in Figure 10-5. Although depicted in a linear fashion, the process will likely be iterative, with each stage having a recursive relationship with the one before it. Companies pursuing enterprise application integration strategies (see Chapter 7) are trying to harness the goals this model depicts by modernizing and integrating all applications across their organizations to create a central repository and holistic view of all aspects of their businesses and customers.

As stated before, data must be collected as close to the point of origin as possible. Employees should be well trained in how to collect accurate data because these data will be used downstream in subsequent processes. Because the hospitality industry uses multiple, disparate systems and collects data from a variety of sources, it is necessary to go through a quality process of data cleansing and standardizing data to ensure what was captured are usable and valid data and that they can be consolidated. Once the data have been approved, the analysis and synthesis can occur. These processes will likely involve statistics, what-if analysis, scenario building, and other forms of data and/or financial modeling. Reporting and communication are important because these functions help to share what is known with people who can interpret or apply that knowledge to make impactful decisions; deliver better, more personalized guest service; and create value and competitive advantage. Finally, there has to be a measurement stage to provide a feedback loop and encourage organizational learning and improvements. In the end, we must be held accountable and able to answer questions like, "Was the effort worth it? Was the original investment recovered?"

4. INFORMATION AS A VALUED ASSET

Information is one of a hospitality firm's most important, yet undervalued, assets due to its intangible value. It is highly coveted as its role is critical in every aspect of the hospitality industry, from guest services to marketing, decision making, administration, and control of the operation or organization. With the hospitality industry increasingly approaching commoditization (i.e., no distinguishing differences in the products and services offered by the companies in the industry), companies must find new ways to differentiate their product and service offerings. Herein lies an important opportunity for the strategic use of information, particularly in the area of guest service. What information is known about guests and how that information is used to create personal, custom, and memorable (think wow) service experiences will be how hospitality companies set themselves apart and win guest loyalty.

The digital economy is powered by an infrastructure of highly sophisticated computer systems and communications networks that collect, analyze, and share information throughout the corporation and its value chain of suppliers and allied partners to all those who need access to that information when and where their needs dictate. This economy is fueled by information and intellectual capital. To some, information might be viewed as a by-product of IT applications, but in reality, it is—or should be—the primary focus, for it is this information that gives IT its value and empowers managers and employees alike to do great things that provide them and their firms a competitive edge.

Information is a critical source of competitive advantage, but it is not just the information that contributes to one's competitive advantage. It is how quickly one can act on this information after finding meaning in it through the discovery of patterns, relationships, and insights—before the competition—to do things that they cannot. Of course, this assumes that an organization is effectively and efficiently gathering the *right* information at the *right* time and by the *right* people. As you can see, there is a lot that one must get right to be successful and outperform the competition. This is why many of today's popular management theorists and consultants suggest focusing on the informational aspects of a business. When these are digitized (i.e., put into an electronic format), new things become possible. Information comes to life through graphics and multimedia and traverses faster throughout an organization, reducing cycle times and time to knowledge. People (e.g., management, employees, suppliers, customers, and partners) then have timely access to the information they need to fulfill their roles in the service delivery process and to make better, more informed decisions.

When we deal with data and information, we must remember four important characteristics. The first is the old adage, "Garbage in equals garbage out." It is imperative that the data collection processes (e.g., reservations, order entry, lead development, etc.) are accurate, complete, consistent, and standardized. Accurate involves the ability to have processes in place to ensure *good* data via proper staff training and automated validation and error checking. Complete implies the ability to connect to various systems to gain all of the data needed, which is a major challenge with the systems in use today. Consistent and standardized suggest that processes, terminology, and data formats should be the same throughout the organization to allow for consolidation and interpretation. These data will be used downstream; for example, for subsequent processes such as check-in, guest profiles, function booking, **data mining** (recall our definition from Chapter 9: detailed statistical analysis and modeling, pattern/trend recognition, and identification of relationships) and marketing campaigns, among others. Therefore, the accuracy of these later activities is only as good as the data collected during the initial guest contact points. Achieving this level of accuracy is a function not only of the systems in place but also the training front line employees receive and the culture of the organization. All guest contact associates must understand and appreciate the important roles data play and their own importance and the contributions they make in collecting and using data to benefit guest service and the overall success of the organization. This is essential to maintaining the integrity of the data.

To avoid service failures and bad (i.e., ineffective) management decisions, we must ensure we have the appropriate procedures and systems in place, and we must train our employees not only on how to collect data but also on the strategic importance of these data. In service businesses like those found in the hospitality industry, data are the raw ingredients used repeatedly in the guest lifecycle for the production of service and the resulting experiences. Thus, to produce flawless service, create positively memorable experiences, and wow guests, our employees require accurate and timely access to reliable data that can then be aggregated, ordered, and converted into usable information.

The second attribute we must remember is that data and information can be perishable. Most data are dynamic, not static. This means that their lives are generally short-lived in terms of their relevance or meaning. Consequently, the value of data can shift over time, given the context and how that data are being applied. Data that have surpassed their useful shelf lives may have limited value in a specific situation or guest encounter, but when they are put in a historical context and used to establish trends or patterns and predict future events, their value takes on different meaning and purpose. The opportunity costs, especially of missed opportunities, are where organizations are really vulnerable. In a time when speed wins, the opportunity costs can be rather high. Therefore, they must be carefully assessed and managed.

The third characteristic is that data and information are context-sensitive. Data without context have no meaning. In order to effectively use data, they must be treated in appropriate contexts for which they were collected and in which they will be applied. Finally, it is also important to remember that there is a humanistic element to data and information as well. Computers can help people organize and process data and information more quickly to find meaning in them, but humans must be able to recognize the value, see the meaning, and know how and when to apply this meaning (and when not to) in their jobs—from making managerial decisions to delivering outstanding guest services to developing successful marketing programs. This also implies their ethical and responsible use, which should never be overlooked.

5. INFORMATION OVERLOAD

A typical hospitality business is information intensive. There is so much information to collect, track, analyze, and report, that a manager's job can often seem daunting as one drowns in paperwork and reports. Some of the challenges associated with running today's operations are trying to wade through reams of reports, e-mails, financial statements, operating statistics, operational log books, and so on. to figure out what's important versus what's not, to separate the important signals from all the noise. Time, of course, never appears to be on our side—especially in hospitality operations where there always seems to be a new crisis brewing. Plus, we are generally faced with numerous distractions and forced to multitask. Ironically, technology is a great contributor to the problems associated with information overload that lead to distracting managers from addressing key priorities, but IT also offers potential solutions to dealing with the challenges of managing large volumes of data and tools to quickly filter, analyze, and report essential information needed, when and where it is needed. If used well, technology can help us manage all aspects of a hospitality business, monitor performance, establish trends, and drive improvement. IT can also help by calling attention to certain patterns, anomalies, or business signals; thereby allowing us to take appropriate and swift intervening action to recognize key individuals (guests or employees) or avert potentially disastrous situations before they get out of control. There are a number of technologies available that aid in the collection, distillation, interpretation, reporting, and communication or dissemination of information. Some of the many technologies include **executive information system (EIS)**, **decision support system (DSS)**, database management system (DBMS) (see Chapter 9), intranets, and the corporate data network. It is important to remember, however, that these systems are only as effective as the data collected and the abilities of those using the systems. The systems are not a substitute for poor management or bad business practices. Moreover, people must also be able to quickly and easily filter and process data in a timely manner, operate the technology applications, make sense of the output, and determine how to sensibly and ethically act. The timely interpretation of data within their context and the transformation of these data into usable and actionable information can drive a firm's competitive advantage. Computers can process information, but people must make decisions and be held accountable. Thus, the industry needs inquisitive managers who are technologically savvy and have great common sense—that is, people who can look at situations, ask intelligent questions, think on their feet, use software applications to model and analyze data, and apply intuition when interpreting results to ensure they make sense and are appropriate given the situation. Answers should never be taken at face value. A reasonableness check should always be applied given the context in which they will be used. All answers should be challenged to ensure they are accurate and appropriate for their context.

6. WORKING SMART

Under the present economic environment, attention must be given to reducing or containing costs. This typically results in having to do more with less as financial resources are rationed and as people resources are eliminated. Under these circumstances, there are fewer staff and fewer managers to operate and manage the many diverse business activities associated with a hospitality enterprise. As managers' time is spread across a wider array of issues and business operations, managers are expected to oversee multiple aspects of the business without necessarily having all of the specific expertise—and certainly not all of the time—required to focus on the many important details to ensure smooth business operations, the consistent delivery of exceptional guest services, and the desired performance levels. Clearly, managers must figure out how to work smart if they are to be effective and productive and how to pay close attention to the numbers while maintaining high visibility across departments. They have little time to spend in their offices reviewing reams of reports, trying to decipher meaning in the numbers, and reflecting on what could have been. The conditions of today require hospitality organizations to apply IT to extend their managers' reach and knowledge across the entire enterprise without necessarily having to have a ubiquitous physical presence to know how the business is performing.

In today's marketplace, the time it takes to acquire knowledge and subsequently act on this knowledge is critical in gaining competitive advantage. Without effective systems and a sound technology infrastructure connecting these systems to each other and to management, the reports generated provide little value. Managers must have real-time access to up-to-the-minute data and information to make informed decisions. When these are digitized, or put into an electronic format, this real-time access can happen. Not only do data and information move faster around the organization and get shared with more people, but they can also come to life through graphical and multimedia tools. Digitized data can be easily shared, graphed, manipulated, and tied to alarms to identify trends and exceptions. Thus, the computer can do most of the work while freeing up resources to spend time acting upon the results and making decisions that will positively influence the future.

In the past and in many cases even today, a corporate office provides much of the reporting for key operating statistics, financial data, and customer satisfaction surveys. This approach is neither efficient nor timely and can often lead to ineffective decisions. The resulting reports provide **lagging indicators** or historical operating information, making it difficult for managers to determine where and how to intervene to positively influence outcomes. By the time the reports are read, analyzed, and interpreted, the information contained within them is obsolete while the factors contributing to results are long forgotten. As properties become more automated, the local reporting capabilities increase, providing more timely information and alleviating many of the problems cited here. Yet, the number of disparate systems creates difficulties in gaining access to timely, meaningful, and consolidated data. At times, administrative staff re-key data from reports into spreadsheets to create customized and consolidated **flash reports**, a daily snapshot of key performance indicators and operating statistics (e.g., revenue, occupancy, average daily rate, guest satisfaction scores, etc.), for management. Not only is this process inefficient, it is also prone to inaccuracies as a result of data entry errors. As previously mentioned, relevance is an issue due to the time involved in preparing the reports. Unfortunately and perhaps surprisingly to some, these practices, as bad as they are, still exist today. With better systems and technology, these practices are changing, but the hospitality industry still has a long way to go, and the timing will be elongated due to the incompatibilities between many systems in use today and the lack of integrated solutions available for purchase.

Through advances in technology such as more open and integrated systems, greater organizational connectivity, and better reporting and analysis tools, the situation has greatly improved, giving managers access to more timely data as well as tools to help interpret the results quickly and effectively. With these tools, managers spend less time buried in reports and more time proactively managing the business.

7. TOOLS THAT CAN HELP

All hospitality systems are designed to help us collect, manage, share, and interpret data, but since there are many diverse systems in use today, it can be difficult to aggregate data and report on them. This is especially true when trying to aggregate data across departments, properties, and brands. Consider for example, all the many systems used to run a large ski resort—from the PMS and restaurant POS to the spa and ski lift ticket systems to the resort's Web site. In each case, data about guests, operational statistics, and financial performance are being collected. For a high-level executive to have to monitor and use each of the many systems to understand how a resort is performing would be time consuming, frustrating, and even awkward. These problems are intensified when this same executive must determine performance across properties or brands or within a region where systems are not necessarily standardized.

Fortunately, there are two systems that run behind the scenes whose specific purpose is to help aggregate, analyze, interpret, and report data from multiple systems. These are the executive information system (EIS) and the decision support system (DSS). There are components of each of these embedded in many hospitality systems. However, their functionality in these systems is limited. Therefore, one must turn to specific tools dedicated to meeting these analytical and reporting needs of the business, tools that are more robust and powerful in their modeling capabilities and statistical assessment abilities.

An EIS is a tool that provides key operating data to managers and executives much like a car's dashboard reports important information regarding the health and status of the vehicle to its driver. Like a car's dashboard, an EIS is information central or a command center of sorts. Because the industry lacks a well-integrated system that can fulfill all of an organization's needs, hospitality operations require multiple disparate systems to operate efficiently and effectively. An EIS is a useful tool in polling these systems to collect, consolidate, and report on the various levels of activity in a single operation, within a region, and across the entire company in a common format. Because the system is intended for busy executives at different levels within the firm, the system must be easy to use and report on key performance measures with multiple units of analysis and views of the data (e.g., summary information that can be expanded to show full details). It must provide **drill-down** capabilities to explore increasing levels of detail about the individual components that comprise each of the high-level measures. The system also tends to be visual (i.e., graphical) in nature, using charts to depict trends and performance over time. It also uses color and sound to call attention to key areas. The system can also be integrated with the company's e-mail system or instant messaging system to issue timely alerts to managers (often via their smart phones) when specific action or intervention is required. The system is typically based on the concept of exceptions management. Assuming an executive has little time and few resources, what are the key areas (as denoted by warning signals or **red flags**) requiring immediate attention? However, these exceptions do not always have to highlight negative situations. They can also call attention to positive events; thereby allowing management to recognize and reward outstanding performance.

An EIS is more than a reporting and communications tool. It can be used for analysis, troubleshooting, and scenario building (e.g., what-if analysis). Because it is relatively easy to use, managers can create their own reports as needed without always having to rely on their IT staff. It gives them better control and access to the data they need to perform their jobs. Additional benefits include comparative analysis with similar properties in the chain, variance reports (actual versus budget), and event triggers or alarms. For each critical measure, management can set thresholds or acceptable ranges for performance. If the numbers shift above or below the established limits, alarms are triggered. At the press of a key or the click of a mouse, management has immediate access to real-time summary information and detailed data about their operations. For example, a district manager might be interested in knowing how performance at one particular hotel or restaurant within his or her region compares with similar hotels or restaurants within the region or elsewhere in the company. If it is outperforming others, one might question why and look for reasons and best practices that can be shared with the management teams at comparable hotels. Similarly, if the hotel or restaurant in question is underperforming, one should also look to identify causes and then prepare an appropriate course of action. The goal is to ascertain the root cause—not just the symptoms—of problems so they can be quickly fixed.

A DSS, generally targeted for use by full-time business analysts versus executive managers, has many of the same capabilities of an EIS, but it is more robust and sophisticated for more heavy-duty data analysis, manipulation, and trends forecasting. A DSS is used for multidimensional analytics and multivariate statistics to find relationships and patterns in data. Recalling from Chapter 9, online analytical processing (OLAP) may be utilized to give users the ability to view and extract data from multiple points of view in real time. Working with multidimensional databases, OLAP allows data to be combined and analyzed through complex queries in many different ways, interactively and on an ad hoc basis. Typically, users of OLAP are interested in viewing data by multiple criteria concurrently and are involved with calculation-intensive analyses. As such, the DSS analytical engine and modeling tools tend to be more powerful than what is found in an EIS since the system must wade through voluminous data for mining purposes and to discover patterns and trends by combining and comparing data and using these findings to predict the future. At the heart of a DSS is its statistical tools used for modeling, **simulation**, and **predictive analysis** (trying to forecast future trends, behavior, and outcomes). Whereas an EIS focuses more on communicating performance results, a DSS' primary emphasis is on understanding these results over time and what they mean in terms of the future. They help to interpret these results, predict future market and buyer behavior, and troubleshoot. The system queries tend to be more ad hoc and more complex than those encountered in a typical EIS, and its use is for unveiling important cause-and-effect relationships that can enhance the performance, strategic direction, and value of the firm. A DSS query might look to identify consumers from a specific geographic region with common demographic and psychographic traits who have demonstrated similar purchasing behaviors so that an e-mail target marketing campaign can be launched. In another query, a user might want to know how much money was spent on cleaning supplies across the organization in order to consolidate purchasing and negotiate better volume discounts. These are just a couple of the many possible questions that might be asked of a DSS. The questions can be one time or repetitive, broad or specific, cover a relatively short period or extend over multiple years, but in each case, the questions usually involve an extemporized component.

8. THE BALANCED SCORECARD

Over time, EIS systems have evolved and now focus on providing a **balanced scorecard** (an organizational report card of key performance measures or dashboard of sorts) to top managers, a concept first popularized by Kaplan and Norton (1996). The balanced scorecard may vary from organization to organization, but the underlying premise is the same: ascertaining the health of the business. In assessing performance, organizations should not rely on any single measure but rather on a composite set of measures that take into account the various stakeholders of the firm (i.e., guests, employees, owners and investors, suppliers, franchisees, allied partners, government, and community). The goal is to assemble a comprehensive and integrated measurement system that will allow managers to monitor performance, identify problem areas, develop intervening strategies, chart the performance of the organization against its overarching strategies, and aid in the development of future strategic directions. The system must not only report historical information but also predict future outcomes.

Traditionally, almost exclusive emphasis was given to financial measures. This approach, which overlooked other key measures, has proven problematic for several reasons. These include a historical and inward focus, a tendency to concentrate on short-term results, and an inappropriate assumption that everything can be quantified (Kaplan and Norton, 1996). In the words of Kaplan and Norton (1996, p. 24):

> Financial measures are inadequate for guiding and evaluating organizations' trajectories through competitive environments. They are lagging indicators that fail to capture much of the value that has been created or destroyed by managers' actions . . . [They] tell some, but not all, of the story . . . and they fail to provide adequate guidance for the actions to be taken today and the day after to create future financial value.

Certainly, financial measures are important and must be included, but they represent only one view of the firm. Instead of a single measure or single category of measures, what is proposed is a composite of integrated and telling measures or key indicators (sometimes referred to as **critical success factors**) across a variety of categories tied to each stakeholder group that will provide vital information regarding the health and performance of the organization. For each measurement category, management should define strategic objectives (or drivers), appropriate measures, targets to be achieved, and key initiatives that will be undertaken to achieve the established goals. Table 10-1 provides a worksheet that can be used in the scorecard development process to help identify and document key measures and goals and align them with the firm's strategy.

Table 10-1   Balanced Scorecard Development Worksheet

Measurement Category	Strategic Objectives (Drivers)	Measures	Targets (Goals)	Key Initiatives
Lodging Performance	Increase market share and improve profitability	ADR Occupancy percentage REVPAR Market share	↑ from $159 to $175 ↑ from 62% to 68% ↑ from $130 to $145 ↑ from 15% to 18%	E-mail marketing campaign Weekend getaway promotion Corporate sales blitz
Guest Satisfaction	Improve guest satisfaction score	Guest satisfaction rating	↑ overall satisfaction score from 4.8 to 6.0 ↑ intent to return score from 4.2 to 6.0	Mobile check-in Digital signage In-room technology enhancements Web site redesign
Sustainability	Reduce energy and water consumption	Energy bills and consumption rates per room Water usage	↓ energy bills and per room consumption rates by 10%	In-room energy management system Compact fluorescent light bulbs (CFLs) Motion sensors Water saving devices Energy Star compliance

The measurement categories will likely include financial considerations (e.g., financial ratios, revenues, net profit, actual versus budget variances), operational statistics (e.g., occupancy, ADR, REVPAR), competitive activity and positioning (e.g., market share, rate positioning), internal factors (e.g., efficiencies, cost savings), employee measures (e.g., turnover, overtime, satisfaction ratings), guest perspectives (e.g., repeat business, satisfaction ratings), supplier relationships and performance (e.g., quality, on-time delivery), environmental concerns (e.g., recycling programs, energy consumption), community (e.g., programs sponsored, charitable contributions) external factors (e.g., economic indicators, weather) and assessments for learning and innovation (e.g., training, experimentation, new ideas, research and development). Using the critical success factors, or key determinants of success for the organization, as measured by each stakeholder group, a snapshot of the firm is prepared indicating its overall health and preparedness as well as providing a source of tracking against the firm's defined strategy. The specific measures chosen and the weight assigned to each are important. Their selection should not be taken lightly because they will help a firm articulate its strategic objectives to all those tasked with their implementation and fulfillment. The measures should be an appropriate blend of the firm's critical success factors, focus on internal and external indicators, and include actual results as well as projections and comparisons to budgets and historical results. The measures used will also help to determine how management spends their time and how resources are allocated within the firm. Finally, they provide a basis for benchmarking and can be used to compare against previous results, predetermined goals, and/or against competitors to see if the organization is improving and getting better

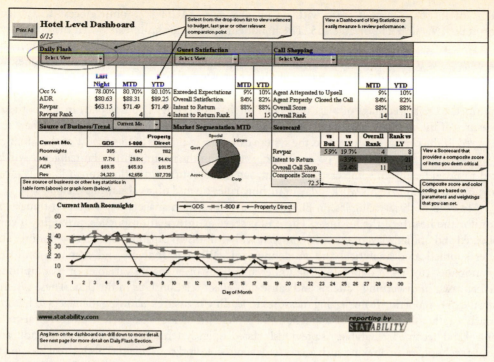

FIGURE 10-6 Sample Balanced Scorecard

over time (Kaplan and Norton, 1996). For an example of a balanced scorecard, please refer to Figure 10-6.

Using such a system provides numerous advantages. First, it improves visibility and communications within the firm, letting employees and managers know how the company is performing with respect to itself, its goals, the marketplace, and the industry as a whole. Second, it allows managers to keep their fingers on the pulse, have up-to-date status information regarding the business, and identify key areas (through early warning indicators like red flags and exception reporting) that require their attention and intervention. Third and finally, a balanced scorecard system provides a source of accountability and control. Remember the old saying, "What gets measured gets done."

To better understand these concepts and determine how to operationalize them, we now turn to two important examples, Toronto-based Four Seasons Hotels and Resorts and Minneapolis-based Carlson Hospitality. Four Seasons Hotels and Resorts has implemented a scorecard system referred to as the *Three P System*, which comprises three very specific measurement categories: people (results to associate opinion surveys), product (service quality), and profit. The data can be collected from the systems installed in all of the company's hotels and resorts around the world and consolidated at the corporate offices in Toronto. The results can then be shared with all those requiring access via the company's intranet. This approach automates the data collection, aggregation, reporting, and dissemination processes, making the information accessible on an as-needed basis. Through the Three P System, Four Seasons carefully monitors its business and maintains the quality and high service standards for which it is known.

Carlson Hospitality (parent to Radisson Hotels and Resorts and Country Inns and Suites) takes the Four Seasons approach one step further by putting critical information directly into the palms of its management team with its proprietary MACH-1 (Mobile Access to Carlson Hospitality, Version 1) portable EIS. The handheld system communicates with the company's core systems such as Curtis-C (central reservations), Harmony (PMS based on Fidelio), and CustomerKare (data warehouse) to gather key performance data. With such a system, it does not matter where a manager is, he or she can always know what is going on and when his or her input or intervention is required. Thresholds (floor and ceiling values) and specific events can be programmed to raise red flags or alert managers of changes (either good or bad) in status to key measures. If the changes are positive, managers can be notified so that they give praise where it is deserved. If the changes are negative, the system can warn managers of the gravity of the situation so that an intervention plan can be developed. Perhaps in the future, artificial intelligence will be used to provide, and in some cases carry out, suggested courses of action, much like advanced yield management systems work today in turning rules on and off as situations dictate.

In both of these examples, an EIS is being used to help managers stay on top of things and monitor the health of the business. These EISs serve as information portals, providing a consolidated and unified view of the data, complete with drill-down capabilities, querying options, and other sophisticated analytical and modeling tools. **What-if analysis** and **scenario-building** functionality (forms of data modeling under situations of changing variables or assumptions) further assist in discerning patterns and cause-and-effect relationships in the data. These systems shift the data reporting from lagging measures to **leading measures**, allowing managers to become proactive rather than reactive, to take action and prevent problems—long before things spiral out of control and become irreparable. As previously stated, open systems, better systems integration, and mobile technology are making such access to data possible and convenient. This is a real blessing to management companies that operate multiple properties under different brands with different core systems. With these technology advances, they now have a way to quickly and automatically consolidate the data without the need to re-key them, making it possible to conduct comparative analyses between current, budgeted, forecasted, and historical information.

9. THE IMPORTANCE OF INFRASTRUCTURE

In order to achieve value from technology, a firm must have an appropriate, capable, reliable, and solid, yet flexible, technology infrastructure in place. Like a building's foundation, the technology infrastructure is the base upon which all technology applications are built. Simply put, the technology infrastructure is *everything* (i.e., people, technology, business processes, training programs, and organizational culture) necessary to support the flow and processing of data and information. It determines a firm's capabilities or limitations. A poor, ineffective, or inappropriate infrastructure will undoubtedly cause problems for the firm; namely, inhibited growth, unrealized potential, service delivery failures, and uninformed decisions. All of these are undesirable and could be catastrophic to the firm. While most of the infrastructure remains behind the scenes, its failure will quickly bring it into the fore. Therefore, one must not underestimate the importance of infrastructure, and one must not skimp in this area. Such shortsightedness almost always causes heartaches and growing pains at a later point in time. Instead, one should pay close attention to the selection, building, and ongoing maintenance and updating of the firm's IT infrastructure. This is not to say that the entire infrastructure has to be purchased at once; it should be scalable, adaptable, and purchased as needed.

The infrastructural elements are discussed throughout this book and will be explored in greater detail in Chapter 11. Of particular note are the systems architecture (hardware and software design, operating systems, and programming languages), network topology and communications protocols, the databases, data warehouses, data mining tools, intranet, security, systems procedures, organizational culture, and human elements. There is a broad range of systems in use within hospitality firms to run operations, link with suppliers and allied partners, and share data throughout the organization and across its value chain, the collection of all of the direct, indirect, and support functions, from supplier to customer, necessary to drive revenues and firm profitability. It is important for systems to be able to talk with one another; that is, share data back and forth with each other as business needs dictate. This sharing can be achieved only if the systems in use are able to talk the same language, which requires defining software, hardware, database, and communications standards at the onset. The data network then becomes the glue that connects various systems together. The databases are the underlying storage cabinets that house all data collected, and, in turn, allow users access to the data through queries, reports, and data sharing with other systems. As one might suspect, successful use of data between systems requires common language, terminology, and formats. In Chapter 9, we introduced data warehouses, mega storage houses for large volumes of complex data and data marts, subsets of a data warehouse with specialized groupings of data. Both of these are powered by sophisticated databases, and when data mining, querying, and reporting tools are applied, the data contained within can be ordered, processed, and analyzed so that key patterns can emerge to provide insights and guidance as to how to grow and better manage the business through new product and services offerings, pricing strategies, marketing campaigns, and so on.

Arguably, what is described here represents an idealistic state. Unfortunately, the hospitality industry is far from attaining such a state given the number and complexity of systems used today and the widespread use of older, outdated technology (i.e., legacy systems). Consequently, applications called middleware are used to assist in the integration—or at least communications—between disparate systems.

The Internet, with its ubiquity and common standards, opens up many doors to providing access to data. Many hospitality systems are becoming Web-enabled; that is, connected to the Web for data sharing and reporting. Security is a critical, yet sometimes overlooked, element of the infrastructure, especially when it comes to wireless technologies and applications. Data are a corporate asset, and like any other important asset vital to a firm's success and competitive advantage, data should be protected. Access should be limited to only those who need it, when and where they require such access. Firewalls, passwords, and encryption, among other things, are all part of the security infrastructure. Finally, when looking at the technology infrastructure, one should not overlook the organizational culture and humanistic elements (including support network) that play such vital roles in the attitudes towards and usage of IT throughout the firm. While it may not be necessary for hospitality managers to fully understand the technical ins and outs of their companies' IT infrastructure, it is essential for them to know the physical capabilities and limitations of this infrastructure. It will define what is and what is not possible.

10. Summary

In an Information Age, competition is based on information, the time it takes to acquire this information, how the organization and its employees act on this information, and how soon they act. The possibilities and applications for business intelligence are virtually endless. Think about how business intelligence can help you to better

manage and allocate resources, control operating costs, improve operational efficiencies and services offered, and drive revenue-enhancing opportunities. To manage the business by the numbers, IT and a good technology infrastructure are required along with highly capable managers. A performance measurement and monitoring system is an ideal application to assist managers in carrying out their duties and should become standard parts of every organization's technology applications portfolio. While business intelligence tools are great assets for managers, they do not replace the need for good, strong, intelligent managers. Software applications can process the data, but someone still needs to interpret the results and make the decisions.

Because information is perishable, timely access is critical, and since the quantity of information is often excessive, tools are needed to help filter out the noise from the substance. An EIS and DSS are key tools in a firm's business intelligence arsenal. They can offer different views of data, drill-down capabilities, and powerful analysis and reporting tools to help interpret meaning from the data, thereby reducing the time involved in analyzing data and the level of statistical **knowledge** required by managers. To provide value, these systems must provide meaningful information for a well-defined set of measures and managerial questions so that managers can quickly address the issue(s) at hand. These systems must also allow some customization to meet user preferences and job needs. A more effective and productive manager, someone who is constantly in the know and armed with up-to-the minute data, can spread himself or herself further across the organization and make better (i.e., fact-based versus gut-based)

decisions. By being more informed, managers are in better control of their environment. They can, therefore, better coach their employees and raise the level of accountability for all departments, teams, and managers around the resort. To a large extent, management can now be done on an exception basis, but one must keep in mind that an exception does not necessarily have to imply a negative situation or identify an underachiever. It can also be used to recognize positive results, star performers, and factors contributing to the organization's success. Remember, the power is in the information and our ability to interpret and apply that information at the *right* times in appropriate and ethical manners.

Consider decision making on a continuum anchored by gut instinct on one end and disciplined analytics on the other (see Figure 10-7). Decision variables such as type of decision, cost, what's at stake, past history, risks, and so on may determine how decisions are made and where they fall on this continuum. Generally speaking, decision making should be disciplined, not based simply on conjecture or a gut feeling. Oftentimes, the risks of making incorrect decisions are too great to allow such a casual or uninformed approach. It is much easier to gain approval and resources when decisions are well researched and driven by data than when they are based upon hunches or opinions alone. That said, it is also important to remember that information is not

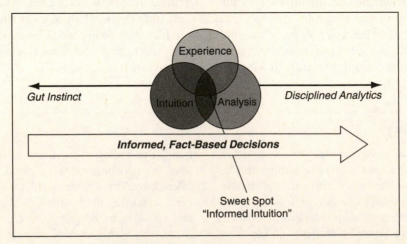

FIGURE 10-7 Applying Discipline and Rigor to Decision-Making

always perfect or complete, and that there is not always enough time or resources to capture and analyze all of the information needed or wanted to make decisions. Managers must be comfortable with some level of ambiguity or uncertainty while relying on the accessible information and the analysis of this information that can be completed within the available time. As a complement, they must also apply their experience, judgment, and intuition to make well-informed decisions. Thus, there is a delicate balance to the amount of time and discipline used to make decisions and the need to be agile, entrepreneurial, and sometime spontaneous. Most business decisions (especially significant ones) will likely be made somewhere in the middle of the continuum rather than at the ends with a bias towards some appropriate level of disciplined research and analysis. This balance is illustrated in Figure 10-7.

Leading business strategists suggest that the key to winning the future is to develop industry foresight and to stake one's territorial claim before anyone else. Following this advice, however, is not as easy as it may sound, especially when one takes into account how quickly things change in the high-tech era. Each day, the seeds of change are sewn. By using disciplined approaches and capable IT, these seeds can be spotted early on as they germinate, sprout, and grow into something big. IT applications are essential in helping us wade through that voluminous data to uncover trends, patterns, and meaning, but remember, technology is not enough. It is how we (and our staff) use the technology and the information it yields that will make a difference. Learning to ask good, intelligent questions, having the systems in place to be able to answer these questions, and knowing how to interpret and apply the answers are important and required traits for hospitality managers. Knowledge, not location, is the key competitive determinant in the digital economy. In sum, applying business intelligence in a hospitality organization is about knowing your business to create value (see Figure 10-8). Continue to learn and improve. Understand your guests and competition, and arm your employees with this information. Offer the right products and services to the right guests at the right time and price. Monetize your guests by making them more loyal and enticing them to purchase upgrades and additional products and services more frequently. Finally, deliver value and personalized services to be unique and to wow your guests. Through information, you can create sustainable competitive advantage.

Moving forward, the playing field and rules of engagement will be quite different than what we have seen in the past. New business models will emerge, especially as the Internet, intranets, and mobile technologies gain in both capabilities and in presence in our industry. It is clear that we are in for some exciting times ahead of us!

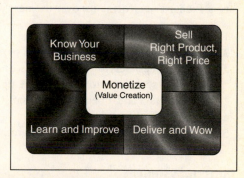

FIGURE 10-8 Business Intelligence Priorities

11. Case Study and Learning Activity

Case Study
Measurement before Management

Richard Sperry works for a major hotel management company. His corporate office has decided that his talents, honed as the head of strategy for the brand, need to be targeted towards the northeastern sector of the United States. This region has forty-five hotels and is presently the corporation's weakest performing region. Of particular concern to his boss is the ability of one of the competitors in the region to respond to market forces more readily, leaving the company at a major disadvantage. One competitor in particular always seems to have its finger on the pulse and adjusts its room rates perfectly to meet shifting demand seen in the region. Its package deals constantly meet with high approvals, and owners couldn't be happier.

Having been burned from the many "if you buy it, they will come," computer solutions offered by many vendors in the dot.com era, management is skeptical of purchasing new systems. Fortunately, Richard has a history of solving problems with little increased spending due to his ability to manage and use information effectively. Management is in clear agreement that the company is presently at a competitive disadvantage. Rather than react to every new offering a competing property may introduce to the marketplace, Richard and his boss concur that the best strategy to compete is to better use information to build a solid foundation of smart business practices blended with quality service offerings. The following four goals have been established and will be used as the basis of measuring Richard's performance over the next year:

1. Increase revenue by 5 percent
2. Increase occupancy percentage by 6 percent
3. Increase Guest Service Index (GSI) scores to 3.5 (on a scale of 1 to 5, with 5 being the most satisfied and 1 being the least satisfied)
4. Decrease food costs by 5 percent
5. Reduce employee turnover by 15 percent

Current Systems

Luckily for Richard, each hotel recently upgraded its technology applications portfolio. Currently, each property shares a similar network infrastructure and common OS. High-speed Internet access is available at all properties on personal computers running Windows. Software, despite being upgraded, has not been standardized throughout the company. Among the forty-five hotels in Richard's region, there are three different PMSs, four different restaurant POS systems, and three different

database architectures in use. Additionally, word processing, spreadsheet, and other productivity software differ from property to property. Browser software is equally divided in the company between Internet Explorer and Firefox.

Current Procedures

Report compilation and dissemination requires each hotel's night auditor to fax weekly flash reports to the regional office where the numbers are entered manually into spreadsheet so that a consolidated report for the region can be prepared. Comment cards, the sole measurement for GSI scores, are mailed to the corporate office each week. The corporate office compiles the scores to create the GSI index and then mails a printed report to the regional office each month. The food and beverage director submits bi-weekly purchasing histories and nightly sales data to the on-site controller who compiles the data and e-mails a series of reports to the regional office. Each month, the regional office e-mails a series of summary financial and operating reports to the corporate office and each property in the region detailing actual performance versus budget and year-to-date statistics. These reports are then reviewed by the general manager and become the subject of discussion in executive committee meetings at each hotel.

Richard has some great ideas for a new strategy. He knows that he has to be able to measure what he is about to manage. Our learning activity is based on that theme.

Learning Activity

1. What are the key problems facing Richard Sperry and his organization as described in this scenario? If you were in Richard's shoes, how might you go about addressing these challenges? What would be your strategy and why? Be sure to provide appropriate justification and a specific (i.e., detailed and measurable) action plan.
2. Before any action is taken, what managerial measures must be implemented for the company's five goals, and how should these

be implemented? What procedural changes are required at each property and at the regional and corporate offices? How should these changes be introduced, and who should lead the change effort?

3. Would any of data require access restriction? If so, who should have access, and to which data?

4. Evaluate the technology applications portfolio and infrastructure for Richard Sperry's company. What are its strengths and limitations?

In what ways is technology being used effectively? Where is there room for improvement? What changes would you suggest and why?

5. If you were to design a balanced scorecard approach for measuring and monitoring performance and the overall health of the organization for Richard Sperry's company, how would you go about it? Where would you start? What issues might you face, and how can you overcome them? What would your proposed balanced scorecard look like?

12. Key Terms

Balanced scorecard
Business intelligence
Cause-and-effect
Critical success factors
Customer analytics
Data
Data hierarchy
Data mining
Decision support system (DSS)
Drill-down

Executive information system (EIS)
Flash Reports
Information
Informationalize
Information asymmetry
IT infrastructure
Knowledge management
Lagging indicators
Leading measures

Online analytical processing (OLAP)
Predictive analysis
Red flags
Scenario-building
Simulation
Value chain
What-if analysis
Wisdom

13. Chapter Questions

1. What are the characteristics of and differences between data and information? Why is it important to distinguish between the two, and how can one convert data into usable information?

2. Why should a business intelligence system be part of a hospitality organization's IT portfolio? Prepare a compelling business case to convince a skeptical hospitality industry executive why he or she should commit resources to secure and implement a business intelligence solution?

3. Why do hospitality managers feel a sense of information overload? How can they cope? What strategies and techniques will you use as a manager to avoid succumbing to information overload?

4. As a hospitality manager in an information economy, what are the important traits for you to possess? What information would you consider essential to

be a successful manager? How would you use this information?

5. What are the core IT infrastructural components to a company's information systems and why are they so important? What roles can the Web, intranets, and mobile technologies play?

6. Is information the basis of competition in today's marketplace? Can information provide competitive advantage? If so, how?

7. About what issues associated with data collection should a hospitality manager be aware? How can hospitality organizations improve the quality of their data?

8. Select a hospitality organization or department within a hospitality organization. For that organization or department, design an ideal balanced

scorecard? What measurement categories and measures would you use and why?

9. What are the differences between an executive information system (EIS) and a decision support system (DSS)?

10. How is IT raising the bar of accountability, changing the way we manage operations, and contributing to performance of employees and the firm as a whole? How do we, as managers, know what questions to ask and where to find their answers?

11. What are knowledge management systems, and how do they differ from a series of databases? Why do organizations need them (in other words, what are the driving forces? what are the primary applications; and what's their business value?), and how do you tangibly measure their benefits and ROI?

12. Why should people share information? How does sharing information change its value?

13. What are the ethical considerations involving the use of data and information that managers should take into account? Why are these important?

14. How can hospitality organizations create processes and IT infrastructures for more effective management and enhanced performance and productivity? What is required? What challenges might exist, especially culturally, technically, and organizationally?

15. What factors lead to good (i.e., effective) versus poor (i.e., ineffective) decision-making or decision outcomes?

14. REFERENCES

Davenport, Thomas H. and Harris, Jeanne G. (2007). *Competing on analytics: The new science of winning.* Cambridge: Harvard Business School Publishing.

Gates, Bill (with Hemingway, Collins). (1999). *Business @ the speed of thought: Using a digital nervous system.* New York: Warner Books.

Kaplan, Robert S. and Norton, David P. (1996). *The balanced scorecard: Translating strategy into action.* Boston: Harvard Business School Press.

Lönnqvist, Antti and Pirttimäki, Virpi. (2006, Winter). Measuring business intelligence. *Information Systems Management, 23* (1), 32–40.

Norton, David. (2009, June). SAS Predictive Analytics: Harrah's builds customer loyalty. *Information Management Magazine* [Online]. Available: http://www.information-management.com/issues/2007_59/sas_predictive_analytics-10015490-1.html.

Overby, Stephanie. (2007, June 13). The price is always right. *CIO* [Online]. Available: http://www.cio.com/article/119209/The_Price_Is_Always_Right.

Piliouras, Teresa. (2006, January 9). Harrah's loyalty program impacts entire operation. *PhoCusWright GDX.*

CHAPTER 11

Technology in the Casino Industry

Chapter Contents

INTERVIEW

Michael Cruz, Director of Gaming Laboratory Operations—Pennsylvania Gaming Control Board

Q: Thank you for agreeing to this interview. I think the readers will find it interesting. Can you start by telling us what your degree is in? Where did you go to school?

A: I graduated from Rutgers University in 2003 with my Bachelor of Science in Electrical and Computer Engineering. It wasn't easy because I took eighteen or more credits each semester and worked a part-time job, but I loved the subjects.

Q: Did you plan on getting into the casino industry when you were in college? How did you end up in the industry?

A: The casino industry wasn't even on my radar. I didn't know where I wanted to work. All I knew is that I wanted to work with computers.

When I graduated, the country was going through the aftermath of the dot.com bust. There were very few IT jobs available and I didn't know where I'd find a job. I went to a career fair at Rutgers and just dropped my resume off at the booth of the New Jersey Division of Gaming Enforcement. I didn't even talk to the recruiter. The chief engineer called me and described the job. It sounded interesting so I applied and got it.

I think my resume stood out because I had an internship for each summer. Each was broadly based and two of the internships focused on quality assurance. My classmates tended to take internships in programming. Of course, the Division of Gaming Enforcement ensures the quality assurance of the slot machines on the casino floor so my background was what they were looking for.

Q: Can you describe your career path from school to your current position?

A: I was an Engineer with New Jersey's Division of Gaming Enforcement from 2003 to 2006. When I left in 2006, I held the title of senior engineer. I took the position of manager of slot certification with the Pennsylvania Gaming Control Board in February 2006. Those were busy times. I was deeply involved in opening the first casinos in Pennsylvania— Mohegan Sun at Pocono Downs and Philadelphia Park Racetrack and Casino.

Just a year after being hired, I was promoted to senior manager of Gaming Laboratory Operations in February 2007. I supervised the Lab's role in the opening of Harrah's Chester Casino and Racetrack, Presque Isle Downs and Casino, The Meadows Racetrack and Casino, and Mount Airy Casino Resort. I also directed the opening of the slot machine testing laboratory in our Harrisburg offices in September 2007. They're state of the art and it was a very involved process. The year 2007 was an incredibly busy year.

In January 2008 I was appointed director of Gaming Laboratory Operations which is my position today.

Q: If I may say so, you seem young. How old are you?

A: You're not the first one to notice. I'm 29. I know that seems young, but I received excellent training when I worked at the New Jersey Division of Gaming Enforcement. I was surrounded by top notch people who had been in the field their entire careers. I made a decision early on to learn as much as I could. I like to learn anyway, but I also know that my career advancement depends on my knowledge. Anyone in the IT field has to keep up on the latest developments to advance. I think my rapid rise is proof of that.

Q: That's pretty impressive. Most of the individuals you deal with at the PGCB and in industry are considerably older. Has that ever been a problem?

A: I have never experienced any kind of discrimination due to my age. People respect ability. If someone can do their job and do it well, they get the respect they need.

Q: What do the Gaming Laboratory Operations do at the Pennsylvania Gaming Control Board?

A: One of our main focuses is quality assurance. Act 71 which legalized slot casinos in Pennsylvania set out the overall rules for casino gambling in Pennsylvania. The Pennsylvania Gaming Control Board created regulations which interpreted the intent of the law. The regulations are incredibly detailed. The Laboratory ensures that manufacturers build slot machines that comply with the regulations.

We test in the laboratory to minimize the variables that can affect performance. In other words, does the machine do what it is designed to do without interference? A slot machine cannot be placed on a casino floor without our certification.

I also have technical field representatives. They are based regionally around the state so that they can reach a casino in a reasonable amount of time. They spend most of their time overseeing the moves of slot machines around the casino floor. As you know, casinos are always moving machines in the hope of attracting more play. They can't move their machines unless one of my field representatives is present.

My field representatives will also solve minor problems at the casinos. However, if there is a more involved problem such as a potential software bug, they will report the situation to my staff in the Harrisburg lab. Together they solve the problem.

My field representatives are the first responders when there is an integrity issue. Generally speaking, you may have heard of incidents when customers have tried to tamper with machines or cheat the casinos. In those cases, my employees would be called in immediately. They gather the who, what, where, when, and why of the situation and report back to the lab in Harrisburg. In turn, this allows me to assist any agency in the Commonwealth such as the Pennsylvania State Police, local police, etc. in their resulting investigation.

Q: Why does the Gaming Control Board have a testing lab? Aren't their privately run labs available to do the same work?

A: Act 71 requires an in-house laboratory. I don't know why the law was written that way, but there are three reasons that I can see. First is proximity. Our lab is in downtown Harrisburg. The legislature is across the street. The Gaming Control Board members are in the same building. If there is a question to be answered or a need for an appearance by me or my staff, it can be accommodated quickly. Gaming Laboratories International (GLI) and BMM Compliance are the two largest private testing and certification laboratories. GLI is based in Lakewood, New Jersey, and BMM is in Las Vegas. It isn't nearly as convenient for them to handle questions or appearances.

Secondly, I and my staff are experts on the statute and regulations in effect in Pennsylvania. We have only one jurisdiction to serve and we know it inside and out. We also know of developments in legislation and regulations as they occur. GLI and BMM cannot keep abreast of changes in Pennsylvania's legislation and regulations the way we can.

Finally, we are not for profit. Our motivation is to serve the Commonwealth of Pennsylvania. There are no competing incentives or loyalties.

Q: What is your role in the Laboratory?

A: I steer the ship. I have a competent staff who needs me to set the direction. They are all professionals and do a good job.

I also explain technical issues to individuals who do not have technical knowledge. I have to convert the terminology of slot machines into lay terms so that people understand. I do this for legislators, reporters, Board members, and others. In the process I educate people on the components of a modern slot machine and the Pennsylvania regulations.

I act as a liaison to the press, legislature, Board and others. Whether it is a new law, new regulation, or a breaking story, I am asked to give information and represent the laboratory and the Board. This role overlaps with my role in explaining technical issues. The two can't be separated. In acting as a liaison, technical issues come up and I have to explain.

I love the hands-on work and I miss testing machines. I don't have time to do that anymore, but I find time to troubleshoot in the lab. It keeps me in touch with current machines and helps me maintain a relationship with all my employees.

Q: What did you learn along your career path that prepared you for your current position?

A: I learned a lot especially from the people I worked with in New Jersey. They were a source of knowledge and wisdom. The one thing I learned that has helped me tremendously is an attitude of "firm, but fair."

We have a responsibility to hold manufacturers and casinos to the regulations. If a manufacturer's product or a casino's system doesn't meet the standard, we have to withhold certification. However, I am always willing to discuss possible solutions to the short-comings. You never know where innovation will come from and a shortcoming can create the incentive to develop new ways of doing things. As long as the resulting solution meets the standards in the regulation, we will consider it.

Q: What changes have you seen in the technology of electronic gaming devices since you started in the industry?

A: Networking is the biggest change. Slot machines used to be individual machines. Each was unique in the game it offered and in its appearance. A customer knew they were sitting at a "Reel 'Em In" or an "I Dream of Jeannie" machine.

The next phase of gaming technology which is under review for certification and imple-mentation is server-based gaming. The underlying technology is not proprietary and is avail-able to any manufacturer. The different machines will be linked to a server (client/server network topology—Chapter 4) with CAT5 and CAT6 cables. Using TCP/IP protocols, the server will communicate with the individual units on the casino floor. The server will have a database of approved games. The customer will sit at the machine, select the game they want to play, and it will appear on the screen. The signage on the front of the machine will be delivered via LCD technology so that the appearance of the machine changes with the game selection. The actual frame of the machine will be generic in nature, but unique to each manufacturer.

This is exciting from both the technology standpoint as well as accommodating the needs of the gambling public.

Q: What do you do to stay current?

A: I attend the Global Gaming Expo (G2E) in Las Vegas. It is the largest gaming conference and trade show in the world, held every November. Over twenty-five thousand people from around the world attend and over seven hundred companies and individuals exhibit their products and services.

I spoke on a panel at the 2008 show. I enjoy that, but to stay current I visit the trade show portion. Slot machine manufacturers exhibit machines that vary from concept ma-chines to machines close to regulatory approval. I see what is coming down the pipeline. It prepares me and it offers me a chance to give the manufacturer feedback on how the ma-chine would need to be modified to meet Pennsylvania's regulations.

Manufacturers will contact me during the year as well. They will explain their new products and ideas for products. I'll give them my feedback so they can incorporate changes before they seek approval.

It's a constantly changing field and I have to keep on top of developments. Otherwise, I can't do my job well.

Q: Thank you for taking the time to talk to us. Is there anything you'd like to add?

A: Thank you for asking me to participate. I hope the students reading your book will find what I said interesting and helpful. The only thing I would add is to recommend that stu-dents keep learning throughout their career. I find something new to learn every day. I like to learn so it's easy. But I know that I need to keep learning or my career will stop dead in its tracks. College is just the start. Your whole life is a learning process.

1. INTRODUCTION

Michael provided us with some great insights into the changing faces of gaming technology. The casinos in the early days of legalization in Nevada were nothing more than a saloon with a couple tables and slot machines. Beyond the mechanical components of the slot machines, there was very little technology. Controls were all manually completed. Surveillance was handled by the bar owner or manager who watched his employees to be sure they did not steal and his customers to be sure they did not cheat. Some of the technological changes which have affected casinos filtered in from other businesses such as the use of ATMs. But many changes are related to the core business activities of a casino and originated within the industry.

Most readers of this textbook have not worked in a casino. They may have visited a casino, but they do not understand the inner workings. Because we will be discussing the impact of technology, we need a common vocabulary. First we need to define some terms and processes we will encounter in our discussion.

2. DEFINITIONS

Although technology has had an impact on all areas of casino operations, the greatest impact has been on the slot floor. When someone within the casino industry speaks about the **slot floor**, they are referring to the area of the casino which offers **electronic gaming devices**. These devices are grouped in rows on the same cabinet base called **banks**. The devices in a bank of machines are usually from the same manufacturer, although there may be numerous manufacturers represented on the slot floor overall.

The slot floor usually surrounds a grouping of table games. The table games area is not considered part of the slot floor. In fact, it is referred to as the **pit floor** or **table games floor**. Consequently in a conversation, the participants can refer to the slot floor and the pit floor when talking about the same general area of the casino. To confuse communication further, the term *floor* refers to the entire area of a casino including all gaming activities such as table games, keno, racebook, electronic gaming devices, and **cashier cage**. The context of the conversation is usually a clear indicator of which definition of floor is in use.

The cashier cage is the location on the casino floor that acts as the hub for all activity related to **cash** and **cash equivalents**. Cash is coin and currency distributed by the U.S. government as legal tender. Currency is commonly referred to as *bills*. Cash equivalents are primarily the *chips* of the casino. They are the equivalent of cash because they have value within the casino and are used in the place of cash.

The name *cashier cage* is sometimes shortened to *cage*. The cashier cage acts as a clearing house for customers and other casino departments alike. Customers can come to the cashier cage to purchase chips, exchange chips for cash, or simply get change for large bills. The table games department will come to the cashier cage to obtain a **fill**. A fill is a request for chips that the table games department makes in order to increase the inventory of chips in a table game's **chip rack**. The chip rack is the brass insert in front of the dealer that holds the dealer's chips. At times the number of chips may run low if players are winning. In order to ensure the dealer has enough inventory of chips to service the players, the table games supervisor will request a fill.

The cashier cage is also responsible for the **drop**. The term *drop* has more than one definition. The context of the discussion determines which definition is in use. The most common definition refers to the money which the casino collects from its players. It is the money wagered and lost.

The term *drop* can also mean the process which the casino employs to collect the drop from each table game and electronic gaming device. Most casinos perform this process once a day, although some will perform it once a shift. Several employees from the cashier cage department form a **drop team**. They are accompanied by a security officer who is considered part of the drop team. The drop team systematically goes through the casino and removes drop boxes from table games and **bill validators** from electronic gaming devices. Empty drop boxes and bill validators replace those that are removed (see Figure 11-1).

A drop box is a metal box that is securely attached to the underside of a table game. It has a slit in the top of the box. The slit is aligned with a slit in the table. There is a plastic paddle that rests in this slit at all times. When a customer requests chips for currency, the dealer will make the exchange. The final step is to remove the plastic paddle, lay the currency across the slit, then reinsert the paddle so that the currency is forced into the drop box. The drop box accumulates all the currency exchanged on the table game.

A bill validator is a piece of equipment in an electronic gaming device which scans every bill inserted by a customer. It checks that the bill is whole and not counterfeit. Once it determines a bill is valid, the machine will register the appropriate number of credits and the player may begin playing. The bill validator will store the inserted currency until it is collected by the drop team.

The drop team will take the bill validators and drop boxes to the count room. When coins were used in slot machines, there was a **hard count room** and a **soft count room**. Coins are counted in the hard count room and currency in the soft count room. Obviously, their names came from the characteristics of the drop being counted. Because coins are no longer used, there is simply the count room. Often, the count room and the vault are combined to conserve space and labor.

Returning to the slot floor, electronic gaming devices have a microprocessor chip inside them called a random number generator. It is referred to by the acronym **RNG**. The RNG constantly generates numbers. Each number has an associated outcome. When the player presses the button to activate the spin, the number which the RNG generates at that moment is selected. The outcome associated with that number is displayed on the screen and the player loses or wins.

If a player wins, he or she receives a **payout**. In other words, the machine pays out winnings because the symbols displayed on the screen are considered a winning combination. For example, three diamonds are displayed on a designated path across the screen. This designated path is called the **pay line**. Early slot machines had one or three pay lines. Today's electronic gaming devices can have over fifty pay lines.

FIGURE 11-1 The Drop Team Pushes a Cart Like This One around the Casino as It Collects the Drop Boxes from Table Games and Bill Validators from Electronic Gaming Devices

Table 11-1	Excerpt from a Pay Table of a Liberty Bell Slot Machine			
	Reel 1	**Reel 2**	**Reel 3**	**Payout**
Outcome 1	Cherry	Lemon	Blank	1 coin
Outcome 2	Cherry	Lemon	Bell	1 coin
Outcome 3	Cherry	Lemon	Lemon	1 coin
Outcome 4	Cherry	Lemon	Cherry	1 coin
Outcome 5	Cherry	Cherry	Blank	2 coins
Outcome 6	Cherry	Cherry	Bell	2 coins
Outcome 7	Cherry	Cherry	Lemon	2 coins
Outcome 8	Cherry	Cherry	Cherry	5 coins

The arrangement of the numbers and payouts is called the **pay table**. When slot machines were simpler, the pay table was smaller and easier to visualize. It literally listed all possible combinations of symbols and blanks on a three-reel machine. Because there were twenty stops per reel, there were only eight thousand possible combinations. In most cases, three symbols were needed across the middle line to generate a payout.

Some of the earliest slot machines were manufactured by the Liberty Bell company. They are referred to as *Liberty Bells*. Their symbols were a cherry, a lemon, a bell shaped like the Liberty Bell, and a blank or an absence of a symbol. For example, the excerpt from a pay table of a Liberty Bell machine is in Table 11-1.

Of course, there would be eight thousand entries rather than just four. But eight thousand is nothing compared to today's devices. Due to the RNG, the pay table of an electronic gaming device has over 8 billion possible outcomes. The pay table is literally impossible to write on a piece of paper. It is completely managed in the memory of a computer.

The **pay pattern** refers to the pattern of the pay table. If you were able to write out the pay table of a device, the winning combinations would show a pattern. The pattern would indicate the different ways to win and how many times each winning combination was associated with a number generated by the RNG.

When slot machines were prevalent, they paid out most of their winners from the coins in their **hopper**. The hopper was a storage space inside the machine. The casino would place a starting inventory into the hopper. But the play of customers would maintain it. When a player inserted coins into the machine, the coins would slide down a chute into the hopper. When a player won, the payout would be collected from the hopper mechanically and spilled out into a tray at the bottom of the machine. The hopper would need to be refilled when a player won a payout larger than the inventory of coins in the hopper.

Now that we have defined the various terms and processes we will be using, let's turn our attention to the impact of technology on the casino industry.

3. ELECTRONIC GAMING DEVICES

You will notice I did not use the term slot machine. There is a reason. Charles Fey invented the slot machine in 1887 in San Francisco. It was completely mechanical in nature which was in keeping with the technology of the era. If you recall your American and world history, the nineteenth century was a time of industrialization. Processes formerly done by hand were mechanized. This led to tremendous productivity increases on farms and in factories.

Mechanization was extended to other areas through inventions and innovation. The slot machine is one example. The original slot machines were a novelty meant to pay off in candy and gum. They were placed in drug stores and similar outlets where the customer inserted a coin into a slot on the top of the machine. Gravity pulled the coin down a chute which flipped a lever allowing the customer to pull the handle and release the reels. The reels were powered by strong springs which made them spin. Eventually they would stop. The symbols on the reels corresponded with certain prizes. To win the prize, the same symbol had to appear on each reel along the line etched across the viewing glass.

Slot machines did not change appreciably for nearly one hundred years. The introduction by Bally of electromechanical machines in the 1960s signaled a significant change in slot machine technology. These machines combined mechanical and electrical components. The mechanical switch which allowed handles to be pulled became an electronic sensor. This sensor performed better because it could detect counterfeit coins, otherwise known as slugs. The hopper where the coins for payouts were stored was larger than in strictly mechanical machines. Larger payouts were possible and more payouts could be made without the assistance of slot department employees.

The electronic components also allowed for more combinations on the reel. This, in turn, allowed for more winning combinations along more pay lines. The original slot machines would payout along up to three straight lines from left to right. The electromechanical machines could pay out on the diagonal as well. The electromechanical machines also allowed for a fourth and fifth reel which allowed for additional pay lines. While this seems tame compared to today's electronic gaming devices, these were major advances in terms of meeting customers' needs.

While Bally first introduced the electromechanical machine in 1964, it was years before the market accepted the new machines. Part of the reason is the inertia of any market to embrace change. However, slot machines were offered primarily as an amenity by casinos. Table games generated the majority of revenue and were considered more glamorous. Certainly, it took more skill to play "21" or craps than it did to pull the handle of a slot machine. Initially men gravitated towards the table games. To keep male table games players gambling longer, casinos installed slot machines so the wives and girlfriends of these players would have something to do. If they were occupied, they were less likely to drag their husband or boyfriend away from the tables.

Since casino managers did not see the revenue potential of slot machines nor did they respect the slot player, they did not see a need to look at innovative products. Introducing the new electromechanical machines to the slot floor was also hindered by the slow acceptance of the new machines by the market. Dedicated slot players liked their mechanical machines and did not immediately recognize the benefits of the new machines. For all these reasons, electromechanical machines were not fully integrated into the slot layouts of casinos until the 1980s.

The new machines' electronic components spurred other innovations. More than one machine could be networked to monitor play on several machines. With this capability, **progressive jackpots** were created. A progressive jackpot starts at a minimum dollar amount and advances in size with each coin played on any of the linked machines. If a player has played the full number of coins and hits the requisite combination of symbols, he or she wins the progressive jackpot. Initially set to hit in the thousands of dollars, the progressives were rapidly designed to reach into the hundreds of thousands and millions of dollars.

Once the Nevada Gaming Control Board approved the progressive feature, a further innovation was created. Machines were linked between casinos; sometimes within a market, but other times among different markets. The advantage of linking machines from different markets allowed a company that owned a casino in Las Vegas and Reno to keep the progressive jackpot within the company. The marketing advantage of offering statewide progressives or a progressive that linked machines in Nevada and New Jersey is obvious. As companies expanded into new gaming jurisdictions during the 1990s, this advantage grew in significance.

The innovation in personal computing and video games that occurred in the 1990s spread to slot machines. The technology that produced the Mario Brothers and Nintendo allowed slot machine designers to create video slot machines. No longer were there actual reels, but virtual reels were made to look as if they were spinning. No longer did the mechanical force of a spring propel the reels. Instead the previously discussed RNG was introduced.

Although the customer sees reels spinning, that is only an illusion. The outcome could just as easily be displayed instantaneously. However, tradition and player psychology requires the spinning reels.

It was during this time that the popularity of slot machines began to increase. Because they were more intriguing with larger payouts, they drew from a larger audience. Slot revenue slowly increased until it surpassed table games revenue in Nevada in the 1990s.

The term *slot machine* is obsolete. *Electronic gaming device* is the current nomenclature because it more accurately describes the piece of equipment. The current machines are closer to a video game than the slot machine invented by Charles Fey. They are primarily electronic in nature with very few mechanical parts. They are less machine and more device.

The transformation of slot machines into electronic gaming devices through the introduction of the RNG brought other innovations. Most machines today do not have a handle. Its use as a release for the reels is no longer needed. There are very complex pay lines possible. A pay line can zigzag from top to bottom as it crosses the reels. Some machines have fifty pay lines or more. Winning combinations can pay left to right, right to left, or both. **Bonus rounds** and **scatter pays** are possible due to the computing ability of today's devices.

A bonus round is a feature on a device that takes the player from the starting screen of the device into a new screen. There may or may not be reels. Themed devices such as Star Wars by IGT, Inc., show a completely different screen. Sometimes the bonus round involves player involvement in making choices. Other bonus rounds simply give the player additional free spins. Video clips of favorite shows or movies can be inserted as winnings accumulate. The current complexity of bonus round offerings often bewilders players.

Scatter pays are a simpler form of bonus. Certain symbols must appear on the screen in order to activate the scatter pay. Typically at least three of these symbols must appear. Once they appear, the device will award an arbitrary number of credits to the player's credit balance on the device. There is often animation or a video clip inserted while the credits are being awarded.

4. TICKET IN, TICKET OUT

The most significant innovation, however, has been **Ticket In Ticket Out**. Otherwise referred to as **TITO**, Ticket In Ticket Out has revolutionized the slot department. The capability of the devices now allows for bill validators to be installed so that customers can insert bills instead of coins (see Figure 11-2). The amount of credit is displayed on the screen. The player's bets are deducted from the credit balance when placed and the player's winnings are added to the credit balance. When a customer has finished playing on a machine, they press the "cash out" button. Instead of coins falling out of the bottom of the device like they did on slot machines, a ticket is printed with the dollar amount of credit. One side of the ticket displays the date and time, the dollar amount numerically and alphabetically, a bar code, machine number, name of casino, ticket number, and an ID number. The reverse side is used for marketing purposes, typically

FIGURE 11-2 Ticket In Ticket Out Technology Has Transformed Customer Service, Casino Financial Control, and Slot Department Job Descriptions

displaying the logo of the casino. The customer can take this ticket and insert it into the next device, turn it in at the cashier cage for cash, or insert it into ATM-like machines around the casino which cashes the ticket.

The innovation surrounding TITO has been embraced enthusiastically by the market and the casinos. Customers favor TITO because they do not have to find a slot changeperson to convert their bills into coins. Instead they go directly to the machine they want to play and begin. Currency does not soil their hands the way coins do. Avid slot players used to wear gloves to avoid getting a gray film of filth on their hands. Tickets and bills are much lighter to carry than a bucket of coins. Customers do not have to take a bucket of winnings to the cashier cage to obtain currency. They have the option of presenting their ticket to the cashier cage or an ATM-like machine in a quick transaction. They can easily take the ticket from one machine and insert it into another machine, hence, maximizing their play time.

Casinos have embraced the TITO technology because it improves customer service. Customers maximize their play time rather than waiting in line to change currency into coin or coin into currency. There have been significant labor savings. The position of slot changeperson has been eliminated. Far fewer employees are needed on the floor. Because coins have been nearly eliminated from the casino floor, fewer employees are needed for the drop team and in the count room.

As you learned earlier, the drop team is a group of cashier cage employees who remove drop boxes from table games and bill validators from electronic gaming devices. The drop team makes a sweep through the entire casino removing all drop boxes and bill validators and replacing them with empty drop boxes and bill validators. The drop is then taken to the count room to be counted and entered into the accounting system. Whereas there was a need for a hard count room to count coins and a soft count room to count currency prior to TITO, afterward there are almost no coins to count. Typically, the count rooms are combined into one room with a corresponding reduction in staff. The reduction in staff and in the square footage dedicated to non-revenue producing areas means a significant savings for casinos.

As we also touched on before, depending upon the size of the casino and the volume of play, the drop team may make a round as often as once a shift. Again due to TITO, though, it is more typical that the drop is done once a day, around midnight. The team is accompanied by a security officer to ensure no one tries to steal the drop and to ensure none of the drop team employees embezzles money. Doing the drop less frequently frees up man-hours in the cashier cage and in security for other productive activities and ultimately reduces the staffing levels and labor costs of the casino.

Fewer coins needed on the floor translate into fewer coins needed in inventory. The vault and cashier cage need far fewer coins than before TITO was implemented. Reducing inventory not only frees up funds for other uses, but reduces the carrying costs of inventory.

Casinos also use TITO because of the improved security of funds. The TITO system traces each transaction in a digital record kept by the computer. At any point in time, casino management can determine where money is on the casino floor. If there is a complaint from a customer or a discrepancy with an employee's money handling, the computer provides a very detailed record of cash movement around the casino. In addition, the computer makes a notation every time an electronic gaming device is opened and by whose key. If a device is compromised, management can quickly determine who has been involved.

The integrity of the devices is of paramount importance to the casino. As long as the parts of the old mechanical slot machines were in good condition, the outcomes of the handle pull were random and the number of prizes awarded could be predicted. The casino could reliably generate revenue so long as the machine functioned properly. As you can imagine, mechanical parts wear over time and the outcomes would become less random. In addition, mechanical machines are easier for customers to manipulate. Whether it is a shaking motion to the entire unit or a cheating move such as **slugging** or **fishing**, the integrity of the mechanical machines was difficult to maintain.

Slugging is the use of counterfeit coins. By inserting a counterfeit coin, the cheater hoped to win a payout in legal tender. Essentially, they would win without betting money. Fishing was the use of a coin on a string. The coin was dropped down the slot until it released the handle, and then pulled back up for reuse. Again the hope was to win a payout in legal tender without placing a bet. These two forms of cheating are no longer possible with the new devices.

The new electronic gaming devices are less susceptible to physical manipulation because there are fewer mechanical parts. The electronic components mean that activity in the device is recorded on the central processing unit (CPU) of the device. In fact, if something occurs which is suspect, a message is sent to the CPU and an alert is issued.

It is rare that an innovation improves customer service, reduces expenses, and improves security at the same time. Everyone wins with TITO! The transformation from slot machine to electronic gaming device has been completed, but the future holds more innovation.

As we saw in the interview and learned in Chapter 4, there are devices in the testing stage of certification by gaming regulatory agencies that utilize **server-based gaming**. Essentially, this form of electronic gaming device stores the software for a particular game on a central server. A customer will be able to sit at a unit on the floor and choose the type of game they play. For example, they will be able to select from a menu of games such as Star Wars, Sex in the City, and Indiana Jones. They will be able to switch back and forth as their mood and losing streaks demand.

These server-based systems will be more sophisticated by tracking the customer's preferences more closely and issuing promotional offers right at the unit on the floor. They will allow the customer to make restaurant reservations or search the casino floor for certain machine types. A player will be able to call up a map of the casino floor to locate a bar, restaurant, retail shop, or the front desk. Essentially, the unit becomes a concierge for the player.

The next generation beyond this form of server-based gaming is already in development. This is a handheld unit which allows a player to move around the casino floor and game where they please, including a bar or lounge. This form is more in tune with younger customers who are used to their PlayStations and Xboxes. It is likely that these types of electronic gaming devices will have a higher proportion of skill involved in their play since the market is moving in this direction. Initially, bonus rounds may involve skill on the part of the customer. Further evolution will introduce skilled participation during the regular device activity.

The demand for this kind of electronic gaming device will be market-driven. As individuals move through their teens and adolescence into adulthood, they become potential casino customers. They will look for casino games that reflect their childhood activities. We saw this in the rise in the popularity of poker and we will see this in skill-based electronic gaming devices.

5. FILLS

As explained in the section on definitions, fills are requested by the table games supervisor in order to procure chips from the cashier cage. The chips are needed in an individual dealer's chip rack to maintain his or her inventory of chips so he or she can service the customers properly. It would be embarrassing if a dealer could not make a payout on a winning bet because he or she lacked an adequate number of chips.

The process before computerization was time consuming. The table games supervisor would note how much of each denomination of chips was needed on a slip of paper. He would call the security department and request a security officer. This could sometimes take a considerable amount of time if the security department was busy. The security officer took the slip of paper to the cashier cage and waited for the fill to be completed.

The cashier at the cashier cage would complete a triplicate form called a fill slip. The fill slips were numbered in sequence so that they could be accounted for. The fill slip had spaces for the pit number, table number, name of the requesting table games supervisor, name of the cashier, date, time, dollar amount of each denomination of chips, and more. All the information had to be completed manually.

The cashier placed the requested quantities of chips into a plastic rack or racks. She or he would count down the racks, initial the fill slip, and have the security officer initial the fill slip. This confirmed that the amount being transferred from the responsibility of the cashier to the responsibility of the security officer was indeed correct on the fill slip. She or he would keep two copies of the fill slip. One for her work and one for the cashier cage's master file.

The security officer would take the chips and the remaining copy of the fill slip to the requesting table games supervisor. He or she would accompany the security officer and the chips to the table which needed the chips. The dealer would stop dealing to accept the chips. The dealer would count the chips, confirm whether the fill slip accurately reflected the quantity, initial the fill slip, and place the chips in the chip rack as the security officer and table games supervisor witnessed this process. After placing all the chips in the chip rack, the dealer would force the fill slip into the drop box through the slit in the table top.

The dealer and the table games supervisor would go back to work and the security officer would take the chip racks back to the cashier cage.

With the advent of computerization, this process uses fewer man-hours. The table games supervisor accesses the computer in the pit. He requests a fill by completing an on-screen form. The computer automatically notes the date, time, pit, and requesting table games supervisor. The supervisor enters only the quantity of each denomination of chips and sends. The cashier cage receives the notification instantaneously. The cashier goes about filling the request while he or she waits for the security officer. At the time the request was sent from the pit to the cashier cage, a request for escort was sent to the security department dispatch desk. The dispatch desk notifies the security officer to report to the cashier cage to complete a fill. The officer is also told which pit is requesting the fill.

By the time the security officer arrives at the cashier cage, the fill is complete. The cashier has entered her information into the system and printed the fill slip. She or he keeps a copy for herself or himself and hands one to the security officer. The rest of the process is identical to the earlier process.

As you can see, the cashier and the security officer have reduced the time they spend on fills. In addition, the pit receives the fill much faster than before computers. The reduction of a few minutes might be the difference between an embarrassing moment for the dealer and flawless service delivery.

6. PLAYERS' CLUBS

With the advent of electromechanical machines and then electronic gaming devices, the computerized capability allowed for the development of **players' clubs**. A customer signs up for a casino's players' club either in the casino or online. The casino issues a plastic card similar to a credit card with a magnetic strip on the back. The front displays the player's name and membership number (see Figure 11-3).

When the customer is in the casino, he or she inserts the card into an electronic gaming device. The electronic gaming device accepts the card and displays a message on its display screen. Typically the message welcomes the player and provides the total number of points in his or her account. As the customer plays the device, the computer adds points to the balance according to a predetermined formula based on dollar amount bet. In many casinos, $5 will earn a point.

At any time, the customer can redeem his or her points for comps or retail items in the casino. **Comp** is short for complimentary goods or services. Presenting a players' club card at a restaurant allows the customer to eat for free. Points can be used towards the cost of a hotel room, souvenirs at the gift shop, drinks at a bar, and so on.

Players' clubs motivate customers to be loyal to a particular casino or casino company. If they have a substantial balance in a casino's players' club, they are more likely to return to the casino. Of course, customers factor in many elements when deciding which casinos to patronize. However, once they decide they like a particular casino, they get a players' club card. The complimentary goods and services reinforce their decision to patronize a casino.

These clubs were originally called slot clubs because they had only slot players as members. The technology to accurately track play was available on electromechanical machines and later electronic gaming devices. However, technology is catching up in the table games area. There is now software and hardware available to assist the table games supervisors in tracking players' activities.

The player presents his or her card to the table games supervisor who swipes the card in the system. All the pertinent information and forms appear on the computer screen. The supervisor enters the estimated average bet, type of game played, table game number, and other relevant information.

FIGURE 11-3 Every Casino Has a Players' Club to Encourage Players to Return and Spend More Money

As the supervisor monitors the player's action, he or she can reenter the system and update the information. For example, the player may switch from "21" to craps, may increase his average bet from $100 to $500, or may simultaneously bet on Keno. Each of these changes will affect the comps that the player can earn. By computerizing this information, technology has eased the burden on the table games supervisor.

7. RADIO FREQUENCY IDENTIFICATION

Technology is not sitting still here either. More comprehensive and sophisticated systems are in development which will monitor each bet played and its outcome. We will now look at a gaming application on a theme we discussed in Chapter 9, radio frequency identification or **RFID**. Remember, RFID is a chip which emits a radio frequency. It can be coded to identify the denomination, casino, and other information. By inserting an RFID chip into each chip of the casino, the casino can monitor the movement of each chip.

Sensors at the table games will know when a chip is in play and whether it won or lost by reading its position. If it moves from the player's area to the betting circle, it is in play. If it moves from the betting circle to the player's area, it won. If it moves from the betting circle to the chip rack, it lost. In this way, such a system can assess each bet a player makes and how much they win or lose.

Identifying a chip with a player occurs through radio waves at the table or when the player exchanges currency for chips. The players' club card takes on new significance as an ID as technology changes the tools available to the casino to track play. The improvement in the accuracy of tracking a table games player's action will be incredible.

8. CUSTOMER RELATIONSHIP MANAGEMENT

As we discussed in Chapter 9, **customer relationship management** is familiarly referred to as *CRM*. Just as in hotels and restaurants, CRM is a popular topic for casinos today and arguably done to a higher degree. Casino companies invest a lot of resources into identifying customers and cultivating a relationship with them. The purpose is to establish loyalty with a customer so his or her preferred casino experience is the hosting casino.

It all started with the slot clubs in the 1980s. As described before, the initial attempt was simply to track a slot player's action so that the appropriate comp could be provided. As the devices became more sophisticated and the computing power of computers increased, it was possible to create a database of extensive information on each player's gambling and spending patterns.

Using this information, casinos today send out direct mail pieces, e-mail blasts, tweets, and more to communicate to their customers, based on their prior patterns, that there is an offer that would be of interest to them. Due to the relatively inexpensive cost of using technology to communicate, a casino can customize an offer for nearly each individual.

Suppose a player enjoys staying at Paris Las Vegas, but plays slots at Bally's and goes to see Penn & Teller at the Rio frequently. These three properties are in the Harrah's Entertainment stable of casinos in Las Vegas. Knowing this behavior, Harrah's can send a promotional piece to this player offering a discounted room at Paris, an invitation to a slot tournament at Bally's, and a complimentary upgrade for tickets to Penn & Teller. How could this customer resist such an offer that perfectly matches his or her preferences?

This kind of customized promotion in turn encourages the customer to utilize these offers to return to the casino. All of this encourages loyalty on the part of the players. Of course, some players like more than one casino and receive offers from all of them. Ultimately, the customer wins, but so do the casinos.

9. SURVEILLANCE

Surveillance is the department of the casino which watches all the other departments to ensure that procedures are followed. If everyone follows procedures correctly, the integrity of controls is maintained. Adequate controls are needed to prevent customers from stealing cash and cash equivalents and employees from embezzling the same.

Remember from the introduction, when casino gaming was legalized in Nevada in 1931, the casinos were not much more than saloons with a few table games and a couple slot machines. They were amenities to encourage customers to stay and drink. There was little need for controls since little money was actually involved and the owner or manager could see all the action himself.

However, as casinos expanded into larger facilities after World War II, the manager could not observe all the activity on the casino floor. There was a greater need to observe employees and customers. A separate department was created to fulfill this function. Since most people do not break rules while being watched, the surveillance staff needed to be concealed while observing. Casinos built a gap between the ceiling of the casino and the floor above. They suspended walkways called catwalks in this space. They also installed two-way mirrors in the casino ceiling. Surveillance employees would crawl along the catwalk to a two-way mirror and observe the action below. If they saw any incident of cheating or stealing, they reported it.

As you can imagine, this system was limited by the number of surveillance employees, the number and positioning of the mirrors, the lighting level, and many other factors. A better way was needed.

Cameras were introduced into the casino industry in the 1980s at about the same time electromechanical slot machines were introduced. Camera and video recording technology advanced at the same time. Casinos soon realized that blanketing the ceiling with cameras could cover more square footage with better views. In addition, the new video technology allowed the surveillance department to record the cheating and stealing they saw. Video evidence proved more valuable in court than eyewitness accounts of surveillance employees.

There are two types of cameras. **Fixed cameras** do not move. They point downward and record strictly what is beneath them. These are good for banks of electronic gaming devices or table games. As long as the floor layout does not change, these cameras will capture what they need to see. Fixed cameras are relatively small and inexpensive. The other camera type is the PTZ. PTZ stands for **pan, tilt, and zoom.** These cameras move side to side, up and down, and magnify the view. They are extremely flexible. They can cover more square footage although columns and architectural features of the casino can obstruct their view. They are larger and more expensive than the fixed cameras (see Figure 11-4).

Technology has not rested in the area of surveillance either. Just as video technology went from analog to digital, so has surveillance equipment. Digital cameras in use today offer greater flexibility and better coverage. With analog cameras, what was viewed by the surveillance department was recorded on the videotape. If a particular player at a particular table was being observed, the scene was recorded on the tape.

Unfortunately, something might be happening at another table within the range of the camera that comes to the attention of management after the fact. For example, suppose surveillance is observing a male player on a "21" table in Pit 7. They watch and do not find anything to confirm the suspicion that he is cheating. Later, management has concerns about Pit 8 which is just behind the camera that was used to observe Pit 7. Because the camera was analog and focused on Pit 7, there is no view of Pit 8.

With digital technology, a 360° view is maintained all the time. It is recorded in full. Through the current technology, a surveillance employee can pull up the files for the time period needed and view in any direction by digitally manipulating the computer. In effect, the cameras make every square inch of the casino floor available on a twenty-four-hour basis. As long as the file is maintained on the computer, the video is available.

Storage of a digital record is much smaller and less costly than with analog technology. With analog technology, a large casino had hundreds of cameras focused on the gaming floor, restaurants, public areas, bars, and so on. Each camera was recorded on its own videotape in its own video recorder. The size of the rooms to house this equipment was huge. The cost of the space plus the recorders and tapes was tremendous.

However with digital technology, because digital data is stored on computer hard drives, there is less space needed. A hard drive can record much more than a single VCR, yet they occupy the same space. Fewer hard drives are needed to record the information from the same number of cameras. There are cost savings in equipment costs. Since digital data does not

FIGURE 11-4   A PTZ or Pan, Tilt, Zoom Camera Can View More of the Casino Floor Than a Fixed Camera

require a videotape or other medium, there are cost savings in supplies. Fewer hard drives translate into lower electric bills since hundreds of VCRs require a great deal of power to operate and HVAC is needed to exhaust the heat generated by hundreds of VCRs. All this leads to significant cost savings.

But just as important are the labor savings. Videotapes can record up to twenty-hour hours. After twenty-hour hours, they must be replaced with a blank tape. The process for changing tapes was labor intensive. An employee had to go to each machine and remove the recorded tape and insert a new tape. Imagine the amount of time needed to exchange a new tape for a recorded tape in hundreds of machines. With digital technology there is no exchange needed!

Once again we see where technology has lowered costs and improved performance.

10. SOFTWARE IN THE ENTERPRISE

The casino uses software like all businesses. Advances in back office reporting, utility monitoring software, communications capabilities, and so on, all add to the efficiency of the modern casino. Given the size of modern casinos, particularly in larger markets, computer-driven software is essential to operating these properties.

The latest development in Las Vegas is CityCenter by MGM/Mirage (see Figure 11-5). This meta-resort covers sixty-eight acres and includes four hotels, three residential towers, an

FIGURE 11-5   CityCenter in Las Vegas Is the Latest Example of a Casino Development Whose Size Requires an Extensive Use of Technology to Manage and Operate

FIGURE 11-5 (*Continued*)

FIGURE 11-5 (*Continued*)

extensive high-end retail mall, a casino with all the amenities, public spaces with artwork from significant artists, and more. To manage and control a facility of this size and complexity requires significant technology support. In actuality, this property and any other modern casino would not be possible without computers and software to facility communication, data collection, equipment monitoring, and more.

11. Summary

As with all businesses, technology has had a major impact on the casino industry. If we look back at the start of the casino industry in America, we see there was little demand for technology. To manage and control a small operation, an owner or manager could simply rely on manual procedures and direct observation.

However, as technology has changed, it has opened up possibilities. You have seen how the change in technology of slot machines created more options such as bonus rounds and scatter pays. In the future, skill-based gaming will come to handheld units that will mirror the emerging market's childhood hobby of playing video games. At some point we may see a merging of the casino business and the video game business. Both are referred today as the *gaming industry* which causes some confusion!

Technology has also allowed the casino industry to reduce costs while increasing revenue. Larger facilities with more gaming opportunities are possible. The usual relationship between labor cost and customer service is to add labor cost to improve customer service. TITO has reduced labor cost while improving customer service. Digital technology in surveillance has eliminated the expense of purchasing and maintaining VCRs while improving the effectiveness of the surveillance department.

The history of technological advance in the casino industry has been an unqualified success. The industry and its customers have benefited from technology. The immediate horizon shows more innovation that will produce exciting opportunities. What lies further into the future cannot be dreamed of today just as Charles Fey would not recognize how his slot machine transformed into an electronic gaming device!

12. Case Study and Learning Activity

Case Study

Harrah's Entertainment has a long history in the casino industry. The original Harrah's casino was founded in 1937 when William F. Harrah and his father, John, left their bingo operation in southern California and moved to Reno, Nevada. Nevada had legalized casino gambling in 1931 and the state was just starting to benefit from the tourism boom generated by gambling.

Today it seems odd that he would have chosen Reno over Las Vegas, but Reno was the largest population center of Nevada from the start. The availability of water, timber, and mineral resources drew ranchers, farmers, loggers, and miners to northern Nevada since before statehood in 1864. Virginia City is the site of the Comstock Lode which was a rich vein of silver and gold discovered in the 1860s. It is located 32 miles southeast of Reno. During its heyday, Virginia City was the largest city between St. Louis and San Francisco. The state capitol, Carson City, was founded before statehood and is located 26 miles south of Reno. Lake Tahoe is 45 miles southwest of Reno. Reno is also 200 miles from San Francisco which provided a significant source of commercial activity in the nineteenth century and tourists in the twentieth century.

At the time Bill and his father moved to Reno, Las Vegas was still a small dusty town in the desert. Reno remained the population center in Nevada until Las Vegas surpassed it in the 1950s. It was only logical that they would go to Reno instead of Las Vegas.

Bill opened a bingo hall on Virginia Street and built the business through strict accounting methods, fair treatment of employees, and excellent customer service. When he died in 1978, he left a casino company which was the gold standard of the industry. He had pioneered accounting procedures which ensured the integrity of the operation. These same procedures were adopted by the Gaming Control Board as it wrestled to eliminate the undesirable element from the Las Vegas casinos. He had built Harrah's Lake Tahoe which was a five-Star, five-Diamond property for the first eight years of its existence. He created a corporate culture of excellence based on cutting-edge employee relations practices and high operating standards.

Harrah's was bought by Holiday Inn in 1980. An aggressive expansion program in the 1990s and 2000s led to over fifty casinos in the United States and around the world. The company changed names to Harrah's Entertainment in 1995 when it was split from the descendent of the Holiday Inn company. It is the largest casino company in the world and has the second largest presence in the Las Vegas market. Its most recent acquisition is the Planet Hollywood casino/resort on the Las Vegas Strip.

It was Bill Harrah's insistence on superb customer service that created a culture which sought new and better ways to serve customers. In the 1980s, the introduction of electromechanical slot machines by Bally opened the technological door to innovation. While progressives, more intricate pay lines, more elaborate pay tables, and greater security were impressive benefits of the new technology, the potential for customer service caught the imagination of others at Harrah's.

Computer technology was opening the doors to innovation in all areas of business. It was automating office functions and reducing the number of manual operations. Hotel front desks, restaurants, PBX, and other areas of a hotel and casino were experiencing a revolution in the way business was conducted. As just one example, the night audit (refer to Chapter 7) using the NCR 4200 could take all night. With computers, the process was truncated to a couple hours at most, largely filled with manual tasks making sure all input was complete and correct. It would be inconceivable today to have a five-thousand-room hotel like the MGM Grand in Las Vegas using a manual system of any kind. Computers are essential to modern business.

Those who saw the potential of technology to improve customer service within Harrah's moved to capitalize on the computer technology in the new slot machines. The idea was to track the activity of customers to better know which slot machines were popular. Using this information, the casinos could adjust their slot mix in order to optimize customer satisfaction and maximize slot revenue. The design of the hardware components and imagining the exact method in which such a system would work were developmental hurdles.

Also during the 1980s, the credit card business and banking industry were going through their own technology-driven revolution. Automatic teller machines or ATMs were introduced on a wide scale. They required plastic credit-card size cards with a magnetic strip on the back. As anyone who banks today knows, one inserts the ATM card into the machine to initiate and complete the transaction. The information carried on the magnetic strip indicates to the computer system who is accessing the ATM. It allows the customer to interact with the bank to complete various transactions without the aid of an employee.

This same technology was chosen for what would become a slot club. The initial systems were not without problems. As with any new product line, the hardware and software needed to be perfected. It took years for the hardware and software to function flawlessly. It also took years for industry practitioners to become accustomed to the new technology.

However, it was discovered in the 1990s that the computer was capable of capturing much more information than just which machines were played. The length of time on machine, average bet, and winnings, among other things, were also recorded. It was also discovered that biographical data could be captured by the system. When players signed up for the card, they were asked numerous questions. Many were demographic in nature such as age, address, and telephone number. But soon other questions were added. Preferences for restaurant cuisine and entertainment options were solicited. As the network within which the cards could be used expanded to include restaurants, shops, night clubs, and showrooms, a complete profile of preferences of any particular customer could be sketched from the data in the database.

As we discussed in Chapter 9, the process for culling the profile and preferences of a segment of the market from a database is labeled **data mining**. Like a miner of mineral ore, someone mining a database is sifting through the raw material to find the information of value. The information so gleaned can be used to fine-tune a marketing program to meet the needs of a particular segment. For example, if a customer uses his or her card to play penny slot machines from IGT with a bonus round, to eat in the buffet, to stay in the hotel, and to use the spa, then a flyer with coupons or promotions for just those features can be produced and sent to the customer. With technology today, a flyer unique to each player can be produced and e-mailed at a cost approaching nothing. The result is an incentive tailored to an individual and, therefore, most effective in motivating him or her to return to the casino. Because it costs so little, there is little downside risk to sending out multiple mailings to the entire list of players enrolled in the slot club. Effectively, the slot club databases and data mining have created a prolific number of market segments, each one populated by an individual. This is the ultimate in individual attention for customers.

As we can see, the innovation process started with an idea. The specific technology was copied from a related industry and modified. After the modification, it was fine-tuned in order to meet the emerging needs of the casino industry. Today, Harrah's Entertainment continues to lead the industry in the use of its database for marketing purposes. However, other companies have made great strides to catch up. They must in order to remain competitive. The true beneficiary is the customer. And all this because Bally developed a better slot machine.

Learning Activity

1. What kind of information would you mine from a CRM database of a casino? How would you use that information? Would you want to increase loyalty, increase revenue, or aim for different goal?

2. How could you use the players' club database of a casino to identify a new market segment?

3. In your opinion, what area of the casino will be affected by technology next? Will it result in improved customer service, reduced costs, or increased security?

4. Do you think Harrah's Entertainment would have over fifty casinos if they had the technology of the 1970s? Explain your answer.

5. How does the players' club database of a casino allow it to cross-market different properties? Can those properties be in different markets?

13. Key Terms

Banks	Drop Team	Pit Floor
Bill Validators	Electronic Gaming Device	Players' Club
Bonus Round	Fill	Progressive Jackpot
Cash	Fishing	RNG
Cash Equivalent	Fixed Camera	RFID
Cashier Cage	Hard Count Room	Scatter Pay
Chip Rack	Hopper	Server-Based Gaming
Comp	Pan, Tilt, Zoom Camera	Slot Floor
Customer Relationship	Pay Line	Slugging
Management	Pay Pattern	Soft Count Room
Data Mining	Pay Table	Table Games Floor
Drop	Payout	Ticket In, Ticket Out (TITO)

14. Chapter Questions

1. Name and describe one way in which electronic gaming devices are different from slot machines.
2. Explain one way in which TITO improved customer service, reduced costs, and improved security.
3. Explain how a customer accumulates points in a players' club.
4. Explain how a customer redeems points in a players' club for complimentary goods and services.
5. How do you think RFID will affect the design of tables of a table games pit?
6. Casinos use their players' club database to customize promotional offers for individual guests. What four offers from a casino would you find valuable? How are these different from your parents' four?
7. Research three casino companies' players' club. What is the process to join? How many casinos are in the company? Where are their casinos located? What kind of comps can you receive for redeemed points? Can you redeem your points for cash?
8. What are the relative benefits of fixed cameras over PTZ cameras?
9. Explain the advantage of digital over analog in the surveillance function.
10. An Excel spreadsheet with embedded formulae will recalculate all numbers practically instantaneously when new data is input. This is more efficient and less prone to error than a spreadsheet completed by hand. Speculate which departments within a casino use Excel and how the use of Excel has affected that department's effectiveness.

15. References

Williams, David C. and Kathryn Hashimoto. (2010). Casino Gaming Methods: Games, Probabilities, and Controls, Upper Saddle River, NJ: Prentice Hall.

Durham, Steve and Kathryn Hashimoto. (2010). Casino Financial Controls: Tracking the Flow of Money, Upper Saddle River, NJ: Prentice Hall.

Ross, David. (2008). The Radio Chip. Global Gaming Business, 7 (9), 20–22.

Allison, Willy. (2010). Eyes on ARIA: An Interview with Surveillance Director, Ted Whiting. Global Gaming Business, 9 (2), 36–37.

CHAPTER 12

Technology for the Meetings and Events Industry

Chapter Contents

INTERVIEW

James Spellos, CMP, President of Meeting U.

Q: James, thanks so much for taking time to speak to us. Please tell us about yourself and Meeting U.

A: Sure. Meeting U is a hospitality meetings technology training company. Our goal is to make meetings technology more usable, practical, and more understandable. I started the company in 1999. Wow, I hadn't realized, until I said that, that it's our tenth anniversary.

Q: Ten years? Congratulations! I guess you could say that there have been a lot of changes over the past ten years.

A: Absolutely. Even though the meetings industry is more reactive when it comes to technology, but things are starting to ramp up faster. For example, Hilton just recently made a PR announcement about their new iPhone policy. Ten years ago, the industry relied on databases and software, whereas now, it's all about capturing the burgeoning online community. The industry has transformed from using very traditional marketing approaches (traditional publications and direct mailings) to a social media society.

Q: Oh, yes, social networking. Any comments?

A: Social media allows smaller properties the opportunity to catch up to the larger properties. Twitter offers a lot of business impact and sharing of vast amounts of information. It's almost too much good information, flowing incredibly rapidly. With social networking, you can actually choose what approach you take, whether it's a business approach or a social approach. Even so, you never know what types of connections will be made. You might meet a business connection while socializing, or become friends with your business network. Technology is weaving into our personal branding.

Q: Could you comment about our online persona?

A: We all have a responsibility to be aware of our online persona, and manage our brand. It is up to each of us to review our online information and make sure it's correct. Can we change what's out there? Absolutely. We can change it by being more active in social networking.

This is really where generational differences come into play. Many Generation Y'ers have no fear about replacing face-to-face communication with electronic communication. They don't view social networking as a lack of privacy, but rather how much information can be accessible for little or no cost. They are not necessarily uptight about sharing personal information and putting it out there. Baby Boomers and Gen Xers may have had a negative experience in the past, or experienced fraud, so they are a little slower in adopting social networking. Also, Boomers and Gen Xers have more of a fear of losing their jobs to technology, and sometimes take steps to protect themselves from too many changes.

Q: In your opinion, what one technological innovation changed the meeting/event industry the most?

A: Oh boy, the one innovation . . . I would have to say over the past ten years, it's the mobile device. However, the meetings industry has not yet realized its full potential. Over the past ten years, I'd say that the Web was an important innovation in the late nineties, and in the past few years, it's social media and mobility.

Q: I've read about how the future of meetings technology lies with the interactive Web, or Web 2.0.

A: Definitely. We've already started using the interactive Web. For example, speakers have been posting presentations for comment. However, unusual issues come up when you invite the whole audience to play. We can't necessarily control the outcome—we can't always control comments. There are also ethical considerations. For example, hotel companies could offer incentives to people to write overly positive comments about their property.

Q: Thanks so much for your time! Any last thoughts?

A: As educators, we are using technology to change how people learn. Our audiences are driving the changes and we need to make sure to not be left behind. It's no longer traditions dictating our teaching behaviors. I can't wait to see what's next!

1. INTRODUCTION

It wasn't all that long ago when meetings and events were planned and executed on paper, or without the aid of technology. Now, it is important for a meeting/event planner to be comfortable using various technological advances to maximize a meeting or event's return on investment (ROI). This chapter strives to introduce the reader to various tools and applications used by successful meeting and event planners across the globe.

It's hard to determine when the meetings and events industry began or when the first meeting or event took place. Some argue that the first planners were around during Biblical times, organizing the logistics behind some of the major events of the time, like preparing the animals for the journey on Noah's ark. What most industry experts can agree upon, though, is that the industry has gone through major changes in the twentieth century and will continue to change and develop well into the twenty-first century. Improvements and advances in technology have brought about many of the changes in the meetings and events industry.

In the 1960s and 1970s, the meeting/event manager's role was to ensure there were enough chairs in a meeting room, or enough white wine glasses on a table for a banquet. Today, the meeting/event manager is a very strategic position, utilizing forecasting tools, revenue management, ROI, and expense management. Meeting/event managers use a wide range of technology, from audio and visual equipment to computer applications and communication devices to increase revenue and minimize costs.

This chapter will introduce the reader to audio and visual equipment, computer and online applications, and communication devices used in the meetings and events industry. Upon completion of this chapter, the reader should be able to identify a variety of tools used to plan and execute meetings and events, as well as discuss technological innovations that will impact the future of this segment of the hospitality industry.

2. AUDIO AND VISUAL EQUIPMENT

Technology helps to enhance the environment of meetings and events. Meetings are typically held to communicate a message and/or to increase learning. Every meeting or event requires its attendees to see and hear the presentation. Imagine a wedding without music, or a guest speaker without a microphone! Audio and visual equipment are important components in most meetings and events, regardless of the style of event. Audio and visual equipment help to engage the audience while allowing the presenters or speakers to concentrate on their message.

Audio

A meeting/event manager should become familiar with some of the basic audio equipment needed to produce successful sound at the event. Audio systems help set the tone for the meeting/event and can evoke a variety of emotions. Depending on the needs of the attendees, an event can require the use of microphones, speaker systems, and recording equipment.

A meeting/event manager must determine the number and types of microphones needed for attendees to hear information at a meeting/event. Microphones can be placed in a fixed location, such as on a podium, or can be wireless, to allow a speaker to move around the site. Meeting managers must consider the number of speakers at a meeting/event, as well as the style of the speaker. Fixed microphones are best for a program with many speakers, or speakers that tend to speak strictly from the podium, while wireless microphones are good for energetic speakers that like to move around. The meeting/event manager must also consider microphones needed for audience response.

Additional microphones require additional equipment, such as mixers (mixing or sound boards), for the best audio quality. A meeting manager may want to consider loud speakers and sound systems (depending on audience and room size). Quality is an important component, not just for the audience at the meeting/event, but also for meetings that will be recorded. Recording equipment (cassette or digital recording devices) can be used to record a meeting for future listeners for the purpose of transcriptions.

A meeting/event manager should ensure that the audio technology is working properly in advance of the meeting/event, so the speaker(s) can focus on the message, as opposed to worrying about properly adjusted and working microphones.

Visual

Meeting/event visual equipment used to be limited to an overhead or slide projector. While overhead projectors are still used to display transparencies, the 35-mm slide projectors have mostly been replaced with video projectors and digital display equipment. Video projectors interface with most computer systems (PC and Mac) and commonly use **LCD** (liquid crystal display) technology.

When selecting visual equipment, a meeting/event manager must consider several components based on the event location. It is important to make note of the room size, as well as how large the projection area (or screen) will be. The location of the projector and the amount of natural and room lighting will also assist the meeting/event manager in selecting the most appropriate equipment.

Just as with audio equipment, quality of visual equipment is important for the audience present and for recording the event. Advances in high-definition display and **Image Magnification** (i-mag) allow a clearer display of the presentation. A meeting/event planner must also familiarize himself or herself with different video standards for playback across the world. International standards vary and are not compatible with one another. The **NTSC** (National Television System Committee) format is used in the United States and Canada, the **PAL** (Phase Alternating Line) is used in western Europe and Australia, while the **SECAM** (Sequential Color with Memory) is used in eastern Europe and France.

Virtual Meetings

Since September 11, 2001, the meetings industry has been exploring alternative delivery formats for meetings. When travel was restricted and more difficult, and even now, as the economy has financially limited travel to face-to-face meetings and events, virtual meetings (audio, video, and Web conferencing) have proved to be viable methods of meeting and communicating messages. However, virtual meetings do not (and probably will not) replace all face-to-face meetings, especially those where networking is an important part of the meeting.

Audio conferencing is connecting two or more sites via audio or a phone connection. In an audio conference, there is no need for visual communication. This type of virtual meeting is the most inexpensive alternative, with many service options available. Most beneficial is the short lead-time in planning an audio conference.

Video conferencing involves connecting two or more sites via video transmission. Video conferencing allows images of the multiple locations to be shared, but also increases cost, lead-time, and complexity. A meeting/event manager must determine whether this meeting will involve one- or two-way transmission, include both video and audio, the size of the audience, and the limitations of the locations involved.

Web conferencing allows two or more sites to connect via audio and visual mediums over the Internet. Web conferencing is the fastest growing segment in virtual meetings, as it is very cost-effective, and compatible with most computer systems. Improvements in web conferencing allow presentation displays, desktop sharing, application sharing, live chats, and audience response.

3. DESKTOP AND ONLINE TOOLS

The planning process of meetings/events has certainly become more efficient with the increased use of technology. Computers, both desktop applications and online tools, help to organize and analyze the vast amount of information needed to make the best decisions for a meeting/event. Meeting/event managers make use of desktop applications, SAAS (see Chapter 4) and Web-based applications, the Internet and portals, as well as social networking sites to attract attendees to their next event, and to customize the experience in order to maximize value.

High-Speed Internet Access

High-speed Internet access is commonplace in meeting/event planning offices. However, it is also important to verify Internet availability at the selected meeting/event location.

During the planning phase, meeting/event managers can offer online registration and payment services, housing and travel management, and market surveys and data collection; provide meeting/event program information; and use the Internet to market upcoming meeting/events. Once on-site, staff, attendees, and exhibitors will need to stay in communication with their offices, on-site personnel, and even with their family members. While many exhibitors and attendees will travel with their own wireless-equipped laptops, some will not. Stand-alone Internet kiosks can be rented and/or sponsored for a meeting/event to offer connection opportunities. The Internet can also be used to show presentations and Webinars, before, during, or after a meeting/event. This is becoming increasingly popular.

The meeting/event manager must be prepared to deal with potential issues that heavy reliance on the Internet brings. Connectivity issues and "dead-zones" on-site can frustrate presenters, exhibitors, and attendees. The manager must also address potential for system crashing and integration issues, as well as protection from hackers.

Desktop Applications

The predominant presentation software used in the meetings/events industry is still Microsoft Office. Meeting/event managers use word processing, spreadsheets, database management systems, presentation software, and project management tools to help plan, execute, and evaluate their events.

In 1949, four organizations formed the Convention Liaison Council, whose goal was to enhance the meetings, conventions, and exhibitions industry with the exchange of information, ideas, and best practices. In 2000, the Council changed its name to the Convention Industry Council and now has thirty-four member organizations. The Council has launched many successful initiatives in the meetings/events industry such as the Certified Meeting Professional (CMP) designation and the Accepted Practices Exchange (APEX).

The **APEX** initiative seeks to unite the meetings/events industry by creating and implementing voluntary practices and standards to create efficiencies throughout the industry. APEX focuses on seven core areas: industry terminology, event specifications guides (ESG), request for proposal (RFP) forms, housing and registration practices, contracts, post-event reports (PER), and meeting and site profiles. Interwoven into these core areas are suggested templates and software packages for planners to use. XML (Extensible Markup Language—Chapter 4) is a critical tool that helps APEX templates integrate with MS Office.

Additional information about APEX and meetings/events industry-accepted practices can be found on the Convention Industry Council's Web site at http://www.conventionindustry.org/apex/accepted.htm.

Portals and Online Searching

Meeting/event managers are now turning to the Internet and online search engines to aid in their planning efforts. Site Selection search engines can help meeting/event managers find suitable locations for their events, and even take virtual property tours. Search engines can be Convention and Visitor Bureau (CVB) based, National Sales Office (NSO) based, or third-party based.

Meeting/event managers can post request for proposals (RFP) to the Web, allowing vendors and suppliers to search and review the requests. Industry listservs are also a popular source of information for meeting/event planning and preparation. Many meeting/event industry associations post information for insiders to use, or allow meeting/event managers to subscribe to RSS (real simple syndication—Chapter 5) feeds for up-to-date information, pricing, and availability.

Social Networking

Meeting/event managers are embracing the social networking concept and other interactive online forums to market their meetings/events and provide information to attendees and exhibitors. While social networking began with Generation Y as its target audience, now Generation X and Baby Boomers are using these sites to connect, share ideas, and network.

4. COMMUNICATION DEVICES

Meeting/event managers use a wide variety of technology to communicate prior to a meeting/event, or on-site. Web-based communication devices, such as e-mail, instant messaging and chat rooms, blogs, and RSS feeds have been discussed earlier in this chapter. Many networking terms from Chapter 4 see usage in the meeting and events arena along with some new additions including voice over Internet protocol (VoIP), radio frequency identification (RFID), audience response system (ARS), personal digital assistants (PDA), and Bluetooth.

VoIP

Voice over Internet protocol is used to make phone calls over the Internet. Meeting/event managers can investigate VoIP for their on-site telephone needs, as well as using this for connection to a 911 emergency system.

RFID

Radio frequency identification (see Chapter 9) can be used in attendance management for meetings, events, and exhibits, as well as head counts in food and beverage operations. Including a RFID chip in attendee badges can provide the meeting/event manager with specific data about attendee patterns. For example, the RFID chip can record which exhibits or breakout sessions an attendee visited.

Audience Response Systems

Speakers strive to make their presentations interactive and engaging for the audience. **Audience response systems** allow the audience to participate in a presentation or for the speaker to survey or poll the audience. This is accomplished in a number of ways from embedded buttons at the seat to portable devices handed out beforehand.

PDA

Personal digital assistants can be used as an ID badge on-site at meetings or events. An attendee can provide the PDA information upon registration, and the meeting/event manager can send important updates and messages directly to the attendee's phone.

Bluetooth

Meeting/event planners have only started to explore the uses for Bluetooth technology in meetings and events. Bluetooth can be used for networking as well as communication with other wireless devices such as phones and laptops.

5. THE FUTURE

While it's difficult to keep up with ever-changing technology and all its potential uses in the meetings and events industry, there are some changes we can foresee in the immediate future. With the success of virtual meetings, we will see these meeting types replacing some inefficient meetings. However, technology will never completely eliminate the need for people to meet face to face.

Corbin Ball, of Corbin Ball Associates, discusses some of the upcoming trends in meeting technology on his Web site. Many future innovations in meetings/events technology will center on Web 2.0 (the participatory Web). In the future, meeting/event managers can use **Wikis** (interactive, collaborative Web pages) to track event management details. Wikis provide a common document usable by remote planning teams. Wikis can be used by speakers to upload abstracts, bios, photos, podcasts, video clips, RSS feeds to their blogs, PowerPoint slides, and more.

6. Summary

Meeting/event managers have a wide variety of technology available to them to make planning and execution easier, more efficient, and more cost-effective. Managers can use audio/visual equipment to enhance the program content and set meeting/event tone. Managers can also use computer applications, from desktop software and APEX templates to wireless and handheld communication devices.

Meeting/event technology is always changing and improving. It is important for the meeting/event manager to keep up with the changes and use technology to add value to his or her meetings and events and maximize his or her ROI.

7. Case Study and Learning Activity

Case Study

The Garden Inn is a three hundred-room hotel in a college town, in Central Pennsylvania. The hotel is one of many major hotel chains in the area, but not as well known as the others. Therefore, The Garden Inn tends to be discovered when the other hotels are full.

The Garden Inn has recently renovated its two banquet rooms and its five separate meeting rooms. With these updates, The Garden Inn now has wireless Internet connectivity, PBX phone lines, and state-of-the-art audio/visual equipment. Becky Wilkins, a recent college graduate, is the new conference services manager for The Garden Inn. Becky majored in Hotel, Restaurant, and Institutional Management with a minor in Information Technology in college, and is excited to incorporate new technology into The Garden Inn, especially in how they market for new meeting and banquet business.

Becky works for Marsha Cord. Marsha has been with The Garden Inn for fifteen years, and most recently was promoted to sales director.

Marsha is rather set in her ways, especially where marketing is concerned. Marsha is rather bitter about how so many employees of The Garden Inn seem more interested in their computers and cell phones, than in working hard.

One day, Becky was searching the Web, and reading various RFPs from meeting planners looking to host meetings/events in the college town. Becky was very interested in responding to these requests because she thought The Garden Inn would be a perfect location for some of these events. Becky approaches Marsha for permission to respond to the requests, but Marsha doesn't think soliciting business over the Web is safe.

Learning Activity

1. How can Becky convince Marsha that the Internet produces safe and viable business?
2. How can Becky show Marsha that technology is useful in marketing meetings and events, and not something to be feared?
3. What kinds of things can Becky offer potential clients to entice them to come to The Garden Inn?

8. Key Terms

Audio Conferencing	LCD	Video Conferencing
Audio Response System	NTSC	Web Conferencing
APEX	PAL	Wikis
Image Magnification	SECAM	

9. Chapter Questions

1. What are some of the considerations for a meeting manager when using audio equipment in their meeting/event?
2. When determining what location to hold a meeting/event, what questions should a meeting planner ask about concerning high-speed Internet access?
3. Discuss how communication devices impact the meetings/events industry today, and what their role may be in the future.
4. Should the meeting/event manager select the location of his or her event and then determine the meeting's technology needs? Or, should technology usage be determined prior to site selection? Explain your answer.

10. References

APEX. Convention Industry Council. Retrieved November 30, 2009, from www.conventionindustry.org.

Convention Industry Council. Retrieved November 30, 2009, from www.conventionindustry.org/aboutcic/about.htm.

NTSC. High-tech productions. Retrieved November 30, 2009, from http://www.high-techproductions.com/pal,ntsc.htm.

Palmer, B. (2009, October). Jumping on the bandwidth wagon. Convene (The Magazine of the Professional Convention Management Association), 53–57.

Ramsborg, G. C. (Ed.). (2006). Professional Meeting Management: Comprehensive Strategies for Meetings, Conventions, and Events (5th ed.). Iowa: Kendall/Hunt Publishing.

Technology trends in meetings and events. Meetingsnet.com. Retrieved November 30, 2009, from http://meetingsnet.com/technology/future/top_tech_trends/.

CHAPTER 13

Strategic Hospitality Technology Investment

Chapter Contents

INTERVIEW

Laura Calin is Vice President for MICROS.

Q: Hi Laura, would you mind commenting on what comes after a system is purchased, namely the eLearning function along with a little bit about MICROS?

A: Sure. First Micros. MICROS Systems, Inc. provides enterprise applications for the hospitality and retail industries worldwide. Over 310,000 MICROS systems are currently installed in table and quick service restaurants, hotels, motels, casinos, leisure and entertainment, and retail operations in more than 130 countries, and on all seven continents. In addition, MICROS provides property management systems (PMSs), central reservation, and customer information solutions under the brand MICROS-Fidelio for more than twenty-five thousand hotels worldwide, as well as point of sale, loss prevention, and cross-channel functionality through its MICROS-Retail division for more than ninety thousand retail stores worldwide.

Q: Great. How is MICROS using eLearning in the hotel industry?

A: The MICROS training approach includes instructor-led training along with asynchronous web-based training, or eLearning. The MICROS eLearning solution provides centralized training in a decentralized industry. Hoteliers all over the world have the ability to take initial and refresher training online from the comfort of their office, library, or home. eLearning is the fastest, most cost-effective means to provide OPERA (PMS from MICROS, Chapter 7) how-tos to each hotel employee, when they need it most.

Q: Do some segments on the hotel of the industry use more eLearning than others?

A: Typically, we've seen an increase in use of eLearning across the board from housekeeping to reservationists. The front desk employee has seen more training than others largely because they are in front of the customer more and need "just-in-time" training material at their fingertips.

Q: Does eLearning have or play a role in self-service applications?

A: Yes. We are seeing an increase in the use of kiosks and self-service applications where eLearning is needed for the customer. The eLearning is broken down into more granular bits of knowledge and provided in the form of a "help" section as their navigating the self-service application.

Q: Any thoughts as to how eLearning technology will advance in hotel in the future?

A: We are seeing an influx of the use of mobile devices to check in guest. MICROS is leveraging mobile technology to provide training via iPhones and other mobile devices. The MICROS eLearning solution is flexible enough to be converted to run on mobile devices in the form of electronic job aids, or eGuides. This advancement will provide knowledge when it is needed most to the employee, on the job. Seventy-five percent of training an employee receives is informal training, and the MICROS training solution allows for employees to reference OPERA how-tos at the time they need it.

1. INTRODUCTION

Laura introduces us to some great themes regarding eLearning. Before we can get into eLearning, we must first learn about technology purchases in our industry. Making a purchasing decision relative to a strategic investment in corporate information systems is very different than a consumer technology purchase. When people buy consumer technology, they often tend to start any discussion about which alternative to purchase with a question along the lines of "Which one is best?" The natural follow-up to this is "How much does the best one cost?" followed quickly by "How much do the other ones cost?" And so goes most of the selection process when it comes to buying anything from iPods to automobiles.

As technology consumers, people are programmed to think of quality and functionality as being somehow related, and, at the same time, they equate the most functionality with the best. Although there may be a great deal of validity to this type of thinking when it comes to purchasing MP3 players, it is often misplaced in the world of business-based information systems. This is because when it comes to acquiring technology for your hotel, restaurant, or any other business, it is not nearly as important to get lots of functionality as it is to get the right functionality for your business.

2. REDUCING EXPENSES AND INCREASING PROFITS

The single most important thing to remember when you think about strategic investments in hospitality information technology (IT) is that these investments must generate a positive **return on investment (ROI)** just like any other strategic corporate purchase. In the past, many technology vendors and professionals have tried numerous arguments for why technology investments cannot be measured against a quantitative yardstick for ROI. These arguments are all weak at best and more often simply the result of laziness and ineptitude. This section will discuss ROI first in its most simplistic terms, and then in a more detailed manner.

One thing to always remember is that in order for an IT system to generate a positive ROI, it must either reduce costs or increase revenue in some quantifiable way. If a hospitality professional never remembers anything about detailed ROI calculations or information system minutia, he or she can always fall back on this most basic premise. If an IT system is worthy of the investment required to implement it, the proponent of that system must be able to quantify in a demonstrably objective manner the approximate value of specific savings (i.e., decreased expenses) and/or increased profits that the system will generate.

If you always think about strategic technology investments in terms of increased profits or decreased expenses, you will tend to make better purchase decisions. The problem is that quantifying cash flow based on a system's purported functionality takes time and effort for which many people do not have the skill or aptitude. It is not in the scope of this text to make you an expert in performing such calculations personally, but the following precepts should provide you with the knowledge necessary to make someone else (i.e., the system vendor's salesperson or your accountant) perform an accurate and objective analysis for you.

Decreased Expenses

Decreased expenses, or cost savings, are generally the first element of **payback** or when the purchase actually pays for itself either through new revenue or cost savings those systems try to achieve. Whenever the discussion of decreased expenses begins, business managers have a habit of thinking immediately of staff reductions. This is not completely unwarranted in the hospitality industry because staffing is usually one of the largest controllable costs. In restaurants, labor can be anywhere from 20 to 35 percent of total revenue. In hotels, when the **fixed costs** associated with property depreciation and other fixed asset depreciation and maintenance are excluded, staffing is usually the largest single cost element. Information systems are very often used to make manual processes more efficient or automate labor-intensive tasks, and labor costs are one cost element that needs to be considered when assessing IT investments.

Implementing information systems that provide increased productivity can certainly lead to dramatic reductions in labor costs. However, decreased expenses associated with new IT can come in many shapes and sizes, and labor is not the only place operators can save money from new IT.

1. New technology can decrease the cost of maintaining systems. For instance, newer computer platforms that are more reliable, perform better, and have higher availability of cheap repair parts, and labor can significantly reduce the cost of hardware maintenance contracts.
2. **Recipe management software** can help operators develop recipes that use even quantities of bulk ingredients and therefore reduce food costs by eliminating waste. However, this may not be a solution for higher-end establishments who need quality ingredients.
3. Periodic maintenance systems for kitchen equipment, HVAC, and other fixed assets can significantly reduce the operating costs of these systems.

4. Power control systems designed to monitor electrical usage and turn lights off when a room is vacant or cool buildings earlier in the day can significantly reduce electrical power consumption costs.

There are two important things to remember when looking at potential cost savings provided by an information system:

1. Fixed costs don't usually go down (that's why they are called fixed).
2. Each hotel, restaurant, and club has a unique cost structure.

Every corporate entity in the world has fixed and variable costs. Many times in hospitality, fixed costs are associated with guest service requirements that are not negotiable based on the organization's market position. As a result, a system may be capable of reducing the labor required to perform certain tasks, but may not generate any savings as a result.

For instance, imagine that a vendor can clearly demonstrate that a system reduces the time required to perform some task by 50 percent (from six labor hours to three labor hours). On the surface, this reduction would mean that the system saves $8/hour multiplied by 3 hours multiplied by 365 days per year, or a total of about $8,750 per year (plus overhead and benefits). If the system only cost $10,000, this would appear to be a great deal, or would it? What if your hotel is a small, high-end property and you always have two people on duty at night because guests expect immediate attention twenty-four hours a day. Or maybe it is a low-end hotel in a very bad neighborhood and you always have two people on duty at night for safety reasons. Now imagine that the task in question is performed by the night shift crew, which is otherwise unoccupied for the majority of its shift. In this scenario, even though the system can be clearly shown to reduce labor requirements, because the cost of maintaining the night shift is a fixed cost, and because those resources are not utilized 100 percent in the existing scenario, it is possible that implementing the new system could result in a $10,000 investment with no appreciable cost savings (and therefore a negative ROI).

Increased Gross Profits

There are two important concepts to remember when analyzing a system's potential to increase gross profits.

1. The assessment must include only increases in gross profit, not **gross revenue**. Gross revenue is total sales. Gross profit subtracts expenses or direct costs from gross revenue. Therefore, expenses from the new purchase must be considered.
2. The assessment must be limited to only those gross profits that are directly attributable to the new system and would not be achieved without the system.

Take particular note of the fact that this section is captioned "Increased Gross Profits" and not "Increased Revenue." All too often technology-purchasing agents focus on revenue enhancement, probably at least in part because that is how vendors advertise. In fact, in a properly prepared ROI calculation, revenue exists only in the supporting detailed data. The actual top line ROI calculation is only concerned with increased gross profits.

When analyzing investments, remember that **gross profits** are equal to gross revenue less direct costs. If we use gross revenue in our ROI assessments, potential investments will look much more favorable than they actually are. This is an important point to remember because vendor advertisements for systems rarely include a complete ROI calculation, but very often highlight increased revenue. It is not uncommon to hear someone say, "I installed this new system and my sales went up X percent." The problem with this line of reasoning is that although it is appealing on the surface to say revenues are going up, without knowing the full cost of generating those revenues, it is impossible to determine if the system was a good deal or not.

For example, assume that the cost of implementing a new spa management system is $20,000. To objectively determine whether the new system would help book $50,000 per year in additional spa revenue, you would need to look at the details. If the spa is staffed internally and generates a 50 percent gross margin on every treatment sold, then the $25,000 first-year return makes the purchase decision very easy (assuming all of the projections are verifiable). However, if the spa is run on a contract basis with a 10 percent royalty on total sales, the annual payback of $5,000 may or may not justify a $20,000 investment (depending on the cost of capital and other factors). Although this example is obviously oversimplified, the concept holds true for all forms of potential increased revenue. You must convert incremental gross revenue projections to incremental gross profits before you can assess the potential value of a new information system.

3. SYSTEM EXAMPLES

Different types of systems can generate various forms of revenue for an establishment. Depending on what the system is designed to do, IT can result in higher unit sales volumes or increased gross margins.

Yield management systems can generate higher gross margins on room revenues while **restaurant menu management systems** can generate higher gross margins on food items by substituting less costly ingredients or by using historical sales data to accomplish the following:

- Develop more effective pricing strategies (e.g., menu mix)
- Create a more effective menu mix
- Schedule employees more efficiently
- Improve functionality for offering and controlling promotions (e.g., buy one get one or happy hour pricing)
- Process credit and gift cards more efficiently
- Improve functionality for cross-marketing other services to existing customers (generate coupon for other company-owned restaurants)
- Increase covers or average checks through the implementation of the new system (and by how much)

When analyzing the potential revenue increase, remember to attempt to identify an increase resulting only from the implementation of the new system. Any forecasted revenue increase due to other reasons, such as a change in the market, must be excluded. This is especially difficult if you plan to monitor the system benefits after conversion because additional revenue attributed only to the system is very difficult to quantify.

4. CASH FLOW AND COSTS

There are many formulas for calculating specific cash flow relative to different types of investments, and a good technology investment can and should be reduced to a financial investment equation before a purchase decision is made.

ROI = (Increased Profits + Decreased Costs)/Investment
all cash flow must be adjusted for time and the cost of capital

There may be additional costs associated with operating the new system. These could include the following:

- Hardware/software maintenance due to automating a manual system or an increase over the old system
- Additional labor due to a short-term decrease in productivity after conversion (to be added to the up-front cost since it typically affects costs only during the first year)
- Costs of converting any exhibiting or historical data
- Costs of interfacing the system with other existing applications or devices
- Communication costs
- Consulting services

There are a number of different things to consider when determining the total cost for a new system. The projections should include all costs associated with the project including purchase price, implementation, and training. Some examples might include the following:

Application software	Operating systems
Network operating system	Cabling and/or access points (cost of cable
Workstations/portables	and cost of installation)
Servers	Printers
Uninterrupted power supply (UPS)	Backup system
Network training	Application training
Shipping	Hardware training
Consulting services	Furniture (new, replaced, modified,
Additional payroll during training	or constructed)
and conversion	System selection costs

Although hard cost savings are the numbers that most companies focus on when determining whether or not to move forward with a new IT project, there are other intangible or soft benefits that need to be considered as well. These might include benefits such as improved guest service, employee morale, or image in the marketplace. Although they cannot be included in the calculation, they are very important factors that need to be taken into account. Some examples include the following:

- Better morale from use of a more user-friendly system
- Overall improved productivity from a more efficient system
- Improved job retention rates due to higher overall job satisfaction

5. SYSTEM SELECTION PROCESS

Although the details of how to specify and select an information system are beyond the scope of this chapter, a discussion of the basic system selection process is necessary to fully understand how IT investments are made. The system selection process described here has nine steps. Although many of these steps can be performed in parallel, it is important that each is performed and that step 1 be completed before any other step in the process begins.

1. Verify/develop the conceptual design for the enterprise
2. Define functional and system requirements for the component application(s)/create organizational consensus on the requirements
3. Compile a request for proposal (RFP)
4. Develop a vendor short list
5. Solicit proposals
6. Assess proposals against criteria
7. Visit reference sites
8. Have vendors provide demonstrations
9. Final selection

VERIFY/DEVELOP THE CONCEPTUAL DESIGN FOR THE ENTERPRISE   Selecting a particular application (POS, PMS, CRM, or anything else) without first having reviewed the long-term IT strategy for the entire enterprise is like buying a pair of suit pants without knowing if you have a jacket, tie, or shirt that goes with them. They may be the best pants you've ever bought, but if you can't wear them with anything you own, you've effectively either forced yourself to spend money on items you hadn't planned to purchase or wasted whatever money you spent on the pants. So it is with information systems that each application should fit into an overall plan designed to effectively leverage your use of information to create additional shareholder value.

The world of information capture (collection), processing, storing, and reporting can be, and should be, divided along the same lines as functional operations within the enterprise. One example of how to do this is to divide all your business functions into a matrix, as shown in Figure 13-1.

A soon-to-reopen hotel might purchase many systems that require integration with existing hardware and infrastructure. The hotel wishes to integrate as much of the existing architecture as possible with the new purchases. What requirements of the system and captured data would integrate with what you already have? This is the endeavor of the matrix. Some of the fields have been filled in to serve as a guide in helping you tackle the remaining fields.

All too often, the critical first step is ignored. This is especially true when outside consultants are brought in to assist or when insiders from a single department or business unit perform the selection without interdepartmental involvement. It is absolutely critical to ensure that this first step is performed completely and with a solid look towards future operational and competitive requirements. Additionally, knowing your business today is unfortunately not enough. The successful purchaser will have an eye towards the future. Notice the "Retail Operations" section under "Associated Data Capture Requirements"; you do not know all the data fields to be captured that may be needed in the future, so you leave some room by requesting that certain fields be left blank and able to be named and used at a later date. Not all vendors will allow forward-looking requirements; however, it is vital to negotiate in what you can. As an operational efficiency and cost-saving measure, all systems and matrix-oriented decisions should follow this forward-looking thought process. You could thank yourself one day for the right decisions you made years ago and avoid having to purchase a whole new system.

The end-product(s) of this first step should, at a minimum, include a list of component applications that will be required to create the entire enterprise's information infrastructure, and a solid idea of the system architecture (including communications backbone) that will be used to host and integrate each of the component applications.

Functional Area	Specific Capability Requirements	Associated Data Capture Requirements	Involved Systems/Technologies
Unit operations: Front Office F&B Housekeeping Reservations Engineering			Entire hotel network
Retail Operations (i.e., gift and pro shop)	Standard POS capabilities plus CRM	All relevant fields captured by credit card data with the addition of number of purchases to date and additional preference fields left blank to be named and utilized at a later date	None, however integration with the PMS is needed
Human Resource Management	Live updates on the Web—a must in addition to standard features	All relevant fields from I-9 IRS forms with the addition of property and department-specific fields	Payroll (electronic data interchange)
Financial Management and Control			
Communications			
Decision Support			Revenue, yield management, and CRM

FIGURE 13-1 Purchasing a New System Requires Proper Planning. A Matrix Can Help Keep Information Organized.

DEFINE FUNCTIONAL AND SYSTEM REQUIREMENTS FOR THE COMPONENT APPLICATION(S) AND CREATE ORGANIZATIONAL CONSENSUS ON THE REQUIREMENTS Once a long-term-strategy and architecture for the entire enterprise have been developed and agreed upon, the task of selecting a particular component application can begin in earnest. Although the top level or basic functional and system requirements for each component application should flow from the conceptual enterprise design, the detailed list of requirements necessary to properly evaluate alternative applications must be defined separately for each system. There are several key strategies that are worth employing during this step:

- Don't let management pick the new system. Create a system selection team and solicit both input and active involvement from the people who will actually have to use it. It is always best if you can select several informal leaders early in the process and win them over as champions of the new system by involving them in the selection process.
- It rarely makes good business sense to automate inefficient processes. More to the point, many of the system selection processes are often hampered by the identification of requirements whose only purpose is to preserve some non-value-added function within the organization. A key element of any system requirements definition process is the ability to objectively analyze the processes the system is designed to support and ensure those processes are designed as efficiently as possible.
- Ensure involvement from multiple departments or business units within the organization (even if it appears as though only one unit is really affected or owns the system).
- Clearly define exactly what you need, or you will never be able to accurately or objectively compare which vendor's application is best suited to your business. You should not let your staff begin any serious conversation with any single vendor until you have developed a list of specific requirements.
- Most organizations purchase any type of application once in a long while and then use/amortize it for several years. As a result, the level of knowledge of what is available is relatively low. It is worthwhile to attend a trade show or seminar or spend some time doing research (in-house or with a consultant) so you have an up-to-date perspective of what functional capabilities you should legitimately expect from your new system.
- As you speak with internal staff about requirements, remember to keep expectations in check. There are systems and vendors available that will do anything you want, but everything comes at a cost. When you start thinking about adding "customization" to a packaged system so that you can meet everyone's requirements, you add to the cost of the system.

One approach to defining and building consensus about requirements uses the following steps:

- Speak to colleagues and read articles about systems that have been recently installed in business units similar to your own. Use this research to identify common features expected to be in any system.
- Refer to your own enterprise system design documents to identify minimal system and functional requirements (show stoppers) that you know in advance any system you select will have to have as a minimum.
- Speak informally with one or more vendors (preferably at a trade show or seminar where you can see many vendors' applications in a short period of time), and develop a list of features and functions that appear to be of value for your business.
- Combine all of the preceding to create a master requirements list. You can then use this master list as a group facilitation tool when you start to meet with members of your selection team.
- When meeting with members of your team, allow them to think out of the box and identify new functionality or features, but remind them constantly that everything comes with a price tag and the perfect system they want may not exist.
- Each requirement identified by the group should be prioritized, either relative to other requirements or against some absolute scale. Many people prefer using a scale of 1 to 5, where 5 is a show stopper, 3 is a legitimate need with the potential to add some value, and 1 is a desire with little or no chance of impacting system implementation.

The final output of these steps should be a complete and prioritized list of specific functional and system requirements for the component application.

COMPILE A REQUEST FOR PROPOSAL (RFP)   If a solid enterprise-level strategy and conceptual design have been complemented by a set of clearly defined component application functional and system requirements, compiling an RFP should be relatively simple. Please refer to the RFP appendix for a detailed model. There are several elements worth noting for inclusion:

- Never sign a contract that includes customization on a fee basis. If the system you are purchasing cannot meet all of your organization's requirements out of the box, then your vendor should provide a firm fixed-price agreement to make the necessary modifications.
- Place all of your system and functional requirements in a numbered outline, matrix, or some other format that forces each vendor to address each requirement specifically and discreetly.
- Always make the vendor include a clearly defined timetable for customization and implementation. Ensure the proposed contract documents include a process for remedy if the vendor does not meet the proposed delivery schedule.
- Make each vendor specifically address such support issues as training, help desk, and remote and local software maintenance.
- Make each vendor provide both a historic and a forward-looking build schedule. The historic build schedule should include a notation as to whether builds released during the previous twenty-four months were released on schedule or delayed. Make each vendor supply a specific statement as to whether future builds are included in maintenance costs.
- Make each vendor supply cost information using the same format (provided by your company in the RFP). This prohibits vendors from burying costs in different places and thereby making your selection process more difficult.

DEVELOP A VENDOR SHORT LIST   Developing a vendor short list can be both the easiest and the most short-sighted step in the system selection process. It can be the easiest because you can simply make a list of several systems that you have seen in advertisements and know about. It can be the most short-sighted because you may feel tempted to include any one of the many new and vastly improved products that enter the marketplace every day. Good places to start for lists and further information in this industry are the vendors listed with the AH&LA and the HFTP organization as well as the magazines *Hospitality Upgrade* and *Hospitality Technology*.

Developing a short list of vendors *before* sending out a RFP is an important element of the system selection process for any organization that purchases multiple systems. The reason is that if you constantly ask a long list of vendors to spend their time and resources responding to RFPs and proposing systems, they have little chance of being selected to provide; your organization will lose the credibility necessary to exact complete and earnest responses from multiple vendors.

There are several rules of thumb that people often refer to in the vendor selection process, but in the end, all of them are rules of thumb, none are cast in stone, and rules can never take the place of good old-fashioned research.

One approach to narrowing the field of potential vendors that seems to work well uses the following steps:

- Refer to one or more well-maintained databases of systems like the one you are selecting. (A caution on databases and buyer's guides: the vendors listed in them often fund these guides. There may be several good vendors that do not appear in the guide you are using; therefore, it is important to use either multiple guides or a comprehensive database that does not rely on vendor advertisements for funding.)

- Use the databases to identify a list of vendor systems most likely to match your organization's system and functional requirements.
- Send a *request for information (RFI)* to those vendors that you think are the most suited to your needs. (The purpose of an RFI is to provide vendors a low-cost, low-effort means to supply you just the information necessary to know if they should be on your short list.) Some basic questions that should be included in an RFI refer back to some of those rules of thumb such as the following:
- Can the vendor provide a list of reference installations similar in size and operation to yours, and is the vendor willing to provide a point of contact at each?
- How long has the vendor been in business and can the vendor demonstrate his or her company's financial stability? (Financial stability and time in market should not be sole determining factors for the nonselection of any vendor, but they are elements of risk that stakeholders should be aware of in advance of making a selection decision.)
- Use RFI responses and interviews with reference installations to narrow your list of vendors to five or fewer vendors who appear capable, responsive, and responsible.

SOLICIT PROPOSALS   Soliciting proposals from good vendors is not as easy as you might expect. Vendors with good systems are in high demand and their ability to hire and train additional technical staff is limited by a global shortage of skilled IT personnel. As a result, writing detailed proposals and estimating the cost of significant customizations require the allocation of valuable people who could be working on other (profitable) projects.

You should therefore not expect good vendors to answer detailed RFPs in an unrealistic time frame. This often requires more advanced planning than most organizations are able to muster. It is not unrealistic to include an eight-week period for vendors to respond to your RFP. This is not because it takes eight weeks for a vendor to write a complete response. More often, it is because it takes four weeks for a vendor to determine that your project is worth dedicating the necessary resources to pursue and to ask all the additional questions and clarifications needed to answer your RFP accurately.

ASSESS PROPOSALS AGAINST CRITERIA   Two critical elements of this phase are objectivity and sensitivity analysis.

One approach is to simply start by using the functionality matrix developed during the requirements stage, and ask each member of the selection team to grade each response on a scale of 1 to 5. It is important to make each individual grade each proposal independently. The purpose of independent evaluations instead of a group evaluation in a large meeting is twofold. The first problem with group evaluation is that some of the people will not read all of the proposals thoroughly. The second problem is that some people will allow their own perceptions to be changed without reason.

Eventually, however, the entire team should meet to discuss the results of the individual evaluations and attempt to reach a general consensus on the merits of each vendor's application relative to the specific criteria identified in your RFP. The important point during this meeting is to gain consensus on each specific functional requirement before allowing the conversation to veer towards whose proposal was best. In this respect, it is often of value if the manager responsible for the selection process has somebody to collect and compile all the individual evaluations from team members in advance.

Depending on the size and complexity of the project, the use of simple spreadsheets or complex decision support tools can be of great value. For smaller projects, it is easy to lay out individual evaluations, calculate average scores, and visually see how consistent various team member evaluations were. For larger more complex projects, it may be appropriate to aggregate scores by category of requirement and then determine the average score and standard deviation for each category of requirements.

For smaller projects, placing the average scores in the same spreadsheet as priority for each requirement will quickly generate an objective score for each vendor's proposal. For larger projects, it may be helpful to use a decision support tool that allows you to build a requirements model and then perform sensitivity analysis on your results. The sensitivity analysis allows the selection team to see what the impacts of various requirement prioritization and/or scoring decisions are on the model's outcome. This is very helpful because it allows you to avoid lengthy discussions about decisions that do not change the model's outcome.

VISIT REFERENCE SITES   No matter how close or lopsided the results of your proposal evaluations are, you should always visit at least one vendor reference site for each of your top choices. In addition, you should speak at length with several others via telephone if you don't have the time or resources to visit them.

It is important to bring your prioritized requirements matrix with you when you visit or call the vendor's reference installation sites and to have the same group of people make each visit or phone call.

In addition to seeing if the system truly does all the things you need it to do, some questions you should ask the people at the reference site are the following:

- Did the vendor install the system in accordance with the schedule laid out in the proposal, and if not, was the delay caused by the vendor or the customer?
- Has the vendor supplied the system in accordance with a reliable schedule?
- Have software and hardware maintenance fee increases been reasonable and predictable?
- Does the vendor provide reliable support in terms of help desk availability, on-site hardware service, and other factors? How often does the customer spend extended periods of time on hold, or wait a day and a half for four-hour on-site service?

It is important to visit at least one installation site that is similar to yours. It is acceptable if one site is similar in size and another is a similar type of operation. If, however, the only reference installations the vendor can provide are for enterprises either significantly smaller or those that do completely different things than yours, you ought to consider the additional risk involved in migrating and/or scaling a system from one business to another.

HAVE VENDORS PROVIDE DEMONSTRATIONS   The key to vendor demonstrations is to ensure that you do not buy a system based on the appearance or sales skills of the person presenting the demonstration. The reality in most instances is that the company purchasing a new system is replacing an old, much less functional system. As a result, a good salesperson could make almost any vendor's application look incredibly functional and robust to a room full of operators who have been working with the proverbial bearskins and rocks for several years. It is important to remove this element of subjectivity from the equation.

The simplest way to make vendor demonstrations more useful and informative is to confine the vendor to a script. A favorite is the ice skating analogy:

- Each vendor has 40 (80 or 120 depending on the complexity of the system) minutes to walk you through a series of functions that you have scripted out (based on your RFP and functional requirements document).

- Following the 40-minute compulsory presentation, each vendor gets an additional 20 (40 or 60) minutes to provide a freestyle explanation of what makes his or her solution uniquely suited to your business.

By making the vendors stick to a tightly written and consistent script, you can be sure that each member of the team has the opportunity to personally verify that the vendor's system does in fact perform all of the functions identified in your requirements document. In addition to making sure you will receive what you think you are buying, this element of universal team verification and buy in is often critical to a successful rollout.

A note on vendor demonstrations: Don't ask a vendor to spend the time and money necessary to come to your site and perform a demonstration if you have not determined that this vendor has a viable and competitive alternative for your application. If you have narrowed the field to two vendors that you believe are head and shoulders above the competition in terms of being perfectly suited for your business, you should not ask other vendors to do demonstrations.

Companies will often have policies requiring the comparison of at least three systems to ensure competitive pricing. This is not a bad policy, but analyzing three alternative proposals does not mean making a vendor you have no intention of selecting spend thousands of dollars to do a demonstration.

FINAL SELECTION   Assuming that the vendor's demonstration verifies the information presented in his or her proposal, the final selection process is a foregone conclusion. In cases where the demonstration reveals weaknesses in a particular vendor's application that were not evident (or simply glossed over) in the proposal, final selection is less easy.

If you have more than three good candidates that came out of the proposal analyses (scoring) stage and only one was eliminated during the vendor demonstration, then you might choose to reconvene the selection team to discuss the other alternatives. In the end though, no matter how many selection committees are formed and how much input is received, the manager responsible for the system selection process has to be both willing and able to make a decision.

The final note on system selection is not much different than the final note on buying a car: You have to be willing to walk away. All too often in this business, you find yourself driven by the lure of being one step ahead of the competition, by the dull whine of Wall Street for any kind of news, or simply by employee complaints to jump into system acquisitions that do not make sense. During the past ten years, businesses within every vertical market segment have scrambled to increase capital spending for IT, often with very little real increase in shareholder value or corporate productivity. We now see software prices either stagnating or, in some cases, decreasing as rapidly as hardware prices. If the system you want is not available today at a reasonable price, wait twelve months and try again. It's better to have done the analyses twice and made a good investment, than to have done the analyses once and made a poor one.

6. IMPLEMENTATION

Now that you have purchased the correct system, a proper implementation procedure needs to be adopted whether it is hardware or software. There are ten steps.

1. Choose a project manager from your existing staff. This may or may not be the person who headed up the selection process. As hard as it may be, this must be a capable person who must be relieved of daily duties and given the lead to serve as your liaison with the vendor's

project manager. This person is now the boss and your lifeline to the project's implementation. The project manager will take charge of the remaining steps in cooperation with your entire staff.

2. Set a schedule. This covers coordinating and confirming the specific delivery of the product and associated dates and any needed supplemental items. The contract and vendor schedule needs to be understood. What may be a good date for the vendor may not be for you. Implementation should be done at off hours and off peaks so as not to affect business operations. Weekend nights are often a good time for business hotels, whereas restaurants might want to find a slow weekday. Resorts can adopt a new system during off seasons as can sports arenas and convention centers.

3. Establish a training system. Before tackling your own property, send a select group of staff from various departments to your vendor's site for initial training. From there, develop a training schedule for your property. When will it occur? For how long? What compensation will be given? How about perks? Training can be both a nice break from the daily grind and a chore. Try to make it as comfortable as possible. Training in the hospitality industry is often an afterthought due to high turnover. However, the greatest system in the world is useless if no one knows how to use it. Training needs to be taken very seriously or else all of the careful analysis up to this point can go up in smoke.

4. Meet with the vendor and exchange notes on steps 1 through 3. Resolve any issues to date and request specific information from the vendor on what to expect from the system and related elements during the upcoming time period. Communicate these facts to all involved to keep them in the loop.

5. Stop and analyze. This may seem like a good step to skip. However, you are approaching the point of no return—the implementation phase. Is everything and everyone ready? Has a contingency plan been put in place? An example may be paper records and systems. Likewise, a good rule of thumb is to contact all the stakeholders in the company and remind them in the next few days you are adopting a new system and apologize in advance for any unwelcome occurrences.

6. Start implementation in *one* department. This entire department must adopt the new system. Old ways of doing things replaced by the new system must be discarded. The system must be totally embraced by all. Those in this first department will serve as additional trainers on the new system and importantly play the role of cheerleaders for future departments. These are the people who can spread the word that it wasn't so bad. Keep in mind that change is difficult and that people are creatures of habit. It is important to win allies early.

7. Stop and analyze. Has the new system affected the processing power of any in-place systems? For example, oftentimes new software may take up precious processing power of the CPUs involved to the detriment of other applications. Take care in monitoring all of the systems. It may surprise you that even the climate control systems may have to be fine-tuned to accommodate new additions. Your model for the new system's implementation is being set. Human comfort and settings deserve proper attention, particularly if the system is to be used for long hours.

8. Move on to the next department. With all the expertise and experience gained to date, the next department is usually easier. The important component here is to monitor the communication of the system between these first two departments. Is your network being adversely affected? For example, complex database queries of your entire customer database or large print jobs can tie up a network. Additionally, the connection to your outside network needs to be tested.

9. Stop and analyze again. Again? Yes, the third time is the charm and is critical since enterprise or companywide implementation is next. You are about to turn your whole location over to a new system (if your whole property is involved) and want to make sure that everything is okay.
10. Rollout the system propertywide.

Following these steps is safe and efficient. Oftentimes business requirements and the fast-moving nature of this industry can truncate some of these processes. Stay with these steps as best you can to avoid problems.

7. Summary

Judging by the amount and different types of technology used in the hospitality industry and presented in Chapters 1 through 12, it seems that every current and future manager must have a solid technological knowledge base. However, just as important, a manager must understand business. During the dot.com era in hospitality, many purchasing decisions were based on neat features and functionality of a proposed system under the assumption that future profits would appear one day. During this period, owners were often scared that if they did not have the current technology, their customers would go elsewhere. Many purchases refused to bear fruit. Now, those in charge of making purchases have gone back to basics. Advancements in technology are still respected; however, business considerations come first. Simply put, any new system needs to either increase revenue or reduce costs. Understanding and utilizing financial metrics and definitions such as ROI and

differing cost and profit structures are again the norm for management.

Hospitality is a fast-paced industry where wants and needs of any new purchase often boil down to something that works. Given the capabilities and price tags of solutions available in the marketplace today, more understanding is necessary. In reaching a determination on the potential purchase, a detailed system selection process is needed. From the beginning of the process where exact needs are established, to site visits of the system in use at the end of the process, all steps along the way are crucial and related. This is equally important in the implementation stage where analysis and testing are done along the many steps before it is committed companywide.

With understanding, proper usage, and analysis of the particulars presented in this chapter, the next technology purchase can be a successful one.

8. Case Study and Learning Activity

Case Study

The "411" On ROI

Let's take another look at ROI in this write-up on specific hospitality IT purchases from a leading IT consultant.

By Michael DiLeva, Experior Consulting

When proposing or developing an Information Technology project, there are plenty of acronyms that will be the center of the conversation, such as PMS, POS, CRM, IP, DSL, HSIA, IPTV, etc. The one acronym that we discussed in this chapter may be overlooked early in the process is ROI—Return on Investment.

Unfortunately, the actual implementation and ongoing support of a hospitality IT project is a piece of cake compared to the challenge of estimating ROI. Of course, it's always difficult to model and project the future success of any effort or investment. But projecting IT ROI in Hospitality, however, is further complicated by the fact that, when compared to other industries or businesses, hospitality often adds at least one additional layer to the decision-making process in the form of an owner, management group, asset manager or even the franchisor. So not only are there often more constituents that need to be considered, all of those involved or impacted by the project may have differing—and sometimes even conflicting—goals and may be measured (and even compensated) differently.

So where to begin? The best place to start is to either conduct a self-analysis on your true motivations for the project or document the goals of the sponsoring party if the technology request is coming from an external department. While it sounds overly simplistic, this initial step should help to flush out one of the most common pitfalls of an IT project—that the overall goals were not properly defined. Often, this step will also highlight if the project is merely "technology for technology's sake," or is designed to solve a real need or to advance a core objective of the organization. While not as prevalent in today's era of tight budgets and reduced capital expenditures, recent history is dotted with examples of hotel companies and hotel executives pushing a technology project because of trade publication "buzz," because a competitor was doing it or because the nuances of the technology or product appealed to a particular constituent's personal interests—all of which are recipes for failure.

As an example of how differing constituents often have different objectives or areas of focus, some Owners, Asset Managers, or Controllers may be focused entirely on financial returns and have little interest in a project that does not offer a very high likelihood of crossing a particular hurdle rate (a minimum accepted rate of return). Other owners may take a more strategic and less financially focused approach towards IT investments and be willing to approve them if they improve the guest experience or increase the prestige of the property. Operations staff may be advocating a project for

its impact on their particular area, such as its ability to assist them in meeting their operational goals (such as average speed to answer in the call center) and not necessarily on how those goals translate to financial benefit.

Generally, project goals can be characterized as either Quantitative (i.e., measurable) or Qualitative (i.e., more related to "quality" and as such more indistinct and subject to broad interpretation). Examples of common IT investments and their goals include:

INVESTMENT	GOAL(S)
Energy Management Systems	Reducing energy expenditures
Check-In/Out Kiosks	Reducing guest wait times or Front Desk staffing requirements
Online Booking Software	Reducing booking costs or improving the ease of guest bookings
Maintenance Software Systems	Reducing parts or materials inventory or reducing maintenance cycles
Interactive Television	Eliminating printed materials or automating/digitizing services
Revenue Management Systems	Increasing ADR
Server Consolidation	Reducing maintenance and energy costs
Wiring Upgrade	Maintaining viable systems architecture or enabling other IT options

For investments with Quantitative goals, identifying the precise goal for the project is relatively easy. Tracked metrics like ADR, Speed-To-Answer, and others easily lend themselves to specific numerical goals (increase 10%, decrease

20%, etc.). For investments with Qualitative goals, like "improving guest service," projecting returns is challenging, but not insurmountable. In these scenarios, it's best to attempt to identify any areas where such objectives are measured and guest surveys are the perfect place to start. Usually there are overall categories that summarize guest satisfaction and often such categories include specific queries on the very area that you're attempting to influence. For example, if implementing new Check-In/Out Kiosks, an appropriate goal would be to increase the Guest Survey Score on the question of "How was your check-in process" from an average of 3.9 to 4.25.

After all of this talk about the "Return" component of ROI, however, there are some points to keep in mind regarding the "Investment" component. "Investment" goes far beyond the price quote provided by your technology vendor or the bottom line figure on your Purchase Order. As was stated in this chapter, often, projects involve a myriad of "hidden" costs that, while not immediately evident when contemplating the initiative, nonetheless have a substantial impact.

Some other examples and re-emphasis include:

- *Training:* Is training on the proper use of the new system included in the bid and have you adequately accounted for the costs for associates to participate in training sessions (either in actual "hard" costs in wages paid during training sessions or the "opportunity" cost associated with the tasks that will need to be covered by others while staff is in training)? These include training on both using the technology and communicating the technology to the end-user (i.e., the guest).
- *Maintenance:* Have all of the future maintenance requirements been fully identified?
- *Infrastructure:* Are there any infrastructure upgrades (e.g., HVAC, wiring, network) that are required for the new technology to operate properly?

- *Marketing:* Are there materials that need to be produced (posters, tent cards, direct mail, etc.) to advise the guest about the new technology, the benefits, or how to use it (to borrow a phrase from the great baseball movie "Field of Dreams," don't assume that "if you build it, they will come!")?
- *Processes:* Do new policies and procedures need to be developed around the technology (for example: documenting how housekeepers should properly clean flat-panel televisions or auxiliary media connectivity apparatus)?
- *Legal Fees:* Does your contract require review by outside counsel or does the technology require development of proper legal Terms of Usage?

With so much to keep in mind, calculating ROI can seem intimidating and may even hinder some projects from ever getting off the drawing board. But as former British Prime Minister Tony Blair said, "Don't let the perfect be the enemy of the good." No projects ever go exactly as planned and few ROI projections are ever 100% accurate. Regardless of up-front projections, for some projects, ultimately breaking even may be viewed as a win.

The key, however, is to conduct proper due diligence up-front, define the project, goals, and expected returns as specifically as possible and ensure that everyone on the team is on the same page. As long as you do that, your project will start with a high likelihood of success—and may even help to make the deployment phase a lot less problematic.

Michael DiLeva heads Experior Consulting, a leading firm that helps companies to deliver a superior experience to their customers and greater value to their shareholders by providing a wide range of marketing, strategy, business development, and technology service—including business plan development, database and direct marketing, marketing communications, business process reengineering, technology assessments and planning, and more. DiLeva has nearly twenty years of experi-ence in the hospitality and gaming sectors, and has provided marketing, technology, CRM, network-ing, and consulting services for major hotel com-panies in the United States, France, the United Kingdom, and the United Arab Emirates.

Learning Activity

1. Name three examples of hidden costs.
2. What is the difference between qualitative and quantitative projects?
3. Provide an example of how differing constituents often have different objectives or areas of focus.

9. Key Terms

Fixed Costs	Payback	Restaurant Menu Management System
Gross Profits	Recipe Management Software	
Gross Revenue		Return on Investment (ROI)

10. Chapter Questions

1. What is the difference between a RFI and a RFP?
2. What are the nine steps of system selection?
3. What are the ten steps of implementation?
4. How would you further the ten steps of implemen-tation to multiple sites?
5. How do you calculate ROI?
6. What is the difference between a fixed and variable cost?
7. Name three factors to be cautious of in system selection.

11. References

Brueggeman, William, and Fisher, Jeffrey. (2001). *Real estate finance and investments*. (11th ed.). New York: McGraw-Hill/Irwin.

Horngren, Charles, Sundem, Gary, and Stratton, William. (2002). *Introduction to management accounting*. (12th ed.). Upper Saddle River, NJ: Prentice Hall.

Taylor, Bernard W. (2002). *Introduction to management science*. (7th ed.). Upper Saddle River, NJ: Prentice Hall.

APPENDIX

XYZ Property Point-of-Sale RFP

Proposals in response to this Request for Proposal (RFP) are due by close of business on . . .

CONFIDENTIALITY STATEMENT

This document, its enclosures, attachments, and all other information, spoken or written, made available in regard to any information herein, are confidential and proprietary property of XYZ property. Any disclosure or reproduction of the above referenced information in a verbal, written, photographed, photocopied, electronic, or other manner, without prior written consent of an officer of XYZ property, is prohibited. Even then, those so authorized may only use the information consistent with the consent and only for purposes of addressing the goals, objectives, and requirements contained within this document. All copies of any portion of this document must include this Confidentiality Statement.

Extreme care should be taken in the methods and locations used to review, discuss, and store this document. By receiving this document you assume full responsibility as outlined in this Confidentiality Statement and agree to be bound by all interpretations thereof. Unauthorized disclosure of the information contained herein as described in the previous paragraph, or as a result of eavesdropping of any type, will be your sole responsibility and punishable by the fullest extent allowable by law.

Table of Contents

I. INTRODUCTION

A. Scope

Property XYZ is seeking a feature-rich point-of-sale (POS) system that will support the operational requirements for the food and beverage (F&B) outlets as defined in this request for proposal (RFP). This RFP provides the necessary information for you to prepare a proposal and also provides background information about XYZ. The purpose of the RFP is to effect the successful negotiation, execution, and consummation of a definitive agreement between property XYZ and appropriate bidder(s) to provide XYZ with a POS system.

B. Objectives

To select a full-featured POS System that will address not only the standard POS requirements but also the many unique operational needs of a full-service resort like XYZ, at a minimum, the final solution must:

- Provide a quick, simple, and straightforward solution for entering and tendering guest checks using touch-screen technology.
- Be a user-friendly system that is easy to learn and requires minimal training.
- Provide management with effective controls for day-to-day management.
- Provide comprehensive, timely, and accurate information.
- Provide comprehensive and flexible reporting and inquiry capabilities.
- As much as possible, maintain a paperless system for record keeping.
- Function using handheld devices for all pool-side outlets.
- Provide operational flexibility to meet the day-to-day challenges and procedural adjustments typical of a new opening.
- Be fully functional with all staff properly trained by opening day.

Although price is an important factor in this process, XYZ places great importance on the quality and dependability of the products reviewed. To determine the quality of systems proposed, emphasis will be placed on the following factors:

- Stability and soundness of the programs (i.e., full-featured, robust, and proven reliability)
- System integrity and security
- The vendor's reputation for quality hardware, software, and service with existing customers

C. Property Overview

Insert as much detail about your property here. Include physical layout, number on staff, target market, and so on. For our purposes, XYZ is a restaurant in a five hundred-room hotel with a pool and golf course. Management also runs a second hotel which needs a POS in its restaurant.

D. Project Schedule

The following dates reflect estimated timeframe for POS selection, contract negotiation, and installation for the vendor's use in planning responses. This information is subject to change by XYZ.

Dates	Action
5/27/2012	RFP Sent to Vendors
6/17/2012	RFP Received Back
7/15/2012	Decision Made by Owners
9/1/2012	Contract Signed
9/13/2012	Equipment Ordered
11/15/2012	Installation and Training, site 1
12/15/2012	Grand Opening site 1
6/1/2013	Equipment Ordered, site 2
8/1/2013	Installation and Training, site 2
10/1/2013	Grand Opening, site 2

E. Bidding Guidelines

The bids and proposals in response to this RFP should comply with the following guidelines:

1. All areas of consideration must be answered concisely, following the directions outlined under each subheading. All statements must be supported with concrete examples or explanations. Ambiguous statements such as ". . . all reasonable support" are not acceptable.

2. Vendors who wish to provide information that is not addressed in the RFP are encouraged to do so as an addendum to the proposal. We realize that the approach of each potential vendor will be unique. We have therefore attempted to present the specifications in general terms. Points that we feel are essential, however, are presented in detail.

3. Vendors are encouraged to provide any additional information, insight, thought, and ideas on how the vendor can help XYZ succeed with this project.

4. XYZ reserves the right to introduce additional factors not contained in this RFP in order to obtain the most suitable solution. After submitting a proposal, each vendor must be prepared to have the operational aspects of their proposed system reviewed in detail by XYZ representatives. A portion of this review may be requested without vendor presence.

5. Questions regarding any information herein should be directed to the project manager from XYZ. **Vendors must not contact any XYZ employees directly.**

6. Vendors judged to be the most qualified to fulfill XYZ's requirements will be invited to visit for further discussions. This meeting will include a demonstration of the proposed system. At this time, each bidder must be prepared to elaborate upon and clarify its written proposal.

7. XYZ plans to make its initial selection within thirty to forty-five days following the final vendor demonstration meeting.

8. Failure to comply with any of the RFP response requirements may subject a proposal to rejection.

9. Each vendor must be prepared to include any or all statements made in their proposal in a contract for systems and services, or as an addendum to that contract. Acceptance of proposals from any source in no way obligates XYZ to the vendor. Furthermore, such acceptance is **not** a guarantee of any type for current or future business relations. XYZ reserves the right to accept or reject any and all proposals, in whole or in part, at any time.

10. Each proposal must be signed by a duly authorized officer of the submitting company.

11. Two (2) copies of the response to this RFP must be received at the project manager's office, one (1) hardcopy along with one (1) softcopy, by the date on the cover of this document. Refer to the cover page for complete address information.

12. Any vendor selected to provide systems to XYZ will be required to present an insurance certificate as proof of liability covering the full scope of their work, for at least $1,000,000.

13. Each vendor submitting a proposal must be a direct national representative of the manufacturer, or the actual manufacturer. (If you elect to submit the RFP through your local dealer, please specify the name, address, and number of the dealer chosen to service XYZ)

14. XYZ requires that vendors provide access, via a software escrow agent, to any applicable software source code, in the event that vendor is no longer able to provide effective support or to continue enhancing the product. Please indicate how this would need to be handled.

15. XYZ reserves the right to adjust the project schedule dates at its sole discretion.

16. The vendor's costs for proposal preparation, demonstration, and testing will be the sole responsibility of the vendor.

II. VENDOR INFORMATION

The following information must be supplied by each vendor:

A. General Information

Respond to all questions detailed in "Appendix A—Vendor Questionnaire."

B. Financial

Provide a copy of your latest annual report or audited financial statements including the balance sheet, income statement, and statement of cash flow. As with all information in your response, this data will be held in confidence. Please note that a "call my banker" type response is not acceptable.

C. Experience

Provide a brief background on your company along with major milestones in the company history.

D. References

Provide a list of customers with a similar configuration, preferably local or regional, using the proposed system along with the list of modules currently in use. Please provide at least two of these references for installations completed in the last year. Also please provide a list of similar installations currently in progress.

Please provide the following for each reference.

- Company name
- Company address
- Contact person (management)
- Company telephone number
- Description of system and use
- Date of implementation

E. Literature

Please attach any additional information that describes your product. Describe what is unique about the proposed solution and what sets it apart from other proposals.

III. GENERAL REQUIREMENTS

The following areas detail some of the general requirements to be considered in the identification of the new POS for XYZ:

A. Network Operating Environment

While the network operating system (OS) will not drive the purchase of the POS system, a graphical user interface (GUI) using Windows (insert version needed) at the workstation is the preferred approach. It is critical that vendors should propose the most stable and robust environment for their system with a proven track record. This includes Unix or any form of thin client. All POS terminal locations will be cabled with either Enhanced Cat-5 twisted pair or fiber (still to be determined). The current plan for connecting the networks at the two locations, the country club and the hotel, includes T3 data communications lines.

Server Configuration:
The POS configuration must include the necessary components to ensure that at no time will the system at either location be inoperative in the event of a communications failure between the two locations. For those systems that support continued use of the POS terminal while communication with the server is down, a single server at the hotel is an acceptable configuration. For those that do not, a server will be required at both locations (note "*Section E. Consolidated Reporting*" for this configuration). The POS, however, will operate off a single server at the hotel and the POS systems at both locations must interface to the PMS.

XYZ will be looking to the vendor for assistance with the hardware and networking requirements including:

- Providing specifications for all hardware including terminals, printers, file server, and any other necessary peripherals.
- While XYZ is considering sourcing hardware from a third party, those POS vendors that sell hardware are encouraged to submit hardware prices as well.
- Upon completion of the installation, MIS personnel must be thoroughly trained on all aspects of system maintenance.

B. Device Requirements

Proposed POS terminals should be a PC-based flat-screen active-matrix PC POS terminal with integrated credit card reader. Should be durable, environmentally sealed (protected from spills), and, as much as possible, scratch resistant. Receipt printers should be thermal in the front-of-house, and dot-matrix in back (for two colors) at a minimum. Due to frequent electrical problems in the southern Florida area, surge and UPS protection is critical.

C. Modules

The following POS modules and general functionality are required by XYZ:

- Basic F&B POS functionality in the revenue outlets as defined in section IV—FUNCTIONALITY REQUIREMENTS
- Handheld use for certain outlets
- Comprehensive package tracking (through interface with the PMS)

XYZ will also require the following modules/applications:

- Restaurant management system (RMS) to include:
  - Cash management and reporting
  - Management reporting
  - Inventory and purchasing
  - Report generator
- Retail POS for retail outlets

XYZ is also considering the following applications:

- Frequent diner
- Table management
- Menu management
- Restaurant reservations
- Minibar

Note: As outlined here, XYZ will be selecting numerous F&B-related applications outside of just POS. We realize all vendors will not be able to propose all applications. At a minimum, interfaces with each of these will be required.

D. Interfaces

A very critical component to the POS system will be the interfacing with other hotel systems. Vendors must clearly define the functionality available with each interface:

Depending on the modules being proposed, the new system must provide the following interfaces. Where applicable, vendors currently being considered are listed. Others may be added or removed as necessary.

For all interfaces listed in the following, vendors must provide:

- A detailed description of the features and functionality supported by the interface.
- A listing of those systems to which an interface is already available and installed.

Where applicable, this information should be provided even for those applications being proposed (such as inventory), as XYZ may still decide to purchase the POS system from one vendor and the other system from another.

1. *Property Management System (PMS)*
   Due to the resort nature of XYZ along with the extensive offering of activities and F&B, package tracking will be critical. Any systems that offer enhanced interface functionality to include package handling should provide detailed functionality description. On the average, packages are expected to account for approximately 50 percent of the daily occupancy.

2. *Credit Card Processing*

A single credit card processing system will be used propertywide that has yet to be determined. The selection of this system will be driven by the selected property management system vendor.

3. *In-Room Entertainment*

Interface will be necessary to allow for room service ordering directly through the in-room entertainment system in the guest room. Vendors currently being considered include:

- LodgeNet
- On Command

4. *Minibar*

If an interface is available with any minibar systems, provide system names and functionality.

5. *Golf Tee Time*

If an interface is available with any tee time systems, provide system names and functionality.

6. *Purchasing/Inventory*

7. *Menu Management*

8. *Reservations*

9. *Table Management*

10. *Accounting*

This applies to an interface with Purchasing.

11. *Golf Cart GPS*

Ability to interface with golf cart GPS system to enable F&B ordering while on the golf course. Designed to allow food prep prior to arrival between the ninth and tenth holes. When planning the interface installations, the vendor must:

- Give the XYZ project manager adequate advance notice for all tasks for which the hotel is responsible.
- Vendors must insure that all interfaces will be up and running on each of the opening dates.
- A permanent backup plan must be in place by GoLive so that no postings are lost in the event of a system problem.
- Backup procedures must be detailed in writing.

E. Consolidated Reporting

Due to the unique layout of XYZ, with two separate locations, there are specific reporting requirements that must be supported. Each outlet and each location must be able to report individually and consolidated reporting including both locations must also be available.

IV. FUNCTIONALITY REQUIREMENTS

Please respond to all questions in "Appendix B—Functionality Requirements." While completing the questionnaire, keep in mind all information detailed in sections I through III of this proposal.

For section on "Tracking and Reporting," report samples should be provided.

For other sections, screen captures should be provided as necessary.

To help us better understand your solution, please feel free to add additional descriptions or details as necessary.

If you are able to supply any of the other modules currently being considered (i.e., table management, menu management, reservations, frequent diner, minibar, or retail POS) please provide functionality descriptions for those modules. Provide any screen captures that may help to describe functionality.

V. PROPOSAL FORMAT

All vendors must follow the format described in this section when completing and submitting proposals for consideration. Each section of the proposal must be clearly labeled and separated by an index tab also lettered and labeled as indicated in this section.

The required sections for vendor responses include the following:

A. Vendor Information

B. Scope of Proposal

C. Requirements Matrix

D. Sample Reports and Screen Layouts

E. Operating Environment

F. System Response Time

G. Equipment Configuration

H. Physical and Environmental Requirements

I. Implementation and Training

J. Documentation

K. System Upgrades

L. Contracts

M. System Costs

Section A: Vendor Information

This section should consist of the responses to the questions listed in "II–VENDOR INFORMATION."

Section B: Scope of Proposal

This section of the proposal should be a concise statement of the relevant factors in the vendor's approach to supplying hardware, software, support, and other key elements as each applies to XYZ's requirements and objectives. Briefly describe the proposed system, highlighting major features, functions, and any areas of potential noncompliance with RFP requirements.

State the modules which you are proposing in response to this RFP. Describe the methods that you will use to insure compatibility with the other systems we will be interfacing to.

Section C: Functionality Requirements

This section should consist of the completed requirements form in "Appendix B–Functionality Requirements."

Section D: Sample Reports and Screen Layouts

In Section D, include sample reports and screen layouts.

Section E: Operating Environment

Section E should begin with a description of the proposed operating environment incorporating the requirements as described in "A. Network Operating Environment." Vendor proposals should describe the specific version of the OS that would be installed with the proposed system. Indicate how long the vendor applications have been operating on this version of the OS in a live environment. In addition, please provide the following information:

Languages/Development Tools: Indicate the programming languages used to develop your system. State what other tools are used in developing your system.

Database: Describe the file organization/database structure that is supported by your OS.

Section F: System Response Time

Based on vendor experience, please indicate the following response times assuming a hotel and F&B configuration similar to XYZ that has been operating and accumulating data for one year:

Credit Card Approval: Indicate the wait time for a credit card approval from the time of the card swipe assuming that your recommended method of data communications is in place.

Backup: Indicate the backup time for daily, weekly and monthly, backups.

Daily Processing: If applicable, indicate the processing time required for the end-of-day process.

System Startup: In the event of a system failure, indicate the time for the system to be up and fully functional from the time the server powered up.

Section G: Equipment Configuration:

In Section E, please detail specific information *including itemized cost* for *all* of the hardware that you are proposing referring to "B. Device Requirements" for device types and quantities. If you are not proposing hardware, please indicate the same specifications for equipment that would be required to run your application.

Where applicable, please make sure to include the following information:

File Server(s): model number, speed, memory size, hard disk capacity, and configuration. Include size and model of monitor.

Storage: type (disk, tape) model number, cost, and capacity.

Note: The new system must include the bidder's recommendation for either hardware redundancy or fault tolerance. If the hardware proposed is to be redundant, the recommended hardware configuration should specify all redundant components and their quantities required for redundancy.

POS Terminal: model number, speed, memory size, network card, and hard disk capacity. Include size and type of touch-screen monitor along with information about cash drawer.

Printers: model number(s), speed, size, and required accessories. Please indicate which printers will be connected to the network and those that would be slave printers.

Modems: Please indicate the number and type of modems necessary for the proposed configuration.

Other Hardware: Please provide the necessary details for any other recommended hardware including network hubs and uninterrupted power supplies.

Section H: Physical and Environmental Requirements

In this section, present an outline of technical and preinstallation assistance your firm will provide. Also explain what is required but not provided by your company and how it is normally accomplished.

List all site preparation information including server space requirements, any special mounting methods required, special power requirements (including any need for isolated power circuits), and the number and type of required data communication lines. Please include information on cabling requirements along with electrical, architectural, and other special concerns. Indicate the maximum distance which all peripherals may be located from the computer or control unit.

In addition, describe any environmental requirements for the proposed system, including air conditioning, humidity control, power supply, and so on.

Section I: Implementation and Training

The following table details the staff training requirements for each of the two phases:

Phase I			Phase II		
Department	Staff	Management	Department	Staff	Management

Based on these staffing levels (which only includes staffing numbers for employees that will require system training) and the two opening phases as outlined in "Property Overview," please provide detailed information on the proposed training process for XYZ including:

- A sample installation schedule using a calendar without dates
- Total number of training hours for each phase
- Number of vendor trainers required for each phase

Include the recommended number of days for the following:

- Network installation
- Network training for MIS personnel
- Interface installation
- On-site postconversion support

Please also provide the total cost for all implementation and training services outlined here. Using the following format, summarize the assignments, responsibilities, when due and associated costs, and where applicable, for implementing the proposed system. Systems must be fully functional on the dates outlined in "Property Overview." Add any factors not listed in the implementation schedule that are relevant to a successful implementation including detailed customer responsibilities.

Tasks	Assigned to	Time
XYZ	Vendor	

Section J: Documentation

Provide a list of the user and system operating manuals that will be provided. In addition, please include a copy of the table of contents and index for each. Please state if technical writing assistance will be provided to document XYZ-specific policies and procedures relating to your system. This could include any necessary interface procedures and emergency network procedures, and any necessary checklists (such as night audit or front office management procedures). Indicate your policy for documentation of system enhancements or upgrades, how the user base is updated, how often, and so forth.

Section K: System Upgrades

In this section, please provide the following information regarding software upgrades:

- Are new releases with improved and additional functionality provided on a regular basis? If so, how often?
- How would your company handle system upgrades for an installation of this size?
- What kinds of additional training and implementation services are provided for new releases and at what cost?

Section L: Contracts

In this section include samples of all contracts related to your proposal. Include hardware, software, service, support and supplies contracts, and any information needed to assess the scope of each.

Section M: System Costs

In this section, please include all costs associated with the project as defined in this RFP. Provide the complete itemized cost for each hardware and software component of the proposed system. Include unit cost, extended cost, quantity discount scales, and total cost for each item. Also indicate the length of time the quoted prices are valid.

Please make sure to include the following:

- All applications, modules, and interfaces
- Network OS
- Other required utilities
- Programming—Hourly/daily rate for programmers, consultants, and any other individuals that may be necessary if specialty programming is required
- Installation—Itemize all installation costs
- Other Costs—Itemize any other related costs not already listed

INDEX